National Races

Critical Studies in the History of Anthropology

SERIES EDITORS

Regna Darnell
Robert Oppenheim

National Races

Transnational Power Struggles in the Sciences and Politics of Human Diversity, 1840–1945

Edited by RICHARD MCMAHON

University of Nebraska Press
Lincoln

Library of Congress Cataloging-in-Publication Data

Names: McMahon, Richard (Richard Eoin), editor.
Title: National races: transnational power struggles in the sciences and politics of human diversity, 1840–1945 / edited by Richard McMahon.
Description: Lincoln: University of Nebraska Press, [2019] | Series: Critical studies in the history of anthropology | Includes bibliographical references and index.
Identifiers: LCCN 2018047769
ISBN 9781496205827 (cloth: alk. paper)
ISBN 9781496225849 (paperback)
ISBN 9781496215826 (epub)
ISBN 9781496215833 (mobi)
ISBN 9781496215840 (pdf)
Subjects: LCSH: Physical anthropology—History—19th century. | Physical anthropology—History—20th century. | National characteristics—History—19th century. | National characteristics—History—20th century. | Race—Classification—History—19th century. | Race—Classification—History—20th century. | Nationalism—History—19th century. | Nationalism—History—20th century.
Classification: LCC GN62.8 .N37 2019 | DDC 599.9—dc23
LC record available at https://lccn.loc.gov/2018047769

Set in Minion Pro by E. Cuddy.

Contents

Figures

Series Editors' Introduction

REGNA DARNELL AND STEPHEN O. MURRAY

Richard McMahon and his colleagues deploy the concept of "National Races" to explore the discourses of racism, science, and nationality over the critical century leading up to the Second World War in which these intersections emerged. The discipline of anthropology, through various permutations of biological, cultural, and linguistic classificatory frenzy, has both been implicated by and provided authority for imperial exploitation and political control of marginal populations, both internal and external. McMahon argues that anthropology holds a key role in understanding these relationships because, more than any other discipline, it held the promise of a "universal and supranational language of modernity." When racial types stand as proxies for national identity, the practices of science and scientists are inextricable from the workings of political power and its self-justification. In retrospect, the complexity and internal variability of the racialist arguments used to justify political power dynamics too often has been obscured by a simplistic linear narrative of Nazi anti-Semitism and relegated to a past no longer mindful of the persistence of the slippages of modern nation-states into the comfortable smugness of "national races" in action.

The collective impact of the chapters transcends the expertise of any single scholar, drawing on the widely diverse disciplinary and national backgrounds of the contributors to move beyond conventional narratives of the "core" players: France, Germany, and England. Although most historical scholarship has taken the hegemony of these powerful nations as a given, McMahon and colleagues argue that the extent of local variation across international boundaries is better revealed by a "peripheral" approach that disrupts mainstream histories. Ideas about race, science, and nation adapted themselves uniquely to local constraints and opportunities in each of the national contexts explored, including Poland, Croatia, Finland, Italy, the Balkans, Japan, Greece, Hungary, Russia, and in regard to Jews. The collapse of old empires empowered new nation-states, emergent in Europe especially after 1870, that required a rallying sense of nationness precisely because they were not internally homogeneous (e.g., the Celtic "revival" in Ireland and Cornwall). None of these peripheries developed its version of national races independently of the others and there is no closure to the processes unleashed.

The project is not merely to present a series of case studies. Rather, the intent is comparative and rejects constraints on dynamic process to move across boundaries of nationality, academic discipline, and racial identity. Although many of the exemplars of possible diversity in the working out of these variables are Eastern European, the Japanese empire confronted a racialized Korean subject population in parallel fashion using European models. Moreover, American eugenics arguments were constructed on familiar edifices; Robert Javenka's *Declared Defective: Native Americans, Eugenics and the Myth of Nam Hollow* (CSHOA 2018) brings racialist consequences home for North American readers.

The impacts of these shifting motives and contexts persist into contemporary relationships of race, science, and nation that bedevil our own times. The power of the racialist discourse was such that its justifications continue to masquerade as common sense.

Readers of *Critical Studies in History of Anthropology* will already be familiar with some of the scholars and arguments expanded here: the comparative project builds on previous work by Anton Weiss-Wendt and Rory Yeomans, (*Racial Science in Hitler's new Europe*, CSHOA 2013) and Marina Mogliner (*Homo Imperii: A History of Physical Anthropology in Russia*, CSHOA 2013). Han Vermeulen's *Before Boas: The Science of Ethnography and Ethnology in the German Enlightenment* (CSHOA 2015) continues the project of decentering North America from the racialist discourses developing in Germany in relation to Russia.

National Races

Introduction

Political Identities and Transnational Science

RICHARD MCMAHON

This book explores a century of interaction between politics and transnational race science. This period produced powerful racialized identity discourses whose influences are still felt today. Biological race science had a particular impact on national identity; scholars used characteristics such as bone structure and pigmentation to identify race types and linked certain types to nations, creating what I call "national races," which they implicitly understood to be proxies for those nations. Intimating that these races represented a nation's transhistorical essence, race scholars systematically associated them with its stereotypical characteristics and historical struggles. For example, scholars enduringly associated the tall, blond, blue-eyed, and long-skulled type, which became known as the Nordic, with the German nation and its supposed Teutonic ancestor tribe, in accounts of its prehistoric exploits.

Under the banners of ethnology, anthropology, and then raciology, physicians led the broad coalitions of biological and cultural scholars who developed these political-scientific discourses. Early anthropology also studied the biology and culture of colonial peoples and nonracial subjects such as child development. However, the race classification of modern nations was a key project. This book emphasizes three of its aspects in particular. First, race classification was a complex web of interactions, crossing borders between countries, between science and politics, and between emerging academic disciplines. Second, in this book we foreground scientific practices and, especially, the power relations that infuse them.

Finally, we adopt an innovative peripheral perspective, arguing that Italian or Jewish viewpoints reveal important elements of the diversity and power relations of transnational race science that a more traditional focus on France, Gemany, and Britain neglects.

Eighteenth-century German scholars gave various names, including ethnology, to their systematic description and comparison of peoples by language, history, and culture.[1] Historians like Han Vermeulen and Elizabeth Williams, however, concur with Claude Blanckaert that the ethnology project of classifying modern nations by biological race,[2] which William Edwards launched in Paris in 1829, had "a new and different character" than earlier research on either peoples or human biology.[3]

The present volume starts in the 1840s, when Edwards's ethnological race classification began to mutate into anthropology. Anatomists like Anders Retzius and Samuel Morton then began developing transnational race histories and genealogies that truly centred around physical types. Scientific transnationalism was a powerful counter to nationalism and other political agendas and interacted with them in complex ways. International conferences and other important new fora for transnational debate confronted centrifugal developments like the institutionalization of national scientific establishments and the intensification of nationalist geopolitical tensions after 1870. By 1850 Retzius's broad- versus long-skull distinction had been established internationally as a key index for defining European races.[4] Classifiers henceforth slotted national races into pan-European race taxonomies, histories, and maps. As in linguistic definitions of nations such as the Celtic Irish, transnational racial categories encouraged complex elements of hybridity and heterogeneity, including alien or junior partner races within nations. From the 1860s, for example, classifiers universally associated the French with the dark, round-skulled Celtic type, even after this was rechristened the Celto-Slav in recognition of its transnational distribution. However, they associated it in "synthesis" with northern French blonds.

Three very recent monographs have taken an explicitly transnational approach to nationalist race discourse in the history of anthropology,[5] joining a few earlier articles on selected episodes and aspects.[6] Like most work on anthropology, the books by Carole Reynaud-Paligot and Chris Manias focus on large "core" countries like France, Germany, Britain, and the United States. The present volume, however, approaches the transnational from a complementary perspective, which it shares with my own monograph. The individual chapters primarily use cases that are in some way "peripheral," to reconstruct transnational networks from their edges. This perspective places particular emphasis on the power relations of networks and what membership in them involved. To contextualize these peripheral accounts, my overview chapter sketches the network as a whole, addressing the role of the core more directly.

Blanckaert's account of ethnology fusing together two preexisting traditions of biological classification illuminates the tense science-politics relationship at the heart of race classification and national races. His "scientific" tradition is Enlightenment natural history, which produced our taxonomy of plant and animal species with Latin names, the division of Homo sapiens into physical types such as the Black, White, Caucasian and Mongoloid, and the beginnings of craniology, or the analysis of skull-shape. Craniology became the mainstay of race classification of modern peoples.

Blanckaert's "political" tradition is romantic nationalism, which also seeped into the German-language cultural ethnology of the Enlightenment.[7] The American and French Revolutions placed peoples on the stage of history previously reserved for monarchs, dynasties, and great men. Because national descent was widely understood to be both cultural and biological, making ancient Gauls literally the ancestors of the modern French, several politicized projects competed and collaborated with biological race anthropology to classify modern nations. In his chapter on Jewish race classification in this volume, Amos Morris-Reich profiles a sociologist-demographer and an ethnologist-folklorist as well as a physical anthropologist. Historians used clues in ancient Greek and Roman texts to extend the existence of modern nations by millenia through their ancient ancestor tribes. Antiquity was a crucial factor in legitimizing nations, making them almost eternal political vehicles for destiny. Nineteenth-century linguistic philologists compared languages and reconstructed ancient vocabularies to unearth the even deeper prehistoric past of nations.

Interaction with these other scholarly projects made the "interdisciplinary" (a somewhat anachronistic term in the nineteenth century) project of using biological race classification to explain the history, geography, relationships, and psychologies of nations a vital episode in the development of the social sciences disciplines.[8] Ageliki Lefkaditou's chapter in this book, for example, stresses physical anthropology's collaboration with archaelogy and *laografia* (folklore) in order to root the modern Greek nation in classical Greece.

My aim in this book—and for the July 2014 conference at University College Cork that led to it—is to establish the creation of national races by transnational race classification as an important topic in the histories of racism, science, and, especially, nationalism. After outlining why this project merits this prominence in nationalism and as a transnational project, I argue that it now largely falls into the cracks between these three historiographies. Finally, drawing on insights from the sociology of knowledge and the history and sociology of science, which the book consistently keeps in view, I discuss the concrete practices that shaped race classification.

The Political Importance of Classifying Modern Nations

Historians of nationalism can particularly benefit from understanding the identity discourse produced by race scholars. Directly or indirectly (including through popularization), it exerted a complex and pervasive influence on more mainstream scholarly, political, and public discourses about national identity. Influential contemporary scholars of history, society, and psychology, such as Ernest Renan and Hippolyte Taine in France, had institutional affiliations with race anthropology.[9] Halford Mackinder's seminal 1908 geopolitical paper[10] cited William Ripley's *Races of Europe*,[11] which also appears to have influenced the races in J. R. R. Tolkien's mid-twentieth-century fantasy novels.[12] Benjamin Disraeli told parliament in 1849 that "[r]ace implies difference, difference implies superiority, and superiority leads to predominance."[13] His novels promoted the Caucasian biological race category developed by craniologists, which, unlike language-based Aryan race narratives, reconciled his Jewish and European identities.[14]

Several scientific race classifiers were themselves politicians—like the leading Zionist Arthur Ruppin, whom Amos Morris-Reich profiles in this volume—or had strong political agendas. Maria Rhode's chapter explains that the physiologist Józef Majer began teaching anthropology in Cracow in 1856 for the nationalist reason that, as an optional course, it could be taught in Polish during the Habsburg authorities' Germanicization experiment. Race classifiers also provided conceptual building blocks and scientific cover for the more immediately influential "applied" racial discourses of popular polemicists (like Count Arthur de Gobineau and Houston Stewart Chamberlain) and eugenicists.[15] These discourses shaped the racist nationalist milieu in which Adolf Hitler and other Nazi leaders grew up.

Marina Mogilner points out in her chapter that although classification was "deliberately expressed in a nonnormative language of anthropometric statistics," its structuring logic "of course" made it "a narrative of sorts." Race classifiers contributed to a continuous debate on the origins and family relations of European peoples that dated back to at least the Renaissance; they helped produce discourses of Northern European superiority and Eastern European inferiority, which still infuse Eurosceptic attitudes and debates on EU enlargement, respectively.[16]

Biological classifiers offered nations important gifts, including the invaluable prestige of ancientness. Ageliki Lefkaditou's chapter demonstrates how the late nineteenth-century ethnology of Clon Stephanos reinforced the scientific understanding of Greece "as one of the oldest indigenous nations" by insisting, against previous anthropological orthodoxy, that ancient and modern Greeks shared the same broad skulls. Amos Morris-Reich's chapter emphasizes the centrality to race anthropology of seeking a nation's "original type." This practice preserved the national race concept even after the 1870s, when anthropometric (body measurement) survey evidence decisively proved that the populations of modern nations were physically varied. As Maciej Górny's account of the Ukrainian geographer Stepan Rudnytskyi in this volume shows, Slavic researchers thus sought the original race of the Slavs in order to associate it with their own nation and deny Slavic racial authenticity to rival Slav nations.

Anthropology also lent nations the enormous prestige of modern medicine and science. It established them as scientifically "proven" entities and, as Marina Mogilner says, was itself "understood as a universal and supranational language of modernity." For nineteenth-century Russian scientists, therefore, participating in international scientific anthropology confirmed their country's contested modern European identity, while Greeks sought international prestige by boasting about the scale and international impact of their scrupulous research.

Contributors discuss how comparisons of skull shape, stature, or hair color supported Italian, Yugoslav, Greek, or Polish territorial claims by focusing research on contested territories or identifying an "ethnic substratum" there. Arnaud Nanta's chapter argues that Japanese "colonial" anthropology insisted on the racial similarity of the Japanese to their Korean and other Asian subjects in order to encourage the latter's assimilation into the Japanese Empire.

My chapter also notes the key strategy of associating one's own national race with prestigious categories such as European and Aryan, while dismissing enemy peoples as primitive, pre-Aryan aborigines or, still more pejoratively, as Asiatic Mongoloids. A positive association with history's great men was abidingly popular. Maria Sophia Quine's chapter describes how in 1887 the Italian anthropologist Giustiniano Nicolucci put forward the Etruscan type of illustrious Tuscans such as Dante, Galileo, and Da Vinci as Italy's national race. A variant of this discourse, described by Maciej Górny, explained Germany's 1918 defeat by identifying Allied leaders as blond Aryans.

Classifiers played a particular role in legitimizing politically useful national character stereotypes as scientific race psychologies. Scholars like Boris Zarnik in Yugoslavia and Julian Talko-Hryncewicz in Poland recognized the centrality of environmental and social influences on character and the dearth of reliable and systematically analyzed evidence on racial psychology. Despite this, they confidently discussed the inherited characters of races, such as one particularly "dreamy-minded" group of Jews. National races were attributed "natural" psychological traits such as enterprise, Westernness, or association with social classes (e.g., civilized bourgeois, romantic peasants, conquering nobles).[17] My chapter argues that these characteristics were also associated with ideological responses to modern change, such as progressive liberalism or reactionary conservatism, lending them scientific and national legitimacy. Identifying the national race with a peaceful, industrious Celto-Slav national race could, for example, help justify bourgeois democracy in the nation, while a conquering, aristocratic Nordic race could legitimize enterprise, war, or social hierarchy. Maciej Górny adds that a racial version of the German right-wing "stab-in-the-back" myth claimed that blond Aryan First World War soldiers "fell in the first line," while "less worthy dark-haired types hid in the rear." Rory Yeomans's chapter, meanwhile, describes how the ethnopsychologist Vladimir Dvorniković legitimized resistance to the individualistic ethos of the urban West by allocating the communitarian, justice-oriented psychological traits of Yugoslav peasants to the Dinaric national race.

Race psychology was therefore important for prosecuting divisive ideological politics. It justified slavery in the United States and represented Finland's Civil War as a clash of individualists with "Germanic blood" against "primitive," "Finnish-Slavic," collectivist mongrels. The name of Poland's Sarmatian Race referenced early modern noble origin myths. Górny says Polish anthroposociological research found that it "characterized" the gentry and intellectuals. The pre-Slavic type by contrast typically dropped out of school early.

Scholarly taxonomies of the supposed relations between groups have huge continuing salience for political identities. Catherine Nash argues in this book's conclusion that the prestigious but politically naïve new science of genetics may reanimate the ethnic identity discourses of the race classifiers, especially as geneticists reproduce the interaction of race classification with scientific popularization. Like race classification, genetic research focuses on ethnic origins, migrations, and settlements and highlights biological aspects of identity. For example, Nash's conclusion notes that the discovery of a genetically distinctive population in Cornwall, which has a Celtic linguistic tradition, was heavily publicized. Other cases, where this correlation was not found, were ignored.

This sharply highlights dangers in using the pseudoscience label to bracket obsolete race classification off from respectable current sciences such as genetics. We should instead judge them by the same standards. Race classification's discursive support for terrible abuses makes pseudoscience an appealing critique, and Amos Morris-Reich's chapter stresses the race category's lack of scientific validity. Scientists already recognized this in a UNESCO-organized statement in 1949.[18] However, in other writing, Morris-Reich distinguishes legitimate from pseudoscientific race science in order to investigate post-1945 German science, despite recognizing that "from our current perspective this opposition is problematic."[19] Emphasising pseudoscientific biology distracts from inherent dangers in other scholarly classifications that formulate politicized national identity narratives, whether biological or not. In the 1990s Samuel Huntington attempted to replace Cold War ideological rivalries with a geopolitical classification of civilizations, based largely on religion.[20] This effort potentially offers intellectual ammunition to conservative identity warriors like Donald Trump, Osama bin Laden, and Vladimir Putin. Language groups such as the Slavs, Germanics, and Celts, identified by philologists, are still an important element in national identities and have been mobilized in political projects—for example, pan-Slavism.

Race science, like other scholarly classification enterprises, offers nationalism scholars an extremely rich source for exploring the complexities of emerging national identity discourses, including the old dichotomy of ethnic and civic nationalisms. Race science suggests that complex tensions between inclusive acceptance of diversity and the exclusive ethno-nationalist ideal of identifying a single national ancestor tribe with a single physical type were common. In her chapter Maria Sophia Quine describes how Nicolucci, despite identifying an Etruscan national race, represented Italians as a mix of physical types, bound together by culture. Ageliki Lefkaditou identifies a similar recognition by Stephanos that Greeks were a racial mixture, but within limits; the anthropologist minimized the foreign and especially Slavic racial impact.

I argue that interwar raciology mostly revived to the east of the Rhine after craniology's fin-de-siècle crisis, encouraging ethnoracial understandings of national identity. Nevertheless, our book challenges Hans Kohn's characterization of ethnic nationalism as "eastern" and civic nationalism as "western."[21] As Rory Yeomans notes in the Croatian case, the presentist tendency of nationalist historiography to project today's strongly ethnic nationalism back onto the nineteenth century reinforces this model. However, several chapters in this book make the case that eastern European models of civic ideology have supported multiethnic state projects.

Maciej Górny suggests that warfare impelled Austrians and Poles to represent their ethnic minorities as racially alien and inferior. In calmer periods, however, a more useful identity geopolitics for multiethnic states justified the inclusion of subject peoples within a wider imperial identity. Maria Rhode's chapter explicitly borrows Marina Mogilner's theoretical model of a particularly "imperial" style in Russian nineteenth-century anthropology and extends it westward to at least the German border. This style decentered linguistic ethnicity, relegating it to one of several important overlapping categories such as "confession, legal estate, language, religion, economic status, and loyalty to the regime." For Polish scholars, for example, the gentry (*szlachty*) embodied the nation while peasants and Jews had a problematic role within it.[22]

Rhode's chapter argues that, to manage the "potentially explosive national problem," the tsarist and Habsburg anthropological establishments both marginalized proponents of exclusive nationalism, and that Polish anthropologists took the same line until at least the rise of neo-romantic nationalism throughout the east during the 1890s. Emese Lafferton attributes similar views to anthropologists in Hungary, another "historical nation" with a native aristocracy and traditional claims to a multiethnic polity.[23] Likewise, the major Russian anthropologist and race classifier Aleksei Ivanovskii, discussed in Marina Mogilner's chapter, boasted about the tsarist empire's unmatched "degree of diversity." His novel anthropological "groups" deliberately divided up Slavic peoples like the Russians on a physical basis and associated some of them with various Tartar peoples. Mogilner and Rhode both suggest that Russian anthropology "tamed various nationalizing projects by its members" that threatened their liberal civic national agenda of inclusiveness and solidarity within a multiethnic empire. The inclusive ideologies of multiethnic states had parallels in the Zionist ideology of a single, religiously defined Jewry, embracing culturally diverse Jewish peoples from the diaspora and Palestine. The three central European Jewish classifiers, whom Amos Morris-Reich profiles, all therefore prioritized the racially mixed category of *Volk*, or people, above physical race.

The triumph of ethnic nationalism in the east may thus largely result from the collapse of the Russian, Habsburg, and Ottoman multiethnic state ideologies when these empires disintegrated in 1917–18. However, Rory Yeomans detects that, even afterward, the civic and assimilationist ideology of multiethnic interwar Yugoslavia was stronger than was often portrayed. Yugoslav scholars used the common Dinaric race to unite their country's component nations, but Yeomans says this always had to coexist with representations of the nation as a fruitful biological mixture, sometimes using a special ability to absorb foreign racial elements.

Some evidence in this book suggests that, if anything, nineteenth-century French anthropology was more overtly nationalistic than its eastern counterparts. It may therefore be that the Rhine was indeed a crucial dividing line in the race anthropology of modern nations but that the East switched from being more "civic" than the West in the nineteenth century to more "ethnic" in the twentieth, as eastern empires disintegrated. Ageliki Lefkaditou reports that, as late nineteenth-century Greek anthropology drifted from a French to a German orbit, Stephanos became increasingly reluctant to reach bold ethnological conclusions. This rejection of ambitious speculation, which was the lifeblood of exclusionist ethnic national race narratives, was the hallmark of the insistently empirical and apolitical Baconian scientific ideology that dominated positivist-era central and eastern Europe.[24] As Maria Sophia Quine and Maria Rhode note, Austro-Hungarian race science often preferred to publish masses of observational statistics and identify mixed types rather than reach potentially divisive conclusions about ethnoracial identities. Rhode says Poles, Austrians, and Germans were all reluctant to apply race categories to their own nations.

Nineteenth-century anthropologists did not just support ethnic mixture and assimilation to serve multiethnic imperial ideologies. Several accounts also cast them as political liberals, who welcomed intermixture within civilized modern society.[25] This is central to Quine's portrait of Italian anthropologists like Nicolucci, who fought for the reformist and nationalist ideals of the Risorgimento, argued for the unity of the human species, and opposed characterizations of non-Europeans as biologically inferior. Rhode agrees that, for Russian anthropologists, liberalism involved a "civic" openness to diversity.

Though public sponsorship was crucial for funding and promoting research, race anthropology was not simply a mouthpiece for states. Classifiers did not always serve their interests. Imperial state ideologies, for example, clashed with the ethnic nationalism that animated much race classification. Polish, Czech, and Slovak race classifiers chafed against the "reactionary" Habsburg state.[26] As Maria Rhodes's chapter describes, Izydor Kopernicki fled Poland after taking part in the 1863 nationalist uprising. Positivist transnational loyalties also countered the claims of states; in exile, Kopernicki allegedly worked in Belgrade "to be closer to the Slavic movement, in the womb of a heroic people, fighting gallantly for liberty."[27] As the next section discusses, liberalism was a key transnational ideology among anthropologists, stimulating counterhegemonic discourses.

Joseph Deniker thus escaped to Paris to avoid arrest for political activities in tsarist Russia and the communard Charles Letourneau fled from Paris to Italy.[28]

Transnational Race Discourse

For very practical reasons such as linguistic abilities and access to sources, histories—including of race anthropology—are often country studies. Monographs about the history of German,[29] French,[30]

Greek,[31] Norwegian,[32] and Russian[33] anthropologies and their complex relationships with race and national politics have recently proliferated; Marius Turda, for example, has written extensively on Romania and Hungary.[34] In particular, younger historians are now unearthing this rather unsavory aspect of the national pasts of central and eastern Europe, despite some reservations among older local historians and anthropologists.[35]

The present book, however, insists that the transnational power dynamics of science deeply impact national political identity discourses. The scientific ideology of seeking universal truths places a high value on international consensus, and classifiers had to slot their local observations into wider schemes; therefore, despite the divisive political content of race classification, it was necessarily a transnational project, and classifiers were affected by common transnational factors. My chapter argues that the transnational organization and universalist pretensions of natural and social scientists play a key role in establishing transnational links among the national identity discourses of political practitioners and the public. Maria Sophia Quine stresses that Nicolucci in Naples engaged closely with Anglo-American debates on the supposed racial inferiority of Africans and whether humanity had emerged once or several times as different races. One of the most intriguingly transnational race identities was the Dinaric race, whose story is told in Maciej Górny's and Rory Yeomans's chapters. Joseph Deniker, the son of French immigrants to Russia, devised this racial type in Paris in 1897, recognizing that tall central and eastern European broad-skulls differed from the short broad-skulled Celtic type identified in France. Although German Nordic supremacists like H. F. K. Günther considered broad-skulls inferior, they and Italian classifiers attributed a high racial value to the Dinaric. It allowed them to distinguish broad-skulled, brunet north Italians, Bavarians, and Austrians from the French, Polish, and Russian enemies of the Axis powers. Certain Yugoslav classifiers and Ukrainian nationalists gave their peoples a Dinaric national race for similar reasons.

These transnational debates emerged from transnational networks that were created by factors like scholarly migration. Deniker and

Kopernicki fled into exile, and Quine discusses how the unforced migration of the Swiss biologist Louis Agassiz and the U.S. anatomist Samuel Morton established transatlantic links. Agassiz studied in Paris and took up a chair in natural history at Harvard, while Morton returned to Philadelphia after studying in Edinburgh. Both corresponded with leading British and German contemporaries.

Amos Morris-Reich's Jews were an inherently transnational population, negotiating identities at multiple spatial scales. Catherine Nash says that "genetic heritage" projects market the genetic heterogeneity of countries like the United States and United Kingdom as a national asset in transnational genetic research. All the chapters maintain an awareness of transnational linkages and are tied together by my overview chapter, which traces the networks of classifiers across Europe. Key episodes in race anthropology, like the shift in the field's balance of transnational power from France to Germany at the end of the nineteenth century, can only be fully appreciated from a transnational perspective.

The volume's innovative peripheral perspective offers new transnational insights into the racial narration of national identity in anthropology. As an edited volume, it brings together the expertise on multiple, diverse countries that a peripheral perspective requires; this format has previously been used effectively to study national identity narratives in fields like archaeology,[36] literature,[37] and historiography.[38] Chapters in this volume present the peripheral national viewpoints of Poles, Jews, Japanese, Greeks, Russians, Yugoslavs, and nineteenth-century Americans. My overview identifies core-periphery relations as a key feature of race classification's transnational networks, while Maciej Górny's chapter on the impact of the First World War across central and eastern European race classification demonstrates the value of challenging parochial Western historiographical perspectives. He emphasizes, for example, that, to the east of Germany, transformative war conditions did not end in 1918 but continued for several years.

A peripheral perspective demonstrates the vital agenda-setting role that transnational power relations gave the core, which I locate in northwest European cities. My chapter lists several features distinguishing core from peripheral research, including the quantity of cited publications, production of influential texts, institutional stability, and the esteem in which research was held. I argue that peripheries often communicated with a particular part of the core, in a hub-and-spoke arrangement. Ageliki Lefkaditou and Maria Rhode's chapters discuss the export of methods, classification schemes, and scientific instruments from Vienna to Cracow and from Paris to eastern Europe more generally. The descriptive methods of Poles and Austrians remained somewhat "old-fashioned," compared to Broca's quantitative approach in Paris. My own chapter argues that, in political terms, pan-European race classification schemes were the single most important hegemonic framework that the core established. To acquire legitimization from international authorities, peripheral race classifiers had to slot their own nationalist narratives into these schemes.

Various chapters also stress the institutional fragility of peripheral anthropology. When Kopernicki died in 1891, his Cracow professorial chair remained unoccupied for almost twenty years and in 1915, after Stephanos's "thirty years of continuous efforts," Greek anthropology "remained underappreciated and marginal." Catherine Nash says that the scientific power politics of genetics is still structured around a US-European core.

Scholars like Maria Todorova, however, criticize the concept of periphery for reinforcing demeaning discourses of backwardness.[39] In this volume Maria Sophia Quine insists that, despite dialogue with other countries, the "biological racism of *Risorgimento* science was not an imitation" of a northwest European core but "arose out of native scientific traditions and served national political interests." My chapter argues, in contrast, that Italy's significant contribution to race classification came late but stresses that this is evidence that the geography of power relations was not fixed. I found that countries like Italy and Russia joined the core around the turn of the century and that Poland became a major center in the interwar period. Maciej Górny agrees that the historical influence of "East Central European racial anthropologists" after the First World War "is comparable to that of their German-speaking colleagues.

Peripherality was, therefore, a far from absolute condition. Influence did not exclusively radiate from key international sites. Maria Rhode emphasizes that Russian and Habsburg race anthropology emerged as much from their own "*imperial situations*" as from "transnational science" and that Kopernicki played a double game, using different methodological standards for work he published in Poland and the West. Peripheral scholars leveraged data and exotic skeletal materials from Greece or the thirty-five thousand Polish exiles in Siberia in Paris to win international prominence. Other contributors note crosscutting connections among peripheries, such as interwar Yugoslav links with Italian and Polish scientists. Peripheries could also accept internationally powerful identity narratives while subverting them. Some eastern Europeans attempted, for example, to interpret the highly politicized Nordic race hierarchies in ways that flattered their own national groups. Rory Yeomans says that Vladimir Dvorniković in Yugoslavia proposed the Dinaric as a potential replacement for the Nordic at the apex of international race hierarchies. Eastern Europeans could argue, meanwhile, that if the itinerant Hegelian spirit of global progress had shifted from the ancient Mediterranean to modern northern Europe, the future could bring it east.

A key episode that demonstrates the potentially decisive and independent role of peripheries was Germany's supplanting of France from the late nineteenth century as the leading race classification "power" and its shift toward right-wing nationalism. Contributors do accept Germany's influence in the liberal period over eastern neighbors, including the powerful Moscow school of anthropology. Several chapters identify the intensifying attraction of German and Austro-Hungarian ideas and techniques across eastern Europe, into the interwar period. Stephanos in Greece, for example, ultimately adopted German practices, despite studying in Paris and initially exploiting the international contacts he made there. Maria Rhode says that Austrian anthropology increasingly lost the features that had distinguished it from the German discipline, and Yeomans recognizes German influences on Yugoslavia's 1930s turn toward more exclusivist race ideologies.

The book's peripheral perspective, however, decenters the specifically German character of race anthropology's lurch from apolitical liberal positivism in the second half of the nineteenth century to nationalistic, right-wing raciology in the interwar period. Writers like Andrew Zimmerman identify the roots of raciology's dehumanizing racism in Germany's nineteenth-century anthropology, and especially in a positivist antihumanism that he links with colonial research.[40] Andrew Evans criticizes such "straight lines from the anthropological discourse of the nineteenth century to the Nazi period."[41] He associates them with the key historiographical controversy surrounding the thesis of a German *Sonderweg*, which traces Nazism from a specifically German path of nineteenth-century modernization. Evans instead emphasizes the unique experience of German and Austro-Hungarian anthropology during the First World War, contrasting it to that of the Western countries that largely rejected raciology.

However, the present book demonstrates that the right-wing, racist turn was not at all solely German. In my chapter, I identify a general pan-European cultural lurch toward a new nationalist, anti-Semitic wave of cultural romanticism, amid intensifying political tensions. My statistical analysis of citation suggests that the turn-of-the-century classification community expanded into the Mediterranean and, especially, Eastern Europe, multiplying the nationalist positions that it had to reconcile. Newly independent countries like Poland invested in national race science establishments with a nationalist agenda. Maciej Górny's chapter details how Polish interwar classifiers reinterpreted received categories in Poland's favor, and, like the recently independent Finns, devised nationalist race narratives. He endorses Evans's argument that the brutality of the First World War stimulated the new nationalist race anthropology,[42] but his research on Polish and South Slavic anthropological studies of prisoners of war contests Evans's suggestion that Germans and Austro-Hungarians were uniquely implicated in this abusive project.[43]

This neo-romantic revival accelerated an existing movement toward claiming native rather than illustrious foreign ancestors.[44]

While Górny and Rory Yeomans's chapters identify such narratives in Poland, Finland, and Yugoslavia, Arnaud Nanta says that, from 1940, Japan's inclusive "colonial" race classification ideology was eclipsed by eugenic narratives of exclusively native Japanese origin; according to Nanta, these largely form the basis of current understandings of Japanese national identity.

A peripheral perspective also helps the present volume explore the complex interactions between anthropologies that studied overseas colonial "true inferiors" and the identities and geopolitical interactions of modern nations. Race classifiers often represented neighboring European countries as ancient enemies, but usually recognized them as, at worst, distant relatives on roughly equal rungs of the racial hierarchy. Several chapters in this book emphasize an insistent demarcation of Caucasians from Africans—for instance, to justify slavery in the United States—and by the otherwise liberal Kopernicki in Poland. Yeomans points out that even race scientists who believed race mixture created biologically superior humans would often draw the line at interbreeding with Africans, which could produce "very weak" intellectual capabilities. Asian or Mongoloid racial links could also compromise a people's European status. One motive, therefore, for Virchow's 1876 survey of millions of German schoolchildren was to disprove claims by the French anthropologist Armand de Quatrefages that Prussians were partly descended from savage Mongoloid Finns.[45] For Quatrefages, this explained the barbarous bombing of the Paris Museum of Natural History during the Franco-Prussian War. My chapter describes how early twentieth-century race classifiers increasingly challenged the century-old consensus that Europe's Aryan ancestors had migrated from Asia. These culturally and racially superior blonds must have had a European origin, it was argued.

However, three cases in the book—those of Japanese, Russian, and Jewish anthropologists—particularly connect the largely separate bodies of historical literature on political uses of anthropological race for nationalism and colonialism. The Japanese anthropologists of Arnaud Nanta's account, who were not European but were modern imperialists, applied much the same nationalist racial identity strategies as Europeans did, including explicit racial representations of the self as well as of others. As I argue in this book, race classification originated in Europe but seems to have developed wherever modern science and nationalism emerged.

Marina Mogilner's Russian scientists were very conscious that their country "bordered on the verge of European Otherness" and the Europeanness of Jews was even more contested. Maria Rhode cites liberal Polish anthropologists describing them as "a totally different tribe" despite finding little to distinguish them physically. Nevertheless, Mogilner and Amos Morris-Reich agree that it made political sense for anthropologists of both peoples to blur the distinctions between the colonial and national racial spheres. Mogilner's Russian classifiers incorporated Tartars into the inclusive, racially diverse Russian nation, while Rhode says that Talko-Hryncewicz, working as a "Russian" anthropologist, found no difference between the "fresh brains" of Russians and "Mongoloid" Buryats. Rhode's argument that Hryncewicz imported this inclusive Russian attitude from the colonial frontier to Europe neatly counterpoints Zimmerman's account of German anthropologists importing brutal and objectifying colonial research practices to European POW camps in 1914–18.[46] Morris-Reich's chapter demonstrates the ambiguity among Central European Jewish anthropologists about their racial relationship with Jews from Yemen and other extra-European places. Other chapters report Yugoslav, Russian, Hungarian, and Turkish dabbling with the inclusion of Asiatic race components in their national races. Conservative antimodernists sometimes used Turanianist or Eurasianist national identity ideologies of descent from wild, noble steppe warriors from the east, to symbolically reject Western urban civilization.[47]

Falling between Scholarship of Science, Nationalism, and Racism

Despite all these impacts, a comprehensive 2009 review by the sociologist Rogers Brubaker inventories the severely limited consideration of racial anthropology in the flourishing literature on nationalism.[48] Vast literatures on cultural nationalism, imagology, symbolic geography, and ethnosymbolism examine nationalist discourses in politics and the arts, and, since around 1970, historians have examined the instrumentalization of racialized ancestor groups in the construction of national identities.[49] When race is mentioned, however, scientific race classification of nations is usually neglected in favor of two other race discourses.

The first is the popular, higher-profile race discourses of politicians, historians, novelists, or applied race theorists such as Gobineau, Chamberlain, and the eugenicists.[50] Historians of anthropology can contribute greatly to nationalism studies by demonstrating that, as Chris Manias[51] and Alice Conklin note, these racist scholarly, political, and popular ideas "thrived" within a "force field" of more morally ambiguous and technical anthropological race classification, which "deeply influenced" and scientifically legitimated them.[52] The subtlest forms of nationalist classification technique, such as boosting the prestige of one's national race by establishing it as one of a small number of fundamental Caucasian types, are only readily apparent to historians of the nicities of scientific taxonomy.

The second focus of nationalism scholars in Brubaker's survey, and the subject of most historical work about racial anthropology, is colonial peoples.[53] A plausible explanation is that scholars quite naturally seek the origins of present racism. Whereas anti-Semitism and color racism unfortunately remain culturally salient, racialized understandings of the characters and geopolitical rivalries of modern developed nations have, thankfully, almost disappeared since 1945. Historians of racism and anthropology therefore concentrate on how race science justified episodes like the Holocaust and colonialism, rather than on European races and nationalism.[54] When scholars like George Stocking Jr. began to examine race anthropology in the late 1960s, for example, they studied how scientists in Europe's overseas colonies reinforced the radical differences between superior "whites" and inferior "natives."[55] From the late 1980s, successors like Blanckaert interjected that much of race anthropology, especially in continental Europe, actually focused on nationalism and the distinctions between different white races, but this remains underemphasized in the field. It is barely hinted at, for example, in the chapters on nineteenth century France,[56] Germany,[57] and even on race in Henrika Kuklick's general history of anthropology.[58] Arguing that the race concept emerged from "perceived differences within European society" and was "only later" systematically applied to skin color differences, Kenan Malik therefore criticizes "an almost axiomatic belief among historians, anthropologists and sociologists" that it "arose out of [European overseas] colonialism."[59]

A second presentist focus, reinforced by the prominence of professional anthropologists—such as Stocking among historians of the discipline—is on the origins of the current globally dominant paradigms of cultural and physical anthropology. To a great extent, these emerged from (or reacted against) specifically English-speaking nineteenth-century studies of the cultural and biological evolution of supposedly "premodern" societies. Histories like Kuklick's therefore focus on this research tradition and associate scientific racism in physical anthropology with evolving Darwinian hierarchies. The race science of modern nations, by contrast, is an intellectual dead end that largely emerged from continental Europe and stressed the immutability of ancient national races rather than their evolution.[60] Though historiographically neglected, this fixist racial typology was, as Maciej Górny's chapter argues, a powerful tool for "symbolic distancing from the enemy." My own chapter describes how anthropological classifiers legitimized modern confrontations as new episodes in an eternal rivalry; by the end of the nineteenth century, they associated Germans and Austrians with a tall, blond, long-skulled Germanic or Nordic national race, while their French and Russian geopolitical enemies shared the short, broad-headed, brunet Celto-Slav or Alpine type. Contemporary accounts of European race history revolved around conflicts between these two races.

Practices

The history of science moved on long ago from merely tracing the emergence and development of ideas. It now studies how routine practices in particular social, cultural, disciplinary, and political contexts create scientific outcomes.[61] Contributors to this book therefore concentrate heavily on how anthropologists established national institutions, networked with colleagues at home and abroad, and carried out research. Race classifiers had to compete with other scholars to organize disciplines and struggle to reconcile scientific ideologies of apoliticism with the need to attract state support. Material conditions reinforced the centrality of politics in the race anthropology of modern nations, whose main public utility, as several classifiers acknowledged, was the very political service of interpreting the nature and history of modern nations.[62] As my chapter argues, its development as a discipline and profession depended on public support for societies and state support for museums, university posts, and mass anthropometric surveys. This created complicated power dynamics. In tsarist Russia race scholars backing the multiethnic imperial state ideology marginalized those promoting ethnic Russian or Ukrainian nationalism. By contrast, separatist nationalists dominated Polish anthropology within the Habsburg Empire. They complained of state discrimination, but were taken entirely seriously by colleagues in the transnational scientific community. That community did, however, marginalize fin-de-siècle right-wing anthroposociologists and often took work from geographical peripheries less seriously.

Geographical context was crucial. Taking Arnaud Nanta's chapter as an example, the practice of teaching Korean students no doubt helped to make Keijō, as the Japanese called Seoul, an important center for Japan's "Colonial" School of anthropology. Ivanovskii and Talko-Hryncewicz's long fieldwork periods in Russia's "imperial borderlands" were very different from the relatively sedentary study of European race. Marina Mogilner describes Ivanovskii as sometimes "going native" and sharing a nomadic life with his study subjects. His inclusive "national" race agenda and Talko-Hryncewicz's use of anthropological categories to blur ethnic differences in Poland may, then, stem in part from the same sympathy with colonial research subjects that the contemporary turn to fieldwork was generating in the social anthropology of Bronisław Malinowski and Marcel Mauss.

Two vital spatial contexts were the transnational scientific community and the nation. Maria Rhode and I both note that the former required common classification practices in order to produce comparable results; the latter demanded a whole series of assumptions to connect races with nations and serve political agendas. A key assumption by anthropological classifiers, including for research design, was that one pure race (a *Kulturträger*) originally "carried" the culture of each modern racially mixed nation. Various contributors report that, in Greek, Japanese, and Polish anthropology, researchers sought traces of the original pure races in isolated, infertile, inaccessible, rural regions, which had avoided foreign immigration, and where it was widely assumed that their vestiges could best be identified. This could turn "particularly backward" areas like Russian-ruled eastern Poland into romantic repositories of Poland's cultural "pure" essence. Catherine Nash argues that this same practice continues in present genetics, denaturalizing immigrants and naturalizing the identity of indigenous locals. The *People of the British Isles* genetics project, for example, sought participants who lived "in the rural locality" where four of their grandparents lived.

Another widespread but implicit scientific assumption was that races must have a "rational" distribution, which allowed them to serve as proxies for the prehistoric geopolitical adventures of nations. Ageliki Lefkaditou reports that contemporary critics therefore complained that, in Stephanos's scheme, "the ethnic elements clashed on all sides and are distributed without any order." Nash says that, even now, scientists identify "clusters of genetic similarity," which some "geneticists, social scientists and public commentators readily relate . . . to racial, ethnic or national groups." For example, the *People of the British Isles* study focused on regional identity. This tended to reify the "politically suspect model of the alignment of genealogy, genetics, geography, culture and national community."

Presentation practices were vital for shaping political messages. Nash notes how the design of maps, diagrams, and labels can associate data with nations and ethnicity. Maciej Górny highlights an Austrian research article that undermined the European credentials of Ukrainians by juxtaposing their photographs with those of Asians and Africans.

In Amos Morris-Reich's account, one Jewish anthropologist merely stood on Jaffa Street in Jerusalem, making "anecdotal observation" of the physical characteristics of passers-by. However, data collection practices often embodied the political projects behind classification. Arnaud Nanta describes Japanese anthropologists, backed by police and public health officials, using force, deception, and bribery to persuade Korean peasants to sign research consent forms that they could not read. POW studies also involved compulsion and violence. Research subjects resisted by giving false answers and avoiding measurement. Maria Rhode identifies Talko-Hryncewicz's "feudal" practices, such as subjecting his family's factory workers to anthropometric testing, as part of her model of imperial anthropology. Meanwhile, Deniker's research practice exemplifies liberal activism in anthropology while maintaining elements of elitism and deceit. Inspired by how political reformers collected data on the social attitudes of Russian peasants, Marina Mogilner says he disguised himself "as a native Russian and a worker (one wearing glasses) to win the peasants' trust."

Race anthropologists nevertheless thought of themselves as scientists, were widely seen as objective experts, and adhered to the scientific procedures of their day. The science-politics relationship was therefore always tense. Though a committed nationalist, Stephanos "refused to enter the realm of day-to-day politics," aiming, like his German colleagues, "to keep science out of the tumult of politics." Disciplinary politics could in any case be just as brutal. According to Ageliki Lefkaditou, the leading French anthropologist Paul Topinard attacked the young Stephanos's conclusions in order to promote his own methodological agenda.

Conclusion

This book's central focus is the historical importance of biological race science for the development of nationalism. Anthropological race classification of modern nations contained a central tension. On the one hand, classifiers were nationalists and explicitly or implicitly used race narratives to promote political agendas; most prominently, they treated specific "national races" as the eternal essences of nations and their proxies in accounts of prehistoric geopolitics. On the other hand, this transnational community of scholars resisted the centrifugal forces of nationalism, thereby revealing unexpected transnational elements in the history of nationalism. The community was held together by the universalist ideal and common project of science, but also by a core area of transnational anthropology clustered around France, Britain, and Germany. This core established institutions, classification schemes, theoretical models, and methodologies for the community as a whole, even if the reception of core influences was always complex and contested. By adopting the perspective of peripheries, the book goes to the heart of the tensions between nationalism and transnationalism, politics and science.

An additional factor encouraging transnational harmony was that scientists in many countries insisted on a "civic" identity discourse, which emphasized that nations were race mixtures, even if one particular type may have had special status because it was historically linked to the nation's ancient original pure-race tribe. Existing histories of race anthropology already emphasize its liberal political bias in the second half of the nineteenth century, welcoming a cosmopolitan, civic mixture of races, ethnicities, classes, and genders in progressive, modern cities. However, the book's peripheral perspective highlights another important and underestimated reason for civic discourse in Western race classification. In 1944 Hans Kohn systematized Ernest Renan's criticism of Germany's ethnic nationalism into a pan-European dichotomy of civic west and ethnic east. By contrast, the present volume shows that, before the rise of *völkisch* and other neo-romantic nationalist ideologies from the 1890s on, the dominant discourses in scientific anthropology across central and eastern Europe were of race mixture and the rejection of exclusivist national races. Ethnic exclusivity threatened not only the social peace of the multiethnic Habsburg and tsarist empires, but the equally multiethnic traditional narratives of the Polish and Hungarian nations. Even the region's Zionist anthropologists understood the Jewish nation as a collection of multiple culturally and racially distinct populations.

A second benefit of the book's peripheral perspective is that studying anthropologists from the edge of the European world, such as the Japanese, Russians, and Jews, reveals surprising complexities in the complicated relationship between colonial and nationalist race science, which are usually studied separately. The Russian case suggests that colonial encounters could even encourage anthropologists to accept inclusive, nondiscriminatory understandings of national identity in Europe.

Neo-romanticism did ultimately establish Kohn's east-west geography, especially after the First World War overthrew the eastern empires and left their multiethnic ideology in ruins. Once again, however, the book's peripheral perspective challenges a key assumption in the historiography. This historiography emphasizes the specifically German roots of the hypernationalist raciology that flourished under Nazism. In this book, we recognize an important shift from a French to a German orbit in central and eastern Europe at this time but suggest that raciology throughout the region largely arose out of domestic neo-romantic culture. At least in this scientific field, the cultural environment that nurtured Nazism was regional rather than specifically German. This finding has clear implications for the intense historiographical controversies about whether Nazism and the Holocaust emerged from specifically German[63] or wider European conditions.[64] Therefore, as in the civic-ethnic debate, history of anthropology can be a key resource for wider nineteenth- and early twentieth-century political history, and especially for understanding the intimate linkages between apparently separate national histories of nationalism.

Notes

1. H. F. Vermeulen, *Before Boas: The Genesis of Ethnography and Ethnology in the German Enlightenment* (Lincoln: University of Nebraska Press, 2015), 1–2, 21.

2. Vermeulen, *Before Boas*, 20; Elizabeth A. Williams, *The Physical and the Moral: Anthropology, Physiology, and Philosophical Medicine in France, 1750–1850* (Cambridge: Cambridge University Press, 2002), 180, 228; Claude Blanckaert, "On the Origins of French Ethnology: William Edwards and the Doctrine of Race," in *Bodies, Bones, Behaviour: Essays on Biological Anthropology*, ed. George W. Stocking Jr. (Madison: University of Wisconsin Press, 1988), 19.

3. William Edwards, "Des Caractères Physiologiques des Races Humaines considérés dans leur rapports avec l'histoire: Lettre à M. Amédée Thierry, auteur de l'histoire des Gaulois," *Mémoires de la Société Ethnologique*, 1 (1841), 1–108; Williams, *Physical and the Moral*, 180.

4. Claude Blanckaert, "L'indice céphalique et l'ethnogénie européenne: A. Retzius, P. Broca, F. Pruner-Bey (1840–1870)," *Bulletins et Mémoires de la Société d'Anthropologie de Paris*, n.s., nos. 3–4 (1989): 166–67.

5. Carole Reynaud-Paligot, *De l'identité nationale: Science, race et politique en Europe et aux Etats-Unis XIXe-XXe siècle* (Paris: Presses Universitaires de France, 2011); Chris Manias, *Race, Science, and the Nation: Reconstructing the Ancient Past in Britain, France, and Germany, 1800–1914* (New York: Routledge, 2013); Richard McMahon, *The Races of Europe: Construction of National Identities in the Social Sciences, 1839–1939* (London: Palgrave Macmillan, 2016).

6. For example, Andrea Orsucci, "Ariani, indogermani, stirpi mediterranee: aspetti del dibattito sulle razze europee (1870–1914)," *Cromohs*, 3 (1998): www.unifi.it/riviste/cromohs; Blanckaert, "L'indice céphalique," 165–202; Pauline M. H. Mazumdar, "Blood and Soil: The Serology of the Aryan Racial State," *Bulletin of the History of Medicine* 64, no. 2 (1990): 187–219; Elizabeth Fee, "Nineteenth-Century Craniology: The Study of the Female Skull," *Bulletin of the History of Medicine* 53, no. 3 (1979): 415–33; Rory Yeomans, "Of 'Yugoslav Barbarians' and Croatian Gentlemen Scholars: Nationalist Ideology and Racial Anthropology in Interwar Yugoslavia," in *Blood and Homeland: Eugenics and Racial Nationalism in Central and Southeast Europe, 1900–1940*, ed. Marius Turda and Paul J. Weindling (Budapest: Central European University Press, 2007), 83–122; Richard McMahon, "Anthropological Race Psychology, 1820–1945: A Common European System of Ethnic Identity Narratives," *Nations and Nationalism* 15, no. 4 (2009): 575–96; and Richard McMahon, "Networks, Narratives, and Territory in Anthropological Race Classification: Towards a More Comprehensive Historical Geography of Europe's Culture," *History of the Human Sciences* 24, no. 1 (2011): 70–94.

7. Vermeulen, *Before Boas*, 21.

8. Carole Reynaud-Paligot, *La république raciale: paradigme racial et idéologie républicaine (1860–1930)* (Paris: Presses Universitaires de France, 2006), 128–46.

9. Reynaud-Paligot, *La république raciale*, 151.

10. Halford J. Mackinder, *The Scope and Methods of Geography and The Geographical Pivot of History* (London: Royal Geographical Society, [1904] 1951), 36.

11. William Ripley, *The Races of Europe: A Sociological Study* (London: Kegan Paul, Trench, Trubner, 1900).

12. Dimitra Fimi, *Tolkien, Race, and Cultural History: From Fairies to Hobbits* (Basingstoke: Palgrave Macmillan, 2008), 144–45.

13. Cited in Herbert H. Odom, "Generalizations on Race in Nineteenth-Century Physical Anthropology," *Isis* 58, no. 1 (1967): 9.

14. Bruce Baum, *The Rise and Fall of the Caucasian Race: A Political History of Racial Identity* (New York: New York University Press, 2006), 113–15.

15. Alice L. Conklin, *In the Museum of Man: Race, Anthropology, and Empire in France, 1850–1950* (Ithaca NY: Cornell University Press, 2013), 10–11; Manias, *Race, Science, and the Nation*, 10.

16. Richard McMahon, "How Culture and History Shape Europe's Differentiated Integration: The Cases of Liberal International Relations and Northern Euroscepticism," in *Post-identity? Culture and European Integration*, ed. Richard McMahon (London: Routledge, 2013), 191–211.

17. McMahon, "Race Psychology," 576, 586–89.

18. Historians, however, question the decisiveness of this break and demonstrate that biologists took decades to repudiate the race concept. Neven Sesardic, "Confusions about Race: A New Installment," *Studies in History and Philosophy of Science Part C: Studies in History and Philosophy of Biological and Biomedical Sciences* 44, no. 3 (2013): 287–93, 288; L. Lieberman, B. W. Stevenson, and L. T. Reynolds, "Race and Anthropology: A Core Concept without Consensus," *Anthropology and Education Quarterly* 20, no. 2 (1989): 67–73, 68.

19. "Taboo and Classification: Post-1945 German Racial Writing on Jews," *Leo Baeck Institute Yearbook* 58, no. 1 (2013): 195–215.

20. Samuel P. Huntington, "The Clash of Civilizations?" *Foreign Affairs* (Summer 1993): 22–49.

21. Hans Kohn, *The Idea of Nationalism: A Study in Its Origins and Background* (Piscataway nj: Transaction, [1944] 1961).

22. Kenan Malik, *The Meaning of Race: Race, History, and Culture in Western Society* (Houndmills: Macmillan, 1996), 121; Kazimierz Stołyhwo, "Sto Lat Antropologii Polskiej 1856–1956: Benedykt Dybowski," *Materiały i Prace Antropologiczne* 35 (1957): 15–18; Władisław Olechnowicz, "Charakterystyka antropologyczna ludnosci gubernii lubelskiej z dodatkiem uwag o głownych u Sławian na północ i wschód od Karpat zamieszkałych," *Zbior Wiadomosci do Antropologii Krajowej* 17, no. 88 (1893): 9, 34.

23. Emese Lafferton, "The Magyar Moustache: The Faces of Hungarian State Formation, 1867–1918," *Studies in History and Philosophy of Science Part C: Studies in History and Philosophy of Biological and Biomedical Sciences* 38, no. 4 (2007): 712.

24. Andrew Zimmerman, *Anthropology and Antihumanism in Imperial Germany* (Chicago: University of Chicago Press, 2010), 114–16, 118; Andrew D. Evans, *Anthropology at War: World War I and the Science of Race in Germany* (Chicago: University of Chicago Press, 2010), 66, 69.

25. McMahon, *Races of Europe*, 32–33.

26. J. Matiegka, "Histoire de l'anthropologique physique en Tchécoslovaquie," *Anthropologie* 2 supplement (1924): 6–8; A. Stocky, "La développement de la science préhistorique tchèque," *Anthropologie* 2 supplement (1924): 55.

27. Michał Godycki, "Sto Lat Antropologii Polskiej 1856–1956: Izydor Kopernicki," *Materiały i Prace Antropologiczne* (1956): 12–13, 28; Stołyhwo, "Sto Lat," 6–7, 12, 16.

28. Laurent Mucchielli, "Durkheimiens dans le contexte 'fin de siècle' (1885–1902)," accessed May 25, 2014, http://laurent.mucchielli.free.fr/raciologie.htm.

29. Uwe Hoßfeld, *Geschichte der biologischen Anthropologie in Deutschland: von den Anfängen bis in die Nachkriegszeit* (Stuttgart: Franz Steiner, 2005).

30. Reynaud-Paligot, *La république raciale.*

31. Sevasti Trubeta, *Physical Anthropology, Race, and Eugenics in Greece (1880s–1970s)* (Leiden: Brill, 2013).

32. Jon Røyne, *Kyllingstad, Measuring the Master Race: Physical Anthropology in Norway, 1890–1945* (Cambridge: OpenBook, 2015).

33. Marina Mogilner, *Homo Imperii: A History of Physical Anthropology in Russia* (Lincoln: University of Nebraska Press, 2013).

34. For example, Marius Turda, "Entangled Traditions of Race: Physical Anthropology in Hungary and Romania, 1900–1940," *Focaal* 58, no. 3 (2010): 32–46.

35. Björn M. Felder, ""God forgives—but Nature never will': Racial Identity, Racial Anthropology, and Eugenics in Latvia 1918–1940," in *Baltic Eugenics: Bio-Politics, Race, and Nation in Interwar Estonia, Latvia, and Lithuania, 1918–1940*, ed. Björn M. Felder and Paul J. Weindling (Amsterdam: Rodopi, 2013), 118; Mogilner, *Homo Imperii*, 1–2, 375; Marius Turda, "From Craniology to Serology: Racial Anthropology in Interwar Hungary and Romania," *Journal of the History of the Behavioral Sciences* 43, no. 4 (2007): 362.

36. Margarita Díaz-Andreu and Timothy Champion, eds., *Nationalism and Archaeology in Europe* (London: UCL Press, 1996).

37. Manfred Beller and Joseph Theodoor Leerssen, eds., *Imagology: The Cultural Construction and Literary Representation of National Characters: A Critical Survey* (Amsterdam: Rodopi, 2007).

38. Stefan Berger, Mark Donovan, and Kevin Passmore, eds., *Writing National Histories: Western Europe since 1800* (London: Routledge, 2002).

39. "The Trap of Backwardness: Modernity, Temporality, and the Study of Eastern European Nationalism," *Slavic Review* 64, no. 1 (2005): 146–47.

40. Zimmerman, *Anthropology and Antihumanism*, 239–40.

41. Evans, *Anthropology at War*, 4–5, 13–16.

42. Evans, *Anthropology at War*, 3.

43. Evans, *Anthropology at War*, 13.

44. McMahon, *Races of Europe*, 170.

45. Chris Manias, "The Race Prussienne Controversy: Scientific Internationalism and the Nation," *Isis* 100, no. 4 (2009): 753.

46. Zimmerman, *Anthropology and Antihumanism*, 243–44.

47. McMahon, *Races of Europe*, 195–96.

48. Rogers Brubaker, "Ethnicity, Race, and Nationalism," *Annual Review of Sociology* 35 (2009): 25–26; an important exception is research since the 1970s on Nazi Nordic supremacism. See Geoffrey G. Field, "Nordic Racism," *Journal of the History of Ideas* 38, no. 3 (1977): 523.

49. Beller and Leerssen, eds., *Imagology*; Athena Leoussi, ed., *Nationalism and Ethnosymbolism: History, Culture, and Ethnicity in the Formation of Nations* (Edinburgh:

Edinburgh University Press, 2006); Sorin Antohi, "Introduction: Symbolic Geographies, Comparative Histories," *East Central Europe* 32, nos. 1–2 (2005): 1–3.

50. Joep Leerssen, *Remembrance and Imagination: Patterns in the Historical and Literary Represenatation of Ireland in the Nineteenth Century* (Cork: Cork University Press and Field Day, 1996), 95–96; Manias, *Race, Science, and the Nation*, 10.

51. Manias, *Race, Science, and the Nation*, 10.

52. Conklin, *Museum of Man*, 10–11.

53. Manias, "Race prussienne," 737; "Ethnicity, Race, and Nationalism," 25–26.

54. Neil MacMaster, *Racism in Europe* (Houndsmill: Palgrave Macmillan, 2001), 5.

55. Manias, *Race, Science, and the Nation*, 103, 114–15; Jonathan Marks, "The Legacy of Serological Studies in American Physical Anthropology," *History and Philosophy of the Life Sciences* 18, no. 3 (1996): 345; Evans, *Anthropology at War*, 5.

56. Emmanuelle Sibeud, "The Metamorphosis of Ethnology in France, 1839–1930," in *A New History of Anthropology*, ed. Henrika Kucklick, 96–110 (Malden MA: Blackwell, 2008).

57. H. Glenn Penny, "Traditions in the German Language," in *A New History of Anthropology*, 79–95.

58. Thomas F. Glick, "The Anthropology of Race Across the Darwinian Revolution," in *A New History of Anthropology*, 225–41.

59. Malik, *Meaning of Race*, 81–82.

60. Manias, *Race, Science, and the Nation*, 114–15.

61. Christian Büger and Frank Gadinger, "Reassembling and Dissecting: International Relations Practice from a Science Studies Perspective," *International Studies Perspectives* 8, no. 1 (2007): 97, 103.

62. William Edwards, "Caractères Physiologiques," 2; Félix-Henri de Ranse, "Sur l'utilité que peut présenter l'étude comparative des idiomes patois dans les recherches relatives à l'ethnologie," *Bulletins de la Société d'Anthropologie de Paris*, ser. 2, vol. 1 (1866): 478; William Z. Ripley, *A Selected Bibliography of the Anthropology and Ethnology of Europe* (Boston: Public Library,1899), vii–viii ; Jan Czekanowski, *Człowiek w czasie i przestrzenie* (Warsaw: Państwowe Wydawnictwo Naukowe, 1967), 20.

63. Evans, *Anthropology at War*, 4.

64. Antony Polonsky and Joanna B. Michlic, eds., *The Neighbors Respond: The Controversy over the Jedwabne Massacre in Poland* (Princeton: Princeton University Press, 2009).

ONE

Transnational Network, Transnational Narratives

Scientific Race Classifications and National Identities

RICHARD MCMAHON

In the century or so before the Second World War, now largely forgotten pan-European transnational communities of scientists attempted to classify European nations by biological race. Though these scientists declared themselves apolitical positivists, they systematically gave scientific legitimacy to narratives that supported nationalist agendas. One of my purposes in this chapter is to persuade students of nationalism of scholarship's role in creating complex transnational elements in national identity narratives. My other purpose is to provide an overview of transnational race classification as a whole. This will contextualize the other chapters of this book, which are mostly case studies of individual peripheral countries and their transnational connections. The broad-brush approach of the present chapter is particularly necessary for the target audience of students of nationalism, who have until now given scant attention to scientific race classification.[1] This has instead largely been the remit of historians of science, and, particularly, of anthropology. The race classification of Europeans was strongly associated with anthropology in the nineteenth and early twentieth centuries, even though many race scientists consciously recognized it as a distinct project.[2]

A scientific ideology of universal positive truth and the practical need to establish an infant academic discipline impelled race classifiers to work across borders as a consensual community, adopting common schemes of European race history and geography. They read one another's work, visited one another, often studied and sometimes took up posts abroad, established transnational institutions such as conference series and authoritative journals, and exchanged skulls, casts, and other materials. One nineteenth-century Freiburg anatomist exchanged material with Italian, Austrian, Hungarian, German, Dutch, Scandinavian, Russian, and American colleagues.[3] Human sciences powerfully molded national narratives into transnational forms, in part by classifying nations within transnational categories. Early nineteenth-century linguistic classifiers, for example, formulated family groupings of Slavic, Latin, or Germanic nations, which became a key element in European national identities. Race classifiers similarly linked nations with transnational European races like the tall blond Nordic.

Transnational geography is a complex and contested issue. Globalization gave a powerful stimulus to transnational analyses of nationalism.[4] Theorists such as Paul Virilio, Manuel Castells, and Arjun Appadurai discussed it in the 1990s as the abolition or transcendence of space, a borderless world, "space of flows" or global civil society in which location lost its meaning.[5] The present chapter challenges this homogenizing geography. I show that race classifiers developed nationalist narratives within the context and constraints of multiple overlapping transnational patterns of connection and influence, including from geopolitics and patterns of networking. Political and cultural traditions influenced the transnational diffusion of political ideas, and the geography of modernization shaped power relations in science. Industrial northwest Europe thus produced the most internationally influential racial identity narratives.

The distinctive contribution of this chapter is to detail these specific European geographies, rather than just identify, as much research on nationalism does, general "nomothetic" explanatory factors.[6] I use qualitative discourse analysis of scholarly texts and quantitative analysis of race classification's citation network to map concrete, large-scale spatial and temporal patterns of race classification, such as the gradually changing geography of its core-periphery relations.

A very diverse historical sociology tradition has examined concrete transnational spatial patterns as a key factor in European history, and they are crucial to debates about nationalism.[7] Hans Kohn's 1944 association of civic nationalism with western Europe and ethnic nationalism with eastern Europe, for example, remains "widely employed" but "vastly criticized."[8] Scholars also continue to trace and dispute the diffusion of "consecutive waves" of nationalism "as they surged out from their West European heartlands,"[9] and to recognize the explicit and implicit nesting of national identities within larger identity categories such as European or Slavic.[10] Studying the concrete spatial patterns of race classification can throw light on important theoretical questions,[11] such as the old debate among historians and sociologists about whether nationalism spread through transnational diffusion of ideas among elites or emerged from wider modern structural change.[12] This chapter finds evidence for both arguments.

"Ideographic" scholars, who insist on the distinctiveness of each individual case, are wary of large-scale patterns, in part for moral reasons. Transnational geographical analyses may, for example, lend themselves "to ethnocentric caricature" of "uncivilized" eastern European ethnic nationalism, and, therefore, "should set off alarm bells."[13] As a broad overview, this chapter cannot note every exception and contradiction, but I regularly highlight examples to emphasize that large patterns and complex detail exist simultaneously. There are patterns at all scales. If, for nomothetic or ideographic reasons, scholars ignore transnational patterns, they risk falling, by default, into the "territorial trap" of "methodological nationalism," treating the familiar, uniform grid of functionally equivalent nations as the only geography that matters.[14]

History of science has begun to move toward mapping transnational patterns. Interest in spatiality flourished among historians of science from the mid-1990s.[15] However, they tended to write ideographic studies of how scientific knowledge was produced or received in particular labs, expeditions, or museums, while drawing general nomothetic conclusions about these kinds of place, space, or site.[16] More "social scientific" work, which identifies large-scale networks and other transnational spatial patterns in scientific communities, has also multiplied over the past decade, however. For example, bibliometrists, who have long analyzed social networks of citation, are now developing computerized tools to visualize networks cartographically.[17] These intrusions have generated some friction with more "humanistic" historical geography but introduce extremely fruitful new agendas.[18] The relationship of power and politics to science, a major theme of the present chapter, is emphasized in particular.[19] World systems theorists, for instance, examine transnational scientific networks to help understand a concrete global core-periphery geography of power relations.[20]

After briefly outlining the history of race classification, the chapter identifies transnational factors in, first, its organization as a community of scholars; and, second, in narratives about racialized national identity.

Race Classifications of Modern Nations

History of science stresses the institutions, context, and praxis of scientists. The establishment of the ethnological societies of Paris (1839), New York (1842), and London (1843) was in these terms a foundational moment, beginning a tradition of biological race classification that later continued under the banners of anthropology and raciology.[21] Though nineteenth-century ethnology and anthropology were not exclusively devoted to the race classification of Europeans, it was a central concern, especially in continental Europe.[22]

The new project of ethnological race classification took its name from a mostly German and linguistic project of studying peoples. It combined two Enlightenment traditions: biological taxonomy and nationalism. Eighteenth-century taxonomists like Carl Linnaeus had identified human races as part of their project of classifying the world's species. From 1775 Johann Friedrich Blumenbach used skull shape as a criterion for doing so. From the mid-nineteenth century this craniology became the enduring central method of race classification. As eighteenth-century cultural ethnology had already recognized, nationalism made peoples, rather than great men or dynasties, the central actors in world history.[23] Mobilized in the American and French Revolutions and in resistance to Napoleonic imperialism, as well as popularized by writers like Sir Walter Scott and François-René de Chateaubriand, nationalism transformed European politics and scholarship, and stimulated new programs of studying Europe's popular customs, languages, national histories, and races.

Race classification of European peoples, therefore, combined political and scientific impulses. As practitioners often recognized, their essential contribution to society was to interpret political relations, especially between nations. At least three factors ensured and maintained this strategic linkage with politics.[24]

First, scientists mostly belonged to the bourgeois intellectual elites, who initiated nationalism in its various forms. Several of Italy's leading anthropologists manned nationalist barricades, for example, and even took public office as liberal nationalist politicians.[25]

Second, in order to study races, which were conceived from the beginning as complexes of physical biology, mental traits, culture, and political identity, biologists had to collaborate with scholars of nonbiological factors such as history, language, society, human geography, and culture. While historians used classical texts to link nations with ancestor tribes like the Celts or Teutons, biological races extended these still further back into prehistory. The new ethnology therefore included scholars of culture, biology, and, often, a combination of these interests.

Third, the history of race classifiers suggests that the public and politicians rewarded classification projects that provided them with the political answers they sought. Scholarship that gave nations and their geopolitical alliances and enmities the legitimacy of ancientness and science, interpreted modern change, and justified national territorial claims consequently thrived. The public flocked to join its scholarly societies and states supported its institutions. Italy thus established its first professorial chairs in anthropology in 1860–69, immediately after national unification.[26] Interwar fascist governments, and newly independent central European states gave generous support to nationalist race anthropology at universities.[27] These well-resourced institutions were then able to successfully promote their nationalist agendas within the transnational discipline.

In the 1860s the new interdisciplinary coalition of anthropology decisively supplanted ethnology as the leading scientific base of race classification. While anthropology's leaders—such as Paul Broca in Paris and Rudolf Virchow in Berlin—reoriented classification more decisively toward biology and craniology and away from cultural evidence, they permanently established the distinction between broad and long skulls, theorized by the Swedish anatomist Anders Retzius in 1840, as the key index of European race classification.[28] In particular, they distanced themselves from philology, whose race taxonomies stubbornly diverged from those of craniology.[29] To study European racial history, anthropology instead relied heavily on archaeology, which unearthed skeletal remains alongside cultural materials. The liberal Virchow, for example, though often preferring to discuss types rather than essential races, was deeply concerned with identifying Slavic or Teutonic racial skull shapes in prehistoric burials.[30]

Race anthropology participated successfully in the late nineteenth-century institutionalization of academic disciplines that largely created our present-day landscape of social sciences and humanities. University professorships started to be established in large number from the 1870s on in particular, including six at Broca's Ècole d'Anthropologie in 1876, providing anthropologists with systematic training and a career structure. States also sponsored museums and massive anthropometric (body measurement) surveys of schoolchildren and army recruits. From its initial heartland in the industrialized countries of northwest Europe, the anthropology of European races expanded to Mediterranean and central and eastern European countries.

Paradoxically, these very successes almost destroyed the anthropological race project at the end of the century. Institutionalization gave disciplines that collaborated on race classification—including history, geography, and archaeology—the autonomy and confidence to concentrate on the problems that arose from their own methodologies and subject matters.[31] Sociologists like Emile Durkheim clashed with racial sociologists, rejecting their anti-Semitic conservative politics and demanding social rather than race-biological explanations for social phenomena. By 1910 Durkheimians had excluded race anthropologists from the young discipline of sociology.[32] Physical and cultural anthropologists, whose interests never entirely coincided, developed into more distinctly separate disciplines that often actively marginalized devotees of race classification.

Institutionalization also strengthened the role of national establishments within race anthropology, shifting this scholarly community from transnationalism toward a more international form of organization. Scientific race classification never escaped the tension between hegemonic transnational and national ideas about the racial identity of nations, but, whereas transnationalism had encouraged common narratives about European racial history and geography, *inter*nationalism stimulated competing national ones. In the 1860s and 1870s, for example, Rudolf Virchow in Germany accepted the mental superiority of the broad-skulled "Celtic" race, which was more associated with France than with Germany; subsequently, however, Germans increasingly insisted on the superiority of the "Germanic" Nordic blond.[33] In Italy in the 1890s, Giuseppe Sergi also distanced his compatriots from the "French" Celts, linking Italians instead with the previously neglected Mediterranean race type.[34] In a series of turn-of-the-century articles, Joseph Deniker, a Russian anthropologist working in Paris, used new data pouring in from central and eastern Europe to identify two important new race types there: the Eastern and the Dinaric. The former (later known as Easteuropean or East-Baltic) was adopted as an important component of national biology in Russia, Poland, Latvia, and, especially, in Finland.[35] Meanwhile, Yugoslav, Ukrainian, and Austrian classifiers identified their nations with Deniker's Dinaric Race.[36] Sometimes, as the case of interwar Poland exemplifies, different schools within countries disputed which race to associate with the nation, often reflecting their different ideological standpoints and transnational links.[37]

Bitter and intensifying geopolitical rivalries—especially after the 1870–71 war between race anthropology's two "great powers," France and Germany—exacerbated this centrifugal trend. Armand de Quatrefages's notorious 1871 pamphlet *La Race Prussienne* characterized Prussians as racially distinct from and inferior to southern Germans.[38] It was written as a response to France's defeat in the Franco-Prussian War and included a fold-out map showing the barbaric Prussian bombardment of the Muséum d'histoire naturelle, where Quatrefages was professor of anthropology. This polemic against Prussian "barbarism" and militarism demonstrated just how emotionally and politically charged racial classifications could be.

Several contemporaries and historians argue that the vast quantities of human physical measurement data that anthropologists amassed ultimately constituted another Pyrrhic success.[39] It became increasingly clear that race traits corresponded neither with socially relevant factors, such as class and nation, nor with one another. Race scientists were discovering what mid-twentieth-century genetics confirmed: that characteristics were inherited separately, rather than in racial complexes that somehow hung together in heredity.

Despite these difficulties, anthropological race classification of Europeans revived yet again in the 1910s as raciology (*Rassenkunde* in German). This used Mendelian genetics, rediscovered in 1900, to give classification a new scientific basis and legitimacy, following its crisis, it used new statistical techniques to sort populations into Deniker's predefined race types. Its reconstituted interdisciplinary coalition included sero-anthropology, a new Mendelian race classification discipline based on blood group, as well as archaeology, folklore research, and many other cultural research fields.

This new coalition also responded to a new political mood. Its key binding force was extreme right-wing neo-romantic nationalism. This cultural movement gathered momentum during the 1880s and 1890s, producing immensely popular nonscientific race theorists like Houston Stewart Chamberlain, who attacked the apoliticism of positivist scientific classifiers.[40] Neo-romantics feared that cosmopolitan, liberal modernity and its values of egalitarianism and democracy threatened traditional national cultures that were rooted in rural hierarchies, in which patriarchal aristocrats ruled deferential peasants, whom the neo-romantics represented as having an ancient mystical connection to the native soil. The German *völkisch* movement, epitomized in Wagner's operas—of "men with flowing beards, who wanted to drink mead out of horns" and "women who liked playing valkyries"—is particularly well known and representative of this trend.[41] It arose out of pan-Germanism, lifestyle reform, the esoteric subculture, organized anti-Semitism, and the national culture movement and was obsessed with "pagan Nordic antiquity," runes (like the swastika), the archaic *Fraktur* script, and racially pure descent from ancient Teutons. Neo-romanticism, however, and its characteristic iconography of an eternal peasantry and noble ancestors emerged in contemporary nationalism from Ireland to Romania.[42] Nationalism, political conservatism, an emphasis on race, celebration of the blond Nordic race in particular, disdain toward other European races, and intense anti-Semitism bridged the apparent incompatibilities between emotive neo-romanticism and modern scientific raciology. These factors appear, in different combinations and to different degrees, in the work of raciologists including Jan Czekanowski in Poland,[43] Viktor Bunak in Russia,[44] and Georges Montandon in France.[45]

A Transnational Community of Scientists

I argue that transnational patterns in narration of nationalism stem in part from the organization of race classifiers of Europeans as a transnational community. I analyzed this community using mixed methods. I first qualitatively researched the lives and institutions of the most authoritative scholars within the transnational community and, through case studies of Irish, Polish, and Romanian classifiers, examined scientists on its periphery. I then combined this with quantitative analysis of contemporary bibliographies and of my own databases of anthropological institutions (societies, journals, university posts, museums, international congresses, mass surveys).[46] My central quantitative resource was a database of citation among a group of the 126 most cited (therefore, authoritative or canonical) texts on race classification of Europeans. After initially choosing some of these on the basis of histories of race classification, I snowballed twice to expand the group, each time adding those texts that the previous selection cited most often. I then recorded details of 6,059 references that these texts made to other texts.

The present section uses these quantitative data to identify three sets of broad patterns in the transnational classification community's structure. These are: spatial patterns of core-periphery power relations—a key influence on race classifiers' nationalist narratives; important changes over time in this geography of power; and spatial patterns in the influence of older cultural geographies.

Core-Periphery Relations

Anthropology flourished in cities with "universities, modern libraries, and a significant layer of educated society."[47] From beginning to end, therefore (according to my citation database and two important contemporary bibliographies), the places of publication were heavily concentrated in the northwest European heartland of nineteenth-century industrialization (see fig. 1).[48] This constituted the classification community's core area.

The snowball methodology that I used to compile my citation database tends to emphasize a centralized, hierarchical transnational economy of respect, attention, and authority. I record the work that a central, intercommunicating group of authorities considered important enough to cite, rather than the overall quantities (or quality) of work produced. Peripheral classifiers frequently resented their marginalization within these power relations but strongly recognized their existence. My qualitative studies also confirm that texts from peripheral areas were not only neglected by the center, but were fewer in number.[49] This offers strong empirical confirmation that race scientists represented nations in response to discourses that were hegemonic within the transnational scientific community as well as to nationalist discourses.

The "production chain" of classification allocated peripheral scholars a specific role. Grand pan-European schemes of history and geography represented the prestigious apex of classification. Those that were cited heavily in my database were generally by leading theorists with senior academic posts in prestigious core institutions. Pan-European schemes by scholars in places like Romania were ignored abroad and often even within their own countries. Peripheral classifiers were frequently treated as mere gatherers of anthropometric raw data. Quite often, the core preferred to use data collected in periph-

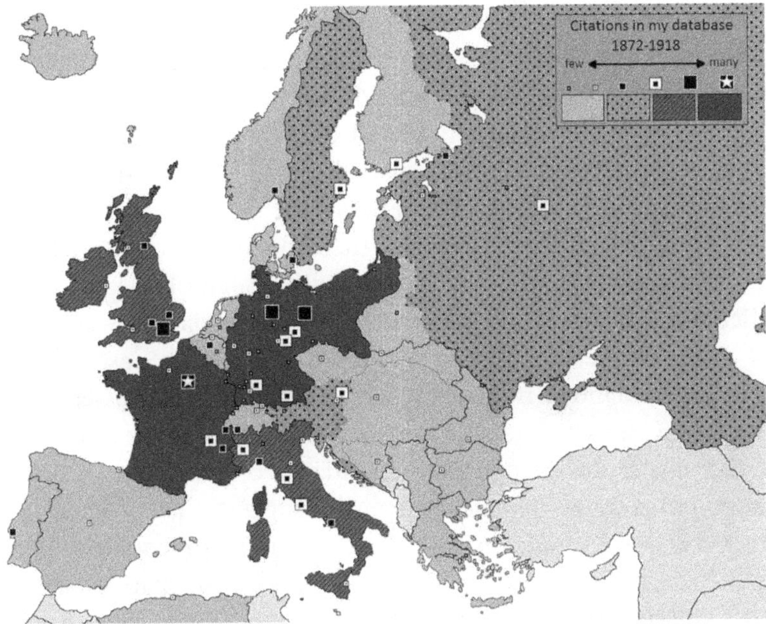

Fig 1. Publications on race classification of Europeans, 1872–1918, based on the author's citations database research. Darker tones and larger symbols indicate more publications.

eries by non-natives. Eugène Pittard of Geneva and Viktor Lebzelter of Vienna were therefore among the most widely cited experts on Romania. Local representatives of ethnically distinct imperial elites mostly reported on Ireland, Slovenia, and the Baltic States, while foreigners' accounts were the only acknowledged source of data on a few ultra-peripheral countries, like Albania, Bosnia, and Turkey. Other countries (Hungary, Russia) moved from representation by foreigners to reporting by natives.

The races in authoritative pan-European schemes were generally identified on the basis of local evidence within a core country, and then extrapolated to the rest of Europe. Retzius identified his universally accepted 1840 distinction between long-skulled Aryan invaders and primitive broad-skulled European natives on the basis of comparing the crania of Swedes and Finns.[50] French scholars originally used a short, dark, broad-skulled French type as the basis of the Celtic or Alpine race, which, according to the influential classifier William Ripley, all late nineteenth-century classifiers identified as dominating Europe's inland regions.[51]

Several other characteristics typified peripheral classification. Professorships were established remarkably early in places like Moscow (1876), Naples (1880), and Budapest (1881), but peripheral institutions tended to be less stable than their core equivalents. When key professors of anthropology in Cracow (1891) and Budapest (1902) died, for instance, their chairs were left unoccupied.[52]

Peripheral texts were also very often cited in race classification's international lingua francas: French, German, and, to a lesser extent, English. Core scholars, like the Swedes and Dutch, are more often cited in their own language than citizens of Spain, a much more populous country.[53] Language data also suggests that, whereas contacts between scholars within the core tended to form a complex web, peripheries were often attached to this web by sparser contacts, in a hub-and-spoke pattern that linked them almost exclusively to a particular section of the core. For example, over half the texts by Czech and Hungarian scholars in my citation database were in German (see fig. 2). Irish race classifiers, meanwhile, almost exclusively cited British works, whereas their British colleagues often had more cosmopolitan continental contacts.

Demonstrating the crucial role of concrete transnational networks in science, Irish classifiers adopted British narratives of blond superiority, ignoring French and Italian race models that appear to have had more potential for Irish nationalist narratives.[54] Czekanowski, Poland's foremost raciologist, borrowed a Nordicist hierarchy from Germany, despite his nationalist opposition to German raciological theories.

Changes within the Core

As mentioned earlier, the core expanded from the late nineteenth century to take in some Mediterranean and central and eastern European countries. Before the 1890s, classifiers from French-, German-, and English-speaking countries dominate my canon and monopolize a comprehensive historical list of race schemes compiled by

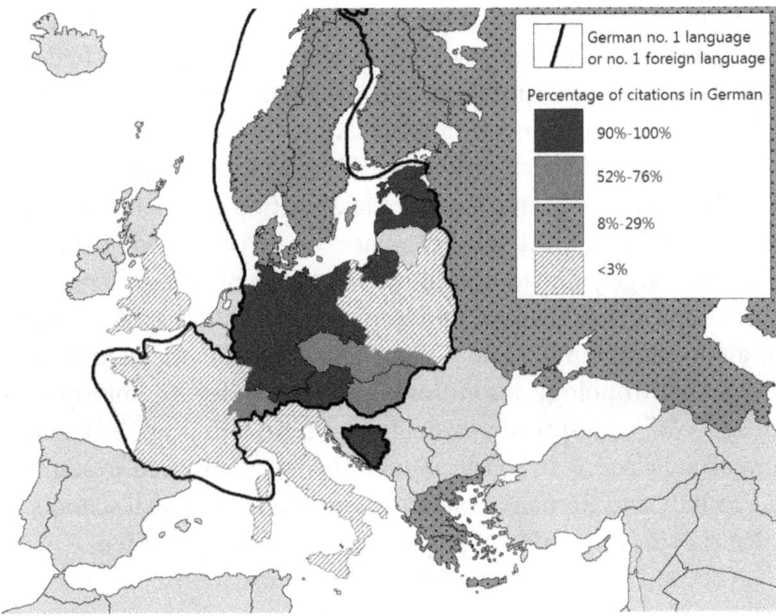

Fig 2. German language publications on race classification of Europeans, based on the author's citations database research.

the German raciologist Egon von Eickstedt in 1937.[55] However, geographical diversity then increased greatly. Eickstedt's list of schemes introduced Slavic writers (Russian, Polish, and Slovene) from 1889 and scholars from six new countries in the twentieth century. In my own canon of influential schemes, nine of the twenty-four post-1900 classifiers were Italian, Polish, Scandinavian, or Dutch. Within the big three language zones, American, Austrian, and Swiss contributions increased.

The expanding classification community produced several new classification "powers." My database had few Italian works until after unification in 1859–60 and the subsequent institutionalization of anthropology. Italian language texts rose from 2 percent in 1853–71 to 27 percent and second place in 1906–18, while publication in Italy went from 5–6 percent in 1872–1905 to 29 percent and top place in 1906–18. Italian schemes account for half those of countries that entered Eickstedt's canon in the twentieth century.

American publications, meanwhile, had small percentages in my database until after 1900, when they sometimes reached the 8–9 percent range. American publication centers expanded from a Swedish to a British scale after 1918.

An intermittent trickle of works from Poland was cited from 1824, but the country became a major classification center in the interwar years, accounting for a dramatic 7.5 percent of my database. This was largely due to Czekanowski's Lwów or "Polish" typological school, which Yugoslav and Romanian classifiers acknowledged as an important influence.[56] In 1938 one Romanian raciologist rated Polish anthropology second only to German for its "multiplicity of schools," widespread university institutionalization, "extremely important place . . . in Polish culture," and "very advanced" research.[57] As in Italy and Romania, however, rival Polish regional schools of race classification and anthropology were sharply divided.

A second dramatic change shifted the transnational community's center of gravity eastward at about the turn of the twentieth century from France to Germany, reflecting transformations in both western and central Europe. Along the Atlantic coast, overseas colonialism diverted anthropologists from their previous concentration on European race.[58] An evolutionary scale in which cultural development was paralleled with physical development, and specifically with pigmentation, was a keystone of racist colonial anthropology. However, this jarred with the craniology-based race fixity that had always been central to the European race classification project of extending nations, essentially unchanged, back into prehistory.[59] A new, early twentieth-century generation of colonial anthropologists like Bronisław Malinowski, Marcel Mauss, and Franz Boas responded to craniological evidence that the race concept was scientifically invalid by establishing new British, French, and American disciplines of cultural or social anthropology. These liberal disciplines decisively rejected race, racism, and anti-Semitism and progressively marginalized race science in the anthropological communities of the west.

By contrast, Matti Bunzl and Glenn Penny argue that after Germany lost its colonies in 1918, its colonial anthropology "never recovered."[60] Thomas Schippers contrasts this "rather small" interwar *Völkerkunde* with the indirect "great stimulus" that Germany's "moral collapse" provided to neo-romantic *Volkskunde*, or folklore studies, making it the country's principal cultural research field and a disciplinary ally of raciology.[61] As a result, Germany converged with countries further east, which never had overseas colonies, and revived race classification as raciology in the early twentieth century.

Older Cultural Geographies

Spatial correlation suggests that an older cultural geography of civic and ethnic nationalism may help to explain the concentration of neo-romantic nationalism and, later, of raciology in central and eastern Europe. It has long been recognized that nationalists in these areas mostly defined nations in racial or cultural terms, because their initial political agendas focused on overthrowing old dynastic states, such as the Habsburg Empire and minor German principalities.[62] French, British, and Dutch nationalists, by contrast, aimed to preserve old dynastic frontiers and were therefore more likely to equate nation with state citizenship.

Nationalist traditions of opposition or support for existing states strongly correlated with the tendency of classifiers to identify one or multiple national races, respectively. Classifiers consistently associated Germans with the Nordic blond, for example, while France was usually represented as a racial synthesis. However, these correlations were far from automatic. Mid-nineteenth-century Anglo-Saxonism powerfully promoted an intensely ethnic understanding of Britain's solely Germanic ancestry. Ireland never developed a flourishing raciology, despite its intensely neo-romantic antistate nationalism.[63] Meanwhile, in the 1920s, Russia became an important center of raciology and its sister science of serology, despite the strength of civic nationalism in support of empire, which Marina Mogilner's chapter in this volume emphasizes.[64] Again demonstrating the power of transnational hegemonic discourse in race anthropology, this suggests that core-periphery network connections could trump the historical baggage of civic or ethnic nationalism. Irish race classification was highly dependent on British ties and probably drew on the Anglo-Saxonist tradition,[65] while Russia had strong links with Germany and Slavic central Europe.[66]

Religion was another older cultural tradition that apparently affected the development of the race classification community and its institutionalization, especially in countries with Romance languages. The Catholic Church in this period was extremely conservative, opposing modernity, liberalism, science, and, especially, human biology. This drove race anthropologists, many of whom were politically engaged, into the arms of liberal reformers. As a result, the reformist regimes that came to power after liberal victories like Italian unification (1859–60), the French Third Republic (1870), and the Portuguese Republican Revolution (1911) founded new university chairs in anthropology.[67] Institutions thus often appeared earlier in these countries than in more industrially developed ones like the United Kingdom and Germany, where the Protestant establishment was less conservative and more open to science.[68] Nonconformist Quakers played an important role in English ethnology and Protestants were prominent in French anthropology.[69] Virchow, a politician who coined the term *Kulturkampf* to campaign against the Catholic Church, was a liberal race scientist, who opposed extreme nationalism. He countered Quatrefages's linkage of German barbarism with Finnish racial origin by making "special trips to Finland and Livonia" and identifying exceptionally fair-pigmented populations there.[70]

Irish nationalism became very closely identified with socially conservative Catholicism rather than anti-Catholic liberalism. Partly as a result, Irish race classification was strongly based in the humanities.[71] Catholicism may also have helped to make Polish and Austrian raciology less politically extreme than in Germany.[72] However, Polish classifiers firmly embraced Western modernity as part of their national identity and established biological race classification as a nationalist science.[73]

Transnational Narratives

Though classifiers initially focused on racially explaining their own nations, they invariably ended up incorporating national races into wider transnational family trees, maps, and historical accounts. Powerful core countries usually established the broad lines of the most transnationally authoritative syntheses in a way that flattered their own supposed ancestors. Peripheral and weaker national establishments exploited or inventively interpreted these schemes to maximize their own nation's prestige. Transnational debates about the Aryans and race psychology illustrate these dynamics.

The Aryans

The Indo-European language family, identified by the philologist William Jones in 1786, included most European languages, as well as Asian languages like Persian and Hindi. Like the racial terms White and Caucasian, it became a synonym for a common, superior, European identity and an object of transnational debate. Narratives of descent from superior Indo-European invaders from Asia legitimized Europe's own overseas colonialism.[74] In the context of ethnology, which initially assumed that people, language group, and biological race could be equated, Indo-Europeans were quickly racialized as the Aryan Race, their name taken from ancient Indian texts. Drawing especially on classical accounts of the Gauls and Teutons who battled the Roman Empire, these Aryans were assumed from very early on to be tall, warlike blonds.[75] Retzius reinforced this race narrative in 1840 by giving the Aryans, whose descendants he believed now predominated in western Europe, long skulls.[76] He said eastern Europeans, by contrast, were descended from primitive, broad-skulled European natives, who had abandoned their own languages when conquered by Aryans.

This Aryan-native dichotomy repeatedly reemerged in transnational race classification discourse. Linguistically non-Indo-European peoples like the Basques, Lapps, and Finns were particularly vulnerable to being bundled together into a common category of pathetic racial vestiges in classifications like those of Retzius and his Scandinavian colleagues, and the 1860s Mongoloid theories of Franz Pruner-Bey and Quatrefages.[77] The British and French "Celtic Fringes," which were also experiencing cultural retreat and political subjugation, were sometimes included in such categories and had to struggle to have their languages recognized as Indo-European. The philologist

Adolphe Pictet regretted that some of his colleagues left the "poor Celtic languages" out of the "vast and beautiful" Indo-European language family, which produced "the masterpieces which most honoured the intellectual and poetic genius of" humanity.[78] Classifiers also often identified the supposedly dark-featured urban proletariat as part of this vestige race.[79]

Retzius's long-skulled Aryan theory remained the scientific orthodoxy for two decades, until it was challenged by Broca in France. Broca's research in 1859–60, as well as subsequent French studies, found that most French people, except in the northeast, were relatively short, broad-skulled, and dark.[80] This was a disaster for the French, because Gallic Celtic ancestry had been established since the French Revolution, and especially after 1830, as a keystone of French national identity, and the broad-skulled type was not considered Celtic.[81] If Celts were linguistically Indo-European, they should be tall, long-skulled, blond, racial Aryans.

Broca's solution was a terminological ruse. He noted that Julius Caesar, whom he considered a reliable, ethnologically aware source, reported a tribal confederation in south central France that called itself the Celts. Science should, therefore, use this racial term for their short, dark, broad-skulled descendants in this region.[82] This reinstated so-called "Celts" as ancestors of the French. In the 1870s Broca's students went further. Identifying a wedge of these broad-skulls stretching from central Asia across a broad upland central belt of Europe to France, they argued that these were the descendants of the ancient Aryan immigrants.[83] The Aryans were broad-skulls and Europe's tall, blond long-skulls were primitive natives whom they had pushed into barren Scandinavia.

French prominence in race classification established broad-skulled Aryans as the transnational scientific orthodoxy until at least 1900, including among liberal German scholars such as Virchow.[84] Eastern European scholars like Anatoli Bogdanov in Russia, Isidor Kopernicki in Poland,[85] and the Romanian Alexandru Obedenariu[86] were particularly happy to associate their nations with what Broca's student Paul Topinard renamed the Celto-Slav race (see fig. 3).[87] It upgraded them to the status of superior racial Ary-

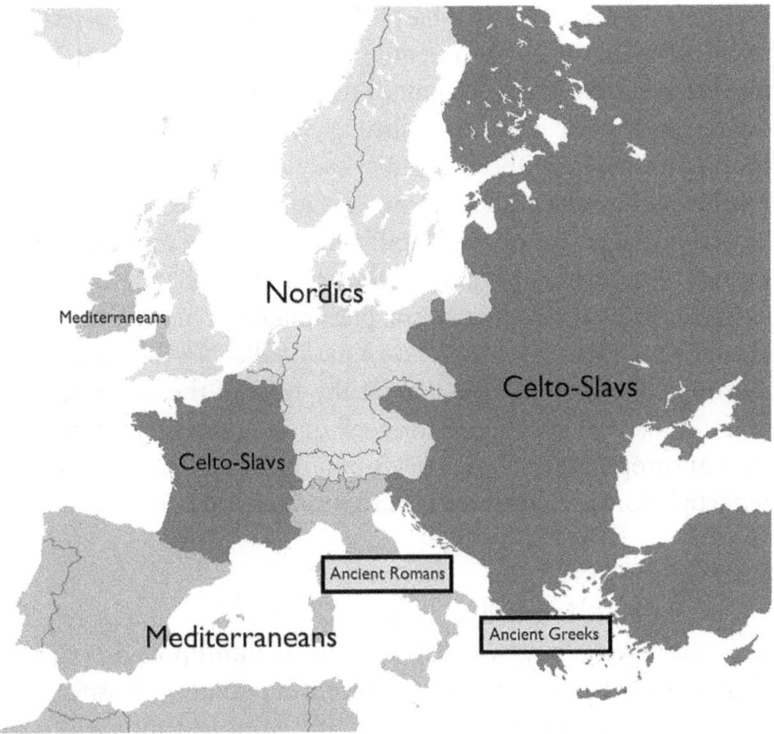

Fig 3. National races in the late nineteenth century, according to consensus opinion within the transnational classification community.

ans and linked them with the prestigious civilization of France. It also perfectly supported contemporary geopolitics. France sympathized with the nationalist struggles of Poles, Czechs, Yugoslavs, and Romanians against German or Habsburg rule and formed a military alliance with Russia against Germany in 1894. The millennial Celto-Slav struggle against (Germanic) Nordics legitimized these geopolitical alliances by extending them into the immemorial past.

The broad-skulled Aryan orthodoxy did not go unchallenged, however.[88] Anglophone writers never entirely abandoned blond Aryans and, on the continent—beginning as a parascientific fringe narrative in the 1880s—neo-romantic writers increasingly insisted that the Aryans were indeed tall, long-skulled blonds.[89] In this heyday of colonialism, however, blond Aryans were not traced from inferior Asia. Instead, this race had forged its superior characteristics in the challenging environment of chilly northern Europe. In the most extreme Nordicist accounts, little bands then spread throughout the prehistoric world, establishing civilizations like those of the Incas and Chinese.[90] The Germanic conquest of the Western Roman Empire and modern colonialism were more recent exploits of this illustrious race, which was the only one capable of founding civilizations. Nordic blood explained the art of the Italian Renaissance, and Jesus too was a Nordic Aryan, presumably on his mother's side.[91] Gustaf Kossinna's extreme *völkisch* nationalist Nordicism came to dominate German archaeology at the turn of the century,[92] and by 1918 this *völkisch* culture was well on its way to capturing German anthropology.[93] H. G. Wells's popular 1920 *Outline of History* reported Nordic Aryans from Europe as scientific fact.[94]

Race Psychology

The attribution of particular mental characteristics to races, referred to as race psychology by interwar German anthropologists such as H. F. K. Günther, was a perennial preoccupation in classification. It was closely linked to the project of allocating specific social roles to races, which right-wing fin-de-siècle anthroposociologists like Georges Vacher de Lapouge in France and Otto Ammon in Germany influentially reinforced with statistical correlations between racial and social data. Anthroposociologists and interwar raciologists often found Nordics better represented among elite classes and the Easteuropean type among proletarians.[95]

Physical race classifiers were periodically forced to abandon racial measures that did not correspond to their other race indices or were shown not to be fixed across generations. However, psychological measurements were proposed and discredited with particular frequency. By analogy with muscles, for example, mid-nineteenth-century anthropologists proposed skull volume (calculated by filling with seed) and size (absolute and proportional to body size) as intelligence indices.[96] Painstaking research discredited these theories by finding plenty of unexceptional individuals and colonial natives with big or heavy brains.[97] An Irish anthropologist in 1896, meanwhile, correlated "mental power" with wider skull sutures, arguing that "intense cerebration acts almost mechanically on the brain-cap, tending by its throbbing to keep the frontal sutures free till late in life."[98]

Despite the repeated failure of such measures, race classifiers continued to propose psycho-physical types. They drew on evidence such as folk sayings and descriptions in novels, while recognizing the scientific inadequacy of such evidence.[99] Most presumed that race psychological differences existed, and that "*some*" measurement would ultimately be found to accurately indicate "innate ability," arranging races in their "proper position in the social scale."[100] Race classifiers often insisted that race psychologies recognized difference rather than hierarchy, but, very often, ideas of superiority and inferiority were implicit at the very least.

The compass points were used to indicate two main systems of hierarchy in Europe. Broadly speaking, Atlantic and Mediterranean coastal countries tended to link superiority with pigmentation.[101] Racial value declined from the blond north, via the industrially underdeveloped Catholic Mediterranean, to Africa and apes.[102] This line could be kinked to include Ireland's "Iberian race" of "Black Kelts"—long-skulled like the Mediterraneans—as an intermediate stage.[103] The English anthropologist John Beddoe said the "most exquisite examples" of Ireland's "Sancho Panza" type never submitted to measurement: "Though the head is large, the intelligence is low."[104]

Scholars from Europe's interior and east more frequently stressed the inferiority of the Asiatic or Mongoloid east. This was reinforced by contemporary fears of the yellow peril from rising Japan and Chinese immigration into the United States and Australia, plus narratives of Ottoman decadence and the supposed Middle-Eastern racial origin of Jews.[105] Liberal German anthropologists like Virchow[106] and Julien Kollmann, for example, hastened to insist that broad skulls and "brunette complexion" were "legitimate appurtenances of white men," and did not "incorporate" them "into the yellow" "alien race."[107] The central racial index of sero-anthropology, meanwhile, contrasted blood group B, the Asiatic or "Asiatic-African property," concentrated in southeast Asia, to the superior group A, which was most common in northwest Europe.[108] Russian scholars bridled at attributions of their people's barbarism to racial infusions from repeated eastern steppe invaders. The raciologist Bunak insisted that medieval Russians hid "in the woods" to minimize contact with the "foreign" Turkish culture, adding that "the well-known French saying 'scratch a Russian and you will find a Tartar' is anthropologically meaningless."[109] These anti-eastern and anti-southern tendencies were far from mutually exclusive. The Scottish anthropologist Robert Knox, for example, declared that the Celtic race shared by Ireland (where "[c]ivilized man cannot sink lower") and France had "no accumulative habits; restless, treacherous, uncertain."[110] He was also, however, terrified of the "savage Asiatic despotism," "physical degradation," and "brute-force, represented by the East, by" "[s]winish," racially "abject" Russia.[111]

A second important transnational spatial pattern in race psychology was the structuring role of the Germanic-Nordic race. This was due to at least three factors. First, German, British, and American preeminence in economics and geopolitics in this period allowed Nordic-Germanics to convincingly portray themselves as the epitome of successful modernization, against which that of other peoples should be measured. Second, the identification of blond elites in largely non-Nordic nations reinforced this transnational role. Spanish and French aristocrats sometimes claimed descent from Germanic Visigoths and Franks, who had overrun the Western Roman Empire.[112] Third, the somewhat central geographical position of Germanic peoples in Europe, abutting Finns, Slavs, Latins, and Insular Celts, encouraged the creation of common non-Germanic race categories. Britain's mid-nineteenth-century Anglo-Saxonist race discourse represented the French and Irish "Celts" as "under every circumstance . . . precisely the same."[113] A fin-de-siècle Irish race writer linked the humour and "daring imagination" of Irish and Slavic peasants.[114]

Contrasts with the Germanic race psychology were tightly intertwined with ideological responses to modern change.[115] Race psychology offered a scientific basis to ideas of national character that played an important political role in adapting to modernity. Associating one's nation with the enterprising, conquering, aristocratic, and individualistic Nordic race could be used to legitimize existing social hierarchies, militarism, colonialism, and laissez-faire economics.[116] The Celto-Slav, by contrast, was generally portrayed as a patient, peaceful, industrious bourgeois, worker, or peasant, with strong collective tendencies.[117] This race psychology was used to suggest that liberal democracy and an activist state were natural to racially Celto-Slav peoples.

In less industrially developed eastern Europe, Celto-Slavists found it harder to claim urban modernity. However, they could exploit antimodern, elitist Nordicist fears that a dark industrial proletariat was swamping the aristocratic blond, whose children withered "in the fatal atmosphere of" towns.[118] Easterners could argue that their industrious, egalitarian, peaceful, and demographically booming peasantry was the perfect basis for building modern greatness in the future.[119] Here, they could exploit Hegel's idea of the World Spirit (*Weltgeist*), which had alighted in the classical Mediterranean, bringing greatness to Greece and Rome, and which now resided in the powerful Germanic north but might soon move eastward.[120] Russia's Bolsheviks, who owed a crucial philosophical debt to Hegel, drew heavily on this vision of future modern greatness.

Nordicists used this Hegelian narrative to contrast the decadent Mediterranean "man of the past," with the blond "man of the future," but Latins countered with their own narrative of racial talent for civilization.[121] Mussolini declared in 1934 that "thirty centuries of history allow us to contemplate with a scornful pity, transalpine doctrines supported by the descendants of men who did not know how to write, when Rome had Caesar, Virgil and Augustus."[122] The anthropologist Sergi fully accepted that the Mediterranean race were not conquering Aryans but portrayed the latter as savage barbarians who had destroyed Mediterranean civilization.[123] Narratives like this exploited the transnationally powerful old discourse of *ex oriente lux*, the idea that European civilization emerged from the east, in Aryan India, the Biblical Holy Land, or among the Babylonian and Egyptian progenitors of Greece and Rome.[124]

These competing modern ideological associations did not necessarily undermine transnationalism in race classification. German Nordicists and French Celto-Slavists often agreed on the stereotypical characteristics of both races, while applying different normative perspectives. Nordicists, therefore, interpreted the mutually accepted traits of the Celto-Slav pejoratively, emphasizing their petit-bourgeois conformism, conservatism, banality, "petty thrift," and lack of individual initiative and "real talent."[125] This consensus allowed a pan-European system of contrasting race psychologies to progressively emerge. Celto-Slav race narratives united Slavs and French in the 1870s. By the end of the century continental stereotypes of the wild, gregarious Germanic warrior had fused with the stern, orderly, "peaceable," "plodding, industrious" bourgeois or scientist of mid-nineteenth-century Anglo-Saxonist myth to create a new cold, efficient, militaristic late nineteenth-century Nordic aristocrat.[126] Later Nordicists adopted the "glorious deeds" of war and bellicose "fanaticism" that Anglo-Saxonists had once projected onto the Celtic race.[127]

A key narrative device in national responses to modern change was a representation of modern mixture among different European races as desirable or problematic. Ethnic nationalism, neo-romanticism, and Nordicism all strongly emphasized the value of race purity. Nordicists claimed modern superiority, while embracing antimodern, anti-urban, and anti-liberal neo-romanticism. They squared this circle by declaring that their modern success arose directly from their racial qualities.[128] Nordicists, therefore, worried deeply that the blurring social and ethnic boundaries of cosmopolitan modern urban civilization threatened the racial purity that brought them their triumphs. They believed blond "ruling classes" of ancient civilizations from India to Greece and Rome had fallen because "mixture with darker natives" adulterated their "Indo-European blood."[129]

By contrast, Italian, French, and (especially once Anglo-Saxonism declined in the later nineteenth century) British classifiers placed a strong emphasis on race mixture as a driver of successful civilization. In Britain this was associated with political ideas of national integration. To promote the integration of the United Kingdom, for example, British liberals like Thomas Huxley argued that the

British and Irish were both racial mixtures of Celts and Teutons.[130] Meanwhile, by combining dark broad-skulls with a supposedly Celtic blond strain, the French national race fusion included both the common people and the blond elites.[131]

Complex syntheses often blurred the distinction between narratives of purity and mixture. In supposedly ethnic nationalist eastern Europe, Poles, Russians, and Latvians were all somewhat open to partial descent from ancient Finnish natives of their countries, though these were distinctly junior parties in their national race fusions.[132] Eastern European scholars were, however, much more resistant to the idea of more recent racial infusions from Germans or Tartars.[133] In "civic nationalist" western Europe, meanwhile, there was an enduring consensus that interbreeding with inferior non-Europeans was undesirable. Though French race classifiers accepted France was a racial synthesis, Teutonic ancestors constituted a step too far. French blonds were instead Celts.[134] Late nineteenth-century Catholic Celticists in Ireland and many Greek scholars produced a still more complex amalgam of mixture and purity, claiming that their race had a special ability to maintain purity while absorbing foreign inputs.[135]

Some parts of Europe produced neo-romantic race narratives that rejected both modernity and Nordicism. Central and eastern European political movements like Eurasianism and Turanianism characterized local national races in very similar aristocratic terms as the Nordic but traced their noble, conquering ancestors to the Eurasian steppe rather than to Scandinavia.[136] This discourse could draw on older narratives like that of the early modern Polish gentry class, which claimed descent from Sarmatian steppe warriors.[137] The Russian poet Alexander Blok summed up the steppe warrior narrative in a 1918 poem, *The Scythians*:

> You are millions, we are multitudes
> And multitudes and multitudes.
> Come fight! Yea, we are Scythians
> Yea, Asiatics, a slant-eyed greedy brood.

In Ireland, Slavic countries and, to some extent, in Mediterranean countries, urban neo-romantics explained the political conquest and cultural retreat of their national races—preserved especially among the poorest and most isolated peasants—by claiming that they were distracted by their better nature.[138] They were more spiritual, sensitive, and connected to their emotions and, through the national soil, to nature. Thus, the literary critic Matthew Arnold made Celts "nature's own children," in communion with its "delicate magic" and "intimate life . . . her weird power and her fairy charm."[139]

Conclusion

In the project of classifying Europeans by race, transnational interactions among individuals and institutions (e.g., journals, textbooks, conferences) were not uniformly distributed. They had centers, zones of particular activity, and other specific spatial patterns, that all changed over time. As I stated at the start of this chapter, one of its purposes is to sketch the complex transnational mechanics of these broad patterns, contextualizing the episodes described in the other chapters.

Race classification, like any scientific project, needed research institutions, funding, specific technical resources, suitably educated people, and a social demand for the particular new knowledge that classifiers produced. Race classification's transnational core was, therefore, quickly and enduringly established in the industrial heartland of northwest Europe; it produced research methods and instruments, training institutions, prestigious journals, and authoritative works, which scholars from less institutionally endowed regions used. These core areas and the canonical European race schemes that they produced therefore reinforced transnational approaches to research and imbued them with relations of power. Transnational, nationalist, and state hierarchies of scientific prestige and influence all reinforced or undermined one another in complex patterns, creating both hegemonic race narratives and marginalized ones. As in all transnational patterns, the geography of race classification changed over time. The community expanded greatly at the turn of the twentieth century and its centre of gravity shifted decisively to Germany.

Older cultural geographies also shaped the transnational geography of race classification. Catholicism, for example, strongly influenced institutionalization in Latin countries. Meanwhile, raciology and antimodern narratives that emphasized race purity appear to have emerged largely in areas where nationalist movements opposed older dynastic state frontiers.

Patterns of local nationalism, then, helped shape classification practice. However, the transnationalism of race classification also influenced nationalism. Race classifiers reinforced the earlier philological project of allocating peoples to transnational groupings such as the Celts, Germanics, Latins, and Slavs, creating a European geography in which the powerful Germanics/Nordics had a special central position. In particular, race science played an important role in creating a pan-European transnational pattern of race psychologies, which was structured around the relationship between the Germanic-Nordic and its Others. As race psychologies elaborated and provided legitimacy to stereotypical ideas of national character, this system helped to infuse national identity with a transnational structure.

This chapter's other purpose is to emphasize to students of nationalism the role of the sciences in the development of nationalist narratives and, especially, their important contribution to making nationalism transnational. Science has a special ideological and organizational bias toward transnationalism. Scholars communicate and collaborate with peers, at home or abroad, in a common quest for universal truths. A transnational subject matter encouraged classifiers to organize themselves transnationally. Their transnational organisation in turn encouraged transnationalism in race narratives. As cross-border communication between early nationally focused investigators revealed that physical types extended across national borders, classification soon broadened its scope to consider the racial history and geography of Europe (and the world) as a whole. Pan-European debates about the Aryan, therefore, discussed a continent-wide history and geography.

Nationalism strained against transnationalism. The institutionalization of education and research in the later nineteenth century tended to create national establishments in the social sciences, which were free to concentrate on specifically national themes and develop distinctive national narratives. This is most marked in disciplines such as eugenics and professional history. However, in the period of international tension from the Franco-Prussian War of 1870–71 onward, race classification was also increasingly organized in a series of fiercely competing national establishments. The nationalist perspective was intensified by the project's central social function of justifying national identities.

Even amid the paranoid geopolitical tensions and intense nationalist passions of the 1930s, classification retained a strong transnational element. The relative weakness of its national establishments, compared to history and eugenics, required stronger transnational links, while the natural science identity of race classifiers reinforced their ideology of scientific universalism. Scholars read work by foreign colleagues, migrated (including to flee Nazi persecution), studied abroad, and exchanged ideas (and recriminations) at international conferences. Nationalist disputes intensified sympathy among allied countries, but, curiously, also sometimes stimulated interaction between foes. Intense disputes about the racial history of contested German-Polish borderlands, for example, forced nationalist scholars on both sides to closely follow and respond to one another's work.[140] The core-periphery organization of anthropology also reinforced shared transnational narratives. A shared system of race psychologies, meanwhile, survived, despite classifiers insulting one another's national race traits, in part because competing modern ideologies permitted different normative interpretations of these traits. This exemplifies the intricate interaction between national and transnational influences on race scholars' narration of national identity.

Notes

1. Rogers Brubaker, "Ethnicity, Race, and Nationalism," *Annual Review of Sociology* 35 (2009): 25–26.

2. William Z. Ripley, *A Selected Bibliography of the Anthropology and Ethnology of Europe* (Boston: Public Library, 1899), vii–viii.

3. Eugen Fischer, "Die Anfange der Anthropologie an der Universitat Freiburg," *Anthropologische Anzeiger* (1926): 100.

4. Ulf Hedetoft, "The Nation-state Meets the World: National Identities in the Context of Transnationality and Cultural Globalization," *European Journal of Social Theory*

2, no. 1 (1999): 71–72; Katherine Verdery, "Transnationalism, Nationalism, Citizenship, and Property: Eastern Europe since 1989," *American Ethnologist* 25, no. 2 (1998): 291–92.

5. Victoria Bernal, "Eritrea Goes Global: Reflections on Nationalism in a Transnational Era," *Cultural Anthropology* 19, no. 1 (2004): 4; Paul Virilio, "Speed and Information: Cyberspace Alarm!" *Ctheory* 18 (1995): http://www.ctheory.net/articles.aspx?id=72; Katharyne Mitchell, "Transnational Discourse: Bringing Geography Back In," *Antipode* 29, no. 2 (1997): 103; Jackie Smith and Dawn Wiest, "The Uneven Geography of Global Civil Society: National and Global Influences on Transnational Association," *Social Forces* 84, no. 2 (2005): 621.

6. For example, Joep Leerssen, "The Rhetoric of National Character: A Programmatic Survey," *Poetics Today* 21, no. 2 (2000): 278–79; and George Schöpflin, *Nations, Identity, Power: The New Politics of Europe* (London: Hurst, 2000), 90–98.

7. For example, Stein Rokkan, "Territories, Centres, and Peripheries: Towards a Geoethnic-Geoeconomic-Geopolitical Model of Differentiation within Western Europe," in *Centre and Periphery: Spatial Variation in Politics*, ed. Jean Gottmann (Beverly Hills CA: Sage, 1980), 163–204; Göran Therborn, *European Modernity and Beyond: The Trajectory of European Societies, 1945–2000* (London: Sage, 1995); and Franco Moretti, *Atlas of the European Novel: 1800–1900* (London: Verso, 1999).

8. Xosé-Manoel Núñez, "Nations and Territorial Identities in Europe: Transnational Reflections," *European History Quarterly* 40, no. 4 (2010): 670; Gal Ariely, "Nationhood across Europe: The Civic-Ethnic Framework and the Distinction between Western and Eastern Europe," *Perspectives on European Politics and Society* 14, no. 1 (2013): 123–25.

9. Anthony D. Smith, "The Diffusion of Nationalism: Some Historical and Sociological Perspectives," *British Journal of Sociology* (1978): 236; Slobodan Drakulic, "Whence Nationalism?," *Nations and Nationalism* 14, no. 2 (2008): 226.

10. Prasenjit Duara, "Transnationalism and the Predicament of Sovereignty: China, 1900–1945," *American Historical Review* 102, no. 4 (1997): 1033.

11. Even certain scholars of globalization agree (Mitchell, "Transnational Discourse," 104–5; Smith and Wiest, "Uneven Geography," 622–23).

12. Drakulic, "Whence Nationalism?," 226; Prasenjit Duara, *Rescuing History from the Nation: Questioning Narratives of Modern China* (Chicago: University of Chicago Press, 1996), 8.

13. Stephen Shulman, "Challenging the Civic/Ethnic and West/East Dichotomies in the Study of Nationalism," *Comparative Political Studies* 35, no. 5 (2002): 558; Núñez, "Transnational Reflections," 670.

14. John Agnew, "The Territorial Trap: The Geographical Assumptions of International Relations Theory," *Review of International Political Economy* 1, no. 1 (1994): 53–80.

15. Simon Naylor, "Introduction: Historical Geographies of Science: Places, Contexts, Cartographies," *British Journal for the History of Science* 38, no. 1 (2005): 2.

16. For example, Lawrence Dritsas, "From Lake Nyassa to Philadelphia: A Geography of the Zambesi Expedition, 1858–64," *British Journal for the History of Science* 38, no. 1 (2005): 36.

17. Loet Leydesdorff and Olle Persson, "Mapping the Geography of Science: Distribution Patterns and Networks of Relations among Cities and Institutes," *Journal of the American Society for Information Science and Technology* 61, no. 8 (2010): 1622–34.

18. Peter J. Taylor, Michael Hoyler, and David M. Evans, "A Geohistorical Study of 'The Rise of Modern Science': Mapping Scientific Practice through Urban Networks, 1500–1900," *Minerva* 46, no. 4 (2008): 394; David N. Livingstone, "Text, Talk, and Testimony: Geographical Reflections on Scientific Habits—An Afterword," *British Journal for the History of Science* 38, no. 1 (2005): 95.

19. Heike Jöns, "Academic Travel from Cambridge University and the Formation of Centres of Knowledge, 1885–1954," *Journal of Historical Geography* 34, no. 2 (2008): 341.

20. Taylor, Hoyler, and Evans, "A Geohistorical Study," 392.

21. Claude Blanckaert, "On the Origins of French Ethnology: William Edwards and the Doctrine of Race," in *Bodies, Bones, Behaviour: Essays on Biological Anthropology*, ed. George W. Stocking Jr. (Madison: University of Wisconsin Press, 1988), 38–46.

22. Chris Manias, *Race, Science, and the Nation: Reconstructing the Ancient Past in Britain, France, and Germany, 1800–1914* (New York: Routledge, 2013), 114–15.

23. H. F. Vermeulen, *Before Boas: The Genesis of Ethnography and Ethnology in the German Enlightenment* (Lincoln: University of Nebraska Press, 2015), 21.

24. William Edwards, "Des Caractères Physiologiques des Races Humaines considérés dans leur rapports avec l'histoire: Lettre à M. Amédée Thierry, auteur de l'histoire des Gaulois," *Mémoires de la Société Ethnologique* 1 (1841): 2; William Z. Ripley, *A Selected Bibliography of the Anthropology and Ethnology of Europe* (Boston: Public Library, 1899), vii–viii ; Jan Czekanowski, *Człowiek w czasie i przestrzenie* (Warsaw: Państwowe Wydawnictwo Naukowe, 1967), 20.

25. Maria Sophia Quine, "Making Italians: Aryanism and Anthropology in Italy during the Risorgimento," in *Crafting Humans: From Genesis to Eugenics and Beyond*, ed. Marius Turda (Göttingen: V&R unipress, 2013), 130, 141.

26. Quine, "Making Italians," 130, 141.

27. Iordache Făcăoaru, "Contribuţii la studiul rasial a studenţilor minoritari din România," *Buletinul Eugenic şi Biopolitic* 9, nos. 1–2 (1938): 209–15; Ilse Schwidetzky, "Die Rassenforschung in Polen," *Zeitschrift für Rassenkunde und ihre Nachbargebiete* 1 (1935): 80–82; Egon Freiherr von Eickstedt, "Geschichte der anthropolgische Namengabung und Klassifikation (unter Betonung von Sudasien): Teil II," *Zeitschrift für Rassenkunde* 6 (1937): 36–96, 88; Björn M. Felder, "'God forgives—but Nature never will': Racial Identity, Racial Anthropology, and Eugenics in Latvia, 1918–1940," in *Baltic Eugenics: Bio-Politics, Race and Nation in Interwar Estonia, Latvia and Lithuania 1918–1940*, ed. Björn M. Felder and Paul J. Weindling (Amsterdam: Rodopi, 2013), 120.

28. Claude Blanckaert, "L'indice céphalique et l'ethnogénie européenne: A. Retzius, P. Broca, F. Pruner-Bey (1840–1870)," *Bulletins et Mémoires de la Société d'Anthropologie de Paris* n.s., nos. 3–4 (1989): 166–67.

29. Schwidetzky, "Die Rassenforschung," 79.

30. Rudolf Virchow, " Menschliche Schädel aus Krakauer Höhlen," *Zeitschrift für Ethnologie. Verhandlungen der Berliner Gesellschaft für Anthropologie, Ethnologie und Urgeschichte* 5 (1873): 196.

31. Benoit Massin, "From Virchow to Fischer: Physical Anthropology and Modern Race Theories in Wilhelmine Germany," in *Volksgeist as Method and Ethic: Essays on Boasian Ethnography and the German Anthropological Tradition*, ed. George W. Stocking Jr. (Madison: University of Wisconsin Press, 1996), 128.

32. Laurent Mucchielli, "Sociologie versus anthropologie raciale: L'engagement des sociologues durkheimiens dans le contexte 'fin de siècle' (1885–1914)," *Gradhiva: Revue d'histoire et d'archives de l'anthropologie* 21 (1997): 77–95.

33. Ludwig Woltmann, *Politische Anthropologie: Eine Untersuchung über den Einfluss der Descendenztheorie auf die Lehre von der politischen Entwicklung der Völker* (Jena: Eugen Diederichs, 1903), 293.

34. Giuseppe Sergi, *Specie e Varietà Umane: Saggio di una sistematica antropologica* (Turin: Fratelli Bocca, 1900), 169, 209–10.

35. Aira Kemilainen, *Suomalaiset, Outo Pohjolan Kansa: Rotuteoriat ja kansallinen identiteetti* (Helsinki: SHS, 1994), 402–3; Kaarlo Hildén, "Über die sog. ostbaltische Rasse," *Institut International d'Anthropologie: IIIe Session Amsterdam 20–29 Septembre 1927* (Paris: Librarie E. Nourry, 1928), 220–23; Kazimierz Stołyhwo, "Über die sog. ostbaltische Rasse," *Institut International d'Anthropologie*, 224; Viktor V. Bunak, "Neues Material zur Aussonderung anthropologoscher Typen unter der Bevölkerung Osteuropas," *Zeitschrift für Morphologie und Anthropologie* 30 (1932): 464–66, 471–74, 491–93; Felder, "God forgives," 125.

36. Rory Yeomans, "'Of Yugoslav 'Barbarians' and Croatian Gentlemen Scholars: Nationalist Ideology and Racial Anthropology in Interwar Yugoslavia," in *Blood and Homeland: Eugenics and Racial Nationalism in Central and Southeast Europe, 1900–1940*, ed. Marius Turda and Paul J. Weindling (Budapest: Central European University Press, 2007), 94–97; Egon Freiherr von Eickstedt, *Rassenkunde und Rassengeschichte der Menschheit* (Stuttgart: Ferdinand Enke, 1934), 365; Marina Mogilner, *Homo Imperii: A History of Physical Anthropology in Russia* (Lincoln: University of Nebraska Press, 2013), 215, 366.

37. Bronisław Jasicki, "Sto Lat Antropologii Polskiej 1856–1956: Ośrodek krakowski w latach 1908–1956," *Polska Akademia Nauk: Zakład Antropologii: Materiały i Prace Antropologiczne* 33 (1957): 32–37.

38. Armand de Quatrefages, *La Race Prussienne* (Paris: Librarie Hachette & Cie, 1871).

39. Massin, "Virchow to Fischer," 106; Gustaf Retzius, "The So-Called North European Race of Mankind: A Review of, and Views on, the Development of Some Anthropological Questions," *Journal of the Royal Anthropological Institute of Great Britain and Ireland* 39, no. 2 (1909): 278.

40. Kenan Malik, *The Meaning of Race: Race, History, and Culture in Western Society* (Houndmills: Macmillan, 1996), 120; Houston Steward Chamberlain, *Die Grundlagen des neunzehnten Jahrhunderts* (Munich: F. Bruckmann K.-G., [1899] 1938), 313, 317–18.

41. Uwe Puschner, "Die Germanenideologie im Kontext der völkischen Weltanschauung," *Göttinger Forum für Altertumswissenschaft* 4 (2001): 87–89; Bernard Mees, "Völkische Altnordistik: The Politics of Nordic Studies in the German-Speaking Countries, 1926–45," in *Old Norse Myths, Literature, and Society: 11th International Saga Conference 2–7 July 2000, University of Sydney*, ed. Geraldine Barnes and Margaret Clunies Ross (Sydney: Centre for Medieval Studies, University of Sydney, 2000), 317.

42. John Hutchinson, *The Dynamics of Cultural Nationalism: The Gaelic Revival and the Creation of the Irish National State* (London: Allen & Unwin, 1987), 130–34; Marius Turda, "Deciding the National Capital: Budapest, Vienna, Bucharest, and Transylvanian Romanian Political Culture," in *Tradition and Modernity in Romanian Culture and Civilization 1600–2000*, ed. Kurt W. Treptow (Iaşi: Centre for Romanian Studies, 2001), 106.

43. Jan Czekanowski, "The Racial Structure of Silesia," *Baltic and Scandinavian Countries* 3.2.6 (1937): 227–32; Jan Czekanowski, *Antropologia polska w międzywojennym dwudziestoleciu 1919–1939* (Warsaw: Towarzystwo Naukowe Warszawskie, 1948), 16–17.

44. Bunak, "Bevölkerung Osteuropas," 468.

45. George Montandon, *La race, les races: Mise au point d'éthnologie somatique* (Paris: Payot, 1933), 99, 247–49, 272.

46. William Z. Ripley, *A Selected Bibliography of the Anthropology and Ethnology of Europe* (Boston: Public Library, 1899); Giulio Cogni, "Note Bibliografiche Informative," in *Piccola Bibliografia Razziale*, ed. Giulio Cogni and Guido Landra, 35–71 (Rome: Ulpiano, 1939).

47. Mogilner, *Homo Imperii*, 76.

48. Ripley, *Selected Bibliography*, and Cogni, "Note Bibliografiche."

49. For example, St. M. Milcu, "Dezvoltarea Cercetărilor de Antropologie în Ţara Noastră," *Probleme De Antropologie* 1 (1954): 8–12, 17–19; C. R. Browne, "Report of the Work Done in the Anthropometric Laboratory of Trinity College, Dublin, From 1891 to 1898," *Proceedings of the Royal Irish Academy* 3, no. 5 (1900): 269.

50. William Z. Ripley, *The Races of Europe: A Sociological Study* (London: Kegan Paul, Trench, Trubner, 1900), 462; Blanckaert, "L'indice céphalique," 188; Paul Broca, "Qu'est-ce que les Celtes?," *Bulletins de la Société d'Anthropologie de Paris* 19 (1864): 463.

51. Richard McMahon, *The Races of Europe: Construction of National Identities in the Social Sciences, 1839–1939* (London: Palgrave Macmillan, 2016), 463–64.

52. Schwidetzky, "Die Rassenforschung," 79; János Nemeskéri, "The History of Physical Anthropology in Hungary," in *Toward a Science of Man*, T. H. Thoresen (The Hague: Mouton, 1975), 139.

53. However, larger countries also tended to be cited more often in their own languages.

54. McMahon, *The Races of Europe*, 253–62.

55. Eickstedt, "anthropolgische Namengabung."

56. Bodo Skjerl, "Die rassische Gliederung der Menschheit," *Zeitschrift für Rassenkunde und ihre Nachbargebiete* [Stuttgart] 4 (1936): 285, 299; Ioan G. Botez, *Con-*

tribuţiuni la studiul taliei si al indicelui cefalic în Moldova de nord şi Bucovina (Iaşi: Institut de Arte Grafice Brawo, 1938), 9.

57. Iordache Făcaoăru, "Contribuţii la studiul rasial a studenţilor minoritari din România," *Buletinul Eugenic şi Biopolitic* 9, nos. 1–2 (1938): 209.

58. McMahon, *The Races of Europe*, 60.

59. Manias, *Race, Science, and the Nation*, 114.

60. "Introduction: Rethinking German Anthropology, Colonialism, and Race," in *Worldly Provincialism: German Anthropology in the Age of Empire*, H. Glenn Penny and Matti Bunzl (Ann Arbor: University of Michigan Press, 2003), 6.

61. "A History of Paradoxes: Anthropologies of Europe," in *Fieldwork and Footnotes: Studies in the History of European Anthropology*, Han F. Vermeulen and Arturo Alvarez Roldan (London: Routledge, 1995), 235–46.

62. Craig Calhoun, "Introduction to the Transaction Edition," in *The Idea of Nationalism: A Study in Its Origins and Background*, ed. Hans Kohn (New Brunswick NJ: Transaction, 2008), xxxiii.

63. L. P. Curtis Jr., *Anglo-Saxons and Celts: A Study of Anti-Irish Prejudice in Victorian England* (Bridgeport CT: Conference on British Studies at the University of Bridgeport, 1968), 108, 111–12; Elizabeth Fee, "Nineteenth-Century Craniology: The Study of the Female Skull," *Bulletin of the History of Medicine* 53, no. 3 (1979): 425.

64. Claudio Pogliano, *L'ossessione della razza: Antropologia e genetica nel xx secolo* (Pisa: Edizioni della Normale, 2005), 492; Egon Freiherr von Eickstedt, *Die Forschung am Menschen: Teil 1: Geschichte und Methoden der Anthropologie* (Stuttgart: Ferdinand Enke, 1940), 174; W. H. Schneider, "The History of Research on Blood Group Genetics: Initial Discovery and Diffusion," *History and Philosophy of the Life Sciences* 18, no. 3 (1996): 302.

65. McMahon, *The Races of Europe*, 260, 267.

66. Mogilner, *Homo Imperii*, 32, 37, 40, 58, 60–67, 80–81, 93, 101, 110, 137–38, 355, 365.

67. Făcaoăru, "studenţilor minoritari," 211; Quine, "Making Italians," 130, 141; J. Harvey, "L'evolution transformée: Positivistes et materialistes dans la Societé d'Anthropologie de Paris du Second Empire à la IIIe Republique," in *Histoires de l'Anthropologie (XVIe-XIXe siècles): Colloque: La Practique de l'Anthropologie Aujourd'hui*, ed. Britta Rupp-Eisenreich (Paris: Klincksieck, 1984), 400, 402; Michael Hammond, "Anthropology as a Weapon of Social Combat in Late-Nineteenth-Century France," *Journal of the History of the Behavioural Sciences* 16 (1980): 126.

68. George W. Stocking Jr., *Victorian Anthropology* (New York: Free Press, 1991), 267; Massin, "Virchow to Fischer," 84–85.

69. Denise Ferembach, "History of Human Biology in France: Part 1: The Early Years," *International Association of Human Biologists, Occasional Papers* 2, no. 1 (1986): 24.

70. Rudolf Virchow, "Race Formation and Heredity," in *This is Race: An Anthology Selected from the International Literature on the Races of Man*, ed. Earl W. Count (New York: Schuman, 1950), 184; Massin, "Virchow to Fischer," 80, 100.

71. Curtis, *Anglo-Saxons and Celts*, 114–15; Hutchinson, *Gaelic Revival*, 124, 135.

72. Stanisław Klimek, *Rasa w zjawiskach społecznych* (Lwów: Wydawnictwo Instytutu Wyższej Kultury Religijnej, 1939), 39.

73. Klimek, *Rasa w zjawiskach społecznych*, 35–36; Stanislaw Żejmo-Żejmis, "Zespoly kulturowe Europy," *Czasopismo Geograficzne* 11 (1933): 58, 65–66.

74. Reginald Horsman, "Origins of Racial Anglo-Saxonism in Great Britain before 1850," *Journal of the History of Ideas* 37, no. 3 (1976): 393.

75. Louis-Achille Bonté, "Sur les origines européennes," *Bulletins de la Société d'Anthropologie de Paris* 5 (1864): 280; Paul Broca, *Recherches sur l'Ethnologie de la France, Mémoires d'Anthropologie I* (Paris: C. Reinwald, [1859] 1871): 365–69.

76. Anders Retzius, *Ethnologische Schriften von Anders Retzius: Nach dem Tode des Verfassers gesammelt* (Stockholm: P. A. Norstedt & Soner, 1864), 3. This book contained a selection of Retzius's articles from 1842–56.

77. Ripley, *Races of Europe*, 462; Blanckaert, "L'indice céphalique," 188; Broca, "les Celtes?," 463; Quatrefages, *La Race Prussienne*, 44–46, 49–50; Armand de Quatrefages, *Histoire générale des races humaines: Introduction à l'étude des races humaines* (Paris: A. Hennuyer, 1889), 301, 313, 455–57.

78. Adolphe Pictet, "Lettres à M. A. W. de Schegel, sur l'affinité des langues celtiques avec le sanscrit," *Journal Asiatique* ser. 3, vol. 2 (March and May 1836): 264.

79. Retzius, "North European Race," 300–301; John Beddoe, "Colour and Race," *Journal of the Anthropological Institute of Great Britain and Ireland* 35 (1905): 237.

80. Broca, *l'Ethnologie de la France*, 284–85, 300.

81. Ivan Hannaford, *Race: The History of an Idea in the West* (Baltimore: Johns Hopkins University Press, 1996), 288. Early modern French nobles had claimed Germanic Frankish ancestry in order to defend their privileges against royal autocracy. In response, revolutionary ideologues claimed the Gauls as ancestors of the common people. The Abbé Sieyès incited the third estate in 1798 to send "back into the forests of Germania all these families who maintain the insane claim to have issued from the race of conquerors." Anne-Marie Thiesse, *La création des identités nationales: Europe XVIIIe-Xxe siècle* (Paris: Editions du Seuil, 2001), 51; Michael Dietler, "'Our Ancestors the Gauls': Archaeology, Ethnic Nationalism, and the Manipulation of Celtic Identity in Modern Europe," *American Anthropologist* 96, no. 3 (1994): 587.

82. Paul Broca, "Sur les Celtes," *Bulletins de la Société d'Anthropologie de Paris* 19 (1864a): 557–58.

83. Jan Czekanowski, *Zarys Historii Antropologii Polskiej* (Cracow: Polska Akademia Umiejetnośći, 1948), 19; Paul Topinard, *Éléments d'Anthropologie Générale* (Paris: Delahaye & Levosnier, 1885), 403–5.

84. Woltmann, *Politische Anthropologie*, 292–93.

85. Czekanowski, *Zarys*, 19; Topinard, *Éléments*, 403–5.

86. M. G. Obédénare, "Les Celtes de l'Europe orientale," *Revue d'Anthropologie* 6 (1877): 253.

87. Emile Houzé, "Les charactères physiques des races européennes," *Bulletin de la Societé d'Anthropologie de Bruxelles* 2 (1883): 88, 96.

88. McMahon, *The Races of Europe*, 199–201.

89. Neil MacMaster, *Racism in Europe* (Houndsmill: Palgrave Macmillan, 2001), 33, 53, 80; Augustus Henry Keane, *Man: Past and Present*, rev. ed., A. Hingston Quiggin and A. C. Haddon (Cambridge: At the University Press [1899] 1920), 504; John V. Day, "Aryanism," in *History of Physical Anthropology: An Encyclopedia*, vol. 1, ed. Frank Spencer (New York: Garland, 1997), 109; Houzé, "Races européennes," 86–87.

90. Woltmann, *Politische Anthropologie*, 287–90.

91. Woltmann, *Politische Anthropologie*, 289.

92. Karel Sklenář, *Archaeology in Central Europe: The First 500 Years* (Leicester: Leicester University Press, 1983), 131–32, 135.

93. Massin, "Virchow to Fischer," 80, 114, 142.

94. H. G. Wells, *The Outline of History: Being a Plain History of Life and Mankind* (New York: Macmillan, 1920), 152.

95. Eickstedt, *Rassenkunde*, 352; Hans F. K. Günther, *Kleine Rassenkunde des Deutsches Volkes* (München: J. F. Lehmanns, 1933), 59–60, 93.

96. Julian Huxley and Alfred Cort Haddon, *We Europeans: A Survey of "Racial" Problems* (London: Jonathan Cape, 1935), 42–43; Fee, "Female Skull," 420–22.

97. G. Banu, *L'hygiène de la race: Etude de biologie héréditaire et de normalisation de la race* (Bucharesti: M. O. Imprimeria nationala, 1939), 204–5.

98. Augustus Henry Keane, *Ethnology*, 2nd rev. ed. (Cambridge: At the University Press, 1896), 44–45.

99. Günther, *Kleine Rassenkunde*, 93; Hans-Jürgen Lutzhöft, *Der Nordische Gedanke in Deutschland 1920–1940* (Stuttgart: Ernst Klett, 1971), 108–9.

100. Malik, *Meaning of Race*, 88; John Grattan, "Notes on the Human Remains Discovered within the Round Towers of Ulster: With Some Additional Contributions towards a 'Crania Hibernica,'" *Ulster Journal of Archaeology* 6 (1858): 27; Laurent Mucchielli, "Sociologie versus anthropologie raciale," 2; Nélia Dias, *Le Musée d'Ethnographie du Trocadero (1878–1908): Anthropologie et Muséologie en France* (Paris: Editions du Centre National de la Recherche Scientifique, 1991), 22.

101. Tzvetan Todorov, *On Human Diversity: Nationalism, Racism, and Exoticism in French Thought* (Cambridge MA: Harvard University Press, 1993), 102–3; James Cowles Prichard, *Researches into the Physical History of Man* (Chicago: University of Chicago Press, [1813] 1973), 172–73, 235.

102. McMahon, *The Races of Europe*, 257–58.

103. Alfred Cort Haddon, "Studies in Irish Craniology: III, A Neolithic Cist Burial at Oldbridge, County of Meath," *Proceedings of the Royal Irish Academy*, ser. 3, vol. 4 (1896–98): 580–83; John Beddoe, "The Basque and the Kelt: An Examination of Mr. W. Boyd Dawkins' Paper, 'The Northern Range of the Basques' in the *Fortnightly Review*, September 1874," *Journal of the Anthropological Institute of Great Britain and Ireland* 5 (1876): 23–24; John Beddoe, *The Races of Britain: A Contribution to the Anthropology of Western Europe* (London: Hutchinson [1885] 1971), 10, 13, 25–26, 294; Dawkins W. Boyd, "The Basque and the Kelt: An Examination of Mr. Boyd Dawkins' Paper, 'The

Northern Range of the Basques' in the *Fortnightly Review*, September 1874," *Journal of the Anthropological Institute of Great Britain and Ireland* 5 (1876): 21.

104. Beddoe, *Races of Britain*, 10.

105. Iordache Făcăoaru, "Valoarea biorasială a națiunilor europene și a provincilor românești: O primă încercare de ierarhizare etnică," *Buletinul Eugenic și Biopolitic* 14, nos. 9–10 (1943): 292; Malik, *Meaning of Race*, 118–19; Pogliano, *L'ossessione*, 111; Iver B. Neumann, *Uses of the Other: "The East" in European Identity Formation* (Manchester: Manchester University Press, 1999), 82; Ingo Wijworra, "German Archaeology and its Relation to Nationalism and Racism," in *Nationalism and Archaeology in Europe*, ed. Margarita Diaz-Andreu and Timothy Champion (London: UCL Press, 1996), 175–76; Pauline M. H. Mazumdar, "Blood and Soil: The Serology of the Aryan Racial State," *Bulletin of the History of Medicine* 64, no. 2 (1990): 197.

106. Rudolf Virchow, "Race Formation and Heredity," in *This is Race: An Anthology Selected from the International Literature on the Races of Man*, ed. Earl W. Count (New York: Schuman [1896] 1950), 190.

107. Julien Kollmann, "Beitrag zu einer Kraniologie der europäischen Völker," *Archiv für Anthropologie* 14 (1881): 35, 37.

108. L. Hirschfeld and H. Hirschfeld, "Essai d'application des méthodes sérologiques au problème des races," *L'Anthropologie* 29 (1918): 535.

109. Bunak, "Bevölkerung Osteuropas," 492.

110. Robert Knox, *The Races of Men: A Philosophical Enquiry into the Influence of Race over the Destinies of Nations: A Fragment* (London: Henry Renshaw, 1850), 26, 324–25.

111. Knox, *Races of Men*, 5, 60, 321, 363–68.

112. Léon Poliakov, *Le myth aryen* (Paris: Calmann-Lévy, 1971), 24–25, 40–41, 60.

113. Knox, *Races of Men*, 318; Curtis, *Anglo-Saxons and Celts*, 22.

114. James L. MacLoughlin, "The Race-Type in Celtic Literature," *New Ireland Review* 5. no. 2 (1896): 26–38, 81–94.

115. Richard McMahon, "Anthropological Race Psychology 1820–1945: A Common European System of Ethnic Identity Narratives," *Nations and Nationalism* 15, no. 4 (2009): 582–89.

116. Günther, *Kleine Rassenkunde*, 59–61; Eickstedt, *Rassenkunde*, 354–56.

117. Broca, *l'Ethnologie de la France*, 292; Paul Topinard, "Essai de Classification des Races Humaines Actuelles," *Revue d'Anthropologie* 2, no. 1 (1878): 508; Topinard, *Éléments*, 400–401; Alfred Cort Haddon, *The Races of Man* (London: Cambridge at the University Press, 1924), 15, 26, 152; Ripley, *Races of Europe*, 470, 473; Obédénare, "Celtes de l'Europe orientale," 253–54.

118. Retzius, "North European Race," 300–301; Beddoe, "Colour and Race," 237; Elazar Barkan, *The Retreat of Scientific Racism: Changing Concepts of Race in Britain and the United States between the World Wars* (Cambridge: Cambridge University Press, 1992), 26.

119. Jean Cuisenier, *Etnologia Europei* (Iași: Institutul European, 1999), 31; Julian Talko-Hryncewicz, "O czlowieku na ziemiach Polskich," *Przegląd Powszechny* 62 (1914): 191.

120. Neumann, *The East*, 74–79, 100.

121. J. W. Jackson, "The Atlantean Race of Western Europe," *Journal of the Anthropological Institute of Great Britain and Ireland* 2 (1873): 400.

122. Cited in Poliakov, *Le myth aryen*, 84.

123. Sergi, *Specie e Varietà Umane*, 213–14.

124. J. A. N. Périer, "Que les vrais Celtes sont les vrais Galois," *Bulletins de la Société d'Anthropologie de Paris* 5 (1864): 615–16; Franz Pruner-Bey, "Sur l'origine asiatique des Européens," *Bulletins de la Société d'Anthropologie de Paris* 5 (1864): 223–42: 224; V. Gordon Childe, *The Aryans: A Study of Indo-European Origins* (London: Kegan Paul, Trench, Trubner, 1926), 94; Day, "Aryanism," 109; Wijworra, "German Archaeology," 166–67.

125. Günther, *Kleine Rassenkunde*, 64–66; Retzius, "North European Race," 299, 313; Ripley, *Races of Europe*, 529–31, 549–50; Eickstedt, *Rassenkunde*, 376.

126. Knox, *Races of Men*, 53–54; Curtis, *Anglo-Saxons and Celts*, 71; Matthew Arnold, *Lectures and Essays in Criticism* (Ann Arbor: University of Michigan Press, 1962), 341.

127. Knox, *Races of Men*, 26.

128. Woltmann, *Politische Anthropologie*, 260, 272–73, 289.

129. Woltmann, 289; Massin, "Virchow to Fischer," 129; Vanderkindere, "Les charactères physiques des races européennes," *Bulletin de la Societé d'Anthropologie de Bruxelles* 2 (1883): 94, 97.

130. John Wilson Foster, "Nature and Nation in the Nineteenth Century," in *Nature in Ireland: A Scientific and Cultural History*, ed. John Wilson Foster and Helena C. G. Chesney (Dublin: Lilliput, 1997), 434; John Lubbock, "The Nationalities of the United Kingdom: Extracts from Letters to the *Times*," *Journal of the Anthropological Institute of Great Britain and Ireland* 16 (1887): 420; Arnold, *Lectures and Essays*, 296–302.

131. Périer, "vrais Celtes," 624.

132. Felder, "God forgives," 125; Talko-Hryncewicz, "O czlowieku," 193; Mogilner, *Homo Imperii*, 124–25, 176.

133. Bunak, "Bevölkerung Osteuropas," 469, 492–93; Hildén, "ostbaltische Rasse," 220–21, 223; Jan Czekanowski, "Recherches anthropologiques de la Pologne," *Bulletins et Mémoires de la Société d'Anthropologie de Paris* ser. 7, vol. 1(1920): 53.

134. Woltmann, *Politische Anthropologie*, 262; Hannaford, *Race*, 288.

135. Sevasti Trubeta, "Anthropological Discourse and Eugenics in Interwar Greece," in *Blood and Homeland: Eugenics and Racial Nationalism in Central and Southeast Europe, 1900–1940*, ed. Marius Turda and Paul Weindling (Budapest: Central European University Press, 2007), 131; Hutchinson, *Gaelic Revival*, 123; Sophie Bryant, *Celtic Ireland* (London: K. Paul, Trench, 1889), xviii, 27.

136. Peter Bugge, "The Nation Supreme: The Idea of Europe 1914–1945," in *History of the Idea of Europe*, ed. Kevin Wilson and Jan van dar Dussen (Milton Keynes: Open University, 1996), 134; Orlando Figes, *Natasha's Dance: A Cultural History of Russia* (London: Allen Lane, 2002), 414, 423–25.

137. Barbara Tornquist-Plewa, "The Complex of the Unwanted Child: The Meanings of Europe in Polish Discourse," in *The Meaning of Europe*, ed. Mikael af Malmborg and Bo Strath (Oxford: Berg, 2002), 217–19.

138. John V. Kelleher, "Matthew Arnold and the Celtic Revival," in *Perspectives of Criticism*, ed. Harry Levin (Cambridge MA: Harvard University Press, 1950), 216.

139. Arnold, *Lectures and Essays*, 374.

140. Czekanowski, "Silesia," 227–28; Schwidetzky, "Die Rassenforschung."

TWO

The Destiny of Races "Not Yet Called to Civilization"

Giustiniano Nicolucci's Critique of American Polygenism and Defense of Liberal Racism

MARIA SOPHIA QUINE

The concept of race pre-dated the Enlightenment and the French Revolution, but what has become known as "scientific racism," consisting of "learned theories" that speciation and raciation within human groups resulted from history and evolution[1] arose as an integral part of late modernity.[2] From its inception, anthropology made "race" its exclusive preoccupation. Historians have focused mostly upon the "classic" age of scientific racism, which coincided with the era of New Imperialism (1870–1914). During this time, scientific constructs of race proved to be indispensable tools for European expansionism. However, the early nineteenth century—and especially the 1830s–1850s—marked a tremendously important epistemological shift. From the 1720s to the 1830s, humanistic notions of human progress and perfectibility predominated. The rise of evolutionary theory and biological materialism generated novel forms of race-centered social thought that challenged these idealistic presumptions. The idea that all of humanity could be divided into different, primordial entities called races, which possessed quite distinct physical and mental attributes and entirely separate manifest destinies, became dominant within modern science and society. A paradigm of race as a determinant of human behavior and development inscribed itself in Western culture, well before the end of the nineteenth century. Racism constituted a new mechanism, language, technique, and technology of power, politics, policies, and nationalism for societies and governments in the West.

Despite the rise of biological and racial determinism, differences of opinion about the meaning of race existed. These disputes are the principal focus of this chapter. Until the nineteenth century, the doctrine of the unity and common origin of humanity, though not uncontested, held sway. So dominant was the theory of one human family, with a single parentage and descent, that it was widely considered to be a defining principle and first proposition of the new ethnology, founded by the Slovakian historian Adam Franz Kollár (1718–1783), as the study of the world's peoples, nations, and cultures.[3] However, in the nineteenth century, monogenesis became one of the most contested and politicized areas of debate within the emergent anthropology, the self-styled "science of Race" and "science of Skulls." As both a scientific hypothesis and a social value, monogeny has received less attention than it deserves. The two finest examples of pioneering historical works on race science focused exclusively on the United States and Britain—countries that, together with France and Germany, continue to dominate the scholarship.[4] Most of the new literature in the field remains very much concentrated within the traditions of national history.[5] However, science was and remains international in nature and scope, so transnational connectivities and connections, and the dialogues and debates between scientists working in different countries and contexts, are a significant avenue of investigation.

It has long been recognized that many elites in the antebellum United States repudiated the thesis of one human race and searched for scientific justifications for slavery, segregation, and "American Apartheid." They found these rationales in theories of race, culture, and intelligence that rejected Enlightenment egalitarian ideas and denied Asians, Native Americans, and, especially, Africans humanity and personhood. Polygeny in the United States was founded upon the notion that the brain of an adult "Negro" never developed beyond that of the "Caucasian" boy and resembled the brain of the orangutan more than it did that of any human. By the 1840s polygeny was becoming orthodoxy; however, dissent from this doctrine remained vocal in some places and quarters throughout the nineteenth century. This chapter focuses on the repudiation, on scientific, moral, and political grounds, of the so-called American school of anthropology by the founder of what might be called the Italian school of anthropology. Italy is a significant, though neglected, case study in the history of debates about the origins and nature of man. The Broca-Virchow story of mono- and polygenism has figured prominently in the historiography; this interchange took place mainly in the 1870s. Italy challenges the Franco-German centrality in the scholarship and complicates the conventional narrative of "anticlerical polygenism" versus "conservative monogenism" in interesting ways. Through its engagement with Anglophone polygenism in the 1840s and the 1850s, it also introduces surprising and intriguing transnational connections. The more extreme varieties of scientific racism, epitomized by the "social Darwinism" that bolstered the Nazi "Racial State," are very, very familiar. Less well-known, but no less significant, the Italian example is indicative of the persistence of humanistic and liberal-democratic political ideals within certain forms of nineteenth-century anthropology and racial nationalism. Some of the ideas upon which Italian anthropology were founded—particularly those relating to the notion of the plasticity of the brain and body and the transformative and elevating effect of assimilationism upon "lower" races—anticipated the game-changing anti-racism of the German-American anthropologist Franz Boas (1858–1942) in the early twentieth century.[6]

Italy defies some of the most cherished assumptions about nineteenth-century science. The distinguished historian George W. Stocking Jr. assumed that differences in approach to race were attributable to contrasting methodologies. His very influential view was that ethnology was closely affiliated with comparative linguistics and Christian theology and therefore promoted monogenism, while anthropology aligned with comparative anatomy and articulated a polygenetic model based upon a biological conception of race.[7] This is a somewhat formulaic interpretation: ethnology + philology = cultural or ethnic nationalism + monogenism; anthropology + craniology = biological racism and polygenism. A significant supposition behind this interpretation is that monogenism, even in its post-Enlightenment form, remained a religious concept or ideology and that polygenism was secular in nature. Moreover, monogenism is seen as anticipatory or "preparatory" for Darwinism, while polygenism is depicted as intrinsically anti-Darwinian. Though derived from the North American, British, French, and German examples, this viewpoint has become a historical truth which is applied to all of nineteenth-century anthropology.[8] The dominance of this template and its associated mindset can blind scholars to what was actually occurring within science and nationalism. For example, it has become customary to view Italian nationalism as largely "cultural" or "historical" before the 1880s, and, thereafter, racialist or racist only in extremist or fascist forms.[9] Giuseppe Sergi (1841–1936) is portrayed as Italy's first major proponent of a biological conception of race and the chief ideologue of a newly racial and racialized form of nationalism.[10] Epitomizing how persuasive and internalized these misconceptions can be, the revisionist history from the 1990s to the present has been predicated upon an unquestioned belief that "organic" and "biological" concepts of race and nation were essentially "foreign" and "Germanic" in character.[11]

The notion that monogenesis amounted to nothing more than a Christian creed and that religion was its defining feature has become some sort of eternal verity. The underlying assumption is that monogenism was outmoded and backward and polygenism was, by contrast, modern and cutting-edge. The Italian case challenges this deeply ingrained perspective; and it demonstrates too that monogenism was no less "scientific" than polygenism. In Italy, monogenism had far more at its disposal than the "folklore, antiquarianism, and philology" that historians describe as its sole methodological foundation.[12] Following Stocking's lead, scholars have long assumed that nineteenth-century science used skulls and bones only to support polygenism. However, comparative anatomy, craniotomy, and craniology were the tools of monogenism long before they became the weapons of polygenism.

Jeffrey David Feldman has argued that Italy's craze for crania was a brief "phase" that began in the 1870s.[13] He portrayed this enterprise largely as a foreign import and reiterated long-held assumptions about Italy being somehow immune to racism; Germans and

Americans were far more obsessed with "somatic characteristics" than Italians, he claimed, without providing corroborative evidence.[14] This interpretation has no grounding in nineteenth-century Italian science, which, well before the last three decades of the nineteenth century, developed autochthonous modes of defining race that focused on classifying and interpreting physical differences. The biological racism of *Risorgimento* science was not an imitation of what was happening abroad: though it entered into dialogue with that of other countries, it arose out of native scientific traditions and served national political interests. Nineteenth-century ethnology-ethnography-anthropology was a global encounter and Italy was a participant, not a bystander. Feldman's line of reasoning fails to grasp the heterogeneity of anthropology; even in countries like Germany, the overtly racist political agenda of polygenism did not go unchallenged.[15] The history of anthropology still holds many surprises. Some are less heartening than the Italian example explored here. Nineteenth-century controversies over race left a recurring legacy. The racist agenda of polygeny fell into disrepute in the twentieth century, but it has far from disappeared from the culture. Many scientists still regard intelligence as heritable and attribute differences in mean IQ test scores to the presumed determinant of race.[16]

Anthropology and the American Racial Republic

Immanuel Kant's "Of the Different Human Races" (1777) is widely recognized as the first scientific definition of race. Kant developed a theory of race that supported monogeny; he wrote that "Negroes" and "Whites" shared "one line of descent" and belonged to the same "human genus."[17] He gave a doctrinal basis to monogenism by postulating that all humankind was a single species and that the different varieties or races of human beings arose because of social rather than biological causes. The eighteenth century witnessed a cultural shift of tremendous import as white Europeans ceased to see blacks as "exotica" and "noble savages" and began to view them solely through the prism of their bondage as "subjects of scientific inquiry, medical specimens, and objects to be anatomized."[18] In the United States, this transformation saw scientific belief, in the form of polygenism (or pluralism, as it was known by contemporaries), become the defense for white supremacism.

American polygenists examined racial differences anatomically and concluded that "inferior" races were the least advanced from the point of view of intelligence. They defined the "lowest" races as those whose ensemble of significant and determining physical qualities, such as skull shape, body proportions, prognathism, facial angle, and, above all, brain size, most closely resembled those of animals—in particular, apes. By contrast, they described the "highest" races as those whose physical characteristics were the furthest removed from those of apes. They considered the European races superior because, in their opinion, they possessed the greatest intelligence. American polygenists placed the Negro races at the very bottom of the racial hierarchy and argued that blacks were incapable of ever achieving the levels of culture, civilization, and morality found among Europeans. Critically important to their arguments was the idea of the irreversibility and permanence of the inequality of races, which they used to defend slavery and segregation. Essential to the project of American anthropology and polygenism was its nationalizing ambition, evidenced in its depiction of Caucasians as a national race in direct opposition to other inhabitants of the multiracial United States, such as Asians, Native Americans, and Africans.

American polygenists sought to consecrate a racial republic upon the principles of white supremacism, arguing that whites were entitled to be the nation's master race and ruling class by virtue of their innately superior intelligence. The key figure in this endeavor, Samuel George Morton (1799–1851) began, as early as the 1840s, to move away from a monogenic framework. In a lecture delivered in April 1842, Morton noted that physical diversities between races existed, but these had "little or no significance." He was, however, beginning to question the thesis of a single creation and common stock by remarking that differences in skin color occurred and persisted, even when these could not be attributed to the chance and circumstance of environmental factors, such as climate.[19] Morton was gravitating toward a belief in multiple origins, a permanency of type, and a plurality of human races. These views ran contrary to the ideals of equality that had been imparted to him by his Quaker education. He openly admitted that prejudice inclined him in the direction of polygenism. Belief in the absolute and unchangeable inferiority of blacks to whites compelled him to reject long-held moral principles. Armed with only a few cursory observations of some crania, he had come to the conclusion that the mental capacity of the average Caucasian was greater than that of a Negro. He also maintained that this inequality in intelligence arose from a "primeval difference among men; not an accidental occurrence." He now believed that racial inequality and hierarchy were immutable and necessary facets of an all-pervasive divine design and economy of creation, which conferred a ranking order upon all living forms in nature, including man.[20] All men were not born equal.

Morton died in 1851, but not before bequeathing *Crania Americana* (1839) and *Crania Aegyptiaca* (1844), studies that exerted a profound influence upon the development of science, culture, and politics.[21] Though the primary purpose of his 1839 work was to reveal the findings of his study of the crania of "more than 40 Indian nations," stretching from Brazil to the polar regions, Morton devoted attention to the question of the "Negro family of races." He disputed the theory of the African origins of humankind by arguing that the Caucasian, a demonstrably superior being, could not possibly have emanated from a region where the inhabitants were of such low mental ability and base moral character. He acknowledged the contentious nature of his claims but maintained that, while the "advantages of education have inadequately been bestowed on them," blacks were generally ineducable, as instances of "superior mental powers" among them were extremely rare occurrences.[22] Morton's 1844 study compared ancient and modern crania, from the osteological collection of George R. Gliddon, all taken from various sites in Egypt. Morton's central argument was that racial differences in cranial formation were as visible six thousand years ago as they were in 1840, suggesting to him that the ruling class of ancient Egypt, just as in the United States of his day, were "Caucasian," while the lowly slave and servant classes were all "Negroes."[23]

In 1850 Morton formally announced his break with monogenism in letters to colleagues, including Josiah C. Nott (1804–1873), a physician from Alabama and one of Morton's greatest supporters. Morton's convictions that racial differences—what he called the "marks of Race"—were not acquired, but rather existed *ab origine*, led him to contend that the human species had its origin not in one, but in several creations. Morton's work found many devotees. When George R. Gliddon (1809–1857), the Egyptologist, sought to publish, by subscription, an homage to Morton, nearly five hundred individuals came forward with donations to help pay for the volume.[24] According to one of the contributors, Morton's brand of ethnology was a preeminently American science because it arose out of a particular set of national circumstances that made race the most pressing political problem of the day. Furthermore, all anthropology was, ultimately, an American science, because three out of the five major races of mankind lived in America (the "Caucasian," "Ethiopian," and "American"), while Chinese immigration into California brought Americans into contact with a fourth, which he called "Coolie labourers." Henry S. Patterson wrote: "It is manifest that our relation to and management of these people must depend, in great measure, upon their intrinsic race-character. While the contact of the white man seems fatal to the Red American, whose tribes fade away before the onward march of the frontier-man, like the snow in spring (threatening ultimate extinction), the Negro thrives under the shadow of his white master, falls readily into the position assigned him, and exists and multiplies in increased physical well-being."[25]

Followers of Morton argued that his database, which documented and deciphered the myriad of physical, mental, and moral differences between the races, should become the basis of a formal racial profiling system for the whole of the national community. This scientific survey should be used, they contended, to structure society through government action, controlling all aspects of race-related crime, health, education, and welfare policy and legislation. They envisaged a perpetuation of slavery ad infinitum and a codified system of segregation designed to keep all racial groups that were deemed inferior subordinate to the white master race. One of—if not the most—overtly racist and politicized of the American polygenists of his generation, Josiah Nott, proclaimed in *Types of Mankind* that all of human history, from the remotest past to the present day, could be defined as a "War of the Races." The only effective strategy for whites to pursue in the future was enforced racial containment on a grand scale.[26]

Morton's work, Nott stated, provided incontrovertible "proof" that it would be advisable for statesmen to "lay aside all current speculations about the perfectibility of the races" and to deal, in political argument, with the simple facts as they stand."[27] According to Nott, Morton's major contribution to science and politics was his method of measuring brain size, which revealed the unequal intellect of the different races. A head form like "the Greek is never seen on a Negro, nor that of the Negro on the Greek." Absolute uniformity of type was not in the law of Nature; rather, a "gradation of species" existed that was immutable. Morton and Nott both contravened one of the Enlightenment's key conceptualizations—namely, that races were different varieties, not species, of human beings. The "fact" of separate origins, they maintained, led to racial speciation of a pronounced character, and the only sensible conclusion to be upheld, however repugnant it might be to the do-gooders and egalitarians, was that "certain barbarous and savage types can neither be civilized, nor domesticated."[28] Nott quoted the English ethnologist James Cowles Prichard (1786–1848), who lamented the fact that "if these opinions are not every day expressed in this country (England), it is because the avowal of them is restrained by a degree of odium that would be excited by it." A monogenist, Prichard was denounced by Nott for being too cowardly to have done anything to mobilize public opinion in England against the abolitionists, who, with the introduction of antislavery legislation in 1833, were winning the race war for the blacks and against the whites. The English were more reserved than the Americans, Nott stated; capitulation and defeat were not options for white Americans.[29]

The scientific endorsement of political racism was one of the most important developments since the foundation of the American nation. This alliance between science and politics, many polygenists hoped, would, in the not so distant future, usher in an era when they would be able to proudly proclaim the foundation, in perpetuity, of a truly racial republic. The most celebrated race scientist in the United States, Morton attracted attention abroad and formed important European connections. Morton himself had learned the rudiments of his techniques from the phrenologists whom he had met while he studied at Edinburgh University, which granted him a second medical degree in 1823. There, Morton came under the influence of the phrenological teachings of the anatomist John Gregory (1724–1773); he also engaged in a long correspondence with the influential Scottish phrenologist George Combe (1788–1858), who contributed explanatory pieces on Morton's method to *Crania Americana* and *Types of Mankind*. Though Morton's approach differed from phrenology, it shared with it a belief that there was a correlation between brain size and intelligence and morality; significantly, Morton entrusted a trained phrenologist to assist him in the undertaking of his cranial measurements. Combe had also visited the United States in 1838 and stayed for almost two years, during which he managed to convince Morton to soften somewhat his hardline views of the Toltecs of Mexico and the Incans of Peru; Morton conceded that these peoples had produced great civilizations, comparable to that of the Egyptians, but reaffirmed his belief that these were mere anomalies amid barbarism.[30]

Perhaps the most important transatlantic link came through Jean Louis Rodolphe Agassiz (1807–1873), the highly respected zoologist who left Switzerland for a chair in natural history at Harvard University in 1846. Like Morton, Agassiz had spent a short time in Paris, where he learned about classification from the great French master himself, Georges Cuvier (1769–1832).[31] Agassiz corresponded with such distinguished scientists as Friedrich Heinrich Humboldt, Charles Lyell, and Richard Owen. Originally a monogenist, Agassiz found Morton's researches so compelling that he commissioned a series of daguerreotypes of African American slaves by the photographer, J. T. Zealy, in Columbia, South Carolina, in 1850; his aim was to collect further morphological evidence from these images to support Morton's theory of special, distinct creations.[32] He publicly announced his support of pluralism in March 1850, at a meeting of the American Association for the Advancement of Science, held in Charleston, South Carolina. Nott presented a paper on the "purity" of the Jewish race, which he used as a platform to endorse segregation as a means to prevent racial inbreeding.[33] Agassiz's endorsement of these ideas was instrumental in helping to make polygenism into an accepted doctrine in the United States. Until his death, Agassiz did not waiver from his belief in "successive, separate, and independent creations."[34] Agassiz's devotion to the principles of racial inequality and hierarchy was just as dogmatic as was his opposition to Darwinism.[35]

The American school utilized their links to European scholars to authenticate their theories of a natural ranking of the races and to further their political agenda. The term Caucasian was central to the intellectual edifice and political enterprise of the polygenists. Coined by the German philosopher Christoph Meiners (1747–1810) in 1785, the category of a Caucasian race was accepted and disseminated by the great race classifier Johann Friedrich Blumenbach (1752–1840) in the 1790s. In the United States, theorists employed the term, for the most part, to denote "white people" of European descent and to differentiate this group from blacks of African descent, who increasingly became identified as "Negroes" (a word employed by Spanish and Portuguese colonizers from the sixteenth century onward to describe the black-skinned peoples of Africa) in both scientific and ordinary usage. The epithet Caucasian embedded itself so deeply in the culture that it became, by the early twentieth century, a normalized form of self-identification and an official category in national statistics and government documents.[36] Morton and Nott relied heavily upon French sources for their rendering of the Caucasian as the personification of supreme perfection and the Negro as the embodiment of human degradation.[37] They cited the French naturalist and convert to polygenism Julien-Joseph Virey (1775–1846), whose radical classificatory system reduced the number of races down to only two—blacks and whites. Morton and Nott relied heavily upon Virey in their discussions of the Caucasian nature of the Egyptian mummies; their concern was to find proof that whites created Egyptian civilization, while black Africans formed the slave population in ancient Egypt.[38] Many monogenists openly admitted that they found it difficult to dispute the observations of Morton, Nott, and others that, in thousands of years of contact with the Carthaginian, Egyptian, Greek, and Roman civilizations, the Negro had not progressed beyond a stage of primitive savagery.[39] It seemed far easier to argue, as did Georges Pouchet (1833–1894), the French naturalist and polygenist, in his 1858 *De la Pluralité des Races Humaines* (On the Plurality of the Human Races), that races constituted entirely different species with differing mental faculties. After the Civil War, one of the key aspirations of the polygenists was realized as "Jim Crow" state and local laws imposing racial segregation in the South gained federal government sanction in 1896.

Liberal Racism Italian-Style

The Sicilian doctor, naturalist, and polyglot Giustiniano Nicolucci (1819–1904) was an Italian liberal, democrat, and nationalist who established ethnology-ethnography-anthropology as a university-based discipline and as united Italy's first national science, whose self-defined remit was to foster the progress of the nation.[40] He used various languages in his work (including English, French, German, and Latin), traveled abroad, received visiting colleagues, and corresponded with foreign scientists. Aware of trends elsewhere, he devised his own taxonomic system, a mix of craniology and morphology, which became the basis of physical anthropology in Italy, as practiced by one of his most important, self-proclaimed successors, Giuseppe Sergi, who went on to found the distinctive Roman anthropological school and Italy's first eugenics society. Moreover, the "father" of cultural anthropology in Italy, Paolo Mantegazza (1831–1910), who was based in Florence, followed Nicolucci and employed his method and findings. By the 1850s polygenism had become dominant in France in the *anthropologie* organized under the leadership of Paul Broca (1824–1880) and, then, his successor, Paul Topinard (1830–1911). There was a great deal of consensus in France, as in the United States, that variations in brain size and shape indicated differences in the intelligence and morality of the races.[41] At a meeting of the French Anthropology Society in 1878, Mantegazza acknowledged his debt to Nicolucci and stated that his research relied heavily upon the study of the 2,500 crania at his museum in Florence.[42]

Mantegazza very proudly declared that one of his aims was to continue a political and scientific tradition begun by his mentor, Nicolucci. Nicolucci was the first scientist in Italy to conceptualize nation as biological race, to define the Italian race scientifically, to juxtapose this construct of inherent Italian-ness with definitions of "other" national races, and to propound an entirely new kind of racial nationalism. His vast osteological collection was used, by himself and by his followers, to form the basis of anthropological, typological, and classificatory accounts of the biological and cultural attributes of the national race of Italy, among other nations. Italian anthropology's quest in the nineteenth century to raid the tombs of long-dead, illustrious poets, artists, and philosophers and find proof of the innate greatness of the present-day Italian people was made possible by his scientific method, researches, and findings.[43]

It was not an aversion to craniological or "somatic" modes of racial classification that distinguished Italian anthropology at the time of its formation and institutionalization in the 1850s to the 1870s. Italian scientists shared with their colleagues abroad the mania for measuring crania and skeletons. However, Nicolucci and his followers, Mantegazza and Sergi, who founded and fostered anthropology in Italy, all shared a cautious and critical approach to the inflated claims of the new craniometry-craniology. During its brief heyday from the late 1870s to the mid-1880s, the Lombrosian school of criminal anthropology favored simplistic and reductionist approaches but was an anomaly and exception in this regard. Italian anthropology, more broadly, was steeped in scepticism and empiricism. Nicolucci and his successors believed that skull measurements, and, especially, the cephalic index beloved by so many anthropologists as the chief signifier of civilization, were not the best means to classify human races, to decipher their intelligence, or to predict their destiny. The ordering of the races was far too complex a process to be reduced to a single determinant. Unlike many of their American and French counterparts, moreover, Nicolucci and Mantegazza believed that culture and civilization were not beyond the reach of the supposedly inferior races.

Another particularity of Italian anthropology was the persistence of monogenism, due, in no small measure, to Nicolucci. Nicolucci upheld the principles of monogenism from the time that he began producing scientific works, in the 1850s, to the end of his prolific sixty-three-year career in science and medicine.[44] He remained true also to the Mazzinian ideals of a just society that had made him into a patriot and revolutionary during the *Risorgimento*. Like many Italians then and now, he saw Catholicism as a unifying and "civilizing" force that had helped enculturate the disparate Italic "tribes" of the peninsula into one ethnos-nation-race; though not fiercely anticlerical (anticlericalism, more typically, was a trait of the French school of anthropology), he was secular and scientific in outlook. He spoke of God and providence occasionally in his early works, but his mental universe was that of a natural scientist whose true faith resided in nature. With regard to the source of his monogenism, his fiercely left-liberal-democratic politics drove his impassioned moral repugnance for slavery far more than any commitment to Christian scripture.

Nicolucci's greatest work was his monumental study *On Human Races: An Ethnological Study*.[45] He conceived of his ethnology as the study of the "principal racial families of the world" and the effects of nature upon them.[46] The main purpose of this treatise, Nicolucci explained, was to refute the polygenism of Morton and his followers in the United States and Europe. Nicolucci read and cited Morton's works in English; he was highly critical in particular, he wrote, of the notion of innate intelligence.[47] He adhered to a belief in the beauty and wisdom of nature's choice of a pluriformity of the human race; racial inequality existed, he affirmed, but intellect was not an inborn or fixed attribute. He also rejected Morton's representation of the Caucasian race as the preeminent American national race. This was a falsification of history and a justification for oppression, he believed. He supported the Humboldtian theory of a dispersal of a single people from Asia to the Americas and argued that Morton was wrong to have claimed that the primary attributes of Native Americans were indolence and courage. The "red tribes," like other oppressed peoples, such as blacks, Nicolucci maintained, were "not yet called to civilization," but they were entirely civilizable.[48]

The entire foundation for his thinking was monogenism. He wrote: "Many have wondered whether human types are the work of different and successive creations. My deepest conviction compels me absolutely to affirm that all men are members of the same family, or, speaking as a naturalist, are a variety of the same species."[49] There was one human family: "I believe wholly that the human creature," he continued, "was imprinted with only one type, which subsequently through the action of certain external forces operating on the physical form of members of our species, such as climate, underwent a conformation into the many and various configurations that distinguish the races, peoples, and nations of today."[50] Nicolucci wanted to align Italian ethnology with that of James Cowles Prichard, whose *Researches into the Physical History of Mankind* represented for Nicolucci an ethical alternative to the American school, which he found repugnant because it saw black people as less than human.[51] Nicolucci shared Prichard's view, as expressed in his *Natural History of Man*, that all human beings were more than skin and bones and blacks possessed the same morality and intelligence as did whites.[52]

Nicolucci was successful at affiliating his fledgling discipline with what he considered to be progressive thought. That he shared a commitment to monogenism with Prichard was well known in scientific circles; Nicolucci was seen as the "Dr. Prichard of Italy" by the famed polygenist Joseph Barnard Davis (1801–1881), of the Royal College of Surgeons (RCS). Nicolucci and Davis corresponded and collaborated, though their views were diametrically opposed. Davis's research into the brain weight of Negroes, which concluded that blacks were irremediably of low intelligence, provided important supporting evidence for the cause of American polygenism.[53] Despite his differing perspective, Davis recognized the importance and originality of Nicolucci's research. Davis explained to his colleague at the

RCS, Sir William Henry Flower (1831–1899), that Nicolucci's work was akin to that of Prichard. Unlike that of Davis, Flower's own investigations into the primate brain endorsed a monogenist position.[54]

Often overlooked by scholars, monogenists and polygenists employed much the same method. The primary differences resided in their interpretation of data. Davis's *Thesaurus Craniorum* (1867), a catalog of his vast repository of skulls and skeletons, which the RCS eventually purchased, was one of the more extreme examples of nineteenth-century craniology-craniometry, in that it contained twenty-five thousand measurements; however, measuring for the purposes of racial classification and ranking was a widespread and standard tool of analysis. Like Morton, Nicolucci came under the influence of phrenology, which had an important influence upon his technique. One of the more unusual pieces in Nicolucci's osteological collection was a cranium on which none other than Bartolomeo Panizza (1785–1867), the internationally celebrated anatomist, had himself drawn an elaborate design of the complete phrenological system.[55] Panizza's contemporaries credited him with establishing the Pavian school of anatomy and understood that his approach was informed by phrenology.[56] Scholars today recognize Panizza's contribution to neurology, but not his interest in phrenology.[57] Nicolucci's classificatory system owed much to Johann Friedrich Blumenbach, whose celebrated *De generis humani varietate nativa* (1795) Nicolucci read in the original Latin. Although Blumenbach argued that his ideal racial type, the Caucasian, was best represented by Greeks and Italians, Nicolucci rejected the whole construct of the Caucasian race on the grounds that it was being used for objectionable political purposes.[58] The polygenists, he believed, were making spurious claims about the innate intellectual superiority of so-called Caucasians with no real evidence. Nicolucci also criticized the vogue of comparing human skulls to those of chimpanzees, gorillas, and orangutans, in order to determine the proximity of racial types to the apes (on a scale running from the "savage" to the "civilized"); he argued that there were too many differences between man and monkeys for this method to be of any scientific use.[59]

Nicolucci recognized that even widely used methods could be flawed. In his very influential research, Davis measured the internal dimensions of the cranium in order to determine the differing cerebral power (what Nicolucci called "*grandezza cerebrale*," or "cerebral greatness") of the various human races. According to Davis, the average European had a cranial capacity of 1490 cubic centimeters, the average "Oceanian" (Pacific Islander) 1451, the average American "Indian" 1441, the average Asian 1435 , the average African 1396, and the average "Australian" (the Aborigines) 1322. Davis's method of classifying races appealed to many polygenists.[60] Nicolucci pointed out that the numerical results obtained by Davis, Morton, and others (including himself) employing this technique were never the same; also, the figures were never consistent from one study to the next. The type of cranium measured by different scientists could differ depending upon whether it was that of a female or a male, an adult or a child, modern or ancient. Moreover, the instruments used to determine the calculations could vary in type and accuracy. How the scientist positioned the instruments and made the calculation could affect findings. And, most significantly, human bias or error could influence the outcome.[61]

Nicolucci maintained that scientists had yet to demonstrate definitively that whites possessed bigger and better brains than other races. That the size or some other property of the human brain had anything to do with intelligence remained thoroughly unproven, he argued. Nicolucci believed that the Prussian anthropologist and anatomist Thomas von Sömmering (1755–1830) was simply wrong to argue that the "Ethiopian brain" resembled that of the ape and displayed a comparable low level of intellectual ability.[62] Sömmering and others, like Morton, Nicolucci maintained, were corrupting good science. The great German anatomist Friedrich Tiedemann (1781–1861) had first pioneered the study of racial difference and brain measurements. Nicolucci wrote that Tiedemann had come to the right conclusion after exhaustive research and proven that no meaningful difference existed between the brains of whites and blacks; blacks suffered from no physical or mental impediment to their education and advancement.[63]

Many scientists assumed that their measurements were exact and their conclusions unassailable, Nicolucci argued, and were blind to their own mistakes, as well as their own biases. Nicolucci read French translations of the work of Petrus Camper (1722–1789), whose famous concept of the "facial angle" influenced many craniologists. Camper drew diagrams of the facial angles of different species that showed a scale of perfection from monkeys at the bottom to an Apollo-like man at the very top.[64] Camper made a huge mistake, Nicolucci stated, because he used monkeys who had not yet developed their second set of teeth; the polygenists who used Camper's findings to support their arguments in favor of a *scala naturae* in which blacks were destined, by virtue of their inborn qualities, to remain at the bottom were entirely misguided.[65]

Technology, culture, and civilization were not beyond the reach of what Nicolucci described as "undeveloped" peoples. In a free and just society, Nicolucci stated, progress and advancement were attainable for all. It was morally wrong and transparently racist to compare the faculties of blacks to lower animals, he wrote categorically.[66] By any measure—be it the volume of the skull, the dimensions of the cranial cavity, or the weight of the brain—all men were equal in worth, if not in education and opportunity. The brain of a white European may be bigger, but it was no better than that of an Asian or an African. In one of the most powerful passages in his *On Human Races*, Nicolucci wrote that polygenic theories were nothing more than a "pretext for Whites to engage in a traffic in human flesh and to clutch within the shackles of slavery a portion of the human family which is neither no less noble, nor, as created by God, no less dignified or worthy of liberty than the other portion of humanity which oppresses it."[67] Nicolucci wrote, "When we compare the skin of a white man with that of a black man, or a red man, we are inclined to suppose at first sight that each race has had a distinct origin," but this interpretation would be wrong, he concluded; all races were "brothers and children" within the same family. In ways that are not unlike what population geneticists who dispute the concept of race in its entirety write today, Nicolucci described, poetically, what made people human and what bound them together into one big species. He wrote: "What surprises me is not so much the number of differences between races, but the number of similarities that exist."[68]

From Barbarism to Civilization

Nicolucci did not believe that humanity came from a single couple, as described in the Bible. He was no Christian fundamentalist. He maintained that human beings all derived from one stirp or stock, which dispersed widely throughout the globe. Of crucial importance to his stance was the postulate that racial differences were contingent upon history, not biology. Races were not unchanging physical types.

Commentators have remarked that Nicolucci's conception of the mutability of human beings was "Lamarckian," but the reality is more complicated.[69] He would almost certainly have been exposed to the ideas about evolution that were in circulation at the time, in the medical school at Naples, where Nicolucci qualified as a doctor.[70] Nicolucci contemplated questions about the evolution of life forms and liked the idea of a potential progress toward perfection, but he was not really a Lamarckian. He relied heavily upon Cuvier for his understanding of species; he had no conception of the inheritance of acquired characteristics; and he, the scrupulous footnoter, never cited Lamarck once in his *On Human Races*. Very much in keeping with anti-Lamarckian doctrine on the permanence of race, Nicolucci maintained that something constant in racial makeup—a legacy of the "original type," perhaps—was not subject to change.[71]

There was an indirect connection between Nicolucci and Lamarck, however, and that is that both were influenced by the Roman materialist poet-philosopher Lucretius (c.95–55 AD), who is credited with devising the very first theory of evolution. Nicolucci's *On Human Races* shows the very marked influence of Lucretius, who was a follower of Epicurus. Eighteenth-century Italian thinkers had rediscovered Lucretius; Nicolucci quoted him at length in passages in the text on biological evolution. Lucretius's philosophical and epic poem in six books, *On the Nature of Things* (*De Rerum Natura*), presents a cosmological and atomic theory of evolution within the framework of Epicurean physics and cosmology. Lucretius was especially concerned with exploring the process of biological evolution through cultural change. As early man passed through successive stages of life on earth, he believed, human beings evolved, and they created an increasingly complex civilization as a consequence.[72]

Nicolucci's conception of the origin and evolution of life was Lucretian. Nicolucci also shared Lucretius's antipathy for supernaturalism. Lucretius's evolutionary hypothesis rested on the supposition that the universe and life were not created by some divine intelligence with a master plan or purpose. Rather, they were the result of purely random physical events within nature. The existence of different cranial types was a sufficient reason for Nicolucci to believe that new human varieties had somehow sprung like branches from the original root stock. They emanated originally from a single primitive archetype but were modified by a slow and constant action of physical and moral factors. This line of reasoning was central to his thinking and became the linchpin of his fierce refutation of the racist polygenists.

For Nicolucci, processes of biological and cultural evolution were linked. To support this idea, he cited the example of the Turks. In the remote past, he wrote, "nomadic Turks from Central Asia" migrated to Europe. These "Asiatic types with pyramidal skulls" changed physically as they "shunned their wild and vagabond ways and adopted a more civilized and sedentary lifestyle." In Nicolucci's opinion, racial interbreeding with Europeans had no part to play in the transformation of the Turks. Rather, geographic proximity to the Christian countries of Europe caused a gradual social advancement of this people, which was paralleled in a dramatic cranial modification. The "Ottoman Turks of today," he stated definitively, are "Caucasian" rather than "Mongoloid."[73] Through a long process of historical development, Nicolucci maintained, human society became more complex and sophisticated. Language, culture, and technology were the agents bringing progress and civilization to even the least developed of races.

Nicolucci's perspective was developmental rather than evolutionary.[74] He did not think in terms of some evolutionary parabola along which some superior races had advanced, leaving their inferior counterparts behind. He strongly opposed the notion that civilization was beyond the reach of certain races, who were condemned to exist in a semi-barbarous state because of their inherent inability to change. In some of the more forceful passages in his work, Nicolucci criticized the American school along these lines. It was true, he wrote, that the majority of Negroes in Africa were barbaric, a fact revealed by their dominant skull shape, which was "prognathic" in type, and by their religion, which was a lowly form of "foul fetishism." However, in west and central Africa, the civilizing influence of Islam caused crania gradually to conform to the "more elevated forms known in the West." The scientific evidence suggested, moreover, that once black Africans were transported to North America, a "considerable variation in their cranial configuration" began. As they came under the influence of a "superior civilization," they experienced dramatic changes to their physiognomy. A "tendency towards the ovoid shape of skull" was becoming visible, even in "Negroes of pure blood," who were, because of their makeup, members of the most durable and constant of all racial types. Nicolucci noted that such an eminent and trustworthy scientist as Charles Lyell (1796–1875) discovered, during his most recent visit to the United States, that black slaves, particularly those living in close quarters with whites, such as domestic servants, were beginning to "approximate the European model of skull and skeleton."[75]

The Aesthetics of Race

Physiognomy provided Nicolucci with a philosophical system that supported his racial egalitarianism. The work of the natural philosopher Giambattista (also known as Giovanni Battista) della Porta, whose *De Humana Physiognomonia* of 1586 was hugely important in the development of ideas in Italy about the connections between bodily and mental attributes, expressed a distinctly Italian tendency toward aestheticism. Ingrained in the culture from the classical age right through to the Renaissance, the "cult of beauty" eventually found expression in the racial typologies of Nicolucci, who delighted in what he considered the exquisitely superior physical attributes of the Italian race. Artistic sensibilities and judgments informed racial thinking in Italy. A Neapolitan, Battista della Porta established the foundation of physiognomy by devising distinct physiognomic types, which were illustrations based on comparisons between humans and animals. He agreed with the Aristotelian premise that internal qualities depended on external features. Battista della Porta took this further by arguing that physical traits shared by men and animals were indices to their personality and character. In his numerous drawings, some of which were semicomical, he compared the faces of men and animals directly; a famous one shows a sheep and a sheeplike man side by side, in order to illustrate Della Porta's point that the wide and well-defined mouth shared by both indicated stupidity and impiety. Della Porta's influence upon Neapolitan and Italian science and culture was profound and persistent.[76] Nicolucci came into direct contact with physiognomy, as he did phrenology, during his studies in Naples in anatomy and physiology, and he gained through them a lifelong interest in morphology, as a complement to his metric style of craniology.

For Nicolucci, the nobility and excellence of human beings were reflected in their beauty. Beauty was not a "fictional idea" for Nicolucci; rather, it was an "absolute reality," which reflected, naturally, corporeal differences, but also, more profoundly, mental and moral qualities. Surviving right down to the eighteenth and nineteenth centuries, classical and Renaissance humanism was evident in such significant manifestations as the idealist philosophy of Benedetto Croce (1866–1952), which followed physiognomic principles and defined aesthetics as the science of expression.[77] Physiognomy and aesthetics—both "sciences of Beauty," in an Aristotelian-Platonic sense—focused on variations in outward countenance and their connections to the mind and the emotions. Specifically, the idea of beauty as an absolute ideal that could be found in nature held out a promise of human perfectibility that appealed to Nicolucci and others within the Italian schools of anthroplogy.

An aesthetic sensibility, informed by such philosophical considerations, was highly visible in Italian nineteenth-century systems of racial classification.[78] Nicolucci, for example, conceived of races in aesthetic terms. He had a subjective and scientific worldview that was inclined to define and judge the different races according to how aesthetically pleasing he found them. He applied these criteria to his own and to other races; while he found non-European races in general less beautiful than Italian or European ones, certain exceptions could be made, such as for "upper-caste Brahmins." Nicolucci cited travel writers such as Francesco Gemelli (1651–1725), who wrote of India in 1708 that its upper classes and its high-born women were beautiful, fair-skinned, or olive-complexioned, and not unlike Northern Italians or Provençales.[79] At the top of Nicolucci's scale of human perfection, not surprisingly, stood Italians, which represented for him the pinnacle of beauty in appearance and nobility of character.

Behind the chauvinism and Eurocentrism of Nicoluccianism, however, was an abiding belief that social conditions led to the degradation and embrutement of some unfortunate races and that human perfection and goodness were attainable in the realm of man on earth. This was the crux of Nicolucci's philosophical antipathy toward Morton and the whole polygenic outlook, which, in his estimation, degraded all human beings by denying the existence of the infinite possibilities for change, progress, and betterment contained in nature. Physiognomy and aesthetics helped keep the humanistic value of human perfectibility very much an aspiration of Italian science at a time when a theory of a fixed racial hierarchy was gaining ground. Important native traditions of thinking had a major impact in other ways, too; they predisposed nineteenth-century Italian ethnologist-ethnographer-anthropologists to a morphological approach in classification. This contrasted with the obsessionally quantitative perspective of the polygenists, which tended toward a hard-line hereditarian view of the imperfectability of the supposedly inferior races.[80]

National Races in Conflict

At a time when anthropology everywhere was ruled by the cephalic index, which was seen as the primary marker of racial identity, Italian science under Nicolucci's command showed a great deal of independence. Nicolucci played a critical role in the exchange of ideas that helped found and shape scientific traditions within his own country. His work also provided a conduit for the transference of ideas about race from university-based science into nationalist discourse about the nation. Nicolucci's research and writing became the basis for the construction of an Italian national race in the 1850s and the 1860s. Nicolucci classified the racial characteristics of the Italians, as represented in the ancient crania found in burial sites, their present-day physiognomy, and their depiction in sculpture and other media in the visual arts. In so doing, he often entered into open dispute with foreign scholars, who had very different ideas of the "typical" Italian.

A deep strain of fraternalism ran through Nicoluccian monogenism. Nineteenth-century anthropology, however, was often a clash of views about the comparative scale of endowments of the various national races. Encounters between different interpretations of racial superiority were an important part of this dynamic history. One of the most significant of these controversies was a matter of great national pride for many of Nicolucci's countrymen. From the 1860s theorists began to define subgroups of the Caucasian race. In the second half of the nineteenth century, various forms of scientific and political Aryanism, Teutonism, and Nordicism defined Germans as a "great, white master race" with a special genius and an ennobling mission. Writing in the 1890s, Houston Stewart Chamberlain (1855–1927) was, perhaps, the most famous of these thinkers. Following Gobineau in his thinking about the infinite superiority of the Aryan and its most perfect representative, the German, Chamberlain alleged contentiously that Italy was of Germanic origin. Although he disliked all southern Europeans, along with "Slavs," Chamberlain was prepared to accept that some Italians had made an enormous contribution to civilization. Even if they were mere "technical" masterpieces, and, therefore, could not compare favorably to those of the German poets and artists, Chamberlain maintained, the works of Dante and da Vinci deserved commendation. But the very best of Italian culture was the product of Teutonic influence from the time of Charlemagne, who was crowned the first king of Italy in 774 and was the true inheritor of the Roman Imperium and the real architect of a New Rome.[81] Chamberlain was not the first or the last theorist to ascribe a Germanic racial provenance to the Italian nation. He popularized and vulgarized the ideas of Gobineau and of anthropologists such as Otto Ammon (1842–1916) and Georges Vacher de Lapouge (1854–1936).

In some respects, Aryan race theory arose in response to the contempt in which Italian nationalists held the Germans. During the *Risorgimento*, Italian nationalist writers, engaged in lively discussions about how "Italian" the Italian people actually were, produced works that offended German sensibilities. In 1862 Pasquale Villari (1827–1917), the celebrated Italian patriot, revolutionary, and historian, published a very influential pamphlet, aimed at a mass audience. This work compared Italy's great "Latin" culture and civitas with lowly "Germanic" civilization. Tracts like Villari's sought to inspire national pride; he called for a regeneration of Roman and Renaissance virtues and the rebirth of a "Third Rome" in the newly unified Kingdom of Italy.[82] The German-born philologist, Orientalist, and monogenist Friedrich Max Müller (1823–1900) complained that, "in the eyes of the Italians, the Germans are barbarians." Writing in 1870, Müller explored one of the most cherished epochs in the entire history of Italy—the Renaissance. In this discussion he noted that anti-German sentiments ran deep within the Italian collective psyche. In 1458, remarked Müller, Pope Pius II declared that the Germans were an inferior and primitive race of marauders who "do not care for science nor for a knowledge of classical literature, and they have hardly heard the name of Cicero or any other orator." Müller rebutted that, though they laid claim to being the creators of Western civilization and Christendom, the Italians were cultural bandits and mere imitators. The beloved Renaissance was not the work of Italian genius, Müller claimed; rather, it was the product of "Greek refugees" from the Byzantine empire. The cultural artefacts and trifles that the Italians prized so highly, Müller noted, were nothing compared to the military power and might of Germany, which was finally "awakening to its position in the world."[83]

Müller was hugely influential; he helped create the myth of the

"Aryan" as a master race of blond, blue-eyed charioteers migrating across from Asia, vanquishing peoples, and founding the nations of Europe. Perhaps because he was German-born, he appeared to be partial to certain physical features. He himself caused immense offense to Italian nationalists like Nicolucci, with his descriptions of the Italian race as ugly. According to Müller, the typical Italian had a full face, big eyes, a wide and short nose, and a prominent forehead; was of short stature, with a big head in proportion to his torso; and had short arms and a heavy body. Nicolucci retorted that Müller was guilty of propagating a stereotype of the short and stubby Italian that was completely untrue. Nicolucci collected and studied crania from all parts of the country and was responsible for creating a detailed racioethnic profile of the variations over time of the physical characteristics of all the different peoples of Italy.[84]

Modern-day Italians were a mix of different cranial types with differing attributes. Lazians, Tuscans, and the Piedmontese had the largest brain power, measured by the size of the cranial vault, while Sardinians had the smallest. Morphologically speaking, distinctions could be quite pronounced, too, so that the "cerebral hemisphere" of an Italian, like the "divine" Dante (determined by a surviving death mask), possessed a great number of circumvolutions and ravines that were quite individual and, therefore, indicative of his exceptional genius. Italian and European literature was born with Dante, science with Galileo, and art with Michelangelo, Nicolucci wrote. Natives of Tuscany, these great men, along with others like Petrarch, Galileo, da Vinci, and Boccaccio, were all part of Florence and Italy's "magnificent intellectual dominion." The cultural patrimony of Tuscany "had no parallel anywhere in the world," so it was fitting, he believed, that Tuscans should be considered the most representative example of the national race. From skull and skeletal fragments, corroborated by portraits of these illustrious men, as well as evidence drawn from the head shapes on sarcophagi, putti, and vases, Nicolucci argued that Müller was wrong. Far from being short and fat, the Etruscans of the past, the Tuscans of today, and, indeed, all

Italians were tall, well-proportioned, muscular, and strong.[85] The notorious Aryanist, white supremacist, and polygenist Gobineau would have agreed with Nicolucci, for he, too, believed that the "Italians are more beautiful than the Germans or the Swiss, the French, or the Spanish."[86]

Tomb Raiders and National Icons

For Nicolucci, Beauty (conceived as character and countenance) and Civilization (defined as culture and history) were the two most important attributes of race. *Risorgimento* race science under his guardianship demonstrates that the "Idea of Italy" did not lose relevance in the 1840s–1860s, as many scholars maintained for decades.[87] Science served the patriotic cause of national unification well during these decades by helping to create an iconography and a cult of the nation and its idols based upon ethnoracial taxonomy. The Nicoluccian method and approach had a major impact upon Italian nationalism. One of the most enduring and important nationalist discussions centered on the remains of the Tuscan Francesco Petrarch (1304–1374), who was revered as the "father of the Renaissance" and the "first modern poet."

Memorialized as one of Italy's most eminent personages, Petrarch had found little peace in death. In 1630 and 1773 thieves had entered his tomb and stolen bits of his bones to sell as objects of veneration. In 1843 Count Carlo Leoni, a patron of the arts, paid for the restoration of the poet's monumental pink sarcophagus. He described seeing Petrarch's remains: "I alone took and held in my hand the most beautiful, most ample cranium of Petrarch and I showed it to the crowd." In 1855 a surgeon conducted an anthropometric examination of Petrach's skull that reassuringly revealed "the most perfect cerebral organism with the vast intelligence of a poet and politician like Petrarch."[88] Giovanni Canestrini (1835–1900), the famous anatomist, carried out another raid on Petrach's tomb in 1873. Canestrini recounted: "I brought with me distilled water and millet, in order to determine, according to the circumstances, with one or the other of these things, the capacity of the cranium. I brought mercury to reveal the capacity of the eye sockets; clay and gesso to calculate the area of the great occipital wall [the bone at the back of the head]; and all of the necessary instruments to measure exactly the most important cranial and facial angles."[89] Canestrini sought to authenticate the skull by means of the ethnoracial identification techniques devised by Nicolucci. He stated that the skull was "undoubtedly that of an ancient Etruscan type" and was, his "rigorous, scientific method" had shown, none other than that of Petrarch. The cranium belonged to Petrarch, the creator of a truly national culture and one of the very best of the best of the Italian race.[90]

The cranium, though, did not belong to Petrarch, who was, in actuality, the "poet who lost his head." In 2003 a team of scientists based at the University of Padua exhumed the body of Petrarch and undertook genetic analysis through the retrieval of mitochrondrial DNA (mtDNA).[91] Molecular gender determination revealed conclusively that the skeletal remains belonged to a male, while the skull belonged to a female.[92] Canestrini, it seems, had unwittingly examined the remains of some unknown woman, whose skull had been substituted at some point for Petrarch's own. Because he was searching for this, Canestrini had found in fragments of bone incontrovertible "proof" of the genius of the poet and of the race to which he belonged.

Beyond National Races

Nationalist sentiments often lurked beneath race science's illusion of objectivity. New techniques of craniology and craniometry transformed Enlightenment methods of description into formalized systems of scientized and racialized thinking that were divisive. What was paramount for the American polygenists was brain size, which many believed confirmed the natural superiority of the Caucasian. For Nicolucci, by contrast, the Italian represented an ideal of beauty and creativity without equal. However, transnational affiliations also abounded. Nicolucci identified with like-minded individuals abroad, especially in England, where some thinkers shared his antipathy toward the American polygenists and their cohorts in Europe.

In the first half of the nineteenth century, ethnology-ethnography-anthropology committed what Claude Lévi-Strauss called its "original sin" by presuming that "race was essential in understanding what has been termed the 'production of civilization.'"[93] Important new ideas emerged, among which were the twin beliefs that "races were real" and "races were rankable." For the biological determinists who shared Morton's polygenic worldview, black people were destined to remain at the bottom of the hierarchy. Stephen Jay Gould, the first historian to bring American scientific racism to worldwide attention, more recently came under fire himself for allegedly "fudging" his own figures. The charge was that Gould wrongly accused Morton of making inaccurate measurements. Gould's critics were self-styled defenders of science and its method.[94]

No amount of remeasurements will dispel the reality, however, that the most important feature of the work of Morton and his followers was not the measurements themselves, but the interpretation of those data. The causative connection between cranial size and native intelligence was the principal issue at stake. Long before Gould subjected Morton to scrutiny, Nicolucci questioned the veracity and the assumptions of American race science. Within Nicolucci's own methodology, the mania for measuring was there from the start; so, too, was a belief in the inequality of the races. But Nicolucci remained faithful to the principles of humanism, liberalism, monogenism, abolitionism and egalitarianism.[95] Though he made a correlation between the cranium and intelligence, this was never the sine qua non of his science, nor did he ever imagine that the position of blacks in society was anything other than socially and politically constructed. In the 1950s anthropology repudiated its "original sin" and rejected the premises of polygenism; it came to embrace an idea of common descent and unity within humankind that is not all that different from the monogenesis of Nicolucci.[96] However, polygenesis and the right-wing and racist politics behind it have far from disappeared from science and politics, so these issues are just as current today as they were in the nineteenth century.[97]

Notes

1. I would like to thank Michael Reynolds, Marius Turda, and, especially, Richard McMahon for reading and commenting on this work.

2. Marvin Harris, *The Rise of Anthropological Theory: A History of Theories of Culture* (London: Crowell, 1968), 82.

3. Fred W. Voget, *A History of Ethnology* (New York: Holt, Rinehart & Winston, 1975), iv–viii. More on Kollár in Han F. Vermeulen, *Before Boas* (Lincoln: University of Nebraska Press, 2015), 314–21.

4. Stephen Jay Gould, *The Mismeasure of Man* (New York: W. W. Norton, 1981) was largely focused on disproving the veracity of the "Bell Curve"; Nancy Stepan, *The Idea of Race in Science: Great Britain, 1800–1960* (Houndmills: Macmillan, 1982) devoted one chapter to monogenism.

5. See, for example, Satnam Virdee, *Racism, Class, and the Racialized Outsider* (Houndmills: Palgrave Macmillan, 2014).

6. Richard Handler, "Boasian Anthropology and the Critique of American Culture," *American Quarterly* 42, no. 2 (1990): 252–73.

7. George W. Stocking Jr., *Victorian Anthropology* (New York: Free Press, 1987), 50, 63–66; "Bones, Bodies, and Behaviour," in *Bones, Bodies, and Behaviour: Essays in Biological Anthropology*, ed. George W. Stocking Jr. (Madison: University of Wisconsin Press, 1988), 3–17.

8. Sian Jones, *The Archaeology of Ethnicity: Constructing Identities in the Past and Present*, 2nd ed. (London: Routledge [1997] 2003), 41. Just one example in which this view is uncontested: Richard W. Rees, *Shades of Difference: A History of Ethnicity in America* (Lanham MD: Rowman & Littlefield, 2007), 37–38.

9. Antonino De Francesco, *The Antiquity of the Italian Nation: The Cultural Origins of a Political Myth in Modern Italy, 1796–1943* (Oxford: Oxford University Press, 2013), intro. and chaps. 1–3.

10. Aaron Gillette, *Racial Theories in Fascist Italy* (London: Routledge, 2002), chap. 2.

11. Silvana Patriarca and Lucy Riall, "Introduction: Revisiting the *Risorgimento*," in *The Risorgimento Revisited: Nationalism and Culture in Nineteenth-Century Italy*, ed. Silviana Patriarca and Lucy Riall (Basingstoke: Palgrave Macmillan, 2012), 1–17, 2–3.

12. Mark Bowden, *Pitt-Rivers: The Life and Archaeological Work of Lieutenant-General Augustus Henry Lane Fox Pitt Rivers* (Cambridge: Cambridge University Press, 1991), 44.

13. Pietro Corsi, "Il cervello degli italiani," in *Giovanni Canestrini: Zoologist and Darwinist*, ed. Alessandro Minelli and Sandra Casellato (Venice: Istituto veneto di scienze, 2001), 351–77 also focused on the 1870s as the start date.

14. Jeffrey David Feldman, "The X-Ray and the Relic: Anthropology, Bones, and Bodies in Modern Italy," in *In Corpore: Bodies in Post-Unification Italy*, ed. Loredana Polizzi and Charlotte Ross (Madison NJ: Fairleigh Dickinson University Press, 2007), 107–26, 109 and 122.

15. Benoit Massin, "From Virchow to Fischer: Physical Anthropology and Modern 'Race Theories' in Wilhelmine Germany," in *Volksgeist as Method and Ethic: Essays in Boasian Ethnography and the German Anthropological Tradition*, ed. George W. Stocking Jr. (Madison: University of Wisconsin Press, 1996), 79–154; *Worldly Provincialism: German Anthropology in the Age of Empire*, ed. H. Glenn Penny and Matti Bunzl (Ann Arbor: University of Michigan Press, 2003), 1–30.

16. *The Bell Curve Wars: Race, Intelligence, and the Future of America*, ed. Steven Fraser (New York: Basic Books, 1995).

17. Translation of Kant's "Von der verschiedenen Rassen der Menschen," in *This Is Race*, ed. Earl W. Count (New York: Henry Schuman, 1950), 16–24, 17.

18. Jeanette Eileen Jones, "'On the Brain of the Negro': Race, Abolitionism, and Friedrich Tiedemann's Scientific Discourse on the African Diaspora," in *Germany and the Black Diaspora: Points of Contact, 1250–1914*, ed. Mischa Honeck, Martin Klimke, and Anne Kuhlmann (New York: Berghahn, 2013), 134–52, 139.

19. Samuel George Morton, *An Inquiry into the Distinctive Characteristics of the Aboriginal Race of America at the Annual Meeting of the Boston Society of Natural History, April 27, 1842* (Boston: Boston Society of Natural History, 1842), 6–7.

20. Samuel George Morton, *Brief Remarks on the Diversities of the Human Species, and on Some Kindred Subjects, Being an Introductory Lecture delivered before the Class of Pennsylvania Medical College, in Philadelphia, November 1, 1842* (Philadelphia: Merrihew & Thompson, 1842), 6, 14–15.

21. George Bacon Wood, *A Biographical Memoir of Samuel George Morton, M.D., Prepared by Appointment of the College of Physicians of Philadelphia, and Read before that Body, November 3, 1852 by George B. Wood, M.D.* (Philadelphia: T. K. & P. G. Collins, 1853), 3–19.

22. Samuel George Morton, *Crania Americana, or, a Comparative View of the Skulls of Various Aboriginal Nations of North and South America*, vol. 1, *American Theories of Polygenesis*, edited and with an introduction by R. Bernasconi (Bristol: Thoemmes, 2002), 86–95.

23. Samuel George Morton, *Crania Aegyptiaca, or, Observations on Egyptian Ethnography, derived from Anatomy, History, and the Monuments* (Philadelphia: John Penington, 1844); Gould, *The Mismeasure of Man*, 74–101.

24. Josiah Clark Nott and George R. Gliddon, *Types of Mankind: or, Ethnological Researches Based Upon The Ancient Monuments, Paintings, Scriptures, and Crania of Races, And Upon Their Natural, Geographical, Philological, and Biblical History: Illustrated by Selections from the Inedited Papers of Samuel George Morton, M.D., (Late President of the Academy of Natural Sciences at Philadelphia) and By Additional Contributions from Prof. L. Agassiz, L.L.D.; W. Usher, M.D.; and Prof. H. S Patterson, M.D.*, 6th ed. (Philadelphia: J. B. Lippincott, 1854), x.

25. Henry. S. Patterson, "Memoir of the Life and Scientific Labors of Samuel George Morton," *Types of Mankind*, xvii–lvii, xxxii.

26. Josiah Clark Nott, "Introduction," *Types of Mankind*, 49–61, 52.

27. Nott, "Introduction," 51.

28. Josiah Clark Nott, "Comparative Anatomy of the Races," *Types of Mankind*, 411–65, 422, 460.

29. Nott, "Introduction," 54–56.

30. Bernasconi, "Introduction," *Crania Americana*, v–xv, xv.

31. Marc-Antoine Kaesar, *Un savant séducteur: Louis Agassiz (1807–1873): prophète de la science* (Paris: Vevey, 2007), chap. 1.

32. Elinor Reichlin, "Faces of Slavery," *American Heritage* 28, no. 4 (June 1977): 4–11.

33. Nott later became responsible for the American publication of Arthur de Gobineau's *An Essay on the Inequality of the Human Races* (1853–55). The arch-conservative racist, Aryan supremacist, and French chauvinist Gobineau found American racism unpalatable: *Henry Hötze, Confederate Propagandist: Selected Writings on Revolution, Recognition, and Race*, ed. Lonnie A. Burnett (Tuscaloosa: University of Alabama Press, 2008), 4.

34. E. Lurie, *Louis Agassiz and the Races of Man* (Cambridge MA: Massachusetts Institute of Technology, Publications in the Humanities, 1955), 234–35.

35. Lurie, *Louis Agassiz*, 282.

36. The United States Census Bureau, for example, currently uses racial criteria of labeling alongside those establishing ethnicity (and nationality as "foreigners"). Population statistics today employ six different race categories to define people: White or Caucasian; Black or Negro; American Indian or Alaskan Native; Asian; Native Hawaiian or Other Pacific Islander; or Some Other Race. Outmoded racist nomenclature, dating back to 1820, when census-taking in the United States first began to define people by skin color, has persisted in official goverment terminology. See The Leadership Conference Education Fund, *Race and Ethnicity in the 2020 Census: Improving Data to Capture a Multiethnic America* (Washington DC, November 2014), 4; and David I. Kertzer and Dominique Arel, "Censuses, Identity Formation, and the Struggle for Political Power," in *Census and Identity: The Politics of Race, Ethnicity, and Langiuage in National Censuses*, ed. David I. Kertzer and Dominique Arel (Cambridge: Cambridge University Press, 2001), 1–42.

37. William B. Cohen, *The French Encounter with Africans: White Responses to Blacks (1530–1860)* (Bloomington: Indiana University Press [1980] 2003), 1–4.

38. Bruce D. Baum, *The Rise and Fall of the Caucasian Race: A Political History of Racial Identity* (New York: New York University Press, 2006), chap. 2.

39. J. S. Haller Jr., "The Species Problem: Nineteenth-Century Concepts of Racial Inferiority in the Origin of Man Controversy," *American Anthropologist* 72 (1970): 1319–29, 1323.

40. George W. Stocking Jr., *The Ethnographer's Magic and Other Essays in the History of Anthropology* (Madison: University of Wisconsin Press, 1992) illustrates the difficulty of defining "national paradigms" within anthropology. In the Italian case, Nicolucci and his successors practiced a "national anthropology" that was plural: it had different regional epicenters and distinctive local traditions. Maria Sophia Quine,

"Making Italians: Aryanism and Anthropology in Italy during the *Risorgimento*," in *Crafting Humans: From Genesis to Eugenics and Beyond*, ed. Marius Turda (Göttingen: Vandenhoeck & Ruprecht, 2013), 127–52.

41. Martin S. Staum, *Labeling People: French Scholars on Society, Race, and Empire, 1815–1848* (Montreal: McGill-Queen's University Press, 2003), chap. 5.

42. Paolo Mantegazza, "Concerning the Atrophy and Absence of Wisdom Teeth," Anthropology Society of Paris, Meeting of June 20, 1878, in *Reminiscences of a Frequenter to the 1878–1881 Meetings of the Anthropology Society of Paris*, Robert K. Stevenson (Paris: n.p., 1929), 21–8.

43. Marius Turda and Maria Sophia Quine, *Historicizing Race: A Global History* (London: Bloomsbury Academic, 2017), chap. 3.

44. Nicolucci's monogenism is not explored in the literature on him: see, for example, *Alle origine dell'anthropologia italiana: Giustiniano Nicolucci e il suo tempo*, eds. Francesco G. Fedele and Alberto Baldi (Naples: Guida, 1988).

45. Giustiniano Nicolucci, *Delle razze umane: Saggio etnologico del Dottor Giustiniano Nicolucci*, 2 vols. (Naples: Stamperia e Cartiere del Fibreno, 1857 and 1858).

46. Nicolucci, *Delle razze umane*, vol. 1, vii—viii, 1; vol. 2, 315.

47. Nicolucci, *Delle razze umane*, vol. 1, vii.

48. Nicolucci, *Delle razze umane*, vol. 1, 185.

49. Nicolucci, *Delle razze umane*, vol. 1, iii.

50. Nicolucci, *Delle razze umane*, vol. 2, 315.

51. Nicolucci referenced the fourth edition of James Cowles Prichard's *Researches into the Physical History of Mankind*, 5 vols. (London: Sherwood, Gilbert & Piper, 1837–51) in his *Delle razze umane*, vol. 1, 10–11.

52. Nicolucci cited repeatedly James Cowles Prichard's *The Natural History of Man; Comprising Inquiries into the Modifying Influence of Physical and Moral Agencies on the Different Tribes of the Human Family* (London: H. Ballière, 1843).

53. Antonio Garbiglietti, *The Brain of a Negro: Il cervello di un Negro della Ghinea del Dottore G. B. Davis* (Turin: n.p., 1868).

54. Letter from J. Barnard Davis to William Henry Flower, February 9, 1870, Royal College of Surgeons of England (RCS), Hunterian Museum, MLB, Series 2 (1868–1906), Serial No. 5965.

55. Nicolucci sold the cranium to the RCS; it is listed as number 155 in Nicolucci's catalog, which describes it as a modern one from Pavia. Today, the markings are only faintly visible. The RCS possesses the manuscript original of Nicolucci's catalogue, entitled the *Catalogo di una collezione di Crani Greci ed Italiani, antichi e moderni, posseduta da Giustiniano Nicolucci, in Isola di Sora (Napoli) Italia*, as well as the copy in English, probably made by J. B. Davis, which is entitled the *Catalogue of a Collection of Modern and Ancient Greek and Italian Skulls, the Property of Giustiniano Nicolucci in Isola di Sora (Naples, Italy)*.

56. G. Zoja, *Un centenario memorabile per la scuola anatomica di Pavia: Prelezione al corso di anatomia umana per l'anno scolastico 1885–86* (Pavia: n.p., 1886), 3–14.

57. Stefano Sandrone and Marco Riva, "Bartolomeo Panizza (1785–1867)," *Journal of Neurology*, 261, no. 6 (2014): 1249–50; C. Calcagni and A. Ialongo, "Traccia di studi frenologici eseguito nell'Istituto anatomico romano nel secolo xix," *Ricerca di morfologia* 30 (1994): 171–78.

58. *Delle razze umane*, vol. 1, 19–20.

59. *Delle razze umane*, vol. 1, 30–3.

60. Whereas Morton used mustard seeds, and Broca lead shot, Nicolucci used grains of rice to determine cranial capacity. Giustiniano Nicolucci, "Intorno al cranio di Dante Aligheri: Nota antropologica," *Memoria della R. Accademia di scienze, lettere, ed arti di Modena*, vol. vii (Modena: n.p., 1866).

61. *Lettera del Dottore Cav. Giustiniano Nicolucci al Dottore Cav. Antonio Garbiglietti intorno all'opera del Signor Dottore J. B. Davis intitolata: Thesaurus Craniorum: or Catalogue of the Skulls of the Various Races of Man, in the Collection of Joseph Barnard Davis*, an extract from the *Journal of the Royal Academy of Medicine* 6 (1868): 9.

62. Nicolucci read French translations of the works of Thomas Soemmering; *Delle razze umane*, vol. 1, 22n2.

63. *Delle razze umane*, vol. 1, 2n1.

64. A racial egalitarian, Camper was a professor of anatomy and an artist whose *Űber den natűrlichen Unterschied der Gesichtszűge* was posthumously published in 1792: Miriam Claude Meijer, *Race and Aesthetics in the Anthropology of Petrus Camper, 1722–1789* (Amsterdam: Rodopi, 1999).

65. *Delle razze umane*, vol. 1, 19, 322.

66. Mexicans, Peruvians, and the Chinese had relatively small brains, Nicolucci noted. While Mexicans and Peruvians were yet to be civilized, uncivilized, the Chinese possessed one of the most ancient and advanced civilizations in the world: *Delle razze umane*, vol. 1, 24.

67. *Delle razze umane*, vol. 1, 22–23.

68. *Delle razze umane*, vol. 1, 33, 330–31.

69. F. G. Fedele, "Giustiniano Nicolucci e la fondazione dell'antropologia in Italia," *Alle origini dell' antropologia italiana* (1988): 37–60, 46.

70. Pietro Corsi, "Lamarck en Italie," *Revue d'Histoire des Sciences* 38, no. 1 (1984): 47–64.

71. *Delle razze umane*, vol. 1, 4–8.

72. Harris, *The Rise of Anthropological Theory*, 26–27.

73. *Delle razze umane*, vol.1, 16–17; vol. 2, 316.

74. His developmentalism was comparable to the diffusionism of Adolf Bastian (1826–1905): Klaus-Peter Koepping, *Adolf Bastian and the Psychic Unity of Mankind: The Foundations of Anthropology in Nineteenth-Century Germany* (St. Lucia: University of Queensland Press, 1983).

75. *Delle razze umane*, vol.1, 17–18.

76. By contrast, historians of modern Germany have drawn direct lines of descent from physiognomic thought to Nazi racial typologies: Richard T. Gray, *About Face:*

German Physiognomic Thought from Lavater to Auschwitz (Detroit: Wayne State University Press, 2004).

77. Benedetto Croce, *L'Estetica come scienza dell'espressione e linquistica generale*, vol. 1, *Teoria*, vol. 2, *Storia*, (Milan: Adelphi, 1902); the tendency to discern character from appearance was also evident, of course, in the work of Lombroso.

78. Vincenzo Gioberti, *Essay on the Beautiful: Elements of Aesthetic Philosophy*, trans. Edward Thomas (London: Simpkin & Marshall, 1860), chap. 2; though a philosophical treatise, this too explored racial categories in relation to beauty.

79. *Delle razze umane*, vol. 2, 62 and 78.

80. Cesare Fornari, *Di Giovanni Battista della Porta e delle sue scoperte: Discorso del prof. Cesare Fornari nel R. Liceo Giordano Bruno in Maddaloni il 17 Marzo 1871* (Naples: Fratelli de Angelis, 1871).

81. Houston Stewart Chamberlain, *The Foundations of the Nineteenth Century*, 2 vols., trans. J. Lees and intro. by Lord Redesdale (London: John Lane [1899] 1911), vol. 1, chaps. 2 and 6.

82. Pasquale Villari, *L'Italia, la civiltà latina, la civiltà germanica: osservazioni storiche* (Florence: Felice Le Monnier, 1862), 12–15, 79.

83. F. Max Müller, *Chips from a German Workshop: Essays on Literature, Biography, and Antiquities*, vol. 3 (London: Longmans, Green, 1870), 65.

84. Quine, "Making Italians," 136–39.

85. Giustiniano Nicolucci, *Antropologia dell'Italia nell'evo antico e nel modern* (Naples: n,p., 1887), 42–44, 99.

86. *Delle razze umane*, vol. 2, book 6, 316–17 (misprinted in the text). *Gobineau: Selected Political Writings*, ed. and intro. by M. D. Biddiss (London, 1970), 114.

87. Alberto Mario Banti, "Le invasioni barbariche e le origini delle nazioni," *Immagini della nazione nell'Italia del Risorgimento*, ed. Alberto Mario Banti and Roberto Bizzocchi (Rome: Carroci, 2002), 21–44.

88. Canestrini, *Le ossa di Francesco Petrarca: Studio anthropologico*, 1–6, 9.

89. Canestrini, *Le ossa di Francesco Petrarca*. 14–6, 19.

90. Canestrini, *Le ossa di Francesco Petrarca*, 81–2.

91. Bruce Johnston, "Putting a Face to Humanist Petrarch," *Telegraph*, 2 November 2003.

92. John Hooper, "Petrarch—The Poet Who Lost His Head," *Guardian*, 6 April 2004.

93. George J. Armelagos and Dennis P. Van Gerven, "A Century of Skeletal Biology and Paleopathology: Contrasts, Contraditctions, and Conflicts," *American Anthropologist* 105, no. 1 (2003): 51–62, 52.

94. Jason E. Lewis, David DeGusta, Marc R. Meyer et al., "The Mismeasure of Science: Stephen Jay Gould versus Samuel George Morton on Skulls and Bias," PLOS Biology Blog, July 7, 2011, https://journals.plos.org/plosbiology/article?id=10.1371/journal.pbio.1001071.

95. On the "antihumanist worldview" of German anthropology, see Andrew Zimmerman, *Anthropology and Antihumanism in Imperial Germany* (Chicago: University of Chicago Press, 2001), 1.

96. Michelle Brattain, "Race, Racism, and Antiracism: UNESCO and the Politics of Presenting Science to the Postwar Public," *American Historical Review* 112 (2007): 1386–1413.

97. S. Fuller, "Science's Twin Taboos: Is It Premature to Declare that the Debates about the Role of Religion and Race in Science Are Closed?," *EMBO Reports* 9, no. 10 (2008): 938–42 pointed out that one of the codiscoverers of DNA, J. D. Watson was forced to resign from his prestigious post in the Cold Springs Harbor Research Laboratory in New York after he stated publicly that he believed that aid money was wasted in Africa because of the low intelligence of Africans.

THREE

A Matter of Place, Space, and People

Cracow Anthropology, 1870–1920

MARIA RHODE

Studies of nineteenth-century Poland usually describe Polish culture and science as a field of national struggle for identity while showing evidence of resistance to oppression and foreign dominance in unfavorable circumstances.[1] Divided between the Russian and Habsburg Empires and the modernizing Prussian state, Polish cultural and academic elites, from the late eighteenth century onward, usually presented themselves as defenders of the Polish tradition and the Polish nation, an imagined community being shaped in complex ways during the nineteenth century.[2] This national focus characterizes not only the Polish elites' self-representation but is also the dominant framework of Polish historiography.[3]

Polish anthropology, the subject of this chapter, did indeed shape a particular space of national knowledge. Cracow anthropology thus transgressed the borders of the Habsburg state to research provinces of imperial Russia, which had belonged to the early modern territory of Poland-Lithuania. However, culture and science did not develop in an isolated national space. Scientists declaring Polish nationality traveled extensively and were part of a transnational community that produced and shared modern scientific methods and standards. They visited European universities in the East and West, kept in touch with European debates, and adapted them to their special traditions and aims. A third and more rarely recognized context of scientists working in Cracow and making "Polish" anthropology is that of the imperial situation in the Habsburg and Russian Empires. This multiple entanglement of transnational scholarly network connections, the imperial frameworks of the Russian and the Habsburg states, and the context of nation-building makes the Polish scientific engagement particularly interesting for the investigation of processes of cultural and knowledge transfers in an analytic frame of cultural history focusing on space production.[4]

In this chapter, I propose looking at the process of knowledge production in Cracow during the Habsburg Empire and the Second Polish Republic, especially the race concept of its anthropologists, in a way that combines the three perspectives or spaces listed above: national, transnational, and imperial.[5]

Without denying the interconnectedness of nationalism and transnationalism, and starting from a certain geographical place, the spatial perspective adopted here enables the inclusion of local factors, which can be as crucial for the production of knowledge and space as nation or profession.[6] This helps us come to a broader understanding of Polish scientific landscape. Doing so, I employ the concept of entanglement, an approach that has only recently been in practice in historiography about "Polish" science. [7] Following the insight that transnational and international territorial geographies of nations influenced the race science community, while race science itself influenced the geography of nationalism—as convincingly shown by Richard McMahon—I point in particular to the specificity of a local (Galician-Cracow) culture of knowledge as the result of this complex entanglement.[8] This does not mean that Cracow anthropology is just another part of an international network. Almost the opposite is the case. Its specificity is as much due to the local, imperial, and national as to the transnational space of knowledge production.

Using the term "imperial situation," coined by Marina Mogilner for the Russian case, I will argue that Cracow race concepts emerged from the Habsburg and Russian imperial situations, and the political identity of race scientists there, as much as from transnational science.[9] The Polish anthropology established in Cracow represented a specific merging of different spaces of knowledge into a global scientific space, shaped by international standards, the imperial framing, and a local tradition. This anthropology had multiple applications: it could serve as a means of national self-assertion, as evidence for scientific modernity, and as an optimistic vision of a culturally diverse traditional society.

The chapter traces the development of Polish physical anthropology from the 1870s to the end of the First World War in Habsburg-controlled southern Poland, or Galicia, a province that centered on Cracow and Lwów (now Lviv in Ukraine). The chapter focuses on the Cracow anthropology circle grouped around the city's Academy of Learning (Akademia Umiejętności) and Jagiellonian University, which was the premier site of Polish anthropology until the rise of the Lwów school in the 1920s, and a prominent challenger to Lwów thereafter. Showing the methods, techniques, publication strategies, and aims of the researchers who belonged to this group, this chapter analyzes an important part of the history of Polish anthropology and highlights the process by which Polish anthropology developed a specific race concept and on its political and societal contexts. It analyzes the race classification schemes, groups, and territories that the researchers decided to concentrate on and points to particular national, transnational, and imperial spaces in which they were located. I will argue that different geographies of knowledge contributed to particular productions of space and that, in this process of knowledge and space production, place played a decisive role. In so doing, the specificity of the Cracow case on the one hand, and its closeness to other contemporary concepts and debates on the other, will be demonstrated.

The first part of the chapter will present the "imperial" models of race science of the Romanov and Habsburg Empires. The second part analyzes the beginning of anthropological research in Cracow in the second half of the nineteenth century, led by Józef Majer (1809–1899) and Izydor Kopernicki (1825–1891), and the establishment of local research methods and practiques.

The third section concentrates on publication strategies that shaped different spaces of communication and specific spaces of knowledge. The chapter then considers three particularly clear illustrations of the interaction between these spaces. One is the contrast between the Cracow race concepts relating to black people and the local population. The second is the local response to the crisis in European anthropology at the end of the century, personalized by the physician, anthropologist, and archaeologist Julian Talko Hryncewicz.[10] The third is the dynamization of the discipline by the First World War.

Imperial Anthropologies: The Russian and Habsburg Model

Austrian race discourse has not yet been analyzed in a transnational context.[11] However, like its Russian equivalent, which Mogilner describes, it participated in wider European debates about race. Nineteenth-century Russian and Habsburg anthropologists were strongly committed to liberal race concepts. Dominant Russian discourse on race, led by the "Russian Virchow," the Moscow anthropologist Dimitri Anuchin (1843–1923), differentiated between biological (racial) and national or cultural qualities. It denied the existence of racial hierarchies and preferred the term "physical type" to "race." Its mantra was the mixed type, its utopian political vision, mixture and kinship.[12] Russian liberal anthropologists were devoted to the idea of a liberal society, guaranteeing civil rights to all inhabitants—a vision at odds with the country's autocratic government. Nationalists and colonialists could also be found within Russian anthropology, but they remained on the margins.

Viennese liberal anthropologists—for example, Carl von Rokitansky/Karel Rokitánsky (1804–1878), the president of the Viennese Anthropological Society; his assistant Emil Zuckerkandl (1849–1910); and Felix von Luschan (1854–1924), a researcher who heavily influenced both German and Austrian anthropology—similarly established a paradigm of imperial diversity and denied the existence of racial or ethnic-biological hierarchies within the empire's population.[13] They spoke of somatic types and varieties rather than races and perceived different ethnolinguistic groups as nationalities or tribes, rather than nations.[14] The mixed type was also a key principle in the liberal and anational anthropology of the Habsburg Empire. [15]

This was the liberal anti-essentialism of the German anthropologial leader Rudolf Virchow.[16] While Mogilner acknowledges Virchow's influence on Anuchin, language and identity made Austrian and German race discourses extremely similar. Historians therefore tend to regard Austrian anthropology as a part of a germanophone unity and as a predecessor of *völkisch* thinking.[17]

Yet Habsburg and Russian race concepts emerged as much from a specific *imperial situation* and the political identity of their race scientists as from transnational science. Growing national movements challenged the political unity and harmony of both empires by asserting their ethnic distinctiveness and demanding self-determination, or at least autonomy. Some conservative imperialists embraced the new nationalism, insisting on the prerogatives of the Russian or Austrian-German ethnic groups, while others defended the old "feudal" hierarchies, in which class strata and religion rather than ethnicity were the key political distinctions. The liberal anthropologists' acknowledgement and acceptance of linguistic and cultural diversity within an inclusive society constituted an alternative strategy. From the 1860s on they initiated intensive studies within the Habsburg state, gradually introducing race as an epistemic category to conceptualize the empire's diverse population.[18] Liberal anthropologists were uncomfortable with the conservative state, at least in Russia. In Austria, however, their position, intentionally or not, supported the official imperial mantra of unity in diversity (*Einheit in der Vielheit*). This was the response of the supranational monarchy to the potentially explosive national problem.[19] This form of anthropology was therefore not imperial in a sense of being close to officials or "the state," but rather because it paralleled the supranational Habsburg project of depoliticizing ethnic groups by recognizing their cultural distinctiveness.[20]

Meanwhile, German and Austrian anthropology, though never entirely separate, only gradually drew closer. A recent study on the Viennese Anthropological Society shows that the Austrian anthropology grouped around this institution cannot be fully identified with its German counterpart, though Virchow was a prominent figure in both societies and countries.[21] Austrian anthropology was to a high degree devoted to the idea of a universal mankind and tried to explain the differences between people by the impact of environment (mountains and climate), an idea that Virchow clearly rejected.[22] It was less anti-Darwinist than its German counterpart. Among the Austrian race researchers were some German nationalists like Augustin Weisbach (1837–1914), who believed in race hierarchies on the global level as well as within the Habsburg Empire.[23] These researchers initially published in the scientific journals of Germany rather than in the organ of the Viennese society.[24] After both Germans and Austrians shifted gradually toward an exclusive, *völkisch* anthropology at the start of the twentieth century, however, the difference between them faded.

Polish conservative and liberal elite ideas about how society should develop and their adherence to the principle of a sovereign, undivided state resembled the inclusive, traditional, supranational concepts of the Habsburg and Russian Empires. In all three cases, the idea of citizenship centered around social strata (state or class) rather than ethnicity. Until the second half of the nineteenth century, in Polish discourse the term citizen (*obywatel*) was reserved for gentry-landowners only, regardless of their ethnic origin. Various political concepts broadened their meanings to different degrees during the second half of the century, to include the peasant majority. The conservative camp in Galician politics stressed the leading role of the gentry in the national movement and its civilizing mission among the peasants, theoretically including them in the nation.[25] In fact, conservative Galician gentry members and the ruling elites regarded peasant deputies as inappropriate and compromising and found their presence in the public space of the cities uncomfortable.[26] This attitude was contested by a left-wing populism only at the end of the 1880s.[27] The idea of ethnicity based on common origin and culture, as the condition for being part of the national community, would await the nationalistic wave of the 1890s.[28]

Establishing Methods and Categories: Nineteenth-Century Cracow Anthropology between the Paris School and a Local Model

In the territory ruled by the Polish-Lithuanian nobility until the eighteenth century (roughly present-day eastern Poland, Lithuania, western Ukraine, and Belarus), anthropology was first established in the 1850s as a part of medical training in Habsburg-controlled Galicia. Its founding was particularly nationally charged, as it was the only lecture to be presented in Polish, whereas all the compulsory courses had to be taught in German.[29] Józef Majer, a renowned physiologist who introduced anthropology lectures in Cracow in 1856 and taught the subject until 1873, is said to have chosen this new field of medical science as a protest against the Germanization project of the Austrian authorities and to show that Polish was a language capable of facing the challenges of modern scientific terminology.[30] His younger colleague Izydor Kopernicki, a member of the impoverished gentry of the Kresy (the western gubernias of the Russian Empire that had belonged to the old Poland-Lithuania), had been heavily engaged in the national and social uprising of 1863, and therefore had to emigrate.[31] Kopernicki was not only involved in the "national cause" in the field of politics; his correspondence with Poles abroad and his activities in Cracow demonstrate his activism for an expressly Polish science. After moving to Galicia from his exile in Bucharest in 1871, he was intensely devoted to the idea of Poland having its "own" science. To some degree he succeeded, for in the nineteenth-century Russian Empire Cracow anthropology was perceived as a Polish school.[32] Trying to convince the Polish zoologist and anthropologist Benedykt Dybowski (1833–1930) to return from Siberia, where he was about to start a scientific expedition, Kopernicki appealed to Dybowski's national duty.[33] It was time for Dybowski, Kopernicki wrote, to stop being regarded as "the famous Russian naturalist"[34] and come back to Poland, which in this context meant semiautonomous Galicia.[35]

Despite this national frame, Majer and Kopernicki were members of a transnational community of scientists and kept abreast of European novelties.[36] Their classification of peoples derived from the French school of anthropology, established by Paul Broca (1824–1880) and Jean Louis Armand de Quatrefages (1810–1892).[37] In the international network of anthropology, both researchers functioned more as individuals than as members of a Polish anthropological community, which would only really emerge later, after national independence.[38]

A transnational space thus shaped the scientific practice (methods, questions, and practices) of both researchers, but could be nationalized in discourse. Both levels were therefore interconnected. Kopernicki, while working in Bucharest's Coltea hospital and writing for the German *Archiv für Anthropologie*, for example, presented himself as a homeless European researcher and emphasized both his exile status and his European connections.[39]

Nineteenth-century Cracow anthropology centered around the medical faculty of Jagiellonian University and the Anthropological Commission of the Academy of Learning.[40] This commission was founded in 1873 and united physicians, historians, naturalists, and teachers. Like its sister association, the *Anthropologische Gesellschaft Wien,* in Vienna, the capital of the empire, it perceived anthropology as a science of mankind, including archaeology, history, and ethnology.[41] Financed by the Cracow bourgeoisie and intelligentsia rather than by the Habsburg state, the academy regarded itself as a substitute for a national institution and was, to quite a large degree, supported by members of the Polish intelligentsia from the Russian part of the former Polish-Lithuanian state.[42] Not only the Anthropological Commission's financing, but also its focus of interest transgressed the territorial borders of Galicia and the Habsburg Empire. Research concentrated on Kopernicki's ancestral homeland, the Kresy, as well as on Galicia. In the commission's work, anthropology had multiple, partially contradictory facets: it was a means of national self-assertion, it served as evidence for modernity, and it produced a vision of a civic, supranational, and traditionally structured society.

The academy's members shaped a space of knowledge produced by history in multiple ways. The representation of the region as particularly backward and therefore representing the "pure" essence of Polish culture, but extremely challenged by progress, put the scientists in the position of modernists and located them in the space of modern science.[43] Chosing to investigate the lands lost by Poland in the eighteenth century reinforced geographical imaginings of a Poland defined by its former territory and implied a revisionist desire to reclaim this territory.[44] This definition of Polish nationality on the basis of territory rather than ethnicity had two partially contradictory consequences. First, it created a modern liberal image of a civic (*obywatelski*), ethnically inclusive Poland. Cracow anthropologists were therefore interested in nearly all the Kresy's inhabitants—Lithuanians, Belorussians, Ukrainians, Poles, and, to some degree, Jews. This civic notion, however, insistently represented these ethnic groups as cultural peoples rather than political nations. The second consequence of this territorial frame was to reinforce the traditional feudal structuring of Kresy society according to social role, confession, and, to an extent, language. Catholic, Polish-speaking gentry ruled Orthodox and Uniate Belarusian and Ukrainian-speaking peasants, while Jews, Armenians, and Gypsies provided trading or artisanal services.

Until the 1870s all Polish nationalist political programs accepted this historically based territorial definition of Poland. They focused on social strata, and especially the degree to which peasants and Jews should and could be integrated into the nation, rather than on "national" competition between local ethnic groups.[45] Here, the national and imperial analytical frames that this article proposes blur into one another. The Poles, like the Hungarians, were what nineteenth-century political theory referred to as "historic nations," with native aristocracies and living traditions of self-rule. Both thus found themselves in the same position as the Austrians and Russians, of discursively representing their territorially defined countries as "modern," ethnicity-blind, and civic, and as traditional spaces of feudal social relations. Ernese Lafferton therefore presents Hungarian anthropology at the period as sharing many of the same national preoccupations and representations as the Poles, Austrians, and Mogilner's Russians.[46]

The Cracow Anthropological Commission's instructions for anthropological observation established additional, new, "scientific," and modern criteria for the description of the local population. Besides the mere quantity of linguistic, religious, and social groups, their physical characteristics such as eye, hair and skin color, shape of the head, face and nose, and stature were to be noted.[47] However, this international, modern, scientific approach, and especially its methods and tools, were modified when applied to the conditions "at home" in Poland, producing ambiguity instead of the positivist principle of clarity of proof. For the new positivist anthropology that had been established by the Société d'Anthropologie de Paris, standardized methods, including measuring practices and instruments, were crucial in producing reliable evidence, especially in quantitative form. Researchers believed that the same methods applied to equivalent objects with standard instruments should produce the same objective and therefore comparable results. This was a core principle of positivist anthropology. Kopernicki shared these standards and was part of a transnational space of knowledge; he contributed to debates about measuring methods and instruments in the *Bulletins de la Société d'anthropologie de Paris*.[48] On the other hand, despite his training in Paris, he was quite open-minded in the choice of instruments and procedures—a key tool of objectivity—to be used in Austrian Galicia. Instead of using a stick measure on springs and a setsquare, he would accept a tape and a smooth plank.[49] Nor did he insist (with one exception, the cranium) on figures and indices. Actual head forms can be judged by inspection, he wrote, and described as long or short. Faces could be classified as long, round, or oval, the last being the most beautiful.[50]

The specific place where anthropology was carried out, and the public addressed by the researchers, therefore determined the geographical space of investigation and modified the analytical tools, taxonomies, and schemes of classification in a considerable way, without challenging the credibility of the results. Kopernicki's and Majer's results were cited as a reliable reference in several European journals and it took thirty years before their methods and instruments were contested.[51] The context of knowledge production in the Austrian Empire—the imperial frame—seems to be extremely useful to explain this simplification of tools and the parity given to measurement *and* description. Emphasizing description and intuition, rather than merely measurement as a means of evidence, corresponded to the practice of researchers like Zuckerkandl or even Weisbach.[52] Taking into account that Majer and Kopernicki were members and correspondents of the Viennese Anthropological Society and that the major researchers there knew each other's studies, an impact of the Viennese practice is quite likely. Kopernicki himself does not mention this, however, probably due to his patriotic self-fashioning. Access to the imperial circulation of knowledge—which, in its sympathy for intuition and description, was quite old-fashioned in comparison to Broca's insistence on figures—therefore shaped the Galician practice of producing anthropological knowledge about the domestic population.

A specific merging of different spaces of knowledge, shaped by international standards and local tradition into a glocal scientific space, can also be noticed in Kopernicki's remarks on skin color. Adopting and adapting the French chromatic scale and referring to traditional categories of social classification, he stated: "As 'among the inhabitants of our land, skin does not have particular colors and differs only in the grade of the suntan of white skin, three terms should be sufficient for description, white, beautiful white without any suntan, buff, similar to the usual skin of our peasants, swarthy, . . . like the so called Eastern skin, common for Jews and Armenians and most typical for gypsies.'"[53]

The categories and aesthetic hierarchies that he introduced for describing skin color corresponded on the one hand with the European tradition that was established by Johann Friedrich Blumenbach (1752–1840), and combined aesthetic terms with quantitative "facts." On the other hand it integrated the dominant, traditional (European) noble ideal of beauty and especially Poland's traditional social categories of state and religion (peasants, Jews, and Armenians).[54] So, to some degree, new science and old tradition went hand in hand, reinforcing each other in establishing anthropological categories in Polish anthropology of Galicia.

The dominance of traditional categories can also be observed in another field. In his instructions for measurement, Kopernicki recommended concentrating on the peasant when gathering physical data, despite this not being a normative part of the Paris model.[55] This was not just a reaction to the country's demography, but a political statement. Taking into consideration that, after the peasantry failed to support the nationalist rebellion of 1846, the figure of the peasant—which elite scholarship had until then rarely considered beyond a Romantic frame—became the main issue of public and scientific, especially ethnological, interest, Kopernicki's anthropological focus on the peasant is not very surprising.[56] His own political opinion and the fact that Oskar Kolberg (1814–1890), a key figure in Polish ethnology, was his close friend and colleague in the Anthropological Commission, probably additionally helped to guide this specific interest.[57] This example shows that, as much as a universal frame of methods and aims formed the space of knowledge production, personal networks, traditions, and political attitudes structured the selection of objects and, by this, the production of anthropological knowledge. Place reveals itself thus as crucial in this process.

Spaces of Communication

Rules of knowledge production varied according to place or context—for example, in publication practices and strategies. Kopernicki used different rules and standards when communicating with western scholars and with the Polish-speaking public and scientific community. When submitting articles for the Société d'Anthropologie de Paris or the Anthropological Institute of Great Britain and Ireland, he followed all their rules and classified skin and hair color using western European, and especially French and London school models, such as the French school chromatic scale.[58] In Polish writing, as shown above, he introduced a simplified, "local" classification, which used highly intuitive rather than strictly scientific, objective, measurable evidence. His Polish texts also neglected the inductive method, a key principle of the new positivist anthropology, especially in Virchow's Germany. He thus fixed norm and deviation before examination, classifying red and flaxen hair as unusual, and black, brunet, and blond as common.[59] Though produced by the same scientist, anthropological knowledge differed depending on the public to whom it was addressed. For the process of knowledge production not only place, but communication spaces, mattered.

Shared Spaces: Extra-European Races

In certain domains, however, Kopernicki was a very typical, transnational European anthropologist—for example, in his practices with regard to non-European subject matter.

Like his colleagues in western Europe, he was very aware of the epistemological significance and the cultural capital of objects and collections. Although for a long time in a fragile academic position himself, he was a key mediator in the international exchange of crania, bones and academic positions between Siberia and western Europe.[60] In the absence of a classical colonial connection, learned members of the Polish Siberian diaspora—which as a whole consisted of about 35,000 men condemned to exile after the upheavals of 1830 and 1863–64—became crucial deliverers of non-European anthropological and ethnographical "material."[61] So, paving his way to the Société d'anthropologie de Paris, Kopernicki presented Franz Pruner-Bey (1808–1882), the renowned German-French anthropologist, with a Gilyak skull received from a Polish Siberian exile.[62] In addition, he ordered "skulls, skeletons and so on" from Dybowski in Kamchatka[63] and established an anthropological collection of about 360 crania and over 2,000 photographs in Cracow.[64]

Despite the lack of Habsburg—and, of course, Polish—colonies, Kopernicki contributed to the race discourse concerning black people by delivering "an engrossing lecture" on the "Anatomico-anthropological Observations upon the Body of a Negro" at the Congress of Polish Physicians and Naturalists in Cracow, held in 1870.[65] There, in a well-attended exhibition, a plaster cast of the bust, leg, and arm of "a handsome, quite strong 35-year-old Negro" presented "typical racial characteristics" to visitors.[66] Kopernicki also published his results in the Polish organ of the Cracow Scientific Society and a direct translation in the Journal of Anthropology, the organ of the London Anthropological Society. Doing so, he must have assumed a great deal of shared knowledge concerning the black race in both scientific communities. Discussing the dissection results, Kopernicki stuck to the Paris anthropological standards—cephalic index and chromatic scale—as crucial tools of evidence and credibility.

In his report he reproduced nearly all elements of the western scientific race discourse concerning black people, including the most contrary positions in postulating or denying black people's inferiority.[67] On the one hand, Kopernicki saw "the constant and *invariable characters*[68] which are proper to the negro race, as the feminie [*sic*] of the body, . . . , the character of the hair, . . . , the smallness of the encephalic mass, . . . , the greatly developed genital organs, . . . the shortness of the great toe."[69] On the other, he cautiously contradicted Broca's interpretation of brain size as a proof of the inferiority of black people. He also emphasized the impact of (European) culture and environment on intelligence long before Franz Boas's studies on culture and body (1912).[70] "Notwithstanding all its exiguity as to its mass," Kopernicki stated,

> the conformation of the brain of our Negro, did not present any of those characters which are generally considered as signs of inferiority. . . . In a word, it seems to us . . . that Nature has wronged our Negro, by giving him a too limited quantity of cerebral mass; but that his cerebral organs have, in consequence of his ulterior education, acquired a certain degree of maturity and perfection, to [*sic*] which he could not have attained in the midst of his own people.[71]

Discussing the characteristics of a black man, Kopernicki used race as a self-evident epistemic category and ascribed racial characteristics to nearly all parts and organs of the body. Though questioning black people's biologically determined intellectual inferiority, he was nevertheless fixated on the difference between black and white races and accepted a self-evident cultural hierarchy. In this context, a shared space of imagination about black people weighed more than place, no matter whether or not it was part of a colonial state. Race as an adequate concept for his own nation, however, was not self-evident at all.

The Domestic People in an Imperial Frame: The Surveys of 1875–1876 and 1885

Along the same lines as other European countries, the academy aimed at inquiring into "the physical properties of the domestic population (*ludność krajowa*) and its three main nationalities (*narodowość*), the Polish, the Ruthenian, and the Jewish." It carried out its survey before that of the Vienna Anthropological Society, though with a much smaller study population of about five and a half thousand recruits and prisoners.[72] Unlike Virchow's huge investigation, which was a reaction to Quatrefage's provocative statement about the alleged Finish origin of the Prussians, the academy's plan was not motivated by an immediate national dispute, but it is quite likely that the French-German scientific conflict did not escape its notice.[73] In its questionnaire, the "nationalities" were determined by language, which was an accepted imperial practice.[74] It published the results in 1876, focusing particularly on correlations between geographical districts and physical traits.[75] Both the assumption of environmental influence on the body, especially of mountains and valleys, and the a priori division of the population into national or "tribal" categories, was typical of Austrian imperial anthropology.[76] Majer and Kopernicki also shared the opinion dominant in Austrian discourse that it remained to be discovered whether skin color was a matter of heredity or environment.[77] Cracow anthropology was in this aspect part of the landscape of imperial knowledge. Broca's polygenist race science, by contrast, attributed variation to race mixture and discounted environmental impacts.[78]

The academy's material was presented in the order of body size; circumference of the chest; skin, eye, and hair color; and form (*budowa*) of the head and face, expressed by the cephalic index and facial angle according to the standards of the Société d'Anthropologie de Paris, and subdivided by nationality and place.

Majer's contribution to the prestigious *Kronprinzenwerk*, a voluminous official tour d'horizon of the empire's population, demonstrate the entanglement of imperial Austrian and Cracow anthropology.[79] However, Majer and Kopernicki resembled both Austrians and German colleagues like Virchow, in finding race a difficult term to apply in the local context; it was more appropriate for classifying non-Europeans. They stated: "We cannot speak of race characteristics; the skin of all inhabitants always has the color of the white race."[80] Despite rejecting a priori the observation of any racial characteristics in the domestic population, which obviously meant that white skin was treated as a norm and its lack as race, they nevertheless used the term race, mostly in the sense of somatic group. The transfer of classification schemes regarded as useful to distance the colonial other did not properly work in a site regarded as homogenous because formed by nature over the course of centuries.

However, there was an exception: the Jews. Majer and Kopernicki essentialized the Jewish population, as a "totally different tribe," not tied enough to the land "to allow the place to leave a mark on them in any possible way." They found their physical examination, therefore, "particularly interesting."[81] Still, in their concept, cultural otherness did not a priori implicate a physical distinctiveness. In their studies of the inhabitants of Galicia, Majer and Kopernicki came to the final conclusion that "the brachycephalic type is an extremely distinctive common trait of *all*[82] nationalities."[83] The only significant difference they found was the nose. One-third of the Jews were classified as having a hooked nose, compared to only one-sixteenth within the Polish and Ruthenian population.[84] But, according to their measurements, two-thirds of the Jews did have a straight nose or were snub-nosed.[85] The survey did not even objectify the stereotypical Jewish nose, nor was there a hint of any correlation of physical with cultural characteristics.

Both anthropologists repeated their investigation in 1885.[86] In some details, concerning the forehead and occiput, and the supposed correlation between brachycephalic forms and a hilly environment, their results differed from those achieved in 1875–76. In general, however, Majer and Kopernicki also found this time that "Poles, Ruthenians, and Jews, undoubtedly brachycephalic in different degree, are also undoubtedly of mixed race."[87]

Kopernicki's and Majer's writing introduced race as a conglomerate of physical features, and nationality as a complementary category for classifying populations. Like other liberal anthropologists—for example, Virchow and Luschan—Kopernicki did not see any congruence between nationality and race. In a separate publication of the same year (1885), dealing only with cranial characteristics, he used the term race synonymously with variety (*varietés hybrides*).[88]

The juxtaposition of Kopernicki's racial classification in the case of the Galician population and his racist interpretation when dealing with a black corpse demonstrates both the modification of scientific concepts *and* their continuity. In some cases, when a transnational space of knowledge dominated the process of knowledge production concerning a shared other, place did not matter. The only spatial distinction that mattered here was the one between Europeans and non-Europeans.

Cracow Anthropology before and during the Great War: Julian Talko-Hryncewicz and His Assistants

Place did matter for the institutionalization of anthropology at universities, however. This was a late and uncertain development throughout both eastern European empires. After Kopernicki's death in 1891, university teaching of anthropology in Cracow discontinued for almost twenty years, although the academic community lobbied to establish a chair in anthropology from the end of the 1890s.[89] Finally, in 1908, Julian Talko-Hryncewicz (1850–1936), a Polish scientist from the Russian Empire and Kopernicki's longstanding correspondent, received an appointment as a professor of anthropology at the prestigious Jagiellonian University.[90] Though Vienna's officials and some Polish modernizers considered Galicia one of the most economically underdeveloped and exotic spaces of the Habsburg Empire, this modern discipline was nevertheless reestablished there a whole five years before the academic institutionalization of anthropology at Vienna University under Rudolf Pöch (1870–1921).[91]

Talko-Hryncewicz moved to Cracow during the decisive years of the European crisis in liberal, physical anthropology, especially in craniology, when, in spite of extremely detailed measurements of the skull, no consensus about race could be achieved.[92] He physically joined the local scientific community in a situation that in many aspects differed from the political and societal conditions of the founding period of Cracow anthropology. Positivism as an epistemic principle and a guarantee for social progress and liberalism were challenged by neo-romanticism and socialism.[93] Nationalistic movements became stronger in all parts of Europe, including the Habsburg Empire.[94] In Galicia, the Ukrainian national movement especially challenged the idea of a Polish nation uniting Polish aristocrats and Ukrainian peasants, whereas the Polish Peasant Party (*Stronnictwo Ludowe*) advocated a polyethnic Poland based on a strong peasant class, diminishing the significance of nobility.[95]

Coming from a country that, unlike Galicia or an imagined or historical Poland, counted more than one hundred nationalities, human diversity was part of Talko-Hryncewicz's everyday life and was one of his core research fields since at least since 1892, when he moved from the Kiev gubernia to Kiakhta in eastern Siberia.[96] What do this "Russian" scientist's answer to the crisis and contribution to Cracow anthropology tell us about the geography of Polish race science and about the imperial race anthropology as a coherent category?

Talko-Hryncewicz was a member of at least three scientific communities: an imperial Russian, a Galician-Polish, and a transnational space of knowledge. Long before exchanging research in Russian-Chinese Kiakhta for a base in Galician-Polish Cracow in 1908, he was elected a corresponding member of the Cracow Academy of Learning (1892) and had been placing his articles in the publication series of its Anthropological Commission since 1886.[97] His publications nationalized knowledge by featuring research subjects from Kiev gubernia, within the historical territory of the former Polish-Lithuanian Commonwealth.[98] His medical and anthropological articles, written in Polish, appeared not only in scientific and popular journals in Austrian-Polish Galicia, but also in the Russian-ruled former Kingdom of Poland,[99] in the western gubernias of the Russian Empire,[100] and in St. Petersburg, the core of the Russian state.[101] Hryncewicz's publication strategies point to the opportunities of multiethnicity in the Russian Empire, which allowed him to continue using Polish as the language of publication even in places that had never been part of the Polish-Lithuanian commonwealth (e.g., St. Petersburg, with its significant Polish diaspora). However, he could also switch to Russian and be regarded as a member of the Russian scientific community, which did not take account of the researcher's nationality.[102] Being part of both scientific communities, he participated in imperial Russian discourse as well as in the Galician-Polish space of knowledge.

Talko-Hryncewicz had studied at Kiev University, corresponded with Dmitri Anuchin, and kept in touch with the Imperial Archaeological Commission in St. Petersburg.[103] He was a member of the anthropological section of the Imperial Society of the Lovers of Natural Science, Anthropology and Ethnography (IOLEAE) and the Imperial Russian Geographical Society,[104] which honored him with a gold medal for his studies on the Transbaikal and Mongolian regions in 1904.[105] Mogilner, the most profound expert on the Russian race discourse, has classified him as a representative of the anthropology of multinationalism, which was, to a significant degree, shaped by the dominant liberal anthropological discourse.[106]

This was an optimistic and inclusive conceptualization of physical anthropology, in which, Hryncewicz wrote, "nations, cultures and peoples do not matter."[107] It could also have been articulated in a similar way by Rudolf Virchow or Felix von Luschan in Germany.[108] It was part of a transnational space of knowledge produced by a generation of researchers born in the 1850s and committed to liberalism.[109]

It naturally shaped how he refered to race when working in Kiakhta and in Cracow. Among the inhabitants of Lithuania and the Ukraine, as well as of those of the Transbaikal region,[110] Hryncewicz analyzed European and non-European peoples, who, according to (western) European taxonomy, were representatives of different races.[111] They belonged either to Blumenbach's Caucasian or Mongolic varieties (varietates), or, according to Deniker's newer classifications, based on the combination of somatic traits, to a multitude of races and secondary races.[112] However, for leading anthropologists of the Russian Empire, Russians and Tatars, for example, belonged to the same anthropological type (see Mogilner's chapter in this volume).[113] Working at the geographical edge of the Russian Empire but being part of its scientific core, Talko-Hryncewicz participated in its dominant race discourse. His conceptualization of human diversity did not construct any part of the empire's population as others, because, according to his anthropological results, all were related.[114] Not even his studies comparing the "fresh brains" of Buryats, whom European taxonomies classified as of Mongolic race, with those of "Russians" (a category including Poles and Jews) delivered any evidence for significant racial difference.[115] In his papers based on the Asian material and published in Cracow, Talko-Hryncewicz used the term race to discuss ancient populations; in relation to living people he more often spoke of groups or types.[116] This classification was part of the dominant imperial Russian as well as the Austrian discourse. Here, imperial situations and scientific spaces merged. However, it differed from the western, or, at least, the French model, which well into the early twentieth century postulated fixed original races.[117]

In his works written for the Cracow Academy in the 1890s and dealing with the population of the former Polish-Lithuanian territory, references to the term race also appear extremely rarely. It is a category used alongside other group taxonomies, such as tribe (*plemię*), ethnographic element (*pierwiastek etnograficzny*), people or nation (*naród*), and stock (*ród*).[118] Despite a nationalistic shift in Polish politics there is no hint of a modern, ethno-nationalist framing. The Russian imperial situation as well as a Polish traditional concept of society seem to have dominated Hryncewicz's anthropological work in this period.

His decision to focus on the historical territory of Poland when writing for the Cracow Academy does seem to have had an explicit national bias, but the proximity of the material and the influence of the financing institution also account for this. His practice for acquiring anthropological material points to feudal traditions of using subordinates. To a high degree, when not using his patients, Talko-Hryncewicz fell back on family and friends for the acquisition of research objects when living in Ukraine (Kiev gubernia) or in Lithuania.[119] Here, the feudal order of the Russian state and the feudal tradition of the Polish-Lithuanian commonwealth enabled him to use his family's position of power to organize so-called factory campaigns, in which workers were obliged to undergo anthropological measurement.

The results of his analysis can hardly be classified as nationalizing, in the sense of creating a biologic uniformity, when referring to the historical Polish-Lithuanian territory. He identified internal diversity within the Ukrainian, Belorussian, and Lithuanian groups that he studied and pointed to similarities between the population of neighboring territories that did not belong to historical Poland—for example, between Latvians, Lithuanians, and Finns.[120] This approach followed the liberal Russian paradigm of kinship and mixture. Here, scientific, imperial, liberal, and traditional cultural spaces merged, regardless of the place of knowledge production, be it Cracow or Kiakhta.

In the years before the First World War, in a specific amalgam of traditional concepts and modern, transnational taxonomies, Cracow anthropology (re)feudalized rather than nationalized the social body and produced a specifically biased space of anthropological knowledge, determined by the self-representation of Polish nobility as the true embodiment of Polishness. In Cracow, as well as taking up the Galician and Austrian tradition of seeking correlations between growth and environment,[121] Talko-Hryncewicz focused sharply on the nobility, to which he himself belonged, in contrast to other socioethnic groups.[122] Unlike his former contributions to the academy's series, he not only concentrated on the geographical space of the former Polish state, but by choosing a specific social group—the nobility—he indirectly emphasized its (vanishing) significance and its (challenged) exceptional status. His writing also developed the idea of physical aristocracy, which he ascribed to ethnic Poles. In his *Poles of the Kingdom of Poland in the Light of Present Anthropological Research* (1912), a study based on Russian, western European, and his own results on ethnic Poles, he concluded: "Admittedly, Poles of both sexes have a weaker physique than other Slavic peoples (Great-Russians, Ruthenians), but they surpass them in a general harmony, and proportionality, which occurs in the cranial and facial measurements. This gives Poles distinct characteristics of aristocracy among the family of Slavic peoples."[123]

This conclusion seems even more surprising, given that it was based to a great extent on measurements carried out in the factories of Warsaw.[124] Within a nationally charged space it can be seen as an attempt to harmonize the social body, dismembered by deep social changes. From a broader perspective it fits the picture painted by Emese Lafferton of Hungarian anthropology, which tried to integrate a nationalist but inclusive agenda with an aesthetic ideal.[125] Could his differentiation between the lower classes and the intelligentsia be classified as part of modern anthroposociology, which also correlated social class and race in the contemporary West? This seems unlikely. Hryncewicz did not refer to such studies as Georges Vacher de Lapouge's (1854–1936) *Race et milieu social* (1909), or Otto Ammon's (1842–1916) *Die natürliche Auslese beim Menschen* (1893), and, unlike them, he did not draw any connections between an alleged Nordic/fair anthropological type and a successful urban existence.[126]

By the beginning of the twentieth century in Poland, race, a term that made Kopernicki uneasy when applied to his "own" population, had become an established category for groups of people, based on distinct physical traits. In his 1913 book *Man in Our Lands*, Talko-Hryncewicz applied the term race and referred to the most recent international anthropological works, such as Joseph Deniker's classification of races. In keeping with liberal anthropological tradition, Talko-Hryncewicz emphasized the mixed character of every race. He underlined the positive influence of "new blood" to stop degeneration, which can be regarded as a response to the pessimistic degeneration discourse and the fear of mixture in western European populist and scientific racism.[127] Talko-Hryncewicz reacted to the European crisis in anthropology by postulating more research, which would require further types to be established and new classifications. Categories developed in the West would not work in the East.[128] Not an ethnographical turn like in France or a genetic one like in Germany, but an old-fashioned (by then) trust in positivist science based on a greater amount of data shaped the Cracow model at the turn of the century.

During his years in Cracow before the Great War, Talko-Hryncewicz contributed to the production of sociogeographical space that structured anthropological knowledge in a way that combined transnational taxonomies, implications of an imperial situation, and a local academic tradition. But it was not just tradition and transnationalism that played a part in Talko-Hryncewicz's concept of anthropological types or races. There are also elements of neo-romanticism, a Polish variant of modernism, with a strong center in Cracow, to be found in his writing.[129] Although professional physical anthropology did not link somatic to mental traits, Hryncewicz's "ethnographic" representation, as part of the general description, often essentialized peoples. For example, he ascribed "something Mongol-Asiatic" to the Ukrainians or presented light type Karaite Jews as "dreamy-minded."[130]

The First World War

First World War prisoner-of-war (POW) studies were a major anthropological undertaking in several countries, especially Austria-Hungary and Germany, offering a convenient opportunity to examine geographically diverse populations.[131] During the war, Cracow and Viennese anthropologists profited in terms of resources for the production of knowledge, from the Habsburg authorities' generally favorable attitude toward large-scale measurement surveys.[132]

Though Poles like Talko-Hryncewicz and Adam Wrzosek (1875–1965) participated in this research, it was far less significant for them than for Viennese and German colleagues. From 1914 onward Wrzosek, assistant to the chair in general and experimental pathology since 1901 and Hryncewicz's deputy during his absence in Cracow, coordinated POW research, collecting measurements and taking photographs and plaster masks.[133] Wrzosek, who graduated from Kiev University and had been trained in Paris and Zurich, would become one of the most eager organizers of anthropology in post-war Poland, initiating its official organ, *Antropologia Polska*. Talko-Hryncewicz himself spent the years between 1914 and 1918 in Tsarist, later Soviet Russia, as the outbreak of the war had surprised him during field studies in Lithuania.[134] However, after his return to Cracow in 1918, he also studied "soldiers of different nationalities" at the Dąbie POW camp near Cracow and compared them with the data he collected in the Buryat hospital in Petersburg between 1915 and

1917.[135] At first glance, the situation in Cracow seems to fit the Austrian or the German pattern; thousands of POWs served as "anthropological material" and the Ministry of Education supported the research by additional means.[136] However, the local situation was different. Unlike their colleagues in Vienna and Berlin, the war was not a starting point for the academic careers of Galician anthropologists.[137] Adam Wrzosek did not even mention his wartime measurements when he applied for a chair in experimental pathology at Warsaw University in 1918.[138] Similarly, neither Jan Czekanowski (1854–1924)—the future star of the Polish anthropological school and ethnography professor in Lwów since 1913—nor his students participated in any POW studies, even though Czekanowski was on good terms with Felix von Luschan, the key figure in German POW research.[139] Ludwik Hirszfeld's (1884–1954) studies in Thessaloniki, which were partially based on POWs, advanced his career enormously. However, this seems to have been more the exception than the rule and, as a blood-group anthropologist, his professional connections with traditional anthropology were tenuous.[140] Though part of the imperial frame, the Cracow/Galician situation was specific.

Conclusion

The knowledge production of Cracow-style anthropology from the second half of the nineteenth century onward shows its closeness to European debates and methods. However, its specificity derives from the fact of its researchers being embedded in an imperial Austrian and Russian scientific and political space, an imperial situation as well as in a Polish national and societal discourse. More simple measuring devices replaced standardized scales, markers, and instruments (a key reqirement of the positivist approach to anthropology) when Poles researched Austrian-Polish Galicia. Race—a crucial epistemic criterion in nineteenth-century western anthropology—was gradually introduced as a concept for describing common somatic traits of the local, Galician, Lithuanian, or Ukrainian population. For the leading Cracow anthropologists, especially Kopernicki, race initially seems to have been a more appropriate term for dealing with black people than with Poles, Ruthenians, or Jews. Here he copied nearly all the assumptions of the western European race discourse, producing a basic division between black and white races. Applying the race concept to the local inhabitants of Poland, however, Cracow anthropologists emphasized the unity of the social body by showing the similarity of each established somatic group without introducing any hierarchies.

The juxtaposition of Kopernicki's racial classification in the case of the Galician population and his racist interpretation when dealing with black people demonstrates that the elasticity or rigidity of scientific concepts depended not only on the place where they were used, but also on the very object of inquiry and the space of communication. The subject of inquiry itself sometimes depended on the researcher's conceptual geography. Polish anthropologists therefore generally preferred to research what they considered Polish lands.

In the nineteenth century, Cracow-style anthropology was tightly connected to institutions—the academy and the university—but it also profited from the feudal character of the Austrian and Russian Empires, as well as from the feudal tradition of the old Polish-Lithuanian Commonwealth. The researchers (most of them of noble origin) acquired their anthropological material not only by using institutional authority, but also through their positions of power in society. In the years before the First World War, Cracow anthropology (re)feudalized rather than nationalized the social body by initially concentrating on the peasant, later on the nobility, and constructing a difference between the intelligentsia and the "people." Being part of the Austrian empire, it shared the mantra of unity in diversity, adapting it to a historically shaped space of a civic nation under Polish dominance. The overlapping similarities with and the divergence from the Austrian model concerning the low significance of wartime measurements for further academic careers, however, show the impact of place within a transnational space of knowledge.

Notes

I would like to thank Rebekka Habermas for her suggestions and Richard McMahon for reading, proofreading, and patiently commenting on this work.

1. For example: Bogdan Suchodolski, *Historia nauki polskiej 1795–1862*, vol. 3 (Wrocław: Ossolineum, 1991); Norman Davies, *God's Playground. A History of Poland*:

Vol. 2: 1795 to the Present (Oxford: Oxford University Press, 1982); Jarosław Cabaj, *Walczyć nauką za sprawy Ojczyzny. Zjazdy ponadzaborowe polskich środowisk naukowych i zawodowych jako czynnik integroacji narodowej (1864–1917)* (Siedlce: Wydawnictwo Akademii Podlaskiej, 2007); Julian Dybiec, *Nie tylko szablą: Nauka i kultura polska w walce o utrzymanie tożsamości narodowej 1795–1918* (Cracow: Księgarnia Akademicka, 2004).

2. Piotr Wandycz, *The Lands of Partitioned Poland, 1795–1918* (Seattle: University of Washington Press, 1974); Brian Porter, *When Nationalism Began to Hate: Imagining Modern Politics in Nineteenth Century Poland* (Oxford: Oxford University Press, 2002).

3. For example: Adam Wrzosek, "Projekt I: Kopernickiego urządzenia zakładu antropologii na wydziale lekarskim w uniwersytecie Jagiellońskim," *Archiwum historii i filozofii medycyny* 3, no. 2 (1925): 266–73, 266.

4. Roger Chartier, "Culture as Appropriation: Popular Culture Uses in Early Modern France," in *Understanding Popular Culture: Europe from the Middle Ages to the Nineteenth Century*, ed. Steven L. Kaplan (Berlin: Walter de Gruyter, 1984), 229–54; *De la comparaison á l'histoire croisée*, ed. Etienne François and Bénédicte Zimmermann (Paris: Seuil, 2004); Michael Werner and Bénédicte Zimmermann, "Beyond Comparison: Histoire croisée and the Challenge of Reflexivity," *History and Theory* 45 (2006): 30–50.

5. *The Spatial Turn: Interdisciplinary Perspectives*, ed. Barney Warf and Santa Arias (New York: Routledge, 2008).

6. Among a huge number of recent studies taking a spatial approach I mention only two: Felix Driver, *Geography Militant: Cultures of Exploration and Empire* (Oxford: Blackwell, 2001); and Kapil Raj, *Relocating Modern Science: Circulations and the Construction of Knowledge in South Asia and Europe, 1650–1900* (Basingstoke: Palgrave Macmillan, 2007).

7. For example, sections in *Imperienvergleich: Beispiele und Ansätze aus osteuropäischer Perspektive*, ed. Guido Hausmann and Angela Rustemeyer (Wiesbaden: Harrasowitz, 2009); and *The Nationalization of Scientific Knowledge in the Habsburg Empire, 1848–1918*, ed. Mitchell G. Ash and Jan Surmann (Basingstoke: Palgrave Macmillan, 2012).

8. Richard McMahon, "Networks, Narratives, and Territory in Anthropological Race Classification: Towards a More Comprehensive Historical Geography of Europe's Culture," *History of the Human Sciences* 24, no. 1 (2011): 70–95, 72.

9. Marina Mogilner, "Russian Physical Anthropology in Search of Imperial Race: Liberalism and Modern Scientific Imagination in the Imperial Situation," *Ab Imperio* 1 (2007): 191–223, 195; Jan Surman, "The Circulation of Scientific Knowledge in the Late Habsburg Monarchy: Multicultural Perspectives on Imperial Scholarship," *Austrian History Yearbook* 46 (2015): 163–82, 163–64.

10. Kazimierz Stołyhwo, "Julian Talko-Hryncewicz," *Polski Słownik Biograficzny* 10 (1962–64): 55–56.

11. Important studies contributing to this issue are: Christian Feest, "The Origins of Professional Anthropology in Vienna," in *Kulturwissenschaften im Vielvölkerstaat.*

Zur Geschichte der Ethnologie und verwandter Gebiete in Österreich, ca. 1780 bis 1918, ed. Britta Rupp-Eisenreich and Justin Stagl (Cologne: Böhlau, 1995), 113–31; and Karl Pusman, *Die Wissenschaften vom Menschen auf Wiener Boden (1870–1959): Die anthropologische Gesellschaft in Wien und die anthropologischen Disziplinen im Fokus von Wissenschaftsgeschichte, Wissenschafts-und Verdrängungspolitik* (Vienna: LIT Verlag, 2008).

12. Susi Frank, "Anthropologie als Instrument imperialer Identitätsstiftung: Russisch-sibirische Rassetheorien zwischen 1860 und 1890," in *Kultur in der Geschichte Russlands: Räume, Medien, Identitäten, Lebenswelten*, ed. Bianca Pietrow-Ennker (Göttingen: Vandenhoeck & Ruprecht, 2007), 203–23.

13. Maria Teschner-Nicola, "Felix von Luschan und die Wiener Anthropologische Gesellschaft," in *Felix von Luschan (1854–1924): Leben und Wirken eines Universalgelehrten*, ed. Peter Ruggendorfer and Hubert Szemethy (Vienna: Böhlau, 2009), 55–80.

14. Irene Ranzmaier, *Die anthropologische Gesellschaft in Wien und die akademische Etablierung anthropologischer Disziplinen an der Universität Wien, 1870–1930* (Vienna: Böhlau, 2013).

15. Ranzmaier, *Die anthropologische Gesellschaft*, 83.

16. Andrew D. Evans, *Anthropology at War: World War I and the Science of Race in Germany* (Chicago: University of Chicago Press, 2010).

17. This tendency can be seen in Brigitte Fuchs, *"Rasse," "Volk," Geschlecht: Anthropologische Diskurse 1850–1960* (Frankfurt: Campus, 2003); and Pusman, *Die Wissenschaften vom Menschen.*

18. Fuchs, *"Rasse," "Volk," Geschlecht*, 136, 151.

19. Peter Stachel, "Die Harmonisierung nationalpolitischer Gegensätze und die Anfänge der Ethographie in Österreich," in *Geschichte der österreichischen Humanwissenschaften—Bd. 4: Geschichte und fremde Kulturen*, ed. Karl Acham (Vienna: Passagen Verlag, 2002), 232–368; Katharina Weigand: "Die österreichisch—ungarische Monarchie in Wort und Bild. Ein kulturpolitisches Instrument am Ende des 19. Jahrhunderts," in *Ethnographie in Serie: Zu Produktion und Rezeption der österreichisch-ungarischen Monarchie in Wort und Bild*, ed. Jurij Fikfak and Reinhard Johler (Vienna: Institut für europäische Ethnologie 2008), 62–80; Moritz Csáky, "Die Vielfalt der Monarchie und die nationalen Probleme," in *Nation, Ethnizität und Staat in Mitteleuropa*, ed. Urs Altermatt and Erhard Busek (Vienna: Böhlau, 1996), 44–64.

20. Karl Langner, "Programm für ethnographische Untersuchungen, speziell auf dem Gebiete Österreichs," *Mitteilungen der Anthropologischen Gesellschaft in Wien* 13 (1883): 183–85; Jan Surman, "Imperial Knowledge? Die Wissenschaften in der späten Habsburger Monarchie zwischen Kolonialismus, Nationalismus, und Imperialismus," *Wiener Zeitschrift für Geschichte der Neuzeit* 9, no. 2 (2009): 119–33, 126.

21. Ranzmaier, *Die anthropologische Gesellschaft*, 9.

22. Rudolf Virchow, "Vortrag des Hrn. Virchow," in *Tageblatt der 58. Versammlung Deutscher Naturforscher und Ärzte in Straßburg, 18.–23. September 1885*, ed. J. Stilling (Strassburg: G. Fischbach, 1885), 540–55.

23. Augustin Weisbach, *Körpermessungen verschiedener Menschenrassen. Europäischer Rassenwahn und Anthropometrie im 19. Jahrhundert*, ed. Reinhard Krüger (Berlin: Weidler Buchverlag, 2002).

24. Fuchs, *"Rasse," "Volk," Geschlecht*, 152; Augustin Weisbach, "Die Gewichtsverhältnisse der Gehirne österreichischer Völker mit Rücksicht auf Körpergröße, Alter, Geschlecht und Krankheiten, "*Archiv für Anthropologie* 1 (1867): 191–218, 285–319; Augustin Weisbach, *Körpermessungen verschiedener Menschenrassen* (Berlin: Wiegandt, Hempel & Parey, 1877) [*Zeitschrift für Ethnologie* supplement].

25. Kai Struve, "Citizenship and National Identity: The Peasants of Galicia during the Nineteenth century," in *Societal Change and Ideological Formation Among the Rural Population of the Baltic Area 1880–1939*, ed. Piotr Wawrzeniuk (Huddinge: Södertörn högskola, 2008), 75–93, 84.

26. Struve, "Citizenship and National Identity," 86.

27. Keely Stauter-Halsted, "Rural Myth and the Modern Nation," in *Staging the Past: The Politics of Commemoration in Habsburg Central Europe, 1848 to the Present*, ed. Maria Bucur and Nancy Wingfield (West Lafayette IN: Purdue University Press, 2001), 153–77; Peter Brock, *Bolesław Wysłouch, Pioneer of Polish Populism in Nationalism and Populism in Partitioned Poland: Selected Essays* (London: Orbis, 1973), 181–211.

28. Porter, *When Nationalism.*

29. Jan Hulewicz, "Józef Majer (1808–1899)," *Polski Słownik Biograficzny* 19 (1974): 161–64; Tadeusz Bielicki, Tadeusz Krupiński, and Jan Strzałko, "Historia antropologii polskiej," *Przegląd Antropologiczny* 53, nos. 1–2 (1987): 3–28, 4.

30. Hulewicz, "Józef Majer," 162. Bielicki, Krupiński, and Strzałko, "Historia," 4; Józef Majer *Niemiecko-polski słownik wyrazów lekarskich, ułożony przez Józefa Majera i Frederyka Skobla* (Cracow: D. E. Friedlein, 1842).

31. Michał Godycki, *Sto lat antropologii polskiej Izydor Kopernicki* (Wrocław: PWN, 1956), 12–13.

32. Marina Mogilner, *Homo imperii ocherki istorii fizicheskoi antropologii v Rossii (konets XIX—nachalo XX veka)* (Moscow: Novoe literaturnoe obozrenie, 2008), 154.

33. Gabriel Brzęk, *Benedykt Dybowski: Życie i dzieło* (Warsaw: Polskie Wydawnictwo Ludoznawcze, 1994). According to his pupils, Dybowski also offered lectures in anthropology during his academic life in Lwów. Letter from K. Stołyhwo to A. Wrzosek, January 12, 1953, AAN Poznań, A. Wrzosek Collection, P 3 70, Part II, Box 21.

34. Adam Wrzosek, "Listy Izydora Kopernickiego do Benedykta Dybowskiego," *Przegląd Antropologiczny* 26 (1960): 110, 122. Kopernicki used the German expression "des berühmten Naturforschers Dr. B. v. Dybowsky."

35. *Die Habsburgermonarchie 1848–1918. Vol. III: Die Völker des Reiches*, ed. Adam Wandruschka and Peter Urbanitsch (Vienna: Verlag der österreichischen Akademie der Wissenschaften, 1980), 522–54.

36. Majer was a member of the Vienna Anthropological Society (Anthropologische Gesellschaft Wien) and of the Society of Friends of the Sciences (Towarzystwo Przyjaciół Nauk) in Poznań (Posen) in the Duchy of Prussia. Kopernicki was a cor-

responding member of the Société d'Anthropologie de Paris and a member of the Anthropological Institute of Great Britian and Ireland.

37. Claude Blanckaert, *De la race á l'évolution: Paul Broca et l'anthropologie française (1850–1900)* (Paris: Harmattan, 2009), 111–35.

38. Richard McMahon, *The Races of Europe: Construction of National Identities in the Social Sciences, 1839–1939* (London: Palgrave Macmillan, 2016), 287–98.

39. Izydor Kopernicki, "Ueber den Bau der Zigeunerschädel," *Archiv für Anthropologie* 5 (1872): 267–320, 275, 278.

40. Jan Hulewicz, *Akademia umiejętności w Krakowie 1873–1918: zarys dziejów* (Wrocław: Ossolineum, 1958), 33; Adam Orlik, "Zbiór Wiadomości do Antropologii Krajowej—historia czasopisma," http://wiedzaiedukacja.eu/archives/57946, May 18, 2017.

41. Hulewicz, *Akademia*, 33; Ranzmaier, *Die Anthropologische Gesellschaftt*; Christian Feest, "The Origins of Professional Anthropology in Vienna."

42. Hulewicz, *Akademia*, 45–58, 75.

43. Orlik, "Zbiór."

44. Tadeusz Chrzanowski, *Kresy obszary tęsknot*, 2nd ed. (Cracow: Wydawnictwo Literackie, 2009).

45. Maciej Janowski, *Polish Liberal Thought before 1918* (Budapest: Central European University Press, 2004), 172, 212.

46. Emese Lafferton, "The Magyyar Moustache: The Faces of Hungarian State Formation, 1867–1918," *Studies in History and Philosophy of Biological and Biomedical Sciences* 38 (2007): 706–32, 707–8.

47. Izydor Kopernicki, "Instrukcya dla robiących spostrzeżenia antropologiczne na osobach żywych," *Rozprawy i Sprawozdania z posiedzień wydziału matematyczno-przyrodniczego Akademii Umiejętności* 2 (1875): 23–35.

48. Izydor Kopernicki, "Déscription d'un nouveau crâniographe: étude crâniographique des races," *Bulletins de la Société d'anthropologie de Paris*, ser. 2, vol. 2 (1867): 2, 559–71.

49. Kopernicki, "Instrukcya," 24–25.

50. Kopernicki, "Instrukcya," 28.

51. Ivan Franko, "Eine ethnologische Expedition in das Bojkenland," *Zeitschrift für österreichische Volkskunde* 11 (1905): 17–32, 17.

52. Fuchs, *"Rasse," "Volk," Geschlecht*, 141–42. Augustin Weisbach, "Die Zigeuner," *Mitteilungen der Anthropologischen Gesellschaft in Wien* 19 (1889): 3, 107–17, 107.

53. Kopernicki, "Instrukcya," 26. Kopernicki's aesthetic glorification of whiteness corresponds almost literally with Blumenbach's. Johann Friedrich Blumenbach, "On the Natural Variety of Mankind," in *Anthropological Treatises of Johann Friedrich Blumenbach*, ed. T. Bendyshe (London: Longman, 1865), 214.

54. Johann Friedrich Blumenbach, *De generis humani varietate nativa*, 3rd ed. (Göttingen: Vandenhoek et Ruprescht [1775] 1795), section 4; Nell I. Painter, *The History of White People* (New York: Norton, 2010), 72–90.

55. Kopernicki, "Instrukcya," 31; Paul Broca, *Instructions crânioloquiques et crâniométriques de la Société d'anthropologie de Paris* (Paris: G. Masson, 1875), 54–56.

56. Kai Struve, *Bauern und Nation in Galizien: über Zugehörigkeit und soziale Emanzipation im 19. Jahrhundert* (Göttingen: Vandenhoeck & Ruprecht, 2005); Zbigniew Jasiewicz and David Slattery, "Ethnography and Anthropology: The Case of Polish Ethnology," in *Fieldwork and Footnotes: Studies in the History of European Anthropology*, ed. Han Vermeulen and Arturo Alvarez Roldán (London: Routledge, 1995), 185–201, 187–88.

57. Maria Turczynowiczowa, "Henryk Oskar Kolberg (1814–1890)," *Polski Słownik Biograficzny* 13 (1967–68): 300–304.

58. Izydor Kopernicki, "Anatomico-Anthropological Observations upon the Body of a Negro," *Journal of Anthropology* 1 (1871): 3, 245–58, 246.

59. Kopernicki, "Instrukcya," 26.

60. After moving from Romania to Galicia, Kopernicki earned his living as a doctor at a spa in Rabka (Galicia) and Marienbad (Bohemia). He was appointed lecturer (professor ad personam, without a chair) at the Jagiellonian University only in 1886, six years before his death: Godycki, *Sto lat*, 17.

61. Andrew Gentes, "Siberian Exile and the 1863 Polish Insurrections according to Russian Sources," *Jahrbücher für Geschichte Osteuropas* 51 (2003): 2, 197–217, 198.

62. Franz Pruner-Bey, "Description d'un crâne de Ghiliak et note sur les Ghiliaks," *Bulletins de la Société d'Anthropologie de Paris*, ser. 2, vol. 2 (1867): 571–79, 572.

63. Kopernicki to Dybowski, November 21 and 28, 1880, Izydor Kopernicki, Listy do Jana Karlowicza, Adama Honorego Kirkora i Benedykta Dybowskiego, *Przegląd Antropologiczny* 26 (1960): 59–132, 118; Izydor Kopernicki, "O kościach i czaszkach Ajnosów," *Pamiętnik Akademii Umiejętności w Krakowie* 7 (1882): 27–68.

64. Godycki, *Sto lat*, 16–17.

65. Józef Majer, *Pamiętnik pierwszego zjazdu lekarzy i przyrodników polskich odbytego w r. 1869 w Krakowie* (Cracow: Drukarnia C. K. Uniwers, 1870), 60; Izydor Kopernicki, "Anatomiczno-antropologiczne spostrzeżenia nad Murzynem, Rzecz czytana na pierwszym zjeździe Lekarzy i Przyrodników Polskich w Krakowie," *Rocznik Cesarsk. Król. Towarzystwa Naukowego Krakowskiego* 3 (1871): 19, 75–100. Kopernicki published the article also in the *British Journal of Anthropology* in the same year: Isidor Kopernicki, "Anatomico-Anthropological Observations upon the Body of a Negro," *Journal of Anthropology* 1 (1871): 3, 245–58.

66. Majer, *Pamiętnik*, 60; Kopernicki, "Anatomiczno-antropologiczne," 57. Kopernicki had exhibited forty "race skulls" in 1870, during the medical naturalist exhibition in Cracow: *Katalog wystawy lekarsko-przyrodniczej w Krakowie* (Cracow: Kornecki, 1870), 35.

67. Kopernicki, "Anatomiczno-antropologiczne," 82; Kopernicki reviewed even quite dated statements of Samuel Thomas Soemmering (1755–1830) and Franz Tiedemann (1781–1861), showing his profound knowledge. Samuel Thomas Soemmering, *Über die Verschiedenheit des Mohren vom Europäer* (Mainz: n.p., 1784). Franz Tiedemann, *On the Brain of the Negro, Compared with That of the European and the Orang-Outang* (London: Taylor, 1836).

68. Author's italics.

69. Kopernicki, "Anatomico-anthropological," 252.

70. Franz Boas, "Changes in the Bodily Form of Descendants of Immigrants," *American Anthropologist* 14 (1912): 3.

71. Kopernicki, "Anatomico-anthropological," 257.

72. Józef Majer, "Program badań antropologicznych," *Rozprawy i Sprawozdania z Posiedzeń Wydziału Matematyczno-Przyrodniczego Akademii Umiejętności* 1 (1874): 67–83; Andrew Zimmerman, "Antisemitism as a Skill: Rudolf Virchow's Schulstatistik and the Racial Composition of Germany," *Central European History* 32 (2001): 4, 409–29; Margit Berner, "Large-Scale Anthropological Surveys in Austria-Hungary," in *Doing Anthropology in Wartime and War Zones. World War I and the Cultural Sciences in Europe*, ed. Reinhard Johler, Christian Marchetti, and Monique Scheer (Bielefeld: transcript Verlag, 2010), 233–54.

73. Christian Schönholz, *Rudolf Virchow und die Wissenschaften vom Menschen. Wissensgenerierung und Anthropologie im 19. Jahrhundert* (Würzburg: Könighausen & Neumann, 2013), 198.

74. Blanckaert, *De la race* á *l'évolution*, 320–28.

75. Izydor Kopernicki and Józef Majer, *Charakterystyka fizyczna ludności galicyjskiej na podstawie spostrzeżeń dokonanych za staraniem Komisyi antropologicznej* (Cracow: Akademia Umiejętności, 1876), 3, 5, 6, 20–21.

76. Pusman, *Die Wissenschaften vom Menschen*, 76–82; Steven Seegel, *Mapping Europe's Borderlands* (Chicago: University of Chicago Press 2012), 181; Angèle Kremer-Marietti, "The Assumption of Climate Causing Human Diversity Was Basic for Monogenists" (L'anthropologie physique et morale en France et ses implications idéologiques), in *Histories de l'anthropologie (XVIe—XIXe siècles)*, ed. Britta Rupp-Eisenreich (Paris: Klincksieck, 1984), 322–33. In Austrian anthropological writing, the term *Stamm* (tribe) is often synonymously used with nationality (*Nationalität*), apparently to minimize the threat of nationalism. Kopernicki and Majer also used the term *szczepowy* (tribal) when refering to Jews: *Charakterystyka fizyczna*, 26, 36.

77. Kopernicki and Majer, *Charakterystyka fizyczna*, 64. Felix v. Luschan, "Die physischen Eigenschaften der wichtigsten Menschenracen: Vortrag gehalten zur Erlangung der Privatdozentur für physische Ethnographie," *Wiener Medizinische Wochenschrift* 41 (1882): 1246.

78. Blanckaert, *De la race*, 341.

79. Józef Majer, "Physische Beschaffenheit der Bevölkerung," in *Die österreichische Monarchie in Wort und Bild: Galizien*, ed. Kronprinz Rudolf (Vienna: K. K. Hof-und Staatsdruckerei, 1898), 239–51; Regina Bendix, "Ethnology, Cultural Reification, and the Dynamics of Difference in the Kronprinzenwerk," in *Creating the Other: Ethnic Conflict and Nationalism in the Habsburg Empire*, ed. Nancy Wingfield (New York: Berghahn, 2003), 149–56.

80. Kopernicki and Majer, *Charakterystyka fizyczna*, 64.

81. Kopernicki and Majer, *Charakterystyka fizyczna*, 26, 36; Kai Struve, "Gentry, Jews, and Peasants: Jews as Others in the Formation of the Modern Polish Nation in

Rural Galicia during the Second Half of the Nineteenth Century," in *Creating the Other: Ethnic Conflict and Nationalism in the Habsburg Empire*, 103–26.

82. Author's italics.

83. Kopernicki and Majer, *Charakterystyka*, 138.

84. Kopernicki and Majer, *Charakterystyka*, 137, 138.

85. The alleged Jewish nose was crucial in the debate on a Jewish type in the Russian Empire: Marina Mogilner, *Homo Imperii: A History of Physical Anthropology in Russia* (Lincoln: University of Nebraska, 2013), 217–50.

86. Izydor Kopernicki and Józef Majer, "Charakterystyka fizyczna ludności galicyjskiej, Serya II," *Zbiór wiadomości do antropologji krajowej* 9 (1885): 1–92.

87. Kopernicki and Majer, "Charakterystyka fizyczna," 82.

88. Izydor Kopernicki, *Charakterystyka kraniologiczna ludności galicyjskiej, Serya II* (Cracow: drukarnia uniwersytetu Jagiellońskiego, 1885), 31.

89. Letter of the Dean of the Faculty of Philosophy to the Ministry of Education in Vienna, December 12, 1905, AUJ (Uniwersytet Jagiellónski Cracow), WF II, 176.

90. Kopernicki, "Listy do Juliana Talko-Hryncewicza," 145–55.

91. Larry Wolff, *The Idea of Galicia: History and Fantasy in Habsburg Political Culture* (Stanford: Stanford University Press, 2010); Feest, "The Origins of Professional Anthropology in Vienna," 127.

92. Benoit Massin, "From Virchow to Fischer: Physical Anthropology and 'Modern Race Theories' in Wilhelmian Germany," in *Volksgeist as Method and Ethnic: Essays in Boasian Ethnography and the German Anthropology Tradition*, ed. George Stocking Jr. (Madison: University of Wisconsin Press, 1996), 79–38, 86–87.

93. Julian Krzyżanowski, *Neoromantyzm polski 1890–1918* (Wrocław: Zakład Narodowy im. Ossolińskich, 1971); Lucja Blit, *The Origins of Polish Socialism* (Cambridge: Cambridge University Press, 1971).

94. Pieter Judson, "Marking National Space on the Habsburg Austrian Borderlines, 1880–1918," in *Shatterzone of Empires: Coexistence and Violence in the German, Habsburg, Russian, and Ottoman Borderlands*, ed. Omer Bartov and Eric Weitz (Bloomington: Indiana University Press, 2013), 122–35.

95. Paul R. Magosci, *The Roots of Ukrainian Nationalism: Galicia as Ukraine's Piemont* (Toronto: University of Toronto, 2002); Olga A. Narkiewicz, *Polish Populist Politics: 1867–1970* (London: Croom Helm, 1976).

96. Stołyhwo, "Julian Talko Hryncewicz," 55–56.

97. Zbigniew Wójcik and Jan Staszel, "Związki Juliana Talko-Hryncewicza z Polską Akademią Umiejętności i Uniwersytetem Jagiellońskim w Krakowie," *Prace Komisji historii nauki* PAU 19 (2010): 83–100.

98. Julian Talko Hryncewicz, "Charakterystyka fizyczna ludności żydowskiej Litwy i Rusi na podstawie własnych spostrzeżeń," *Zbiór wiadomości do antropologji krajowej* 16 (1892): 1–62.

99. Julian Talko Hryncewicz, "O antropologii wogóle i zastosowaniu jej u nas," *Wisła* 2 (1888): 247; Julian Talko-Hryncewicz, "Słów parę ze stanowiska antropologii: W kwestii pochodzenia Słowian," *Wisła* 16 (1902): 6, 754–61.

100. *Kurier Litewski*, 1906: 2, 1.

101. Julian Talko Hryncewicz, "Z dziennika lekarza," *Kraj* 37 (1883). J. Talko Hryncewicz, "Antropologii stosunek do medycyny," *Przegląd Lekarski* 43 (1904): 58.

102. Nataliya V. Eilbart, *Juliian Dominikovich Talko-Grincevich—issledovatel' Zabaikal'ia 1850–1936* (Moscow: Nauka, 2003); Maria Blombergowa, *Polscy członkowie rosyjskich towarzystw archeologicznych 1839–1914* (Wrocław: Zakład Narodowy im. Ossolińskich, 1988), 35–36.

103. Blombergowa, *Polscy członkowie*, 36.

104. Stołyhwo, "Julian Talko Hryncewicz," 55–56; Nathaniel Knight, "Science, Empire, and Nationality: Ethnography in the Russian Geographical Society, 1845–1855," in *Imperial Russia: New Histories for the Empire*, ed. Jane Burbank and David L. Ransel (Bloomington: Indiana University Press, 1998), 108–41.

105. Maria Blombergowa, "Juliana Talki-Hryncewicza i Gotfryda Ossowskiego kontakty z cesarską Komisją Archeologiczną w Petersburgu," *Kwartalnik Historii Nauki i Techniki* 2 (1989): 271–82; Mogilner, *Homo imperii*, 201–8.

106. Mogilner, *Homo imperii*, 204–6.

107. Julian Talko-Hryncewicz, *Człowiek na ziemiach naszych*, 3.

108. Pusman, *Wissenschaften vom Menschen*, 77–78.

109. Andre Gingrich, "Liberalism in Imperial Anthropology: Notes on an Implicit Paradigm in Continental European Anthropology before World War I," *Ab Imperio* 1 (2007): 224–39.

110. Ju. Talko-Grintsevich, "K ėtnografii Kitaia," *Protokoly Troitskosavsko-Kiakhtinskago Otdeleniia Priamurskago Otdela Imperatorskago Russkago Geograficheskago Obshchestva* 4 (1895): 4–23; Ju. Talko-Grintsevich, *Zametki po antropologii severnych Kitaitsev* (Moskva: A. I. Mamontov 1902); Ju. Talko-Grintsevich, "Kitaitsy Kiakhtinskago i Urginskago Maimashena," *Trudy Troitskosavsko-Kjakhtinskago Otdeleniia Priamurskogo Otdela Imperatorskago Russkago Geograficheskago Obshchestva* 2 (1899): 2, 3.

111. Cracow anthropologists did not use the term Caucasian; they spoke of the white race. Kopernicki linked skulls of his skull collection with people or nations (Hindu, Czech, Bulgarian, German, Great Russian, Gypsy), rather than with the three or five anthropological races: *Katalog wystawy*, 35.

112. Joseph Deniker, *The Races of Man: An Outline of Anthropology and Ethnography* (London: Scott, 1900), 77, 285, 379.

113. Marina Mogilner, "The Challenge of Transformation and Rationalization. Russian Physical Anthropology of the Nineteenth–Early Twentieth Centuries: Imperial Race, Colonial Other, Degenerate Types, and the Russian Racial Body," in *Empire Speaks Out: Languages of Rationalization and Self—Description in the Russian Empire*, ed. Ilya Gerasimov, Jan Kusber, and Alexander Semyonov (Leiden: Brill, 2009), 155–89, 185–89.

114. Julian Talko-Hryncewicz, "Charakterystyka fizyczna ludów Litwy i Rusi," *Zbiór wiadomości do antropologji krajowej* 17 (1893): 51–72, 171–72.

115. Iu. D. Tal'ko-Grintsevich, "Nekotoryia dannyia o vese mozga zhitelei Zabaikal'ia," *Trudy Troitskosavskago-Kiakhtinskago Otdeleniia Priamurskago Otdela IRGO*

9, no.2 (1906): 51–93, 70; Julian Talko-Hryncewicz, *Z przeżytych dni 1850–1908* (Warsaw: Galewski, 1930), 274.

116. Julian Talko-Hryncewicz, *Materiały do etnologii i antropologii ludów Azji środkowej. Mongołowie, Buriaci i Tungusi* (Cracow: Akademia Umiejętności, 1910), 17, 55, 76–77, 93.

117. Blanckaert, *De la race*, 105–6.

118. Talko-Hryncewicz, "Charakterystyka fizyczna ludów Litwy i Rusi," 56, 58, 60.

119. Talko-Hryncewicz, "Charakterystyka fizyczna ludu ukraińskiego," 3; Talko-Hryncewicz, *Z przeżytych dni*, 201; Talko-Hryncewicz, "Szlachta litewska, studyum antropologiczno-etnologiczne," *Materiały antropologiczne, archeologiczne i etnograficzne Akademii Umiejętności* 12, no. 2 (1912): 3–115, 11–12.

120. Talko-Hryncewicz, "Charakterystyka fizyczna ludów Litwy i Rusi," 171.

121. Julian Talko-Hryncewicz, "Dwa sprawozdania z referatów zrobionych na posiedzeniach Komisji Antropologicznej o badaniach podczas wakacji letnich 1910–1912 Górali polskich przy pomocy p. E. Frankowskiego," *Sprawozdania Akademii Umiejętności Wydz. Mat.-Przyrodniczy za lata 1912–13* 12 (1912): 1, 13–15.

122. Talko-Hryncewicz distinguished between grand land owners, petty nobility, Lithuanians, and Latvians: J. Talko-Hryncewicz, "Szlachta litewska," 3–115; Talko-Hryncewicz, "Przyczynek do historji rodzin szlacheckich na Litwie," *Litwa i Ruś*, 4 (1912): 11.

123. Julian Talko-Hryncewicz, "Polacy Królestwa Polskiego w świetle dotychczasowych badań antropologicznych," *Rozprawy i Sprawozdania z posiedzeń wydziału matematyczno-przyrodniczego Akademii Umiejętności* 12 B, ser. 3 (1912): 241–355, 340, 345.

124. Talko-Hryncewicz integrated the results of the Russian-Jewish researcher Arkadi D. Elkind (1869–1903) and his paper "Privislianskie Poliaki (antropologicheskii i kraniologicheskii ocherk)," *Izvestiia* IOLEAE 40 (1897) [*Trudy antropologicheskogo otdela*, vol. 18], 459–505; See also Mogilner, *Homo imperii*, 206–15.

125. Lafferton, "The Magyar Moustache," 715.

126. George Vacher de Lapouge, *Race et milieu social* (Paris: M. Rivière, 1909). Otto Ammon, *Die natürliche Auslese beim Menschen* (Jena: Fischer, 1893).

127. Julian Talko-Hryncewicz, *Człowiek na ziemiach naszych* (Cracow: Mortkowicz, 1913), 3; Daniel Pic, *Faces of Degeneration: A European Disorder, c. 1848–1918* (Cambridge: Cambridge University Press, 1989).

128. Talko-Hryncewicz, *Człowiek na ziemiach*, 3, 116.

129. Kazimierz Wyka, *Modernizm polski* (Cracow: Wydawnictwo Literackie, 2003).

130. Talko-Hryncewicz, *Człowiek na ziemiach*, 151; Julian Talko-Hryncewicz, "Karaimi vel Karaici litewscy," *Materiały archeologiczne, antropologiczne i etnograficzne* 7 (1904): 44–97, 96.

131. Andrew D. Evans, "Science behind the Lines: The Effects of World War I on Anthropology in Germany," in *Doing Anthropology*, 99–122.

132. Faculty of Philosophy to the Ministry of Education in Vienna (draft), December, 13, 1916, AUJ, WF II 176. The ministry granted financial support for 1917 (copy of a letter from the Ministry of Education in Vienna, January 27, 1917, AUJ, WF II, 176); Berner, "Large-Scale," 249; Viktor Lebzelter, "Anthropolog. Untersuchungen an serbischen Zigeunern," *Mitteilungen der Anthropologischen Gesellschaft in Wien* 52 (1922): 23–42; Maciej Górny, "War on Paper? Physical Anthropology in the Service of States and Nations," in *Legacies of Violence. Eastern Europe's First World War*, ed. Jochen Böhler, Włodzimierz Borodziej, and Joachim von Puttkammer (München: Oldenbourg, 2014), 131–67, 137; Britta Lange, "AfterMath: Anthropological Data from Prisoner-of-War Camps," in *Doing Anthropology*, 311–36.

133. Warsaw University to the Ministry of Religious Issues and General Education (MSRiOP), March, 6, 1918, AAN Warsaw, Akta personalne Adam Wrzosek, microfilm B 15705, 13. Zbigniew Maćkowiak and Michał Musielak, *Adam Wrzosek: życie i działalność* (Poznań: Wydawnictwo Poznańskie, 2000), 22.

134. Talko-Hryncewicz, *Wspomnienia*, 50–163.

135. He conducted 3591 measurements: Talko-Hryncewicz, *Wspomnienia*, 172. The camp in Dąbie has been an Austrian POW camp during the First World War. The repatriation started in the end of October 1918: Hannes Leidinger and Verena Moritz, "Verwaltete Massen. Kriegsgefangene in der Donaumonarchie 1914–1918," in *Kriegsgefangene im Europa des Ersten Weltkriegs*, ed. Jochen Oltmer (Paderborn: Schöning, 2006), 35–66, 66. Since December 1918 it was a Polish camp for Ukrainian and Czech prisoners of war, taken into captivity in the Soviet/Ukrainian war of 1919–20. Zbigniew Karpus, *Jeńcy i internowani rosyjscy i ukraińscy w Polsce w latach 1918–1924: Z dziejów militarno-politycznych wojny polsko-radzieckiej* (Toruń: Marszałek, 1991), 50–52. Since Talko Hryncewicz returned to Cracow in March 1918, it is more likely that he conducted his measurements on First World War captives.

136. Letter from the local government (namiestnictwo) to the dean of the Faculty of Philosophy, June 2, 1918, AUJ, WF II 176. Olga Willerowa, one of Wrzosek's assistants, presented her results based on the measurement of 611 men: Olga Willerowa, "Spostrzeżenia nad barwą oczów, włosów i skóry u Tatarów, Ormian, Gruzinów, Mołdawian, Serbów i Macedończyków," *Przegląd Antropologiczny* 1 (1926): 84–91.

137. Andre Gingrich, "After the Great War: National Reconfigurations of Anthropology in Late Colonial Times," in *Doing Anthropology*, 355–80, 369; Górny, "War on Paper," 136.

138. Warsaw University to the Ministry of Religious Issues and General Education (MSRiOP), March 6, 1918, AAN Warsaw, Akta personalne Adam Wrzosek, microfilm B 15705, 13. He published the results in 1922: Adam Wrzosek, Serbowie. Materiały antropologiczne zebrane w latach 1914–1918, *Wiadomości antropologiczne* 1 (1922): 1, 3–29.

139. Jan Czekanowski spent a significant part of the war (1914–16) in Moravia working on his African material: Andrzej Malinowski, "Antropologia poznańska XX wieku," *Homines hominibus* 1 (2008): 4: 33–74, 50. One of Czekanowski's students, Jan Myd-

larski, who graduated in Lwów in 1922, started his career after the war, but there are no hints that he participated in the POW studies during the war.

140. Maciej Górny and Katrin Steffen, "Böses Blut: Die Blutgruppenforschung und der Serologe Ludwik Hirszfeld in Deutschland und in Polen," *Historie: Jahrbuch des Zentrums für Historische Forschung Berlin der Polnischen Akademie der Wissenschaften* 7 (2013–14): 97–119.

FOUR

Yet Another Greek Tragedy?

Physical Anthropology and the Construction of National Identity in the Late Nineteenth Century

AGELIKI LEFKADITOU

On March 30, 1881, the Greek scholar and Member of Parliament Stephanos Dragoumis (1842–1923)[1] received a letter from Paris seeking assistance in establishing contacts with physicians from his constituency.[2] His correspondent was Clon Stephanos (1854–1915), a young doctor writing an article on Greece to be included in the celebrated *Dictionnaire encyclopédique des sciences médicales*.[3] Encouraged by Dragoumis's positive response, Stephanos sent a second letter, asking for further help with data collection and inquiring "what kind of care has been taken for the skeletons of those who fell at [the Battle of] Chaeronea and whether the bones of each and every one of them are specially kept."[4] This was the first instance in which archaeological human remains became a shared matter of concern for an anthropologist and a politician in Greece.

The historical interest in the Battle of Chaeronia—fought in 338 BC and during which the army of Philip II defeated the coalition of Greek city-states led by Athens and Thebes and gained control of Greece—preceded the exchange between Stephanos and Dragoumis. The relationship of the Macedonians to the Greeks of central and southern Greece remained a much-contested issue until at least the mid-nineteenth century. In the diverse historiographic schemata adopted by Greek historians, the battle signified either the beginning of the Macedonian hegemony, the enslavement of the Greeks, and, consequently, the end of the glorious classical era, or the historical and cultural continuity of the ancient Greek civilization through the achievements of Alexander the Great.[5] For Stephanos, the anthropological examination of the remains could reveal the racial affinity between ancient Macedonians (originally assumed to be a mixture of Illyrians and Greeks) and Greeks of the city-states. For Dragoumis, the challenge was to strengthen national coherence and unity, and by extension reinforce claims for the expansion of the Kingdom of Greece to the north.[6] The private communication about Chaeronea's skeletons, then, introduces anthropology and Stephanos as two new actors in the controversial arena of scholarly accounts of national identity and their political counterparts.

This chapter focuses on the work of Clon Stephanos, the first and only Greek scholar of his time to systematically research the racial origins and constitution of the country's inhabitants.[7] Initially educated as a medical doctor in Athens and greatly interested in prehistoric archaeology, Stephanos encountered anthropology in Paris and was determined to secure the establishment of the discipline at the University of Athens. His scientific praxis brought together craniometry, archaeological findings, historical archives, and linguistic analysis. However, for nation-building, the nascent scientific field had to negotiate its place among hegemonic intellectual resources such as history, archaeology, and folklore studies.[8] At the same time, western European anthropological schools, though an indispensable source for theoretical and methodological innovation, often appeared rather suspicious and critical of local interpretations, especially when these contradicted established authorities and traditions.

Despite Stephanos's positivist approach and adherence to the ideal of scientific objectivity, the inevitable entanglement of anthropology with the defense of the Greek nationalist project affected both the professionalization of this science in Greece and its international credibility.[9] Indeed, it took more than thirty years of continuous effort until a chair of anthropology was established at the University of Athens. Stephanos died before having the opportunity to become a professor and left the discipline at a crossroads. This chapter, then, endeavors to paint a complex picture of the history of the founding of anthropology in Greece: one that appreciates its multiple connections to international and national fields and actors but also acknowledges its difficulties in escaping its peripheral status. Before proceeding any further, however, a brief look at nineteenth-century discussions on Greek national identity is in order.

From Ancient to Modern Greeks

Even before the advent of the War of Independence (1821–32), the arguments for the foundation of a Greek national state were based on identification with ancient Greece, and, most notably, classical antiquity. Reflecting the influence of European Enlightenment ideals and the fascination with classical Greece as well as the need for an exemplar of the administrative, economic, and political organization of the emerging polity, this appropriation was in a sense a historical necessity.[10] Despite the complexities it induced, the revival or rebirth of ancient Greece in the body of the newly established Greek state became its first foundational myth.

The original conception of a resuscitated Greece in its former glory was a product of the educated local and foreign elites, and it largely dismissed or alienated the majority of the Greeks whose direct experience, including their religious feelings, were much closer to that of the Byzantine period or even the Ottoman times. Toward the middle of the century, however, a powerful national narrative was formed, incorporating the classical past, the Hellenistic and Roman periods, the Middle Ages—in the form of the Byzantine Empire—and modern times.[11] This synthetic schema, introduced by Constantinos Paparrigopoulos (1815–1891) in the founding work of modern Greek historiography, the *History of the Greek Nation* (published in multiple volumes from 1860 to 1870), suggested "a cultural and spiritual evolution and continuity."[12] The understanding of the national past now rested on a genealogical connection between the various historical phases of Hellenism and established a conception of national unity through both difference and similarity.[13]

European audiences were not easily swayed. Notwithstanding the romantic sentiment of the great number of Philhellenes who fought during the Greek War of Independence for the revival of Greek democracy and the abolishment of Ottoman occupation, the idyllic image of Greece began to change rapidly shortly thereafter.[14] What was becoming increasingly obvious was that western Europeans were not willing to leave ancient Greece to the current, unfortunate, degraded inhabitants of the country. Ancient Greece and its glorious inhabitants were appropriated as the root of Western civilization, and the Greek national story became redundant.

The most common reference in such discussions is the work of the Austrian scholar Jakob Phillip Fallmerayer (1790–1861), who, in a number of works from the 1830s, variously asserted that not only there was no cultural link between ancient Greeks and the people of the Greek state but also denied any biological affinity.[15] Or, even more pointedly, for Fallmerayer the Slavic presence in Greece guaranteed that not even a drop of ancient Greek blood was left in the veins of modern Greeks. Though he soon became persona non grata and an archenemy of the Greeks, Fallmerayer was certainly not the only European scholar who entertained such views. The French diplomat, writer, fallen aristocrat, and (quite ironically) close friend of the Dragoumis family, Arthur de Gobineau (1816–1882), is often referred to as one of those who have challenged the Greek narration.[16] Indeed, in his study *Essai Sur L'Inégalité Des Races Humaines* (1853–55), Gobineau, expressing a general pessimistic feeling of inevitable societal decay, suggested that ancient civilizations perished as a result of extreme mixture and ascribed the brilliance of ancient Greece to its superior, Aryan aristocracy. Unlike Gobineau, who had no real connections to the world of science and was soon ostracized by French naturalists and anthropologists, several influential nineteenth-century naturalists and physicians variously engaged with the Greek conception of continuity.[17] The following two examples are characteristic.

In 1847 the Swedish anatomist Anders Retzius (1796–1860) published a paper under the title "On the Round, Brachycephalic Skull from Greece."[18] The skull under examination belonged to an eight-year-old individual and reached Retzius through a Swedish diplomat in Athens. Following contemporary practice that supposed a characteristic skull type for each nation, and after comparing the skull to artistic drawings, ancient sculptures, and observation of living Greeks, he reported, "I think I can assume that the brachycephalic skull shape occurred in both the former Greeks and it is common among the present-day ones."[19] Though this seems to suggest a line of continuity, Retzius also adopted Fallmerayer's claims that the current Greek population was mostly of Slavic origin, and, given the prevalence of short skulls among the Slavs, stated that "it would be almost impossible to ascertain a difference between it [a Slavic skull] and a real brachycephalic Greek."[20]

The controversial Scottish anatomist Robert Knox (1791–1862) addressed similar concerns in a series of lectures first published in 1850 under the title *The Races of Men*.[21] For Knox, ancient Greeks were a unique amalgam of Scandinavian or Saxon, Celtic, Slavonian, Gothic, and Oriental elements that mixed with the aboriginal Pelasgi when these races invaded the peninsula.[22] But it was the Scandinavian or Saxon race that "contributed mainly, no doubt, to the formation of the noblest of all men—the statesmen, poets, sculptors, mathematicians, metaphysicians, historians of ancient Greece. But from that land nearly all traces of it have disappeared."[23] Knox's agenda was to advance the idea that "the European races, so called, differ from each other as widely as the Negro does from the Bushman," and in doing so promote the supremacy of the Scandinavians or Saxons.[24] Nevertheless, in this process he established a clear-cut division between the Greeks of the classical period, defined from the times of Homer to Alexander the Great, and the modern inhabitants of the country: "The grand classic face has all but disappeared, and in its place comes out a people with a rounded profile; the nose large and running into the cheeks, like the Jew; the chin receding; the eyebrows arched. Anti-classic in all things, how Greece has fallen."[25]

As previously discussed, mid-nineteenth-century Greek historiography was instrumental in restructuring the originary myths of the newly born nation-state, partly in response to such external challenges. Within this context archaeology, as well as *laografia*, produced the indisputable material evidence in support of the national rhetoric of continuity, either through uncovering and protecting antiquities or collecting, documenting, and classifying folk legends and songs.[26] Antiquity became the "secular religion" of the nation, ancient monuments were its icons, and archaeologists, the people who could interpret the past and mediate between past and present worlds, were its religious leaders.[27] Indeed, only a year after the establishment of the Greek state, the Archaeological Service was founded, while in 1834 the first archaeological law, which regulated excavation permits as well as the ownership and preservation of the antiquities, was enacted. In 1837 the privately funded Archaeological Society in Athens became the second most important pillar of archaeological activity, and a number of foreign schools followed its path.

From the side of laografia studies the great majority of nineteenth-century Greek scholars saw modern culture and identity as rooted in ancient prototypes, and in a circular move constructed their taxonomies and analyzed their carefully gathered data starting from the idea of cultural continuity.[28] In doing so, Greek scholars reinforced the identification with antiquity by reinstating it not as a purely intellectual construct but as a constitutive part of people's imagination and tradition.[29] An indispensable partner in the formation of national science, laografia represented "a disciplinary hybrid, a blend of romantic historicism, methodological evolutionism, and philological scholasticism."[30]

But even though the alliance between historiography, archaeology, and laografia was powerful, Greek scholars were presented with challenges that went beyond mentality or culture and addressed the physical body, or, even more pressingly, made culture coextensive with biology. And this is where Greek anthropology endeavored to find its niche in discussing national origins and identity.

Clon Stephanos in the Anthropological World of Paris

Clon Stephanos entered the world of anthropology after he and his mathematician brother, Kyparissos, moved to Paris in 1878. The apartment the two brothers rented on 28 Rue de l'Arbalète was strategically situated within walking distance of the Muséum d'Histoire Naturelle and the Faculté de Médecine, the two main sites for anthropological research in the city.[31] At the museum, Armand de

Quatrefages (1810–1892) was appointed the world's first professor of anthropology in 1855. At the medical school, the Société d'Anthropologie, founded in 1859 under Paul Broca's (1824–1880) leadership, had managed to establish a laboratory space, a library, a museum, and the first private school for anthropology, the Ècole d'Anthropologie. Both settings allowed for interested members of the public to attend courses without fees or any other entrance requirements, and the school's library was open to everyone.[32]

Stephanos's medical background—typical of most physical anthropologists at the time—and his interest in prehistoric archaeology and history aligned nicely with the original French conception of anthropology, which encompassed the history of nations.[33] It seems, however, that Stephanos had already made a name for himself within the French scholarly community well before his arrival in Paris. Thanks to the excellent relationships between Greek and French archaeologists, his first treatise on mostly unpublished inscriptions from his homeland, the island of Syros, received glowing reviews by *Revue Archéologique*.[34] The study was indeed presented as a work "impossible to be researched with more zeal [and in which the texts] have been transcribed with such extreme care and have been explained with an erudition both precise and abundant."[35] This early publication is indicative of Stephanos's double commitment to inductive empiricism and national themes. Quite similar in terms of methodological approach and research agenda, his second publication focused on the Russian occupation of the Cyclades Islands of the Aegean during the Russo-Turkish war (1768–74).[36] The study meticulously brought to light previously examined documents sent to the people of the Cyclades from the beginning of the Russian occupation in October 1770 until its end in August 1774 and was favorably presented in the *Revue des Questions Historiques*.[37]

Even so, we know very little of Stephanos's actual encounters in Paris. One of his letters to Dragoumis, however, leaves no doubt that he had access to Broca's laboratory or the museum's facilities. "I beg you," Stephanos wrote to Dragoumis, "to take the time to inform me, if—in the case that the local Anthropological Society, or the 'Muséum d'Historie Naturelle,' asks for crania from Megara from modern times—it would be easy for you to see that the French Embassy in Athens would assume responsibility for their shipment."[38] The task was complex. The involvement of a government official in such a situation could only be made possible by complying with the law, but, most important, by assuring the high level of expertise and public profile of the individuals and institutes involved. In any case, Dragoumis responded positively on the basis of their common understanding, and a number of skulls were sent to Paris for anthropological study.[39]

By way of establishing himself within the network of French learned societies, in 1879 Stephanos joined L'Association pour l'Encouragement des Études Greques, through which he already kept close contact with French and Greek intellectuals.[40] But, quite surprisingly, he never became a member of the Société d'Anthropologie. This organization was an ideal meeting ground for younger scholars, and especially medical doctors like himself. However, Stephanos's more conservative Catholic background may have conflicted with the outspoken republicanism, extreme materialism, and anticlericalism of many of the society's members.[41] In any case, Stephanos was elected a member of the more inclusive Association Française pour l'Avancement des Sciences.[42] Given the close relationship and interaction between the two societies, we can safely assume that Stephanos was well positioned in the network of medical doctors that dominated the anthropological society and was familiar with contemporary anthropological debates.

In this context, Stephanos put together his magnum opus, the most comprehensive study of Greece to date and the only such written by a Greek scholar, entitled *La Grèce Au Point De Vue Naturel, Ethnologique, Anthropologique, Démographique et Medical* and published in 1884.[43] The monograph appeared as an extract from the *Dictionnaire encyclopédique des sciences médicales*, to which Stephanos had contributed this remarkably long entry on Greece, as well as a few other shorter articles.[44] The dictionary itself was a massive undertaking of one hundred volumes edited by the French physician Amédée Dechambre (1812–1886) and printed over a period of twenty-five years, from 1864 to 1889. With over 250 authors appearing in the list of contributors, including the names of founding members of the Société d'Anthropologie such as Paul Broca, Eugène Follin, Charles Robin, and Aristide Verneuil, this publication ultimately constituted a map of the whole of the medical world of Paris.[45]

A footnote by Dechambre—truly an unexpected and unique insertion in the whole dictionary—provides both an explanation for Stephanos's lengthy piece and a hint to how he was perceived by his French peers. The importance of this contribution (written by "one of the most educated" young doctors from Greece) for the field of medical geography, noted Dechambre, excuses its length.[46] He went on to express his regret for having asked the author to omit some of the data and stated that he wished that the omitted material would find a different venue for publication. Dechambre's assessment was not exaggerated. Stephanos's thesis was the result of a concerted effort to weave together an unprecedented amount of data on the country's geography, geology, flora, fauna, ethnology, anthropology, demography, hygiene, and pathology. Most of the included measurements came from published international research or Greek scholarly sources, but Stephanos had also managed to establish a local network of informants, which provided him with original data on areas not previously studied.

The Greeks of *La Grèce*

Drawing inspiration from the intellectual tendencies of the time, *La Grèce* provided an entirely numerical description of Greece in line with the contemporary excitement for the positive method. The crucial influence of the French school of anthropology on Stephanos's work is nowhere more evident than in the two chapters devoted to ethnology and anthropology. It is here that he fully embraced the school's characteristic "cult of facts" and the subsequent dismissal of everything that could be perceived as subjective interpretation or mere speculation.[47] His accounts of Greek prehistory and the racial composition of ancient and modern populations are also marked by Broca's early assertion that there is probably no other question "of such interest for us than the origins of our nation."[48] In this sense, the anthropological endeavor to study the past and present of European nations was necessarily intertwined with national historiographies and the processes of national identity formation.

Indeed, in keeping with contemporary anthropological views, which presented European nations as mixtures of diverse racial elements and ethnic groups, Stephanos argued for a modern Greek nation that incorporated Frankish and Albanian elements next to the Greek populations. Yet, according to Stephanos, the courses and fortunes of the Franks and the Albanians had been quite distinct. The first, a mixture of Francophone crusaders, after having lost most of their medieval settlements, were completely assimilated and Hellenized, while some had even adopted Greek Orthodoxy.[49] The integration of the Albanians, on the other hand, was a much slower process, only recently enabled by common military conscription, the development of public education, and the expansion of means of communication. In any case, Stephanos suggested that the Albanians of Greece, though not as great in numbers as often assumed, fought during the Greek War of Independence as if "for their own country" and were "flattered to be considered Greeks."[50] Even if their racial descent, often associated with the prehistoric Illyrians, was different, their presence in the country since at least the fourteenth century, as well as their patriotic feelings, firmly established them as part of the national community.

This same discussion of population movements during the Middle Ages and modern times, however, brought Stephanos's ethnological account even closer to the predominant national responses with regard to Slavic influences on Greece. Following the national agenda set by historians, archaeologists, and folklorists, as well as his own empiricist inclinations, Stephanos took issue especially with the validity of Fallmerayer's historical sources. He did not deny, however, that when those sources were considered literally and in isolation, they did point to significant Slavic incursions toward the south of the Balkan Peninsula. A "general trend for exaggerations dominated the work of Byzantine chronographers," Stephanos wrote, but if their work is supplemented by an analysis of toponyms and language traits it has the potential to clarify the extent of Slavic presence and interactions with the locals.[51] Researching along these lines, he found not only that Slavic toponyms were restricted to specific localities in the Peloponnese—in which, nonetheless, the Greek element remained numerous even during the heyday of invasions—but also that words of Slavic origin were extremely limited even among agricultural populations that had certainly mixed with the Slavs. So, he concluded, "the influence that these tribes exerted on the population of Greece, generally considered, in fact appears to be restricted."[52]

But the reconstruction of the distant ethnological past of Greece was also one of Stephanos's main concerns. Though he shared anthropologists' skepticism about philological accounts of prehistory and the tendency to align prehistoric peoples with modern races, he consistently linked the majority of the prehistoric inhabitants of the Greek peninsula to a dolichocephalic or Mediterranean race: a branch of the Aryan family.[53] And he went even further to propose that the primitive Pelasgians—consisting of various tribes and often considered autochthonous populations—were most likely of Aryan origins even though their place in the European family had not yet been identified. While this model is largely reminiscent of the mid-nineteenth-century Aryan doctrines that were then taken up by turn-of-the-century Germanic or Nordic nationalism, Stephanos remained vague about the birthplace of the Aryan race and avoided any references to Aryan superiority. By contrast, he acknowledged Semitic influences through established Phoenician and Egyptian colonies and infusions dating back to the sixteenth century BC. Thus, the prehistoric peoples of the Greek peninsula represented a mixture, albeit one with predominant Aryan characteristics in its constitution.

For Stephanos, this mixing of peoples continued well after the advent of the tribes recognized as the first Greeks, originally coming from the north or the east and settling on the coasts around the Aegean Sea and in mainland Greece. By further combining mythological genealogies with linguistic variations, which he saw as reflections of the varied and fragmented physical environment, Stephanos suggested common origins and kinship among the various Greek tribes. The indigenous, peaceful, and agricultural Pelasgians were either easily conquered or forced to migrate, and the ones who remained behind mixed with the Greeks and were slowly absorbed. Nowhere in his writings, however, is there a reference to the relative worth of the elements that mixed; unlike early racial classifiers, he avoided stereotypes related to mentality or psychology.[54] Even when referring to the Dorians, antiquity's "Greeks par excellence," Stephanos decidedly stated that they fused from the start with other Greek and foreign tribes.[55]

Nevertheless, he was not fully committed to an idea of complete mixture. As Stephanos emphasized repeatedly, geographic isolation, as well as laws and traditions that either prohibited or discouraged marriages between locals and foreigners, regulated intermixing. Consequently, foreign influence on indigenous elements was not as profound as the number of non-Greeks living in Greek areas might suggest. This idea of checks on mixing, and their relative weakening as we move away from prehistoric times was, as we will see shortly, key in establishing a lineal continuity between ancient and modern Greeks. Though Stephanos, like many of his contemporaries, referred rather vaguely to the terms race, tribe, and variety and to the relationship between language, culture, and physical type, his ethnological work decidedly supported the national community's understanding of Greece as one of the first indigenous nations. But it also categorically belonged to the tradition of western European scholars who saw impurity of blood not as a characteristic of degraded nations, but rather as the driving force of biological and cultural improvement.[56]

In the anthropological chapter *La Grèce* that followed, Stephanos aimed at dissolving the uncertainties of the ethnological storyline introduced by the somewhat ambiguous sources it was based on. Once again Stephanos's understanding of anthropology's scope followed the French tradition, which by the 1880s was focused on rigorous measurements of physical characteristics, predominantly on skulls and heads.[57] The comparison of measurements of ancient and modern skulls, supplemented by those of living inhabitants from various regions of Greece, became his main object of study.[58] The whole venture rested on the routine assumption that, although human groupings were susceptible to evolution and change, and all historical and existing populations had resulted from considerable admixture, certain features remained sufficiently fixed to indicate lineage. But it also rested on accumulating masses of data. Anthropologists all over Europe—having rejected the earlier idea of representative samples and deductive theorizing—were thrown into a relentless pursuit of measurements, which were transformed into indices, and finally arranged in statistical seriations.[59] The Balkan Peninsula, and especially Greece, was of immense interest to these soldiers of facts as both the historical route area of European civilization and a terrain of intense ethnic intermixing, chiefly within the confines of the Ottoman Empire.[60]

In most of his analysis of ancient skulls, Stephanos relied on studies conducted by his most esteemed international colleagues, such as Rudolf Virchow (1821–1902) in Berlin, Giustiniano Nicolucci in Naples (1819–1905), and Armand de Quatrefages (1810–1892) and Sigismond Zaborowski (1851–1928) in Paris. However, by exposing the limited numbers of skulls and areas on which these studies were based, Stephanos undermined the validity of their individual conclusions and their effectiveness in actually representing a population living in such historically and geographically diverse regions. "Thus, we see," he wrote rather polemically, "that for the majority of Greek lands, science does not know even a single skull."[61] This statement, of course, not only cast doubt on the shared belief that all ancient Greeks were dolichocephalic but also argued for the necessity of Stephanos's work. By collectively considering available data and using Broca's divisions of the cephalic index, he managed, albeit barely, to demonstrate the existence of short skulls among classical Greeks.[62] Nevertheless, in a most interesting turn from the empirical reality of skull measurements, Stephanos looked at artistic monuments as further evidence of short-skulled ancient Greeks. Even though art had featured prominently in anthropological accounts of the early and mid-nineteenth century, his contemporaries were rather skeptical of such associations. So was Stephanos. His conviction that, "according to the testimony of ancient authors and monuments of art, it is beyond doubt that a large part of the ancient population of Greece was brachycephalic and especially sub-brachycephalic" could, however, be linked to its importance for the national theme of continuity, as we will see in Stephanos's anthropological treatment of modern populations.[63]

So what did the measurements on modern skulls and living Greeks reveal?[64] In a sentence, modern Greeks appeared predominantly brachycephalic. The obvious puzzle for Stephanos was, therefore, how on the one hand to confirm the continuity between ancient and modern Greeks, and on the other hand to differentiate modern Greeks from neighboring populations, especially the Slavs, who were assumed to have completely dominated ancient elements. So far we have seen that the strategy he followed with regard to the first issue was to suggest that brachycephaly was common in ancient times. To tackle the second question, Stephanos compared averages between both Greeks and Slavs, but also proceeded to a detailed region-by-region analysis to rebut theories of intense local Slavic influence. By way of example, Stephanos focused on the population of the Peloponnese, a region Fallmerayer considered Slavicized from early on, and reported that its mean cephalic index was lower by one unit compared to that of the Slavs. Based on such minute differences, he suggested that, "although the Greek population had experienced the influence of numerous foreign elements during the Middle Ages, sometimes even to a considerable degree, these various influences did not in general succeed in accumulating and profoundly changing the elements of the country."[65] Echoing familiar anthropological narratives, Stephanos concluded that the populations living on fertile plains were much more susceptible to the ravages of epidemics and conquest, while those living on infertile land, such as mountainous areas or islands, retained the Greek racial elements and carried them to the rest of the country through their migrations.[66] Thus, upon his return to Greece, he traveled all around the country, not just to determine the racial composition of modern Greeks, but also to identify these indigenous elements among the people of remote villages, especially inhabitants of high mountains and islands.

The reception of Stephanos's ethnological and anthropological account nicely illustrates the international potential of anthropology as a science that studied humans by objectively accumulating facts, as well as the possible tensions arising from their interpretation. In 1885 Joseph Deniker (1852–1918), the Franco-Russian naturalist and anthropologist, used Stephanos's anthropological data, along with that of Broca, Topinard, Virchow, Retzius, Nicolucci, and others, as a source for a *Grande Encyclopédie* entry on the races of Europe.[67] By splitting European populations into seven groups according to their physical form, Deniker confirmed that the majority of the current population of Greece belonged to "a dark, large in [body]-size, meso-, or sub-brachycephalic" race.[68] Again, in agreement with Stephanos's results, he acknowledged the existence of "a dark, dolichocephalic race of very small size," to which the ancient people of the Peloponnese belonged.[69] Even if not explicitly accepting Stephanos's larger scheme, Deniker entertained the possibility of continuity between ancient and modern Greeks, and, most interestingly, kept Slavs and Greeks apart. In his subsequent study of the cephalic index of the races of Europe, Deniker not only fully endorsed Stephanos's results but also adopted his argument about the likely existence of short-skulled ancient Greeks.[70]

However, the reception of *La Grèce* by Paul Topinard (1830–1911), who had taken over as head of the society and the Ècole d'Anthropologie after Broca's death, was more complex. In 1885 he published a paper on the necessity of adopting a common methodology that would allow comparisons between different sets of craniometric measurements.[71] According to Topinard, in the present situation there was too much discordance between different schools, which disrupted international communication. To strengthen his arguments and demonstrate the advantages of his suggestion, Topinard focused on Broca's method for the measurement of the cephalic index. Stephanos's conclusions from the comparison of the cephalic index of ancient and modern Greeks served as one of the examples he used to prove that the older nomenclature obscured the presentation of data. For him it was evident that there was "profound difference between the ancient and modern population of Greece," especially since Stephanos had not found extremely short-skulled individuals among the former.[72] "This conclusion is too obvious to have escaped Mr. Clon Stephanos," wrote Topinard, but "his nomenclature, modeled on that of Broca and his averages, did not demonstrate it with such sharpness."[73] He went even further, almost completely dismissing Stephanos's main work on measuring the heads of living inhabitants. Topinard suggested that there could be no comparison between cranium and head measurements, as there was no fixed rate of conversion between the two.[74] Considering that this was a much-contested issue with central figures in the field adopting various solutions but also standard practice, Topinard's dismissal appears even harsher.[75]

Topinard's motives for choosing to comment on Stephanos's results are unclear. Was he intrigued by Stephanos's interpretation, and did he want to demonstrate that, stripped down to bare numbers, the only thing it proved was how different ancient and modern Greeks were? Was it easier for him to attack someone outside the society, given its polemical internal workings, in order to establish his own authority? Whatever the answers to these questions, Topinard's reaction exemplifies how anthropological facts about humans were not just discovered; their veracity depended on intricate systems of measurements and observations. But it is also an excellent reminder of the ruthless, patronizing attitude of anthropology of the great centers toward what was perceived as scientific peripheries. Stephanos was as empiricist as his international colleagues; his work depended on their authority both in using the facts they had already collected and in modeling his own research methodology after it. For the interpretation of his results, he again relied on available scientific sources, taking every possible caution against ambiguous inferences. The Greek scholars he cited also belonged to this same positivist tradition. From his perspective, whatever the apparent tension between his scientific and nationalistic vocation, it was paradoxically resolved by a deep commitment to the objective ideals of the former.

To be sure, when Stephanos returned to Athens he was not an unfamiliar face. While still in Paris, he had made sure to send a copy of *La Grèce* to Dragoumis, as well as a short article to be published in a local newspaper.[76] The political situation was also favorable, as Prime Minister Trikoupis (1832–1896), who had himself studied in Paris and spent the early years of his life in England, was determined to modernize all sectors of the Greek state by emulating the countries of western Europe. Stephanos had an important publication and a network of connections to French learned societies. But what is more, he was someone who combined the much-desired scientific expertise and rigor of a Western scholar with the unique interests and alliances that allowed him to be reintegrated into Greek academia. At this point, he was himself a bridge between the transnational world of anthropology and the local arena that looked to the new science for "positive" answers concerning national identity and origins.

Finding a Role for Anthropology at the University of Athens

It did not take long for Stephanos to reap the fruits of his labors. On June 21, 1886, the rector of the University of Athens presented to the university senate an application arguing for the "plausible usefulness of the establishment of an anthropological laboratory."[77] The senate concluded in favor and "worthy of being the director of the laboratory was judged the applicant himself; Mr. Clon Stephanos."[78] With the approval of the Ministry of Ecclesiastical Affairs and Education, the newly appointed Stephanos became the head of the Anthropological Laboratory and Museum.

At the time, almost half a century after its establishment in 1837, the University of Athens was enjoying what most scholars would characterize as its golden age: an era of continuous expansion and a high public profile. Around the main four schools of theology, law, medicine, and philosophy, a constellation of scientific collections and units had become principal loci for the development of scientific disciplines.[79] As historians of modern Greece have amply documented, the University of Athens, its academic personnel, and its students were from the start intimately intertwined with the country's adventurous modernity.[80] This engagement included a decisive role in the construction of *Greekness*. Likewise, Greek scholars, and, even more so, the new generation of scientists, promoted and encouraged their portrayal as soldiers of science, patriotic and humble teachers, or tireless and selfless workers.[81] In this context, the scientific ethos of western Europe and the appropriation of the national past became powerful resources that Greek academics actively used for the legitimization and promotion of their aspirations.

Having experienced the difficulties of anthropology's institutionalization abroad, Stephanos knew early on that the burden of proof for its scientific credentials and national relevance lay with his ability to use both resources. The establishment of the museum was, of course, an important occasion and the single most critical episode in the early history of the discipline in Greece. But anthropology's position still remained precarious. Compared, for example, to the flamboyant ceremony accompanying the founding of the university's observatory, which included gunboat salutes and fervent public speeches, anthropology's inaugural act was rather modest.[82] In response, Stephanos set up a lifelong program that endeavored to balance nationalist and scientific inclinations but also argued for Greek anthropology's importance for the national interdisciplinary and the international disciplinary communities.

In doing so, Stephanos's research continued on the path paved in *La Grèce* and was mainly inspired by the French model of physical anthropology. He used Broca's anthropometric nomenclature and, despite limited funds, ordered the standard laboratory equipment from the renowned French instrument maker Collin.[83] His orders for the museum's library, however, also suggest an important influence by liberal German anthropologists and ethnologists, which would become more evident in the years to follow.[84] Though mainly focusing on measurements and observations on skulls and heads, Stephanos reported that anthropological investigations required "anthropological material in the narrowest sense of the word," but also "auxiliary ethnological material," including predominantly written sources. "For the anthropological and ethnological investigation of the Greek regions, like every other country," he later wrote, "modern science requires a broad work agenda, including whatever possible to shed light or simply contribute to the solution of such issues."[85] With the support of the state he measured thousands of people, mainly Greek and foreign military conscripts and schoolchildren, but also inhabitants of remote villages both within and outside the borders of the Kingdom of Greece. Provided with human remains from Greek and foreign archaeological excavations and graveyards, he also measured numerous skulls, from prehistoric to modern. Finally, while traveling across the country, he collected archival sources on toponyms, genealogy, linguistics, and population movements.

His first report to the university suggested that, through anthropometric research on crania and living inhabitants from all corners of the country, he had been "able to prove anthropologically the preservation of the ancient Greek [dolicochephalic] element, relatively pure" in a number of locations around Attica, on Greek islands such as Naxos and Kefallinia, and in the Peloponnese.[86] At the same time, Stephanos argued that the settlements of peoples belonging to "the great brachycephalic race" during the Bronze Age were responsible for the appearance of short-skulled Greek populations of the purest form, mainly in the northwest of the country. As already discussed, the rest of the population descended from mixing between these early peoples and, to some degree, from foreign invaders. In the same letter, Stephanos also argued that a great percentage of the long-skulled Albanians living in areas of central Greece were of "Greek origins that with time were Albanisized."[87] On the contested issue of Slavic influence, he stressed that, according to the anthropological data, its "effect on the Greek population is presented as very limited."[88]

Stephanos presented his initial results on a cephalic index map based on ten thousand measurements—a figure, he suggested, that only very few other European countries could match, and certainly neither France nor Germany. "This map of Greece surpasses the ones constructed elsewhere," wrote Stephanos, "because of the numerous observations on which it is based, but also because the anthropological data are presented independently of administrative divisions, though these are taken into account for the conclusions."[89] His arguments were convincing enough that the Greek committee for the 1889 Universal Exposition in Paris, headed by Dragoumis, decided to include it among the exhibits of the Greek pavilion.

The map received a silver medal accompanied by an anonymous, mixed review in the *Revue d'Anthropologie*, which found it difficult to read and not very informative on the methods employed.[90] What most puzzled Stephanos's French colleagues, however, was the non-obvious interpretation of the results. In Greece, the reviewer wrote, "it is difficult to establish a general rule, except that brachycephaly is more frequent or higher in the north, where it confirms the influence of the brachycephalic Albanians and Montenegrins."[91] "The ethnic elements clashed on all sides and are distributed without any order," the reviewer continued; "perhaps, the brachycephalic are more frequent in the west and the dolichocephalic in the east, which would be the opposite of what logic would dictate."[92] But even if Stephanos's results did not provide an easily discernible pattern, or at least one that aligned with the more commonly accepted account of a dominant Slavic influence from the north and a Mediterranean influence in the west, the large empirical basis of his work and the use of internationally endorsed methods facilitated its acceptance.

Within the national university, the most explicit endorsement of anthropology as the specialist discipline that could authoritatively substantiate Greek origins can be found in the words of the professor of Greek letters at the University of Athens, Georgios Mistriotis (1840–1916):

> But it is already time that the government and the archaeological society takes care for the salvage of the remains of the Sacred Band of Thebes, who fell at [the battle of] Chaeronea,[93] and which, to our shame, are deteriorating under the influence of the soil and the atmosphere. But even if no one else takes care of these, we think that the National University can provide Mr. Clon Stephanos the resources required for the preservation of the remains of those heroes, which after having been slaughtered while bravely fighting for the freedom of the Greeks, can now to be called upon as undeniable witnesses in the craniological examinations of the ethnological courts to testify for the identity of the Greek race.[94]

For an extreme archaist and a scholar who most vigorously opposed the dominant synthetic narrative of Greek history such as Mistriotis, the anthropological examinations could settle the question of the relationship between Macedonians and the Greeks of the city-states once and for all. Marching toward the end of the century, as Balkan irredentisms clashed, especially in areas such as Macedonia, Stephanos's portrayal of anthropology as the study of "the whole nation"[95] and an indispensable science for understanding "the origins and the subsequent fortunes of the Greek nation" was gaining momentum.[96]

On a more practical level, however, there is very little evidence of the museum acting as more than a repository for anthropological research. The 1893 university guide encouraged "students of medicine, who wish to study their fatherland from an anthropological or ethnological perspective" to visit the museum.[97] Two years later, following a generous donation to its library and the systematic growth of its collections, the museum opened its doors to everyone.[98] While we cannot speculate whether any students took up the task, or how many visitors used the library or viewed its collections, Stephanos often referred to distinguished foreign visitors who studied those collections.[99] We know of two such cases.

In an announcement to the Royal Prussian Academy of Sciences in 1893, Rudolf Virchow mentioned that, during one of his visits to Greece, Stephanos showed him "a skull from Tiryns and five from Chaeronea."[100] In 1897 Achilles Rose (1839–1916), an American medical doctor and Hellenist, wrote an enthusiastic report on the museum. Rose related that he had recently returned from his travels to Greece, where, in one of the vast halls of the academy of Athens, he had discovered the museum: "a treasure . . . the praise of which cannot possibly be exaggerated."[101] The collection of numerous skulls and skeletons acquired by the museum "under the strictest control of men of science," combined with "thousands of archives, documents, deeds, ecclesiastical, fiscal, and family papers, . . . and personal inquiries," could uniquely provide an answer to "the most important part of Hellenic ethnography, . . . a comparison of the ancient type with all the later types of Greece."[102]

Rose's description echoes Stephanos's insistence on the importance of the anthropological museum—an emphasis that should not be understood as exclusively directed toward a national audience, but, most important, as an act of emancipation from Greek anthropology's perceived peripherality. For Stephanos, European anthropological accounts were mostly based not only on limited material but also on skulls of disputable origins. By contrast, his results stemmed from direct, unmediated access to anthropological material. In 1893 he wrote, "The anthropological museum had only few additions this year, since only material from verified and unquestionable origins is being accepted; to that effect no other similar museum is superior to ours."[103] Carefully documenting the acquired material in close cooperation with the most prestigious contemporary archaeologists, he boasted that he brought together "scientific material that the anthropological museums of Europe looked at with envy."[104] It is not difficult to detect the same kind of attitude when Stephanos variously stressed that, either out of necessity or a spirit of innovation, he did not simply emulate foreign anthropological traditions but actively sought to contribute to international scientific efforts. Thus, he worked extensively to determine new points on the skull that would either complement or simplify existing methods,[105] and was the first who sought to associate the frequency of hair and eye color with skull shape among Greek populations.[106]

In a fashion rather typical of anthropologists of his time, he was, however, hesitant to publish any of these results or reach hasty conclusions.[107] Especially as Stephanos's rapprochement with German liberal anthropology grew ever stronger, either through his readings or personal contacts, he increasingly became less assertive and vaguely promised to solve issues of "highest anthropological importance" in future publications.[108] Adhering to his German colleagues' principle "to keep their science out of the tumult of politics," Stephanos, though a committed nationalist, refused to enter the realm of day-to-day politics.[109] Indeed, when in 1892 his compatriots put his name up for election to the Greek Parliament,[110] he issued a statement urging his supporters to champion those candidates who "wish to serve the interests of the country the most during these critical circumstances."[111]

Notwithstanding Stephanos's commitment to "apolitical objectivity,"[112] a royal decree issued in 1899 acutely reaffirmed the museum's national importance by changing its official designation to Museum of Anthropology and Ancient Ancestral Relics.[113] In the aftermath of the humiliating defeat in the 1897 Ottoman-Greek War and the social unrest that followed, the change in the museum's name symbolizes the yearning for a renewed connection with ancestral roots.[114] In the same way that antiquities came to symbolize holy relics and were sanctified, human remains represented the genealogical threads that connected the nation to its past.

This alignment of anthropology with archaeology was particularly reinforced after the 1900s, when Stephanos turned almost exclusively to excavating prehistoric settlements in the Aegean, under the auspices of the Archaeological Society in Athens. The extreme empiricism of Greek archaeology, coupled with Stephanos's loyalty to inductive methods, led him to produce reports that closely resembled documentations of archaeological excavations. Anthropology was almost lost in pages filled with details about the excavated tombs, the position of the skeletons, and the contents of the graves. The bond was further strengthened when, in 1905, Stephanos, as an authority on ancient inscriptions, became an advisor to the society.[115] It was during these years that he published his second and final book.

In 1911, after almost three decades of research, Stephanos published a thin, unimpressive monograph of a mere sixty-seven pages entitled *Contributions to the Physical Anthropology of Greece: The Transverse Cephalic Index*.[116] The contrast to *La Grèce* is striking. The booklet is plainly void of any interpretative conclusions or inferences and limited to the absolutely necessary textual descriptions. The short introduction explains that his results were solely based on head measurements from soldiers and workers aged eighteen to thirty years old and treated according to the internationally acknowledged method of the French school of anthropology. After paying homage to Topinard's taxonomy for presenting variations more clearly, he went on to meticulously document all measurements arranged in seriations.[117]

But the preface of the book perfectly captures his intentions. Stephanos wrote, "After many years of anthropological researches in Greece, I now publish them, as objectively as I can, and as contemporary *Biometrics* [emphasis in original] demands. To combine these researches with ethnological issues would be unworthy of the great times ahead and Anthropology of the future."[118] His rejection of ethnology only strengthens his faith in what later came to be known as the exact sciences. Stephanos saw his endeavors as belonging to a new, emerging trend: the combination of the doctrines of the biometric school with demographical studies that led to the rise of mathematical statistics. In the end, the underwhelming book was the most decisive point in Stephanos's lifelong battle with the elusive ideal of objectivity. Yet the Greek language of the publication did not allow Stephanos's work to be cited by his colleagues abroad and never achieved the status of *La Grèce*.

Concluding Events and Thoughts

On November 10, 1896, Stephanos sent a letter to his "dear and well-respected master," Rudolf Virchow, asking for a response with his opinion on "the necessity of the existence of a university chair of anthropology, especially in the medical school."[119] The timing seemed excellent. The University of Athens was about to reform its organization, and the museum had just been relocated to "a beautiful south-facing hall of the Sinaia Academy, and thus made accessible to all interested visitors."[120] However, although the rector of the university and celebrated professor of chemistry Anastasios Christomanos (1841–1906) eagerly endorsed this claim for a chair of anthropology that same year,[121] it took more than ten years for the school of medicine to submit an official request.[122] This was finally granted by royal decree in 1912.[123] Another two years passed before the medical school finally decided that anthropology belonged to its area of expertise.[124] In a tragic turn of events, Stephanos died a year later, on January 11, 1915, without ever becoming a professor at the university.

The next day, the newspaper *Acropolis*, known for its dramatic coverage, wrote, "A great figure of Modern Greece passed away. Great and unknown. . . . In any other civilized nation a chair would have been established for the Greek sage. . . . He was the great, unacknowledged altruist of Greece. A wonderful philosophical character. A wonderful philosophical genius with a wonderful philosophical ethos. All this, the State—the barbaric and criminal state—failed to put in use. But this overly kind, overly Greek, overly philanthropic man did not complain. He fought. He studied. He wrote."[125] Many such brief obituaries followed; all exalted Stephanos's industriousness, devotion to science, and patriotism. But the one from *Acropolis* is, in all its exaggerations, unexpectedly useful in summing up this chapter.

From a certain perspective, after thirty years of continuous effort, Greek anthropology, much like Stephanos himself, remained underappreciated and marginal within Greek scholarship and intellectual discourse. The pervasive and overpowering reach of history, archaeology, and laografia in producing the country's identity narrative pushed anthropology to the margins. The initial state support and the existence of a large educated elite—despite Greece's fragile economy—did not result in further backing for anthropological research. The university's resources were mainly devoted to the education of doctors, teachers, and lawyers, who staffed the developing public and private sector, and the incentive for students to follow a purely academic—and largely underpaid—pursuit in the style of Stephanos was weak. Yet this is just one side of the story.

Before his death, Stephanos had secured the establishment of two anthropological institutions, a museum and laboratory, and a university chair. His early work in Paris put Greek anthropology on the map of international science, while his later rapprochement with the German tradition foreshadowed its decisive influence on later developments in Greece. Far from being indifferent to theory, he researched, appropriated, and reconstructed theories on the origins and identity of the Greeks and firmly defended the idea of continuity against alternative interpretations. Stephanos's commitment to a positivist scientific model that was highly suspicious of unsupported speculation was not necessarily at odds with the national importance of anthropology. Yet his attempts to professionalize the discipline by adhering to the imperatives of scientific objectivity, which accompanied a growing reluctance to hastily publish his findings, further distanced him from the national mission and ultimately delayed its full institutionalization.

Thus, the story of nineteenth-century Greek physical anthropology is one of both failure and success. As a novel scientific project, it exhibited a remarkable resilience in negotiating the demands of international science and local nationalist endeavors, but Stephanos's death left it with no obvious way forward. His successor, the medical doctor Ioannis Koumaris (1879–1970), inherited a working museum, the possibility of a university appointment, and a strong scientific program. Koumaris would have to convincingly reassert the importance of anthropology for the national interdisciplinary community and reconfigure its place in the international disciplinary terrain.

Acknowledgments

I am grateful to Richard McMahon, Amos Morris-Reich, Jon Røyne Kyllingstad, and Greg Radick for their feedback, and to Christina Fili, for generously sharing her insights and work on Kyparissos Stephanos. I would also like to thank Natalia Vogeikoff-Brogan at the American School of Classical Studies at Athens and Eleftheria Daleziou at Gennadius Library Archives for their valuable research suggestions. The director of the Anthropological Museum of the University of Athens, Professor Theodoros Pitsios, has been very kind in entrusting me with complete access to the museum's archives. This research has been funded by the Research Council of Norway (Project no. 220741/F10).

Notes

1. Stephanos Dragoumis was at the time a member of Parliament. His skills in politics and financial management led him to occupy several governmental posts, including the Ministry of Foreign Affairs and the Ministry of Internal Affairs (1886–90, 1892–93), while he briefly served as prime minister of Greece in 1910.

2. Stephanos N. Dragoumis Papers, March 20, 1881, American School of Classical Studies at Athens (ASCSA), Gennadius Library Archives (GLA), Folder 189.2.109.

3. *Dictionnaire encyclopédique des sciences médicales*, ed. Amédée Dechambre (Paris: G. Masson, 1864–82).

4. Stephanos N. Dragoumis Papers, ASCSA, GLA, Folder 189.2.122 [June 1, 1881].

5. For the incorporation of the Macedonias into national history, see Vangelis D. Karamanolakis, *Η Συγκρότηση της Ιστορικής Επιστήμης και η Διδασκαλία της Ιστορίας στο Πανεπιστήμιο Αθηνών (1837–1932)* (The formation of historical science and history teaching at the University of Athens (1837–1932)) (Athens: IAEN, 2006), 102–5.

6. Stephanos Dragoumis, with family origins from Macedonia, and especially his diplomat son Ion (1878–1920), was heavily involved in Macedonian affairs and the Macedonian Struggle between 1904 and 1908. For a fascinating account of the conflicts over this territory up to the 1990s Macedonian controversy between Greece and the Republic of Macedonia that followed the breakup of Yugoslavia, see Erik Sjöberg, "Battlefields of Memory: The Macedonian Conflict and Greek Historical Culture" (PhD diss., Umeå Universitet, 2006), 26–40.

7. On the prehistory of the field in Greece and early contributions by Greek scholars, see Sevasti Trubeta, *Physical Anthropology, Race, and Eugenics in Greece: 1880s-1970s* (Leiden: Brill, 2013), 159–61.

8. For an example of these interactions from Norway, see Jon Røyne Kyllingstad, *Measuring the Master Race: Physical Anthropology in Norway, 1890–1945* (Cambridge: Open Book, 2014).

9. For similar discussions on the tension between nationalist and internationalist loyalties of anthropologists, see Richard McMahon, "On the Margins of International Science and National Discourse: National Identity Narratives in Romanian Anthropology," *European Review of History: Revue Européene D'histoire* 16, no. 1 (2009): 101–23; Chris Manias, "The Race Prussienne Controversy: Scientific Internationalism and the Nation," *Isis* 100, no. 4 (2009): 733–57.

10. Seminal contributions in this discussion include: Georgios B. Dertilis, *Ιστορία του Ελληνικού Κράτους, 1830–1920* (History of the Greek state, 1830–1920), 2 vols. (Athens: Hestia, 2010), 331–97; Yannis Hamilakis, *The Nation and Its Ruins: Antiquity, Archaeology, and National Imagination in Greece* (Oxford: Oxford University Press, 2007), 57–123; and Antonis Liakos, "The Construction of National Time: The Making of the Modern Greek Historical Imagination," *Mediterranean Historical Review* 16, no. 1 (2001): 27–42. For European perceptions of ancient Greece, see the classical study by Frank M. Turner, *The Greek Heritage in Victorian Britain* (New Haven: Yale University Press, 1981).

11. See Karamanolakis, *The Formation of Historical Science*, 85–168; and Liakos, "National Time," 30–35.

12. Hamilakis, *The Nation and Its Ruins*, 116.

13. This understanding of the past was not simply dominant, but in many ways it was the only way to be a Greek nationalist and remained unchallenged even by socialist and Marxist scholars until at least the mid-twentieth century. See Liakos, "National Time," 37–40.

14. On the perceptions of modern Greeks by European travelers, see David Constantine, *Early Greek Travelers and the Hellenic Ideal* (Cambridge: Cambridge University Press, 1984); Deborah Harlan, "Travel, Pictures, and a Victorian Gentleman in

Greece," *Hesperia* 78, no. 3 (2009): 421–53; and Robert Eisner, *Travelers to an Antique Land: The History and Literature of Travel to Greece* (Ann Arbor: University of Michigan Press, 1991).

15. On Fallmerayer's work and its reception in Greece, see Elli Skopetea, *Φαλμεράυερ: Τεχνάσματα του Αντίπαλου Δέους* (Fallmerayer: Willes of the rival awe) (Athens: Themelio, 1999).

16. On the perception of Gobineau's racial ideas in Greece, see Trubeta, *Physical Anthropology*, 159–61. But also see Steven Kale, "Gobineau, Racism, and Legitimism: A Royalist Heretic in Nineteenth-Century France," *Modern Intellectual History* 7, no. 1 (2010): 33–61, on how Gobineau's ideas have been misrepresented and his influence exaggerated.

17. Carole Reynaud-Palligot, "The Notion of 'Race' in the Nineteenth Century," in *The Invention of Race: Scientific and Popular Representations*, ed. Nicolas Bancel et al. (New York: Routledge, 2014), 87–99, 93–94.

18. Anders Retzius, "Ueber die Runde, Brachycephalische Schädelform der Griechen," in *Ethnologische Schriften*, ed. Anders Retzius (Stockholm: Norstedt & Söner, 1864), 86–89. A few years earlier, Retzius had introduced the division of humans in two main groups, the short-skulled brachycephalic and the long-skulled dolichocephalic, based on the measurement of the cephalic index (i.e., the ratio of the maximum width to the maximum length of a head/skull multiplied by one hundred).

19. Retzius, "Ueber die Runde," 88.

20. Retzius, "Ueber die Runde," 89.

21. Robert Knox, *The Races of Men: A Fragment* (Philadelphia: Lea & Blanchard, 1850). For the influence of Greek sculpture on Knox's work and especially on the development of a physical conception of English national identity, see Athena S. Leoussi, "Myths of Ancestry," *Nations and Nationalism* 7, no. 4 (2001): 467–86.

22. Knox, *The Races of Men*, 270–71.

23. Knox, *The Races of Men*, 41.

24. Knox, *The Races of Men*, 39.

25. Knox, *The Races of Men*, 270–71.

26. Here I use the transliterated term *laografia* instead of "folklore" in agreement with Greek scholars who argue for the idiosyncratic use of the term in Greece, which was closer to the German *Volkskunde*. See Evthymios Papataxiarchis, "From 'National' to 'Social Science': Politics, Ideology, and Disciplinary Formation in Greek Anthropology from the 1940s till the 1980s," in *The Anthropological Field on the Margins of Europe, 1945–1991*, ed. Aleksandar Bošcović and Chris Hann (Zurich: LIT Verlag, 2013), 31–64, 32.

27. Hamilakis, *The Nation and its Ruins*, 39 and 99–103.

28. The founding and still most comprehensive work on the history of the field in Greece is by Michael Herzfeld, *Ours Once More: Folklore, Ideology, and the Making of Modern Greece* (Austin: University of Texas Press, 1982). On this topic, see 121.

29. Hamilakis, *The Nation and its Ruins*, 72–74.

30. Papataxiarchis, "From 'National' to 'Social Science,'" 32.

31. Studies on the history of anthropological institutions in France include: Alice L. Conklin, *In the Museum of Man: Race, Anthropology, and Empire in France, 1850–1950* (Ithaca: Cornell University Press, 2013); Jennifer M. Hecht, *The End of the Soul: Scientific Modernity, Atheism, and Anthropology in France* (New York: Columbia University Press, 2003); Claude Blanckaert, ed., *Les Politiquesde l'Anthropologie: Discours et Pratiques en France, 1860–1940* (Paris: L'Harmattan, 2001); Nélia Dias, "The Visibility of Difference: Nineteenth-Century French Anthropological Collections," in *The Politics of Display: Museums, Science, Culture*, ed. Sharon Mcdonald (London: Routledge, 1998), 31–45; Elizabeth A. Williams, "Anthropological Institutions in Nineteenth-Century France," *Isis* 76, no. 3 (1985): 331–48; and Joy D. Harvey, "Races Specified, Evolution Transformed: The Social Context of Scientific Debates Originating in the Société d'Anthropologie de Paris 1859–1902" (PhD diss., Harvard University, 1983).

32. Paul Broca, Paul Topinard, Théophile Chudzinski, and G. A. Kuhff, "Laboratoire D'Anthropologie, " in *Rapport Sur L'École Pratique Des hautes Études, 1877–1878, 1878–1879* (1877), 125–29. Stephanos does not appear among those who regularly attended the courses and practical exercises at Broca's laboratory from 1877 to 1879, though he could have done so at a later time or not on a regular basis.

33. Paul Broca, "Anthropologie," in *Dictionnaire Encyclopédique Des Sciences Médicales* (Encyclopedical dictionary of the medical sciences), Première Série, Tome cinquième, ed. Amédée Dechambre (Paris: G. Masson, 1864), 276.

34. Clon Stephanos, *Επιγραφαί της Νήσου Σύρου το Πλείστον Ανέκδοτοι, μετά Τοπογραφικόν και Ιστορικών Παρατηρήσεων περί της Αρχαίας Σύρου και Δύο Λιθογραφικών Πλακών* (Inscriptions from the island of Syros mostly unpublished, with topographical and historical observations about ancient Syros, and two lithographic plates) (Athens: Varvarrigou Printing House, 1875).

35. Anonymous, *Revue Archéologique*, n.s., no. 31 (1876): 68.

36. Clon Stephanos, *Ανέκδοτα Έγγραφα Αποσταλλέντα προς τους Κατοίκους των Κυκλάδων κατά την υπό των Ρώσων Κατοχήν Αυτών* (Unpublished documents sent to the inhabitants of Cyclades during the Russian occupation) (Athens: Ermou Printing House, 1878).

37. Anonymous, *Revue de Questions Historiques* 24 (1878): 704.

38. Stephanos N. Dragoumis Papers, ASCSA, GLA, Folder 189.2.137 [September 21, 1881].

39. Stephanos N. Dragoumis Papers, ASCSA, GLA, Folder 189.2.138 [September 26, 1881].

40. "Liste générale des membres au 31 décembre 1890" (General list of members on 31 December 1890), *Revues Études Grecques* 3, no. 10 (1890): 61.

41. Harvey, "Races Specified, Evolution Transformed," 7–112.

42. Association Française pour l'Avancement des Sciences, Congrès La Rochelle, Comptes-rendus de la 11e session, 1882 (French Association for the Advancement of Science, La Rochelle Congress, proceedings of the 11th session, 1882) (Paris, 1883), 817;

Association Française pour l'Avancement des Sciences, Congrès Rouen, Comptes-rendus de la 12e session, 1883 (French Association for the Advancement of Science, La Rochelle Congress, proceedings of the 12th session, 1883) (Paris, 1884), 814–15.

43. Clon Stephanos, *La Grèce Au Point De Vue Naturel, Ethnologique, Anthropologique, Démographique et Médical* (Paris: G. Masson, 1884).

44. Stephanos, "La Grèce," in *Dictionnaire Encyclopédique Des Sciences Médicales*, Quatrième série, Tome dixième, ed. Amédée Dechambre (Paris: G. Masson, 1884), 363–581.

45. Harvey, "Races Specified, Evolution Transformed," 15.

46. Stephanos, *La Grèce*, 363. For on overview of the field of medical geography, and its influence on Greek anthropology, see Trubeta, *Physical Anthropology*, 31–40.

47. Dias, "The Visibility of Difference," 34.

48. Paul Broca, "Recherches Sur L'Ethnologie De La France," *Mémoires De La Société D'Anthroplogie De Paris*, 1 (1860–61): 1–56.

49. Recent studies on the history of Latin Greece include: Nikolaos G. Chrissis and Mike Carr, eds., *Contact and Conflict in Frankish Greece and the Aegean, 1204–1453* (Surrey: Ashgate, 2014); and Nickiphoros I. Tsougarakis and Peter Lock, eds., *A Companion to Latin Greece* (Leiden: Brill, 2014).

50. Stephanos, *La Grèce*, 430.

51. Stephanos, *La Grèce*, 423.

52. Stephanos, *La Grèce*, 427.

53. Manias, "The Race Prussienne Controversy," 743–44.

54. The only derogatory term used by Stephanos was in his description of the Slavs as "barbarians" (e.g., *La Grèce*, 422), which gives away the influence of national sentiments on his otherwise rather detached account.

55. Stephanos, *La Grèce*, 418.

56. For a seminal contribution on the importance of the idea of mixture in European race classifications, see Joshua Goode, *Impurity of Blood Defining Race in Spain, 1870–1930* (Baton Rouge: Louisiana State University Press, 2009).

57. Dias, "The Visibility of Difference," 31.

58. Following standard international practice, the main point of comparison for ancient and modern populations was the cephalic index. Stephanos, however, also discussed other indices suggested by French and German anthropologists, but only briefly considered insufficiently researched characteristics such as eye, hair, or skin color.

59. For an example of the German case on this theme, see Andrew D. Evans, *Anthropology at War: World War I and the Science of Race in Germany* (Chicago: University of Chicago Press, 2010), 66–69.

60. See Trubeta, *Physical Anthropology*, 38.

61. Stephanos, *La Grèce*, 432.

62. The total number of ancient skulls measured did not exceed seventy, but according to Broca even a series of twenty skulls, randomly collected, was enough to offer secure conclusions (see Dias, "The Visibility of Difference," 36).

63. Stephanos, *La Grèce*, 439.

64. For data on modern skulls, Stephanos used studies by authoritative figures such as Quatrefages, Nicolluci, and Augustin Weisbach (1837–1914). Measurements on living inhabitants of the country were taken by the Greek naturalist Nikolaos Apostolides (1856–1919) and Stephanos.

65. Stephanos, *La Grèce*, 439.

66. See, for example, McMahon, "On the Margins of International Science and National Discourse," on Romanian narratives about Transylvanians replenishing the plains after invasions.

67. Joseph Deniker, "Anthropologie et Ethnologie," in *La grande Encyclopédie: Inventaire Raisonné Des Sciences, Des Lettres Et Des Arts*, ed. Andre Berthélot et al. (Paris: Lamirault, 1885–1902), 810.

68. Deniker, "Anthropologie et Ethnologie," 811.

69. Deniker, "Anthropologie et Ethnologie," 811.

70. Joseph Deniker, *Les Races De L'Europe: L'Indice Céphalique En Europe* (Paris: Association Française pour l'Avancement des Sciences, 1897).

71. Paul Topinard, "Du principe général à adopter dans les divisions et nomenclatures de caractères et en particulier de la nomenclature quinaire de l'indice céphalique," *Bulletins de la Société d'anthropologie de Paris* III° Série, tome 9 (1886): 91–108.

72. Topinard, "Du principe général," 102.

73. Topinard, "Du principe général," 102.

74. Topinard, "Du principe général," 101.

75. For a contemporary account on the divergent opinions regarding the relationship between cranial and head indices, see Joseph Deniker, *The Races of Man* (London: Walter Scott, 1900), 73.

76. Stephanos N. Dragoumis Papers, ASCSA, GLA, Folder 190.1.134 [October 5, 1883]. We do not know, however, if Dragoumis did send the article to an Athenian newspaper.

77. Proceedings of the Senate meetings, 1883–86, University of Athens (UOA) Historical Archive, vol. 14, 275.

78. Proceedings of the Senate meetings, 1883–86, UOA Historical Archive.

79. Vangelis Karamanolakis, "The University of Athens and Greek Antiquity (1837–1937)," in *Re-imagining the Past : Antiquity and Modern Greek Culture*, edited by Dimitris Tziovas (Oxford: Oxford University Press, 2014), 112–27.

80. See, for example, Kostas Lappas, Πανεπιστήμιο και Φοιτητές στην Ελλάδα κατά τον 19ο αιώνα (University and students in Greece during the nineteenth century) (Athens: IAEN, 2014).

81. Kostas Tampakis, "Onwards Facing Backwards: The Rhetoric of Science in Nineteenth-century Greece," *British Journal for the History of Science* 47, no. 2 (2014): 226.

82. Tampakis, "Onwards Facing Backwards ," 217–18.

83. Collin's response to Stephanos's order, July 8, 1887, UOA Historical Archive, Anthropological Museum 1886–87, Folder 315–21. For Broca's and Topinard's liaison with specific instrument makers, see Lucile Hoyme, "Physical Anthropology

and Its Instruments: An Historical Study," *Southwestern Journal of Anthropology* 9, no. 4 (1953): 420.

84. Clon Stephanos's Report to the University, undated, UoA Historical Archive, Anthropological Museum 1890–91, Folder 315–21.

85. Report for the Rectorship of Panagiotis Pavlidis, professor of theology, during the academic year 1893–94, Pergamos Digital Library (DL), UOA Historical Archive, *Rector Speeches*, 152.

86. Stephanos's Report, July 24, 1887, UOA Historical Archive, Anthropological Museum 1886–87, Folder 315–21.

87. Stephanos's Report, July 24, 1887, UOA Historical Archive.

88. Stephanos's Report, July 24 1887, UOA Historical Archive.

89. Speeches of Theodoros Afendoulis, rector of the National University during the academic year 1877–88, Pergamos DL, UOA Historical Archive, *Rector Speeches*, 138–39.

90. "Review of Clon Stephanos's Carte De L'Indice Céphalique En Grèce, " *Reveu D'Anthropologie*, série 3, tome 4 (1889): 732–33.

91. "Review of Stephanos's Carte," 733.

92. "Review of Stephanos's Carte," 733.

93. Recall the Battle of Chaeronia mentioned in the chapter's introduction and its importance for the construction of Greek national identity.

94. Report for the Rectorship of Georgios Mistriotis, professor of Greek letters, during the academic year 1890–91, Pergamos DL, UOA Historical Archive, *Rector Speeches*, 84–85.

95. Pergamos DL, *Rector Speeches*, Pavlidis, 154.

96. Report for the Rectorship of A. D. Kyriakos, professor of ecclesiastic history and symbolism, during the academic year 1895–96, Pergamos DL, UOA Historical Archive, *Rector Speeches*, 261.

97. A. Kolialexis and K. Xanthopoulos, *Οδηγός των Φοιτητών του Εθνικού Πανεπιστημίου* (Student guide of the National University) (Athens: Printing House P. D. Sakellariou, 1893), 38.

98. The donation of 1430 volumes was made by the family of Alexandros Paspatis (1814–1892), an internationally educated Greek scholar who had carried out extensive linguistic, archaeological, and historical studies. Pergamos DL, *Rector Speeches*, Kyriakos, 259–60.

99. Report for the Rectorship of Anastasios K. Christomanos, professor of chemistry, during the academic year 1896–97, Pergamos DL, *Rector Speeches*, 269.

100. Rudolf Virchow, "Über Griechische Schädel aus Alter und Neuer Zeit und über einen Schädel von Menidi, der für den des Sophokles gehalten ist," *Sitzungsberichte der Königlich Preußischen Akademie der Wissenschaften zu Berlin* 34 (1893): 677–700.

101. Achille Rose, "Greek Anthropology," *New York Medical Journal*, September 18, 1897, 434.

102. Rose, "Greek Anthropology," 434–35.

103. Before the establishment of the museum, the acquisition of crania—often associated with grave robbery, disputable processes of exportation, or even gifts—by museums, collections, and individual scholars outside Greece was a common phenomenon related to the increased anthropological interest in ancient Greece and the populations of the Balkan peninsula. See also Trubeta, *Physical Anthropology*, 37–39. Report for the Rectorship of Ioannis Pandazidis, professor of Greek philology, during the academic year 1892–1893, Pergamos DL, UOA Historical Archive, *Rector Speeches*, 227.

104. Pergamos DL, *Rector Speeches*, Kyriakos, 61.

105. Report for the Rectorship of Ioannis N. Hatzidakis, professor of mathematics, during the academic year 1894–95, Pergamos DL, *Rector Speeches*, 318; Pergamos DL, *Rector Speeches*, Kyriakos, 260.

106. Pergamos DL, *Rector Speeches*, Pandazidis, 225–27.

107. Evans, *Anthropology at War*, 66.

108. Pergamos DL, *Rector Speeches*, Pandazidis, 227.

109. Evans, *Anthropology at War*, 67.

110. Stephanos's name appeared in the elections list as an independent candidate, which is quite remarkable given the extreme polarization between the modernist party of Trikoupis and the more traditional and conservative party of Theodoros Deliyannis (1820–1905), *Ήλιος* (Sun) 387, Hermoupolis, April 28, 1892, 2.

111. *Πατρίς* (Fatherland) 1350, Hermoupolis, April 30, 1892. The newspaper fervently supported Trikoupis's party and disparaged various independent candidates for secretly working in favor of Deliyannis's election.

112. Evans, *Anthropology at War*, 68.

113. *Εφημερίς της Κυβερνήσεως* (Government gazette) 51:1, March 19, 1899, 2.

114. Thomas W. Gallant, *The Edinburgh History of the Greeks, 1768 to 1913* (Edinburgh: Edinburgh University Press, 2015), 286–326.

115. Λεύκωμα της Εκατονταετηρίδος της εν Αθήναις Αρχαιολογικής Εταιρείας 1837–1937 (Centenary book of the Archaeological Society in Athens), 47.

116. Clon Stephanos, *Συμβολαί εις την Φυσικήν Ανθρωπολογίαν της Ελλάδος: Ο Εγκάρσιος Κεφαλικός Δείκτης* (Contributions to the physical anthropology of Greece: the transverse cephalic index) (Athens: Printing House of the Royal Court A. Raftani, 1911).

117. Recall Topinard's harsh critique on Stephanos's results in *La Grèce*.

118. Stephanos, *Contributions*, preface.

119. Archiv der Berlin-Brandenburgischen Akademie der Wissenschaften, NL Virchow, Nr. 2009. As Stephanos's personal archive was lost after his death, this is the only correspondence between the Greek anthropologist and Virchow, or any other German intellectual that the author has discovered. However, given the German scholar's fascination with Ancient Greece, and especially the tension-ridden interest of classicists, prehistoric archaeologists, and anthropologists; see Suzanne L. Marchand, *Down from Olympus: Archaeology and Philhellenism in Germany, 1750–1970* (Princeton: Princeton University Press, 1996). One may assume more exchanges took place, even though they can not be documented at this moment.

120. Pergamos DL, *Rector Speeches*, Christomanos, 138–39.

121. Pergamos DL, *Rector Speeches*, Christomanos, 70–71.

122. Proceedings of the Meetings of the Faculty of Medicine, March 17, 1912, UOA Historical Archive.

123. *Εφημερίς της Κυβερνήσεως* (Government gazette) 121, April 12, 1912, 1.

124. Proceedings of the Meetings of the Faculty of Medicine, January 17, 1914, UOA Historical Archive.

125. Ακρόπολις (Acropolis), January 12, 1914, 2.

FIVE

Jews between Volk and Rasse

AMOS MORRIS-REICH

Focusing on three Central and Eastern European Jewish authors, this chapter aims to provide a central cross section of the scholarly classification of Jews in terms of *Volk* and *Rasse* in the final decade of the nineteenth century and the first decades of the twentieth. Academic models of human affinity and kinship such as Volk and Rasse are never devoid of a political dimension or entirely separable from cultural and political discourses. This is because the terms, or signifiers, on which they are based derive from and are entwined with the shifting meanings of natural language semantics. The definition of such models and their application is virtually never based on random inductive sampling, but, rather, is applied to social and historical realities that are perceived as given and invested with political meaning. There is always a prior social reality from and against which such models of classifications proceed, and every form of human classification necessarily involves inclusion and exclusion, whether these are vertical, horizontal, implicit, or explicit in form. The historical contextualization of human classifications involves several levels of analysis, including the considerations of present-day historians, the race scientists themselves, and the changing historical ground of both. To explore this multilevel contextualization, the chapter first reconstructs the wider and longer-term contexts of debate on the classification of Jews. This will clarify the underlying questions, assumptions, expectations, and dilemmas that would otherwise be hidden in the lines of argumentation in the three case studies. This wider contextualization and analysis of the cases are combined to avoid a deterministic, teleological, or anachronistic account.

Entwined with other populations and often classified as marginal to or excluded from other national, "racial," religious, or linguistic classes, the classification of European Jews at the end of the nineteenth century provides a particularly complex and ambivalent context of study. Various principles of classification (physical anthropological, linguistic, religious, or other) determined the affinity or distance between different Jewish populations, on the one hand, and between respective Jewish and non-Jewish populations, on the other. Within this framework, demonstrating racial connections or affinities between Hungarian Jews and Algerian Jews, for example, almost certainly meant enlarging, at the same time, the distance between Hungarian Jews and non-Jewish Hungarians. To be members of one class, in this respect, meant necessarily being excluded from (and excluding) others, explicitly or implicitly, from a different but otherwise overlapping class. Looking back from the second decade of the twenty-first century, with our retrospective knowledge of the breakdown of European civilization in the First World War; the reorganization of the densely mixed (linguistically, religiously, ethnically, and socially) lands of Central and Eastern Europe into nation-states; and the collapse of European civilization in the Second World War, including the systematic murder (using race and racial classifications as justifications) of European Jewry and the Sinti and Roma, the pre-Nazi racial discourses of human classification must also be seen as deeply corrupted, motivated by, and to a great extent reducible to political contexts.

But even if the line separating apparently scientific, objective claims from what historian of anti-Semitism Gavin Langmuir calls socially effective "chimerical belief or fantasy" is elusive, reducing such past academic discourses entirely to politics is a form of historical anachronism.[1] Instead, we have to acknowledge that we are operating in muddy waters, where scientific beliefs, forms of classification, and arguments exist alongside, and cannot be differentiated from, ideological and political considerations, which could only be explicit or implicit in retrospect. It should be recalled that all brands of physical anthropology have failed to yield any neatly delimited races or related classifications that everyone could agree on. Whether embedded in notions of racial purity or of racial heterogeneity, whether politically motivated or intended as purely scientific description, the empirical activity of classification has for this reason always been beset with uncertainties and contingencies. Some forms of classification and their applications were already recognized as biased and motivated at the time, in ways that, rather than annulling them, interacted in complex ways with their truth claims. The classification of humans by humans is inherently messy.

Classes (or "types," in linguistic terms) such as "Nordic," "Alpine," "Slav," or "Negroid" were understood by scientists both as natural groupings, already existing in the world, and as the products of scientific discovery. Thus many of these classes or racial types were already standard in the eighteenth-century publications of such writers as Carl Linnaeus, Immanuel Kant, and Johann Friedrich Blumenbach. But the forms of classification as well as the particular classes within them were also dynamic, with numerous new classifications and types—for example, Paul Broca's or Joseph Deniker's attempts to introduce general classifications or the introduction of particular types such as Felix von Luschan's "Armenoid type"—being introduced, thereby reshuffling the already existing classifications to varying degrees. In hindsight it is easy to see that, unlike the situation in other scientific disciplines such as chemistry, scientists could not stabilize their definition of race as a concept; they could not reach agreement on the number of races in the world (or in Europe), or on the principles of classification in practice.

The indexing of actual populations or their assignment to classes (or "tokens," in linguistic terms)—such as the classification of northern Germans as more "Nordic" than southern Germans—contributed to the invention of the very classes that were at the same time being represented as already given (in what Ian Hacking calls the "looping effect of kinds").[2] On a less abstract level, however, the classification of humans by humans always involves motivations, intentions, and expectations (on the part of both classifiers and classified) at varying degrees of explicitness and implicitness and is essentially unstable because its meanings are of necessity unstable and open to various kinds of interpretation and inversion by others. For instance, one physical anthropologist might describe Eastern European Jews as brachycephalic (broad-skulled) rather than dolichocephalic (long-skulled), implying, according to contemporary physical anthropological assumptions, that they are racially closer to their non-Jewish Slavic neighbors than to the Arabian Semites of the Middle East (who in fact may well be the racial heirs of the ancient Hebrews). But another anthropologist could use the same classification to determine the inferiority of the Eastern European Jews to the allegedly superior race of the dolichocephalic Nordic type.

Historically and politically, furthermore, the classification of Jews in late nineteenth- and early twentieth-century Europe was potentially even trickier than some of its contemporary parallels. This is due, first of all, to the anti-Semitism that is never fully absent from the wider European context and, second, to the (sometimes) anomalous position of Jews within the racial discourse based on the assumption (extending such historical, linguistic, and anthropological categories as Teutonic, Slav, or Semitic, discussed in the introduction to this volume) of their non-European—geographical cum racial—origin. Indeed, in linguistic and anthropological discourses the Jews were often assumed to have their geographical and biological origins outside of the lands, societies, or nations in which they resided; this question led to numerous debates and controversies. As a result, and at least partially overlapping the centuries-old Christian conception of Jews, physical anthropology portrayed Jews as aliens.

Jewish and non-Jewish authors sometimes employed the same physical anthropological classes to contradictory ends, whether inclusionary or exclusionary. Moreover, one author's classifications or findings would frequently be interpreted in unanticipated ways by others (amplified by the traveling of ideas across national contexts). Social and political contexts determined the control of such definitional criteria and the significance and policy uptake of such analyses, but positions and arguments could be inverted; the potential for this kind of inversion was known to these authors and therefore, we should assume, would have been a consideration in their arguments and argumentative strategies. In this article I study tensions between classification of Jews in terms of Volk and Rasse in the work of three scientists and scholars: the pioneer of truly "scientific" Jewish race science, Samuel Weissenberg, in the 1890s and first decade of the twentieth century; the founder of Jewish sociology and demography, Arthur Ruppin; and a pioneer of Jewish ethnology and folklore in Palestine, Erich Brauer. While different in terms of their personal and professional backgrounds, together they represent one particular cross section of authors of Jewish background working in Central and Eastern Europe, who share, to a great extent, similar convictions concerning the position of Jews within the categories of Volk and Rasse.[3]

As categories of classification, Volk and Rasse are particularly slippery. In German, the terms Volk and Rasse (the latter being far narrower and strictly biological in its meaning) had a wide spectrum of meanings. Volk could be essentially open and inclusive, or an instrument of delimitation and exclusion. Definitions of Rasse, too, ranged from the descriptive (real but insignificant) to the deterministic (determining the intellectual and moral characteristics of individuals). In the opening of the entry on "Rasse" in the most important source on historical semantics in German, the *Geschichtliche Grundbegriffe*, Werner Conze notes its two semantic fields: as a classificatory concept in biology along the same lines as "genus," "species," or "variety," and as a term designating a social-political group (135).[4] In the opening of the entry on "Volk," Reinhart Koselleck notes how, in a process of mutual exchange, the term Volk is often used at one and the same time both for self-definition and for the exclusion of strangers ("*Selbst-und Fremdwahrnemung werden dabei oft durch dieselben Begriffe wechselseitig konstituiert*") (142). Because of the (varying degrees of) overlap between the concepts of Rasse and Volk, tensions between the two are inherently built into their semantics and pragmatics. Finally, the background of the authors using these terms, their motivations, and the point in time at which they were writing cannot be ignored, because the same classification used by individuals of different backgrounds, at different moments of time, or in different political contexts could bear different implications. A complete mapping of the classifications of Jews using the categories of Volk and Rasse could presumably be undertaken as a form of Venn diagram. The Venn diagram shows all possible logical relations among a finite collection of sets, and in this case that would mean all the different logical possibilities involving definitions of Volk, definitions of Rasse, classifications of Jews, and conclusions derived from the various relationships among these three.

Before we turn to the case studies, however, I would like to present the two main perspectives on the relationship between Volk and Rasse, elucidate the semantic difficulties involved in translating the terms into English, and explain the methodological grounds for pitting the two interpretations against each other.

Volk and Rasse are both central concepts in modern academic, public, and political European discourses. Volk would normally be translated into English as "nation" or "people" and Rasse as "race," but these translations are problematic for several reasons: "nation" does not carry the holistic meanings that Volk has in German, nor does "race" convey the particular meanings of Rasse. Furthermore, in a certain sense the translations confuse some of the original genealogies of the concepts; I will come back to this point below. At the same time, while the genealogies of the two terms are different, they are very often viewed as being co-constitutive concepts in the history of European nationalism.[5] That is, the concept of Rasse is seen as providing the biological or physical substratum of the concept of Volk.

But even if we assume as our starting point that race is the biological substratum of nation, eventually tensions between the two classificatory schemes will surface. Such classificatory schemes have their own internal logic, and the mapping of one onto another will necessarily yield variations, contradictions, or discrepancies. Defining the German Volk according to criteria of language, geography, and culture, for instance, yields a different map than mapping it according to skull shape, height, and skin color would. Hence, as Franz Boas already noted over a hundred years ago, there will never be complete accord among linguistic, national, and racial classifications. (This also applies, of course, to classifications of Jews.) As we look at the inevitable tensions (however small) between the two schemes, the question becomes, how did authors handle such moments of tension, and what can we conclude from this?

In this frame of interpretation, disagreements between the concepts of Volk and Rasse cannot ultimately be understood as anything but a form of confusion.[6] But such moments of disagreement can also lead us to a reconsideration of their fundamental relationship as deeply contradictory. Because this conceptualization is less intuitive, I will spend more time attempting to explain it. My explanation draws on Chris Hutton's work in the history of linguistics and race theory.

To recapitulate Hutton's conceptualization, Volk is defined as a relationship among four elements: language (mother tongue); culture or worldview; lineage, genealogy, or kinship; and territory. The phonocentric concept of Volk can be traced from the Biblical account of the settlement of the earth by Noah's sons, Shem, Ham, and Japheth (Gen. 10:5, 10:20, and 10:31), who were divided "after their families, after their tongues, in their lands, after their nations," and through the complex geographical, linguistic, and spiritual attributes associated with the descendants of each of those sons in medieval and then early modern theorizing.[7] The concept gains its full political and ideological impact in its use by German theorists of Volk (Johann Gottfried von Herder, Johann Gottlieb Fichte) and subsequently within liberal-bourgeois nationalist movements of the nineteenth century. The concept of Volk was central, in different ways, to both Nazism and the Soviet Union.[8]

Hutton contrasts the Volk paradigm with two distinct paradigms of identity, or "semiotic orders." The first of these is "textual-ritual," where the framework for understanding human society and human actions in relation to the social and cosmic order is provided by a set of sacred or institutionally validated texts or by specialized ritual knowledge, either written or oral, subject to interpretation by an elite class of scholar-administrators or priests. In 1807 Napoleon summoned France's Jewish leaders and asked them twelve questions.

One of these was whether Judaism, Jewry, and Jews is a nation or a religion (the assumption behind the question being that Judaism, Jewry, and the Jews could not be both simultaneously). One of the possible answers, from that moment onward, was that Jews were defined according to a certain set of texts and rituals—that is, that Jews were members of a religion. Following Napoleon's question, Jewish history was never the same again, because from that point onward ideologies of Judaism positioned themselves on one side or the other of that distinction (or denied both).[9] The cross section of authors that we deal with in this article give the answer that Jews are a nation, but, as we will see, the possibility that Jewry or Judaism may be a religion after all—with its texts, knowledge, and customs—hovers over the discussion.

The second semiotic order that Hutton contrasts with the concept of Volk is racial anthropology, grounded in the physical human body. The body is understood to be marked by skin color or other salient somatic characteristics, which can be represented at the group level as "physical types" and are understood to be expressed in blood ties, kinship, lineage, race, and so on. Here the human body, rather than language, history, territory, nationality, or self-classification, is the starting point. Racial anthropology in its modern sense is generally traced to the late eighteenth century, where an emergent comparative anatomy met developments in the science of taxonomy (Linnaeus) to produce the beginnings of the modern theory of race (Blumenbach, Kant).[10] The point to emphasize for our purposes here is that in their purest forms, according to Hutton, these approaches reject the language and criteria used in the discourse of Volk in favor of something that is conceptualized as deeper and more real—namely, sets of correlations and connections at the individual and the group level. While, according to the first perspective, in which Rasse is viewed as the biological substratum of Volk, the concepts of Volk and Rasse constitute each other, in this latter interpretation Rasse is not only deeper and more genuine but differs from and contradicts the principle of Volk.[11] By the 1870s academic orthodoxy required racial and linguistic criteria to be distinguished from each other in the theorizing of identity.

But this rendered the construction of coherent historical narratives based on Volk problematic, along with any pretensions to a unified and definitive classification of human diversity.[12] If, according to the first perspective, discrepancies between Volk and Rasse would be seen as minor, according to this latter conceptualization such discrepancies are far larger or even just outright contradictions. The question here is thus: What kind of relationship can we draw between Volk and Rasse in the work of Samuel Weissenberg, Arthur Ruppin, and Erich Brauer?

One last necessary point, before we move to the case studies themselves, pertains to the difficulty in translating Volk and Rasse into English. As Hutton notes, there is a mismatch between the concepts of Volk and Rasse in German and the words and corresponding concepts in English, a mismatch that is accentuated by the reception of National Socialist thought in the English-speaking world. Lacking the centrality of a term equivalent to Volk, English "race" has historically had a much wider set of meanings than are suggested by the current political use of the term (further accentuated by the color line that marks the use of "race" in the U.S. context). The English word race now functions in many contexts as an imagined synonym for German Rasse, but late nineteenth-century English writers, whatever their attitude to the definition and status of the term "Aryan," used "Aryan race."[13] The term "Aryan people" was also widely used, either as an equivalent to Aryan race or to designate one of its subsets. In German, however, by far the most common usage was to pair *arisch* with Volk, and the distinction between Rasse and Volk was absolutely fundamental to German scholarship, into the Nazi era.[14] The term "Aryan race," which in popular English language sources is mistakenly given as underpinning Nazi ideology, is actually being used to translate the phrase *arisches Volk*.[15] Importantly for the general context of discussion, Jews and "Gypsies" (Roma and Sinti) were anomalous with regard to the normative Volk model that created the difference on which race theory came to operate.[16]

In looking at the three cases I discuss here I am very selective; my only intention is to identify and illustrate the existence of tensions between the concepts of Volk and Rasse and to document how the three authors I have chosen dealt with those tensions when they arose. Then, in the final section of the article, taking a step back from the particulars of the tensions in order to appreciate the bigger picture, I will contrast the two perspectives—Volk and Rasse as constitutive of each other or as profoundly conflicting projects—and ask which of the two frames of interpretation for the concepts of Volk and Rasse applies better to the cases seen here, and which of the two they can be claimed to corroborate.

While the tension between Volk and Rasse could be exemplified using any one of a variety of cases, it may be most easily documented in the racial anthropological discourse on Yemenite Jews. The reason for this is that the study of the Jews' racial constitution was based on several assumptions, two of which clashed with regard to modern European Jewry and Yemenite Jews: firstly, that Jews were racially defined, by which it was meant that Jews shared a certain racial, bodily structure, and, secondly, that the Jewish type persevered over time and space. Indeed, a foundational study by Richard Andree insisted upon a great similarity between the physical form of Ashkenazi and Yemenite Jews.[17] Nevertheless, as early as the 1880s, authors began to note that the skull shape of European Jews tended to the brachycephalic while the supposedly Semitic skull, as manifested by the desert Bedouins and Yemenite Jews, was identified as dolichocephalic. Scholars committed to a scientific (racial) account of the Jews thus faced a contradiction. What then was the (racial) relationship between European and Yemenite Jews? If an account of the Jewish Volk could not deny the biological, racial substratum, how could the problem be harmonized if embracing the one excluded the other? And what were the scientific or political implications of this situation?

Over the following decades, several attempts were made to grapple with this problem, none of which succeeded in providing a fully satisfactory answer. On the whole, scientists tended to approach this contradiction by assuming that it was probably the result of incomplete scientific theorizing and insufficient empirical data.[18] In 1892 Felix von Luschan, the non-Jewish Austrian archeologist and ethnologist, set the discussion on the Jews' racial profile on a new path by redefining the racial constitution of the Jews as being mixed from several components. This redefinition allowed for the separation of European Jews from Yemenite Jews. But while this redefinition explained the structure of European Jews it could not explain that of Yemenite Jews. This is the basic framework from which the deliberations of Weissenberg, Ruppin, and Brauer ensued. In reading the three, then, we will try not to lose sight of the larger question of the relationship between Volk and Rasse that was built into this state of affairs.

Case 1: Samuel Weissenberg and Jews between Asian, European, and Middle Eastern Types

The physical anthropological studies by Samuel Weissenberg, published primarily between the mid-1890s and 1908, of European, Asian, and African Jews, point to major differences in skull shape, indicating not only the varied nature of contemporary Jewry but also the structural affinities between Asian Jewries and their surrounding non-Jewish populations. Physical anthropological classifications that were relatively straightforward from one perspective turned out on closer observation to involve the tacit negotiation of several separate but interrelated questions: Were Jews originally a relatively homogenous racial group? If they were, then how does one explain the major differences between Jewries around the world as well as between Jewries and the non-Jewish groups among whom Jews have lived for centuries? Simultaneously, and even more fundamentally, over Weissenberg's discussion hovers the question of whether Jews are a biologically defined racial group or nation or, ultimately, a community bonded rather by religion and culture alone.

Samuel Weissenberg (1867–1928) was a Russian Jewish physician, born in the Ukrainian city of Elizavetgrad and educated in Germany, who expanded the study of the physical anthropology of the Jews to include communities in central Asia and the Middle East. Weissenberg's quest to discover the original Jewish type in terms of Rasse was nonetheless not linked in the same way as Ruppin's studies—for example, to corroborate a Jewish nation, or

Volk. Weissenberg attended the fifth Zionist congress in 1905 but showed a far greater commitment to diaspora Jewry than to Zionism. Without wanting to reduce his scientific work to his biographical trajectory, I would still point out that his gradual shift from the secular Jewish background from which he came to an increasing commitment to Jewish religion may be important for understanding why, for Weissenberg, Rasse seems far more independent from Volk than it is for either Ruppin or Brauer.

In her recent history of Russian physical anthropology, Marina Mogliner emphasizes the Russian contexts of Weissenberg's work, particularly his focus on non-European Jewry in the multinational Russian empire.[19] But John Efron's comprehensive chapter on Weissenberg in *Defenders of the Race* (1994) is more relevant to our discussion here. Weissenberg received his education in Germany; the great majority of his publications were in German rather than in Russian; and, as Efron shows, the wider context in which Weissenberg developed as a physical anthropologist was the harassment of Eastern European immigrants (harassment from which, as John Efron notes, he suffered directly) in Germany and in particular the anti-Semitism that he endured there. Weissenberg's turn to physical anthropology was inseparable from his recognition that the core of the anti-Semitic claim (couched in scientific language) was that the Jew bore physical and mental characteristics that prevented him from living peacefully with Aryans. Weissenberg's career as a physical anthropologist, then, included internal and external motivations that involved his beliefs about the Jewish collectivity as well as anti-Semitic writings on Jews.[20] While the two are unquestionably related, in the following I will focus, as I do for Ruppin and Brauer, far more on the internal issues involved in the question of Jews between Volk and Rasse.

A single question ran through Weissenberg's various physical anthropological studies: of the relationship between contemporary Jewish types and what Weissenberg believed to be the original Jewish type. The starting point of his work is the intersection between his assumption that Jews were at some point in time a pure race (a common theory in then-contemporary race anthropology) and the empirical application of the tools of physical anthropology. Weissenberg was forced to recognize the present physical variety of Jews. His answer to that was that "the Jews do not form one exact anthropological type, but are composed of several types, which are not everywhere the same."[21] But if this was the case, which of the current Jewish types was closest to the original Jewish type, and how did the divergences of the others occur?

Weissenberg pointed to three possible solutions to this question: either Jews were a *Mischvolk* (a "mixed people" or a "mongrel people") from the beginning; Jews absorbed foreign elements through proselytism; or the environment changed Jews' original type. But it is important that Weissenberg, unlike Ruppin, did not believe that the current bond between Jews was racial; for Weissenberg, therefore, the answer to the initial question had no immediate or self-evident ideological or political consequences.

As both Efron and Mogliner point out, Weissenberg's argument that the Caucasus was the site of the origin of European Jews paralleled Blumenbach's 1795 assertion concerning the origin of the European type. Because if Blumenbach spoke of the Caucasus as the racial cradle of the Europeans, Weissenberg's argument implied, first, that Eastern European Jews were European par excellence. Second, it implied that Eastern European Jews were racially separate from the Semitic type in general and Jewish populations characterized as Semitic in particular. Weissenberg alternated between physical anthropology and Jewish folklore. Between 1895 and 1905, for instance, he abandoned physical anthropology for a focus on Jewish cultural anthropology. His political or ideological convictions also changed: before 1900 Weissenberg adhered to the German Jewish liberal view that Jews were part of a community of faith (*Glaubensgenossenschaft*) but no longer a national community (*Nationalgenossenschaft*), while after 1900 he saw the different customs and traditions as belonging to one magnificent Jewry. What is of interest to us here, though, is his physical anthropology. Weissenberg's most important contribution to the physical anthropology of the Jews began in 1908 with a stipend from the Rudolf Virchow Foundation to travel to Turkey, Syria, Egypt, and Palestine to carry out anthropometric studies on Jews, including Samaritans and Karaites; Arabs; and Armenians. In his findings and in his deliberations on those findings, the tensions between the concepts of Rasse and Volk are apparent.

In the measurements that Weissenberg carried out in Jewish communities in Palestine, he was sure he had discovered examples of the original Jewish type. His measurements showed these Jews to be similar to their non-Jewish neighbors, both of them conforming to the long-skulled Semitic type. These findings, Weissenberg argued, refuted von Luschan's argument concerning the Hittite origin of the Jews. Weissenberg's same measurements made plain that European Jews differed markedly from the Semitic type.[22]

Like almost all race scientists, Weissenberg was concerned with the origins of and the relationship between the Sephardim and the Ashkenazim. The central question was how the division between the two had taken place and which of the two was closer to the original Jewish type. If, as Weissenberg maintained, the ancient Israelites had been dolichocephalic (long-skulled), then the Sephardim were closer to them in physical type. Weissenberg believed that the Ashkenazim had deviated from this type by intermixing with the people of the Caucasus, who were brachycephalic, before 586 BC. Modern Ashkenazi Jews were therefore a mixed type.

Weissenberg was also, like other physical anthropologists, particularly interested in the study of Yemenite Jews, and he measured fifty of them in Jaffa and Jerusalem. There were two main schools of thought about the Jews of Yemen: either that they were a distinct race, different from other major Jewish racial types, or that they were racially Arabs who had long ago converted to Judaism;-Weissenberg inclined toward the latter view but remained unsure. After he had compared Yemenite Jews with European Jews, he concluded that "there exists no physical relationship between the European Jews and their Yemenite coreligionists."[23]

Weissenberg's studies of Jews from central Asia also show that, along with religion, language was also completely inseparable from the anthropological study of Jews. In Jerusalem, Weissenberg measured Jews from Bukhara, Samarkand, Merv, and Hart.

Although there were great geographical distances separating their various places of origin, Weissenberg viewed them all as stemming from the same *Stammland* (ancestral homeland), because they all spoke a common dialect of Persian. As their measurements showed great variety in skull shape, however, Weissenberg concluded that they had undergone thorough intermixture with the local central Asian brachycephalic populations and were now anthropologically a mixed group.

A later study of Caucasian Jewish communities drove Weissenberg to the conclusion that the Yemenite Jews had maintained their racial purity while the Jews of the Caucasus had been modified through their encounters with the hyperbrachycephalic Caucasians; he now characterized the latter as "Judaized Caucasians."[24] Only the original Jews of Palestine and the Yemenite Jews, in Weissenberg's view, showed continuity with the original long-skulled Jewish type.

In his analysis of Weissenberg's studies, Efron points to some of their methodological weaknesses. I would like to emphasize the different dynamic between Rasse and Volk in Weissenberg's work. Ruppin and Brauer assumed that the study of Jews in terms of Rasse would delineate the boundaries of the Jewish Volk, the *Volkskörper*, but were driven to differentiate between the "original type," "foreign," and "special" types of Jews, the latter being more marginal to the constitution of the Jewish Volk. Weissenberg, on the other hand, though he spent a large part of his career studying the physical anthropology of various Jewries, undertook those studies more as part of a quest for the original Jewish type and for an understanding of its later permutations than as a way to corroborate the boundaries of the Jews as a Volk. This was because he had doubts about whether there even was such a thing as a Jewish Volk and he was not invested in the creation of a Jewish nation, Zionist or otherwise. As a result, Rasse for Weissenberg was an independent category rather than one subordinated to Volk. Further, his documentation of Jewish variety in terms of Rasse had no immediate or clear consequences. While secular Jews, failing to view Jews as members of a religion, sought another, scientific and objectively documentable common denominator for Jews the world over, Weissenberg, as an observant Jew, could much more easily acknowledge that while different Jewries could be defined racially, Judaism was instead a social category based upon law and custom.

Case 2: Erich Brauer and Yemenite Jews as Arabs of the Jewish Constitution

Erich Brauer's original discipline was ethnology (*Völkerkunde*), in which he wrote a dissertation focusing on the religion of the Herrero, and his basic disposition toward his objects of study remained ethnological when he turned to the study of his coreligionists in Palestine. In other words, although he was very successful in employing the techniques and practices of the cultural anthropologists who were his contemporaries, his position toward non-European Jewries remained external to them. In this sense he differed from Weissenberg, who alternated between folklore (*Volkskunde*) and physical anthropology (*Anthropologie*) and whose basic position was that of an insider studying his peers. This may be at least part of the reason for Brauer's abstention from studying European Jews with the same methods and tools. Brauer also differed from Weissenberg (and from Ruppin, as we shall see below) in the sense that he seems to have been less driven than they were by any general question about or outlook on Jewry or Judaism as a whole. For this reason, the more general aspects of his understanding of Jews in terms of the concepts of Volk and Rasse have to be deduced from his studies of particular Jewries.

Erich Brauer inherited the racial discourse on Jews, with its structural discrepancy between Volk and Rasse, from his predecessors. But his position with respect to this basic structure is nonetheless different because of the combination of his biographical background and his academic education. As a teenager Brauer was involved with Zionism, but as an adult he was far less committed to Zionism than Ruppin was. Brauer, who was born in Berlin in 1895, was to some extent already a marginalized figure during his lifetime.[25] In part this was due to a medical condition: a childhood illness had left him a hunchback. But it was also because he never obtained a permanent academic position. As a Jew in Germany he would not have had more than a slim chance of obtaining an academic position anyway, and when he finally settled in Jerusalem, after the Nazi party secured control of Germany, Jerusalem was flooded with individuals with academic qualifications who could not all be absorbed by the small and newly established Hebrew University.[26] Up to his death, Brauer conducted his research on temporary fellowships and grants.[27]

Brauer started his academic education in Leipzig on the eve of the First World War and subsequently moved between several universities, including a period in Berlin, in 1917, with von Luschan. His doctoral dissertation on the religion of the Herero, written under the supervision of the distinguished Africanist Karl Weulle (1864–1926), director of the Völkerkunde Institut, was submitted in 1923 to the University of Leipzig.[28] Bauer's first trip to Palestine was undertaken on behalf of the Leipzig Museum of Ethnology (Museum für Völkerkunde zu Leipzig) in 1925 in order to collect ethnological objects from the Arab community. From 1927 to 1931 he conducted fieldwork in Jerusalem on the Jews of Bukhara who had settled there. In 1931 he returned to Leipzig and in 1934 published his book *Ethnologie der Jemenitischen Juden* (Ethnology of Yemenite Jews), still the most cited book on the subject outside the Hebrew language. Around this time, however, his supervisor, Weulle, was succeeded by the anti-Semitic Otto Reche, which ended any prospects of employment for Brauer in Leipzig. In 1932 Brauer had been offered a teaching position at the University of Berlin by one of his former teachers, Diedrich Hermann Westermann, but negotiations over the offer ended abruptly as the Nazi party ascended to power. Brauer returned to Palestine once again, more as a refugee than as a Zionist, and this time for good. The nature of and basis for Brauer's travels back and forth between Germany and Palestine therefore changed dramatically in 1933.[29]

Brauer started his Middle Eastern career studying Arab communities in Palestine, only turning to Jewish diasporas in the mid-1920s, and his background and practice, involving both folklore (Volkskunde) and ethnology (Völkerkunde), is crucial in this respect. While Brauer was mostly interested in the cultural dimension of the diasporas that he studied, he took for granted the existence and relevance of racial classifications and dimensions as well. From his base in Jerusalem he studied several Jewish diasporic communities, including Jews from Kurdistan, Afghanistan, and Yemen. The semantics of this characterization, as opposed to "Yemenite Jews," is important.

Brauer was influenced by the *Kulturkreis* theory, which emphasized interrelations between cultures. When he moved to the Jewish context, therefore, he documented the mutual relationships between Jews and their respective environments. His assumption that the different Jewries were part of some Jewish "whole," the Jewish Volk, however, stood in a certain tension to that practice. At the same time, Brauer accepted it as a given that the various specific Jewries were racially defined. But, unlike Ruppin or Weissenberg, he never attempted to elucidate the relationship between the components and the whole. In one sense, his monographs on various Jewries were based on the assumption that each such a diasporic Jewish group was a separate component with more or less permanent boundaries. In another sense, the racial particulars ascribed to certain Jewries were incongruous with those ascribed to others. Brauer, who was not theoretically inclined, does not seem to have reflected on such discrepancies nor attempted to conceptualize them.

In an unpublished four-page document that most likely accompanied the exhibition of this last research project, Brauer noted the absence of knowledge on the peoples among whom Jews live (he used the present tense), reiterated von Luschan's stance about the Jews being comprised of Oriental and Armenoid races, and emphasized that the Jews of the East should be prioritized for study because they were closer to the original Jews (*yehudim rishonim*). In this short text Brauer followed the typological model, writing of individuals as "exemplars" and as "representative" of their race.

In Brauer's work, too, the tension between the classification of Jews in terms of Volk and Rasse can be discerned in his book on Yemenite Jews.[30] Politically speaking, Brauer starts his discussion of Yemenites in medias res, studying Yemenite Jews in British Mandate Palestine in the wider context of the emergence of a Jewish society there. Scientifically, too, his discussion grows out of an already existing anthropological discourse. Brauer's discussion of Yemenite racial features occurs in the third chapter, which is devoted to Yemenite physical anthropology. He opens with an account of a Saturday afternoon on which he is standing on Jaffa Street, in Jerusalem, observing the various people walking down the street. Yemenite Jews, he says, can be distinguished from the colorful tableau of the rest by their short, dark, slender forms ("*diese dunklen, kleinen, schmalgliedrigen Gestalten aus dem bunten Bilde der übrigen herauskennen*"). He complements this anecdotal observation with statistics that point to the smaller average height of the Yemenites (compared to Sephardic Jews), their slender form, dark skin color, long skulls, and the particular shapes of their noses, foreheads, irises, lips and mouths, and hair.[31] At the end of the book are eight tables of photographic reproductions, each containing four to six reproductions, to which Brauer refers throughout this discussion.

By and large, Brauer's discussion of what he takes to be the racial characteristics of Yemenite Jews proceeds by allusions to photographs or photographic tables. For instance, he states that "the lips are not infrequently full (table 1, 5; table 5, 4). The mouth is sometimes broad (table 1, 1)."[32]

Brauer contends that Yemenite Jews do not comprise one pure type, which he attributes to the processes of mixture that this community has undergone over the course of its long history. But, he insists, two African types do stand out particularly clearly in the features of the Yemenites: the Negroid and the Hamitic. In conclusion, Brauer mocks Niebuhr's impressionistic observation of similarity between Yemenite and Polish Jews, commenting: "Niebuhr does not seem to have encountered too many Polish Jews in his life, because anthropologically there is nothing that connects Ashkenazi Jews with Yemenite ones."[33] Brauer emphasizes the differences between the skull shapes of Yemenite and Ashkenazi Jews based on what he takes to be valid anatomical statistical facts, agreeing with von Luschan that the long-skulled Yemenite differs from the short-skulled Jewish archetype (*Urtyp*).[34] Ultimately, then, according to Brauer's anthropological or racial categories, Yemenite Jews are

Arabs. This statement is deeply ambiguous in several ways. Firstly, in labeling them as Arabs, it conflates the anthropological categories he had been using to characterize Yemenite Jews with national categories, so that it is no longer possible to distinguish between Volk and Rasse. Secondly, it is almost impossible to ignore a sense of substitution and inversion here—namely, that in discussing the relationship between Yemenite Jews and the Jewish Volk Brauer is also, implicitly, discussing the relationship between German Jews and the German Volk. In a statement that can be seen as somewhat ironic, coming as it does from an exiled German Jew, Brauer transplants the self-perception of many German Jews—as Germans whose Jewishness is merely a religious identity—to Yemenite Jews. Stating that "the Yemenite Jew . . . is an Arab of the Jewish faith" (*Araber jüdischer Konfession*),[35] Brauer implies that the Jewish nation, the Jewish Volk, is able to contain Yemenite Jews as well, in spite of their different racial structure. The way Brauer goes about substantiating this claim involves a specific dynamic between the concepts of Volk and Rasse.

Participation in the Volk, Brauer stresses, pertains not merely to skull or body form but to attachment (*Verbundensein*) and the will to be a member of a race. This sense of attachment turns Yemenite Jews into a racial group, within the wider Arab environment, and permits their inclusion within the Jewish whole. Anatomically or racially, Yemenite Jews may be Arabs, but their consciousness as Jews makes them part of the Jewish Volk. An inclusive view of the Jewish Volk enables Brauer to see Yemenite Jews as part of the Jewish national project.

Case 3: Jews, Special Types, and Foreign Types

Compared with Weissenberg and Brauer, Arthur Ruppin's political and scientific outlook was both more comprehensive and less ambivalent. Ruppin converted to a Jewish national outlook of the Zionist kind at an early age, while still in Germany, and not only did he remain committed to this outlook for the rest of his life, but he is considered one of the most important Zionist leaders, certainly before 1914, and the most important Central European or

German Zionist leader. Ruppin developed a comprehensive, multifaceted, and multilayered empirical and statistical model for the study of sociological and demographic tendencies in contemporary Jewry. But if his commitment to the Zionist project was based on a firm belief that Jews were a nation and as such should be separated from the non-Jewish nationals among whom they had lived for centuries and from whom they differed racially, to a greater or lesser degree, there were nevertheless, on more practical levels of his work, tensions to be found. For instance, his early belief that Jews were racially different from northern Europeans and far closer to Middle Eastern populations led him to hold that a clearer separation of the populations would be to the benefit of both. But if this early belief led him to a stance that Jews should return to their original homeland, namely Palestine, his belief in the greater racial affinity between Jews and the Arab population now clashed with his national outlook about the necessity of creating a political Jewish body there. Some of the tensions in Ruppin's work, as we will see, could be located at the meeting point between his national and scientific outlooks, which I will illustrate with regard to the concepts of Volk and Rasse.

Considered the founder of modern Jewish sociology and demography, Arthur Ruppin was clearly engaged in a project that focused on the Jewish nation, the Jewish Volk, ranging from birthrates through mixed marriages to patterns and rates of crime. But he also believed, throughout his entire professional career (1903–41), that the modern sociologist of contemporary Jewry also needed to take the biological, racial substratum into account. Although the existence and significance of race in Ruppin's scientific (and political) work is a contested subject among historians, the particulars of the dispute are less important to me here than the recognition that race does exist in his model, so that we can look at the tensions he identifies and analyze how they are addressed within his scientific and political economy.

It is important for our purposes to note that in his first book Ruppin already emphasizes racial union as the Jews' strongest bond. That is, Ruppin understands race as essential to the Jewish *national* constitution. In that book (which came out in two editions, in 1904 and 1911, with significant changes between the two) Ruppin discusses the racial characteristics of the Jews. He claims that the Jews have preserved a high level of racial unity (not to be confused with racial purity) throughout the generations and explains the Jews' proximity to the peoples of the Near East. Race unites the Jews through space and time, so that despite geographical distances the Jews in the West and the East are close to each another. Ruppin also emphasizes the continuity of the "Jewish type" over hundreds of years, under conditions of geographical dispersion. In the second, 1911 edition, of that first book the "racial value of the Jews" becomes even more essential to Ruppin's discussion of Jewish nationalism. The explicit context of the discussion is the Jews' right to exist as a separate *national* unit. Ruppin's nationalist-Zionist view and his view of race are closely connected, but in his scientific and political economies the latter is subordinate to the former.

In his comprehensive overviews of contemporary Jewry, Ruppin affords a racial historical survey of Jews dwelling outside Israel. His belief that Jews are bonded by their racial structure and that the Jewish type is permanent requires him to then explain the differences among Jews living in different diasporas. Ruppin's answer to this challenge is that the Jewish national body is comprised of three distinct major Jewish types, which reflect the basic characteristics of the Jewish racial structure. As he sees it, a similar historical process took place in each of the large centers (Babylonia, Spain, Poland). First, foreign racial elements penetrated the Jewish community; then came a long period of inbreeding until "nearly all the individual differences in these respective areas were erased over the centuries." Ruppin concludes: "We call the three Jewish groups—the Babylonians, Sephardim, and Ashkenazim—original Jewish types. From the racial point of view each group is made up of the three racial bases that constituted the ancient Jews of Eretz Israel . . . Only the proportion changed."[36] Ruppin does not directly discus this, but he was most probably aware of mainstream German race scientists who in the 1920s distinguished between mature mixtures over millennia that (in practice) created new races and immature young "bastard-peoples," which were created by the mixing of individuals of what they considered distant races and were thus illegitimate.

This description can explain differences between major Jewries and has immediate implications for Ruppin's understanding of the composition of the Jewish Volk and its boundaries. Indeed, as a result, some Jewish racial groups, including the Jews of Yemen, the Caucasus, and Bukhara, find themselves entirely outside the Jewish racial type. Ruppin calls these groups "special types" and characterizes the difference between them and the rest of world Jewry in racial terms.[37] Ruppin is also led, as a result of these definitions, to recognize "foreign types" that have emerged through intermixture with northern Europeans.[38] His racial perspective leads Ruppin to investigate the various Jewish groups' degree of adaptation to their respective environments, concluding that the racial differences are smallest where the dominant races are made up of similar racial elements and largest where the dominant races did not partake in the evolution of the Jewish type. This is particularly the case in northern Europe.

Ruppin, then, classifies Jewish groups according to their degree of racial proximity to the nations in whose midst they dwell, this degree of proximity being critical for peaceful relations between different populations.[39] Ruppin, like many others, sees a problem where Jews live in the midst of peoples whose racial makeup is very different from theirs. Even more important, the fact that he takes racial classifications seriously leads Ruppin to categorize Jews in terms of the intersecting notions of Volk and Rasse: he differentiates between those whose racial origin is Jewish, but who for historical reasons are no longer considered part of the Jewish collective (because, whether through intermarriage or conversion, they assimilated into a different collective), and those who are not racially Jewish but are part of the Jewish national body.[40] He puts the Samaritans, the Karaites in the Crimea, the Marranos in Portugal, the Doenmeh in Saloniki, the Jedid al-Islam in Persia, and other Caucasian tribes into the first of these two groups. The Falashas of Ethiopia, the Black Jews of India, the Chinese Jews, and converts to Judaism in Russia and Eretz Israel he places in the second group.

As I noted earlier, the subject of Rasse in Ruppin's work is contested. The majority of Ruppin scholars (myself included) believes that Ruppin adhered to a soft determinism, drawn from physical anthropology, in his racial outlook. The majority of scholars thus views his notion of race as descriptive, in the sense that his effort was directed at classifying Jewish populations according to what he took to be their physical characteristics. A minority of scholars, however, views Ruppin as adhering to a far more radical conception of race, one that is drawn from contemporary anti-Semitic authors who did not simply seek to describe populations but had determined that humanity was comprised of groups that were inherently unequal in their human value, hierarchically ordered, and who believed Jews, as a racial phenomenon, to be an ultimate force of evil in the world. The majority of scholars sees Ruppin's classification of Jewish populations, which is offered in the context of his historical survey of the Jewish people, as having no consequences for the relative positions of those populations within the Jewish Volk. But for the minority of scholars, such a historical survey is not merely descriptive but determines the inherent inferiority of specific populations within the Jewish Volk: if Ashkenazi Jews are described as stemming primarily from the Hittite branch of Jewry, while the Yemenite Jews are descended from the Semitic type, Ruppin is actually suggesting that the latter are inferior to the former. I will return to the intersection between the concepts of Volk and Rasse in my conclusion, but here I simply want to emphasize that the majority of scholars agrees that the intersection between Rasse and Volk has ramifications for Ruppin's scientific and political outlooks, but that the two categories are not on a par for him and that he never loses sight of the fact, neither in his scientific model nor in his political project, that the racial is subordinate to the national.

Conclusion

This experiment in the contextualization of Jews as positioned between the concepts of Volk and Rasse can be viewed as a historical instrument, applicable as well to other, related contexts. I have discussed three authors—Samuel Weissenberg, Erich Brauer, and Arthur Ruppin—and pointed to incongruities in their work between classifications of Jews in terms of Rasse and in terms of Volk. To introduce that discussion, I posited two contradictory frames of analysis for analyzing the relationship between the concepts of Volk and Rasse. According to the first, Volk and Rasse are categories constitutive of each other; according to the second, Volk and Rasse stand in contradiction to each other. According to the first, Rasse provides the substratum for belonging to the Jewish or German Volk, and in this sense Rasse is subordinate to Volk; according to the second, Rasse determines the classification of an individual or a group irrespective of his or her belonging to a respective Volk and in this sense is independent of and can undermine the classification of the same individual or group by the category of Volk. According to the first, tensions between Rasse and Volk are local and the category of Rasse is ultimately subordinate to that of Volk. According to the second, pragmatic attempts can be made to harmonize the two or minimize the tensions between them but conceptually the two concepts stand in contradiction and Rasse is the principal determining concept, while Volk is essentially subordinate to it. These two contrasting frames of interpretation do not apply equally well to our three test-cases.

Although the three authors discussed here differed in their biographical backgrounds, their scientific agendas, and their political and ideological commitments, I have argued that they should be seen as one cross section with regard to the positioning of Jews between the classificatory categories of Volk and Rasse. All three authors shared a similar asymmetric structure in their outlooks: the category of Volk was implicitly (Weissenberg and Brauer) or explicitly (Ruppin) analytically superior to that of Rasse. While they all took race seriously, all three viewed Jews as a nation and concluded that Jews were racially varied. In no instance was a population excluded from the Jewish Volk based on its supposed racial characteristics.

This chapter covered just one cross section of the classification of Jews in terms of Volk and Rasse. It could be compared to and contrasted with other cross sections, such as the role of Jews within the

German Volk. In the latter cross section scholars like von Luschan, Virchow, and Lazarus insisted on the difference between German Jews and non-Jewish Germans in terms of Rasse, but included German Jews within the German Volk. The most obvious example of this latter frame of analysis is the scientific and political ideology known as the "Nordic Idea." When proponents of the Nordic Idea, from Ludwig Schemann through Houston Stewart Chamberlain to Hans F. K. Günther, mapped their concept of Nordic superiority onto the European populations of central and northern Europe, they acknowledged tensions between the categories of Rasse and Volk, as only a portion of the German population matched the idea of the Nordic type. Although these writers did not tire of trying to justify why the German Volk was the best conduit for the Nordic Rasse despite the clear discrepancies between the two, they never lost sight of the superiority of Rasse as the determining category and the true goal. This analysis of the tensions between the categories of Volk and Rasse can therefore serve as an instrument for the analysis of structures and modalities of classifications in a historical context that might otherwise, in retrospect, seem to have carried standard or homogenous meanings. After all, for this author at least, arguably the most important question hovering over this discussion is this: Do these (or similar) classificatory categories of humans *necessarily* incorporate particular social and political consequences or, on the contrary, are they only contingently and indeterminately related to the many other forces operative in history?

Notes

1. Gavin Langmuir, *Toward a Definition of Antisemitism* (Los Angeles: University of California Press, 1996), 14 (and discussion throughout the book).

2. Ian Hacking, "The Looping Effect of Human Kinds," in *Causal Cognition: A Multi Disciplinary Debate*, ed. Dan Sperber, David Premack, Ann James Premack (New York: Oxford University Press, 1995), 351–83.

3. From the many other possible discussions of Jews between *Volk* and *Rasse*, it is beneficial to differentiate this current cross section from another, exemplified by physical anthropologist Rudolf Virchow, psychologist Moritz Lazarus, or Austrian Felix von Luschan, who in different ways classified German (or European) Jews as German (or European) in terms of *Volk* although different from elements of the non-

Jewish German population in terms of *Rasse*. On Virchow see Andrew Zimmerman, "Anti-Semitism as Skill: Rudolf Virchow's "Schulstatistik" and the Racial Composition of Germany," *Central European History* 32, no. 4 (1999): 409–29; Matti Bunzl, "Völkerpsychologie and German-Jewish Emancipation," in *Worldly Provincialism: German Anthropology in the Age of Empire, ed.* H. Glenn Penny and Matti Bunzl (Ann Arbor: University of Michigan Press, 2003), 47–85; and Till van Rahden, "'Germans of the Jewish Stamm': Visions of Community between Nationalism and Particularism, 1850 to 1933," in *German History from the Margins*, ed. Mark Roseman et al., (Bloomington: Indiana University Press, 2006), 27–48; on von Luschan see my "Photographs and Economies of Demonstration: The Idea of the Jews as a Mixed Race People," *Jewish Social Studies* 20, no. 1 (2014): 150–83.

4. See Werner Conze ("Rasse") and Reinhart Koselleck ("Volk") in *Geschichtliche Grundbegriffe: Historisches Lexikon zur politisch-sozialen Sprache in Deutschland*, ed. Otto Brunner, Werner Conze, and Reinhart Koselleck, (Stuttgart: Klett-Cotta, 1992), 5:135–78 and 7:141–430.

5. Richard McMahon's *The Races of Europe: Construction of National Identities in the Social Sciences 1839–1939* (London: Palgrave Macmillan, 2016) is the most recent major publication in this vein.

6. See Richard McMahon's *The Races of Europe*: "The Nazis never really clarified their racial doctrine" (121).

7. Arno Borst, *Der Turmbau von Babel: Geschichte der Meinungen und Vielfalt der Sprachen und Völker*, 4 vols. (München: Deutscher Taschenbuchverlag, 1995).

8. Graham Smith, "The Soviet State and Nationalities Policy," in *The Nationalities Question in the Post-Soviet States*, ed. Graham Smith (London: Longman, 1996), 2–41; Francine Hirsch, "The Soviet Union as a Work-in-Progress: Ethnographers and the Category *Nationality* in the 1926, 1937, and 1939 Censuses," *Slavic Review* 56 (1997): 251–78.

9. On negational views of Jews see my "Three Paradigms of 'The Negative Jew': 'Identity' from Simmel to Zizek," *Jewish Social Studies* 10, no. 2 (2004): 179–214.

10. Ivan Hannaford, *Race: The History of an Idea in the West* (Baltimore: Johns Hopkins University Press, 1996), 202ff.

11. This tension was not always fully perceived or formulated, but sometimes it was. Hans F. K. Günther, the most popular theoretician of race in Weimar and Nazi Germany, for example, conceded that almost all Germans were *Mischlinge*, "mongrels": "Racial anthropology is in the disagreeable position of having to pronounce the overwhelming majority of Europeans to be of mixed race, to be bastards. This renders it an awkward, disturbing science, making it something discomforting in the manner of that exhortation to 'know thyself.'" Hans F. K. Günther, *Rassenkunde des Deutschen Volkes* (München: J. F. Lehmann, [1922] 1934). Deep in the psyche of the European governing class was the model of the relations between Aryans and Dravidians in India, where the Aryan or Nordic group was threatened by the racially inferior, but numerically superior, teeming dark-skinned masses. Germany, France, Britain, or the United States all faced essentially the same problem, with their mix of superior

and inferior races. This same framework animated the virulent racism of figures like Madison Grant (1865–1937) in the United States. Madison Grant, *The Passing of the Great Race* (New York: Scribner, 1916). Note, however, that explaining social difference through racial disparity of European nations is also found in nineteenth-century democratic historiography.

12. In the case of India, this distinction was summed up as "philology versus ethnology": Friedrich Max Müller, *Biographies of Words and The Home of the Aryas* (London: Longmans, Green, [1887] 1912), 243–51; Herbert Hope Risley, *The People of India* (Calcutta: Thacker, 1908), 6 (and following)

13. Matthew Arnold, *Literature and Dogma: An Essay towards a Better Apprehension of the Bible* (London: Smith, Elder, 1883), 89–90.

14. Heymann Steinthal, "Dialekt, Sprache, Volk, Staat, Rasse," in *Festschrift für Adolf Bastian zu seinem 70: Geburtstag* (Berlin: Dietrich Riemer, 1896), 47–51.

15. Christopher Hutton, "Phonocentrism and the Concept of Volk: The Case of Modern China," in *Ideas of Race in the History of the Humanities*, ed. Amos Morris-Reich and Dirk Rupnow (London: Palgrave Macmillan, 2017), 273–96.

16. On Gypsies in the Nazi era, see Guenther Lewy, *The Nazi Persecution of the Gypsies* (Oxford: Oxford University Press, 2000).

17. Richard Andree, *Zur Volkskunde der Juden* (Bielefeld and Leipzig: Von Velhagen & Klasnig, 1881), 230.

18. See also Samuel Weissenberg, "Die autochthone Bevölkerung Palestinäs in anthropologischer Beziehung," *Zeitschrift für Demographie und Statistik der Juden* 5, no. 9 (1909): 130.

19. Marina Mogliner, *Homo Imperii: A History of Physical Anthropology in Russia* (Lincoln: University of Nebraska Press, 2013).

20. John M. Efron, *Defenders of the Race: Jewish Doctors and Race Science in Fin-de-Siècle Europe* (New Haven: Yale University Press, 1994), 94.

21. Weissenberg, "Die Sudrüssichen Juden," 362.

22. Efron, *Defenders of the Race*, 114–15.

23. Weissenberg, "Die jemenitischen Juden," *Palästina* 7, no. 1 (1910): 321 (translation mine).

24. Weissenberg, "Die kaukasischen Juden."

25. Orit Abuhav, "The Face of Man: On the Contribution of Anthropologists Erich Brauer and Raphael Patai to the Anthropology of Jews," *Jerusalem Studies in Jewish Folklore* 20 (2003): 155–73 [Hebrew].

26. For various reasons physical anthropology and race were not prominent subjects of research and teaching in the 1925 established Hebrew University. Physical anthropology was only introduced to the Hadassah Medial School in the 1950s, when anatomist and physical anthropologist Nico Haas (1927–1988) moved to Israel from Romania and joined the medicine faculty in 1952. The subject of race, however, was studied by Arthur Ruppin, who became a professor in the newly established sociology department in the 1920s. For a brief history of "race" in the early

phase of the Hebrew University see my "Arthur Ruppin's Concept of Race," *Israel Studies* 11, no. 3 (2006): 1–30.

27. Brauer was also marginalized because of his relationship with the renowned scholar of Jewish mysticism Gershom Scholem. Both belonged to the same group of young Berliners from assimilated Jewish backgrounds who were interested in Zionism. The two were close friends and in 1915–16 were members of the "Young Yehuda" movement together. Scholem's advances to Brauer's sister, Greta, were rejected, which complicated their relations when Brauer arrived in Jerusalem, where Scholem was a professor at Hebrew University and Brauer only a temporary affiliated researcher.

28. This study was published in 1925 as *Züge aus der Religion der Herero: Ein Beitrag zur Hamitenfrage.* Institut der Völkerkunde. Erste Reihe: Ethnographie und Ethnologie. (Leipzig: R. Voigtländers Verlag, 1925).

29. For detailed accounts of Brauer's status at Hebrew University, in the fields of Jewish studies, Oriental studies, anthropology, and folklore, see Orit Abuhav, "The Face of Man"; Vered Madar and Dani Schrire, "From Leipzig to Jerusalem: Erich Brauer, a Jewish Ethnographer in Search of a Field," (unpublished manuscript); and Dani Schrire, "From Tribes in Africa to the Communities of the East: Brauer and the 'Return' from Africa to Judaism" (PhD diss., Hebrew University, 2011 [Hebrew]).

30. Erich Brauer, *Ethnologie der Jemenitischen Juden* (Heidelberg: Carl Winters Universitätsbuchhandlung, 1934).

31. Brauer, *Ethnologie der Jemenitischen Juden*, 51–54.

32. Brauer, *Ethnologie der Jemenitischen Juden*, 54.

33. Brauer, *Ethnologie der Jemenitischen Juden*, 55.

34. Brauer, *Ethnologie der Jemenitischen Juden*, 57.

35. Brauer, *Ethnologie der Jemenitischen Juden*, 57. This juncture between racial and national classifications of Yemenite Jews (long-skulled Semites), European Jews (broad-skulled Armenoids), and Arabs (long-skulled Semites) forms various forms of possible relations between national and racial identities. From the context of discussion it is nonetheless clear that what separates Arabs and Jews is their national identity rather than their racial classification. Unlike the German Nordic discourse, furthermore, racial differences are not discussed in hierarchical terms (but it remains an interpretive question whether it is nonetheless implicitly suggested).

36. Arthur Ruppin, *The Sociology of the Jews* (Tel Aviv: Stiebel, 1934), 36 [Hebrew].

37. Ruppin, *The Sociology of the Jews*, 37.

38. Ruppin, *The Sociology of the Jews*, 38.

39. Ruppin, *The Sociology of the Jews*, 40.

40. Ruppin, *The Sociology of the Jews*, 41.

SIX

Classifying Hybridity in Nineteenth- and Early Twentieth-Century Russian Imperial Anthropology

MARINA MOGILNER

The late Professor Rudolf Virchow was right in saying that for western European anthropologists Russia represents a country to which one can apply the words "*ex oriente lux*," because it is exactly here, in Russia, where one finds the keys to the whole range of questions raised by contemporary anthropology.[1]

Narrating Race in the Imperial Context

Over the past decade we have witnessed a sea change in the international history of human sciences in Russia. It is now common knowledge that Russian imperial and Soviet social thought and cultural imagination were permeated with a racialized idiom. As the growing body of new research shows, Russian intellectuals engaged with the concept of race quite early on, at least since the 1830s, when they joined the international discourse on racial specificities. They read European studies of race in original languages, promptly translating works on the subject by the most prominent Western scholars: George Louis de Buffon and Johann Friedrich Blumenbach, Ernest Renan and Gustave Le Bon, Georges Vacher de Lapouge and Rudolf Virchow. Moreover, in the mid-nineteenth century, racialized imagery began spreading from Russian natural sciences to the sphere of the humanities and popular discourse. The Russian imperial government was never a coordinated entity, with a shared political worldview and cultural horizon—at least, it never officially embraced "race" as a legitimate ideological category of difference—which did not preclude individual state agencies from advancing policies and practices explicitly based on the idea of the reality of biological groupness. The early Soviet regime was much more open to experimenting with scientific approaches and modern social engineering. It explicitly, though inconsistently, absorbed the language of biological determinism, while simultaneously undermining it with radical constructivist sociopolitical visions.[2]

By exploring these complex dynamics of extensive imperial and Soviet engagements with race, the latest scholarship opens up a new perspective on Russian and Soviet history and on the transnational phenomenon of "imperial modernity" in general. Beyond a superficial paradox (how can an archaic empire be discussed in terms of its modernity?), there is a challenging research problem of how the classical Foucauldian power-knowledge paradigm functions in the imperial situation. From the vantage point of new imperial history, neither size, expansionist foreign policy, nor authoritarian regime can be seen as a meaningful distinction between a nation-state (such as the Fifth Republic, as the context for all generalizations of Foucault) and an imperial situation. The chief contrast between the two is in their approach to the rationalization of differences. The nation-centered society is structured by social hierarchies and categories of difference based on a single criterion that is identically understood and universally present in all social and spatial loci of the community. For example, ethnicity is not to be confused with an economic status or political orientation, and it is similarly understood everywhere. In this regard, empire is relevant not as a polity, but as a context-setting category: it embraces only partially congruent and mutually "translatable" sociocultural spaces and hierarchies and acts as a "switchman" between different contexts that change the meaning and mode of one's performance and even identity.[3] Depending on the context, "a Pole" can mean ethnicity, gentry status, religion, political views, or regional identity. In the imperial situation, modernity is complicated not by presumably archaic imperial institutions, but by the very multidimensional sphere that distorts the clear Foucauldian (nation-centered) power-knowledge nexus. Multidimensional imperial situations perpetuate hybridity: not necessarily in the sense famously defined by Homi Bhabha, as occurring exclusively within the colonial discourse, but in a more profane sense of producing hybrid—that is complex, hierarchical, relational and situational—identities (see the example with a Pole above). Hybrid identities defined social dynamics in a contiguous heterogeneous Russian empire with blurred boundaries between the metropole and peripheries. In this polity peoples identified themselves and were identified by the state through overlapping classificatory grids that included confession, legal estate, language, region, economic status, and loyalty to the regime—but never explicitly their nationality or race.

The imperial situation in general creates structural preconditions for hybrid performance of modern discourses: however advanced and scientifically sound, by circulating throughout the multidimensional "imperial" sphere of context-sensitive meaning, they produce unexpected consequences. Instead of replacing old unsystematic regimes of human diversity with "regular," rationally organized, and classified population structures, they end up reproducing the original multilayered diversity on a new level of complexity. As a result, both old and modern empires have to operate through regimes of case-specific exclusions rather than through the logic of positively defined and universally applicable rules.[4] The Russian empire, for example, never exercised a unified "nationality policy" toward its different collective subjects. Instead, it dealt with each of them separately, as the so-called national—Jewish, Muslim, etc.—questions, granting exclusive rights and privileges or exclusively denying thereof.

Another important feature of the Russian imperial situation was the dissociation between the centers of political and discursive (knowledge) authority. In this chapter I consider one characteristic case: while in general the imperial regime in St. Petersburg preferred to rely on traditional administrative patterns and not to engage modern knowledge in a systematic way, some state agencies and intellectuals in different regions of the empire developed race science and advanced scientifically sound programs of social engineering. As this case shows, centers of modern knowledge production in the empire did not necessarily condition and reinforce political authority and discursive control, generating instead a more complex political and scholarly dynamics.

The complexity of relationships between knowledge and power revealed itself in how the Russian Empire responded to the challenge of rising nationalism. On the one hand, it suppressed non-Russian national movements and preserved a particularistic imperial approach to its multiple internal regions, peripheries, and subjects. On the other hand, since the late nineteenth century the imperial regime had been engaged in active self-nationalizing as a Russian national power, exhibiting the turn from more inclusive ideologies of "confessional state" or of imperial nation loyal to the dynasty toward a much more exclusive and "scientific" model of the ethnic Russian nation.[5] The imperative of developing systematic, objective, and rational knowledge about the population was a sine qua non for participation in modernity and hence was central to all of the imperial actors, regardless of their political goals.

In the postimperial world of today, the story of "national races" in the Russian Empire can be deconstructed in a postcolonial mode, through a genealogy of postimperial nationalisms and national sciences embedded in their respective imperial situations. However, in this chapter I want to reconstruct a properly imperial case of race science and racial classification that reflected the multidimensional quality of the Russian imperial situation at the turn of the twentieth century. I do not claim that this was a uniquely Russian approach to race and racial classification that would fit the niche reserved in this collection for specific national cases. My task is rather different—to explore the role of the Russian empire as a political and epistemological context for a universal endeavor of modern knowledge production.

Russian race science emerged in the mid-nineteenth century as a field, consciously developed in opposition to ethnography as a "humanist" and subjective discipline.[6] No nationalism or antinationalism played a role in this process. Its founders, natural scientists, embraced evolutionism as a general epistemic framework and Western modernity as a social ideal. They participated in the discourse of race as a master key that unlocked nearly all social, cultural, and political phenomena.[7] For them, the very ability to conceptualize social reality in the language of race and produce a map of subjects and objects of race analysis made Russia a European country and a European empire. Benefiting from the diversity of the Russian empire as a field, Russian race scientists and amateur scholars (physicians, schoolteachers, and other members of the general public interested in race) could participate with equal success in explicitly colonial anthropological studies and in anthropology directed at European populations. Eventually they developed schools of study and research networks that can be identified as colonial or nationalist and, as such, find direct analogues in Western academic and political contexts.[8] Yet, overall, the European science of race as seen from Russia was not racist, and colonial anthropology was not viewed as dominating the scene (probably in part because Russia itself bordered on the verge of European Otherness). Anthropology was rather understood as a universal and supranational language of modernity, a means of scientifically comprehending the laws of human progress and the success of civilization—something that the old humanist and particularistic paradigm of European culture, centered on self-referential textual traditions, was not able to do.[9] As such, the language of race science was also uniquely suitable for representing hybridity as a fundamental human condition in the empire and the basis of a future better humanity.

In what follows, I reconstruct a classificatory discourse that reflected this fundamental "Russian," turn-of-the-century dilemma of universal modernity and imperial hybridity.

The Moscow School of Race Science: Narrating Imperial Modernity

This dilemma informed in particular the so-called Moscow school of physical anthropology—the leading and largest subgroup of Russian anthropologists. It existed as an empire-wide network of scientists and professionals coordinated by the Anthropological Division of the Imperial Moscow University's Society of the Lovers of Natural Sciences, Anthropology, and Ethnography (IOLEAE). The Moscow University chair in anthropology (set up in 1879) and the Moscow University Anthropological Museum were two other important institutional knots in the network.[10] The Moscow school kept a safe distance from the imperial state and this estrangement was mutual. The lack of interest on behalf of the political authorities in the Moscow network's activities only reinforced the missionary zeal of its members. Their self-proclaimed mission was clearly to modernize Russian society and enhance the role of scientific experts; only their version of modernity was a distinctively imperial one. The school successfully tamed the various nationalizing anthropological projects of its members and, equally successfully, derailed attempts to impose "classical" colonial hierarchies of power-knowledge in the empire. The methodology promoted by the Moscow school differentiated between race and culture, advanced the concept of the "mixed physical type," studied "ethnically Russian" and non-Russian population groups, integrated scholars regardless of their ethnoconfessional background (including Jews), and offered a broad and inclusive liberal, epistemological, and ideological framework for their projects.

Moscow liberal anthropology was a science of modern imperialism that—curiously enough—rejected colonialism and experimented with integrationist scientific and (by extension) political and social models. In this regard, it was representative of the larger liberal trend in race science that celebrated diversity within the established political borders of a country, relegating the function of the scientific managing of this diversity to a modern state or, in the Russian case, to a self-organizing community of experts dissatisfied with the existing political regime.[11] Professor Dmitrii Nikolaevich Anuchin, the leader of the Moscow school and the first holder of the Moscow university chair in anthropology, modeled himself and his school after the leading ninteenth-century German physical anthropologist Professor Rudolf Virchow and his liberal race science—regardless of the fact that the principal context of Virchow's anthropological work was not German imperialism but German national unification.[12] The problem of the complex composition of the German people, and their complex racial origin, cultural background, and state loyalties, inspired many of his anthropological projects, which resulted in a picture of racial intermixture of the European population beginning from prehistoric times. Anuchin and other members of the Moscow school wholeheartedly shared this vision. For them, the difference between the German *nationalizing* and Russian *imperial* contexts was not a problem, as both contexts "naturally" implied a focus on interracial interaction and "mixed physical types" and did not provide grounds for constructing racial hierarchies. Anuchin interpreted the programmatic task of Virchow's anthropology as "the study of the type of the German people, or, to be more precise, determining those different types that participated in its formation and, after having mixed over the course of many centuries, produced the contemporary diversity of its physical traits."[13]

This research program could have been unproblematically transferred from Germany to Russia, reconciling imperial and national contexts and agendas. Only after the epoch of Virchow in German race science ended (roughly after 1902), a gradual replacement began "of the previous humanitarian ethics by a biological and selectionist materialism more concerned with the inequalities of evolution than the universal brotherhood or spiritual unity of humankind."[14] This replacement has been accomplished by pupils and younger colleagues of Virchow, who, in a way, preceded the reorientation of Anuchin's students under the early Soviet regime from a liberal anthropology of imperial diversity to a biological materialist anthropology inspired by the new visions of societal progress. Therefore, the classificatory discourse developed by the Moscow school had no direct continuation after the end of the Russian Empire and remained an imperial phenomenon in more than one sense.

This classificatory discourse was hybrid in every possible aspect. Methodologically, it combined a philosophy of accumulation of a totality of "objective" measurements and their mathematically precise comparison and organization with the acceptance of existing historical (arbitrary) borders of the Russian Empire as a natural field for anthropological research, and of imperial population diversity as a value in and of itself. Different human species, racial types, and ethnic groups coexisted as elementary units of classification in this discourse, contributing to its internal inconsistency. The results of comparison and classification produced no pure racial types (one noticeable exception being the Jewish type), thus establishing hybridity and racial miscegenation as the dominant pattern of "natural history" of humankind and of Russian imperial humanity in particular.[15]

As with any other anthropological classification, the classification considered in this chapter was an embodiment of "real science" deliberately expressed in a nonnarrative language of anthropometric statistics. At the same time, it was, of course, a narrative of sorts, for any classification requires a structuring logic that produces meaning. Such a structuring narrative could be formulated within the discipline itself, as was the case with the "natural history of humanity" discourse. It could also be borrowed from another scientific field—for example, the general Darwinian narrative of evolution. Riccardo Nicolosi refers to Darwin's theory as a mode of representation equally observable in nineteenth-century Russian literature and Russian science (arguing along the way that in other "national cases" this parallelism is represented much more vividly).[16] According to Nicolosi, in both domains "Darwin's plot" and rhetoric constitute indispensable elements of argumentation.[17] Developing this logic further, one can identify other "master plots" that participated in structuring anthropometric statistics as a narrative while informing nonscientific discourses. Most of them were appropriated from the fields of ideology and politics. Examples include unique racial genealogies of particular national collectives, or naturalization of differences between peoples or genders,[18] or a justification of European superiority ("all the marvelous discoveries, all the wonders of science and art have been achieved by races who shave," wrote the Russian orientologist of the pre-Darwinian generation Osip Senkovskii, referring to Peter the Great's civilizational choice for Russia).[19]

The role of such metanarratives became more significant when scholars had trouble reaching even a basic consensus regarding the definition of race as their central category of analysis. Different authors of the period defined race through physical but also hereditary moral, intellectual, and cultural attributes. In addition, as a poorly institutionalized and seminormal (in Kuhn's sense) discipline, physical anthropology could not effectively secure hegemonic control over interpretations of race in powerful national and civilizational-colonial political narratives, or in popular discourse. Even if disjoined in the imperial situation, politics participated in the production of modern scientific discourse, and science affected politics. The context-setting role of empire revealed itself through the hybridization of grand narratives, where a typical "antifeudal" critique of dynastic regimes could be infused with radical democratic social visions, nationalism would be amalgamated with socialism, and liberal doctrines of universal political participation would not contradict the acceptance of civilizational differences. The case of race classification analyzed in this chapter explicates the nonlinear relationships between scientific and political interpretations of race in the Russian imperial situation and raises a larger question about modern science's ability to represent the idea of hybridity beyond the constraints of colonial metanarratives of assimilation or contamination.

By the late eighteenth century, all major racial classifications produced in Europe and the United States were becoming factors of Russian intellectual and political debates. Johann Friedrich Blumenbach's 1791 edition of *Handbuch der Naturgeschichte* appeared in Russian translation in 1797.[20] Following Buffon, Blumenbach famously claimed to have established the existence of four (and eventually five) human races: Caucasian, Mongolian, Ethiopian, American, and Malaysian. This scheme served as the basis for further classifications advanced by Russian scholars who, like their Western colleagues, were concerned with the agglomeration of objective anthropometric statistics and with developing scientific explanations of differences and similarities among the human genus. They were, however, equally concerned with securing a place for Slavs among the Caucasians, with making sense of Russianness and the diversity of the imperial population, and with proving Russia's European identity. Both pre-Darwinian and Darwinian anthropology of the nineteenth century developed classificatory discourses and, as Karl Hall writes, "already by mid-century anthropology was acknowledged—in philosophical principle if not in ethnographic practice—as a separate branch of the natural sciences charged with 'classification of the various human tribes.'"[21]

In his pioneering craniometrical studies of skulls of different peoples of the empire (1860s), Professor Anatolii Petrovich Bogdanov, the founding figure of the Moscow school of physical anthropology, followed Paul Broca's classification method based on the form of crania.[22] When in 1899 his successor, Dmitrii Anuchin, wrote an article on race for the major encyclopedic project (Brockhaus and Efron, *Encyclopedic Dictionary*, vol. 26), summarizing the "natural history of humanity" as it had been understood up to that time, he structured his survey as a history of classifications. Anuchin began with Karl Linney and continued with Buffon, Blumenbach, Gottfried Leibniz, Immanuel Kant, Georg Forster, Georges Cuvier, Marie Jean Pierre Flourens, James Cowles Prichard, Thomas Henry Huxley, Anders Retzius, Jean Louis Armand de Quatrefages, Theodor Waitz, Georg Gerland, Ernst Heinrich Haeckel, and Paul Topinard—to name just a few.[23] This classificatory tradition represented not some outdated archive, but operational knowledge that enabled the science of physical anthropology to normalize itself. Anuchin's personal preferences, except for sustained evolutionism and monogenism, were rather eclectic. Thus, he adopted Topinard's 1876 classification, based on the form of nose, hair, and skin color, when he set about the task of composing a racial genealogy of the greatest Russian poet and exemplary Russian, Alexander Pushkin.[24] Anuchin carefully examined all portraits, drawings, and busts for which Pushkin had served as a live model, focusing on presentations of skin color and facial features. And, most important, he studied Pushkin's death mask and an original sample of his hair. The Moscow professor then posited the Abyssinian theory of Pushkin's compromising "blackness," for, unlike African (Negro) blackness,[25] Abyssinian blackness (the Hamitic race) could be classified as belonging to the European racial family.[26] On other occasions, however, Anuchin endorsed Joseph Deniker's 1899 classification of European races or worked with the classification of races in the Russian Empire developed by his junior colleague, Aleksei Ivanovskii—the classifications that most concern us in this chapter. The "Instruction" for Moscow University's doctoral candidates in physical anthropology, composed by Anuchin sometime before 1916 and embracing the newest titles such as the first edition of Rudolf Martin's *Lehrbuch der Anthropologie* (1914), still included all of the above as relevant references. In addition, it "strongly recommended" that students master French, German, and English so as to read standard foreign works "fluently." The seminal work of one of the most prominent and most "Russian" of the Western classifiers on Anuchin's list, *Les Races et Les Peuples* by Joseph Deniker, featured in the "Instruction" in French: "We do have a Russian translation—Anuchin explained—but it is not completely satisfactory."[27]

The French Scholar Joseph Deniker as a Russian Classifier

The years 1899 and 1900, when the twenty-sixth volume of Brockhaus and Efron's *Encyclopedia* containing Anuchin's article on "Race" came out, marked a prominent moment in the history of anthropological classifications. One after another, the two major classifications that set the tone of international debates for many years to come appeared in print: "The Races of Man" by the French scholar Joseph Deniker and "The Races of Europe" by the American scholar William Z. Ripley. It was Deniker's classification from his earlier French publications that occupied the most space in Anuchin's encyclopedic article "Races": almost 25 percent of the text, a whole page listing the characteristics of thirty races (of which thirteen were identified as "main races" and the rest as "subtypes").[28]

The English translation of "The Races of Man" became available in 1900; the Russian translation, which Anuchin did not consider satisfactory, was ready just one year later and published in 1902.[29] The book contained 172 illustrations, a few tables, and two maps, but for the most part it was a textual narrative about the difference between the "sociological" (ethnographic) characteristics of humans and "racial" groups as "somatological units" (and their descriptions). This was a narrative of the progression of science from a descriptive stage to a highly self-reflective stage at which the objective classification of thirty races and subraces arranged into six major "somatological units" became possible. Besides this all-embracing classification system, there was another reason why Deniker's magisterial study became archetypal for Russian physical anthropology. Despite his reliance on statistics of measurements, Deniker did not completely rule out the role of social factors in the formation of human diversity. Some passages in his book seemed to endorse biological reductionism, whereas others suggested that the future of anthropology was in the study of culture.

The dualism of Deniker's classification reflected the fundamental epistemological problem of that time: how to reconcile the individual and unique nature of objects sampled for research with the universal and generalized character of conclusions drawn from the study of these objects. Central to all fields of modern knowledge, this was a debate between the positivist search for general causal explanations and the historicist quest for a hermeneutic understanding of specific individuals and historical moments. In 1894 Wilhelm Windelband famously conceptualized this debate by juxtaposing "nomothetic" (generalizing) to "idiographic" (individualizing and descriptive) sciences as the foundation for the differentiation between natural sciences and the humanities.[30] As Windelband explained later, race science's aspiration to present human history as a general "natural history of humanity" was methodologically unsubstantiated, because human development could be understood only as unique combinations of elements—that is, only in the idiographic mode—whereas "the question of the natural and genetic unity of the human race is irrelevant in history."[31] Windelband specifically denied the possibility of identifying some elemental "general units" such as races or types, insofar as "it is only in lower races without any history that we may find a unity or purity of race."[32] His no-less-famous student and disciple Heinrich Rickert—who was widely read in Russia as a leading Neo-Kantian philosopher, especially in the period between the two revolutions (of 1905 and 1917)—better explained this point with the metaphor of the "in-dividual" (both unique and indivisible) nature of the object of study in natural and social sciences alike. Rickert reconsidered the opposition proposed by Windelband, suggesting that the distinction between nomothetic and idiographic knowledge does not actually correspond to the distinction between natural and social sciences, but only to the two possible analytical strategies applicable to any scholarly inquiry. In both intellectual fields, Rickert claimed, the focus on the unique or general qualities of an object depends on the scholar's personal decision, so neither of the explanatory strategies (or the reality itself) can be value-free: "This is why we must explicitly stress that the world of unified individuals—quite like reality as an object of aesthetic perception or as an object of general concepts—is *only* a specific *conception.* As a third conception, we differentiate it in principle from the natural scientific and aesthetic conception."[33]

Deniker is often credited with proposing the first scientific classification of human races based exclusively on somatic characteristics, but it seems more logical to suggest that, rather than mistakenly "contaminating" his "hardcore science" methodology with relics of more archaic culture-centered theories and geographical neologisms such as Nordic, Alpine, and Dinaric, Deniker in his classification consciously followed Rickert's redefinition of the proverbial opposition between "general" and "particular," and therefore included explicitly "idiographic" elements in the scheme that by definition was expected to be purely "nomothetic." This synthetic quality of Deniker's classification; his explicit problematization of the unit of scientific analysis between ethnography and anthropology; his simultaneous insistence on clarifying a scientifically precise meaning of categories such as "people," "nation," "tribe," "race," and "species";[34] his denial of a uniform "Slavic racial type" in favor of a concept of Slavic peoples as an interblending of "three principal and three secondary races"; and his general conclusion that no geographically isolated group and no pure race existed and that there were always transitional types reproduced and reinforced major debates between Russian race science as a universalizing paradigm and Russian ethnography as a nationalizing cultural discourse.[35] Deniker's axiom that ethnic,national and linguistic groups did not coincide with races (somatic units) was popularized by Anuchin on behalf of the school of liberal anthropology in his standard encyclopedic article, which so extensively cited Deniker's classification of races: "Race characteristics do not coincide with tribal or national (language, religion, customs, belonging to a particular state); representatives of different racial types can exist among the same people, whereas representatives of the same race can be found in different tribes and peoples. Racial types are more or less abstract concepts of characteristics, and live representatives of these types correspond to them only partially."[36]

Technically, Ripley enjoyed the same academic authority among Russian anthropologists as Deniker, and advanced an equally scientific, rather than a political, narrative of race. Although well-known to Russian scholars, the works by this American sociologist and race classifier were never translated into Russian and never enjoyed the same popularity as Deniker's. Perhaps his less nuanced and more schematic approach to races did not accommodate the above-mentioned imperial specificity of Russia and the newest methodological concerns of scholars.[37] Deniker himself criticized Ripley for neglecting Eastern European material (although he included in "The Races of Europe" Anuchin's maps of height distribution in Russia), whereas Ripley, among other criticisms, called Deniker's races "*existent* types" because they combined true racial hereditary factors with idiographic ephemeral and momentary features.[38]

Probably, Joseph Deniker was more popular in Russia also because he was perceived as a "half-Russian" (see note 40). Indeed, he was born in 1852 in the southern Russian town of Astrakhan, one of Russia's many ethnically mixed regions, and received his degree in engineering from the St. Petersburg Technological Institute. In Russia he was often intimately introduced by his Russian name and patronymic, Iosif or Osip Egorovich. The naturalized French "Osip Egorovich" corresponded with his Russian colleagues in Russian, followed Russian-language academic publications in his field, and even received some of them directly from Anatolii Bogdanov, the founder of the Moscow Society of Lovers of Natural Sciences, Anthropology, and Ethnography. Deniker admired Bogdanov as a scholar, and also for "keeping the memory [of Deniker] alive in Russia."[39] He was very happy to find out from Bogdanov that his portrait and a short biography were to be included in the collection of biographies of Russian zoologists and welcomed with great satisfaction the chance to be "added to your biographies as a half-Russian."[40]

In Russia, however, Deniker's portrait and biography was not only found in articles on race classifications or listings of famous natural scientists. Osip–Iosif Deniker was known outside of academic circles as a participant in the revolutionary Populist movement of the 1870s, and as someone who maintained connections with the Russian political emigration in France. Deniker's own recollections of his Russian student youth, presumably written in the late 1880s while he was working on the classification of races, were published in Russia or, rather, in the Soviet Union, posthumously, in a 1924 issue of a special journal dedicated to the history of the revolutionary movement, *Hard Labor and Exile* (*Katorga i ssylka*). Many of those who knew Deniker in the 1870s were still around at the time. The editorial introduction presented "Iosif Egorovich" as a typical member of the Russian intelligentsia with a classic intelligentsia biography:

> Deniker's interest in public activism manifested itself already during his school years. After his arrival in Petersburg, he became a full-fledged and active member of the original small world of radical students. Gatherings, collecting data about the people, self-development circles, publication of books, studies with workers—all these were present in I. E. Deniker's life, and he paid his dues to all. A bit later, in 1874, when charges were pressed against him for propaganda among the people, Deniker was subjected to a police search and questioning—however, by that time he had fled for Europe.[41]

Deniker's memoirs suggest a possible genealogy for his interest in ethnography and anthropology in Russian populism, with its idealization of *narod*—the simple folk, the people. Deniker recalled in particular how impressed he was with the program for the systematic collection of data about the people, distributed by populist propagandists to students before they returned to their provincial hometowns and family estates for summer vacations: "There were questions about salaries in factories and in different crafts, and so on, and about peasants' land allotments, and about their type of landownership, about dues and taxes, and so on, about peasants' attitude toward religion, the tsar, the authorities, and the *kulaks*. . . . I would like to add that many questions pertained to local ethnographic and social conditions."[42]

A son of French natives naturalized in Russia, Deniker had to disguise himself as a native Russian and a worker (but wearing glasses) to win the peasants' trust and actually get these "subalterns" to speak out.[43] This was the situation that he perceived and described in complex terms, as at once cultural, sociological, political, regional, and biological, and with the implicit Rickertian idea of "value" that enabled the generalization of all the different individual peasants and workers whom he met on a riverboat floating to his native Astrakhan as a single *narod*—the people with a unique destiny and soul. Deniker interpreted their uniqueness and wholeness, however, with the help of general scientific categories (economic, social, and ethnographic). As Rickert would formulate later, "It is important to show only that our principle is truly *general*, and therefore that by its means any reality at all—regardless of whether it is physical or psychic—can be analyzed as individuals in the strict sense and the more comprehensive sense."[44]

The Races of Russia

The Moscow professor Aleksei Arsen'evich Ivanovskii (1866–1934) in many ways followed in Deniker's footsteps when he set out to develop an original methodology for the classification of Russian racial types and then attempted to apply his method to classify the peoples of the world. His endeavor signified a new height achieved by Russian physical anthropology by the turn of the twentieth century. Not only was Ivanovskii's approach to perceiving social reality as a multidimensional phenomenon influenced by his observation of the Russian imperial situation (like Deniker's), but he used it as an archetypal case, relying on accumulated data from all over the Russian Empire to produce a general model of global human diversity; he constructed his own version of Deniker's "The Races of Man" exclusively from within the Russian imperial situation.

Ivanovskii was the editor of the *Russian Anthropological Journal*

(*Russkii antropologicheskii zhurnal*)–the mouthpiece of the Moscow school of liberal anthropology. In addition he worked as an assistant at the Moscow University Anthropological Museum and as the secretary of the IOLEAE anthropological division, which literally placed him at the very center of this broad network of specialists and amateur scholars.[45] Together they understood the specificity of the Russian Empire as a place of exceptional diversity (rather than as an epitome of international prestige or domestic grandeur), where, in the words of Dmitry Anuchin, "from Poland on the west to the Amur region and Kamchatka on the east, and from the southern peoples of the Transcaucasia, Central Asia, and bordering Chinese territories to the Lapps, Samoyeds, Tungus, and Chukchi, whose fate brought them to the far north—within these broad limits one physical type gives way to another."[46]

The trope of unique Russian imperial diversity permeates the publications of members of this network. Ivanovskii reproduced it in his dissertation, proudly declaring that "the ethnic composition of Russia's population is characterized by such a degree of diversity—of physical types and cultural stages—that cannot be found in any Western European state."[47] Such a peculiar reason for "imperial pride" produced an unusual formulation of the "white man's burden." According to Ivanovskii, the greatest responsibility of those facing imperial diversity was neither imperialist nor philanthropic, but taxonomic, "to disassemble this composition into its structural elements, to distinguish between the principal and secondary ones, to register features of resemblance and difference among them, and to establish the level of their kinship and interaction."[48] Thus the ultimate goal of exploring actual human diversity was to produce its most accurate map—at once comprehensive and nonreductionist (nomothetic and idiographic), leaving no "tribe that would not be touched by anthropometric compass and tape."[49] It is important to stress that this great modernist scientific utopia itself was modeled as a virtual "empire of knowledge" rather than as a "monological" scheme based on a single criterion of classification. In the enthusiastic formulation of this utopia by Dmitry Anuchin, one can easily identify the "Foucauldian" drive to put the entire society under the supervision of experts, but there is no indication that local forms and "deviations" were seen as subject to any rationalization and normalization in the future, in accordance with any normative scenario: "Just imagine that everywhere in Russia, in different big and small centers, observer-anthropologists are dispersed. They collect data on the variations of types in each district according to a certain system and using certain methods—data on the distribution within the local population of skin color, hair and eye color, height and body proportions, head and facial forms, morphological deviations, physiological, and pathological peculiarities."[50]

Alexei Ivanovskii's contribution to this modernist utopia is hard to overestimate. As the secretary of the anthropological division, he coordinated and assisted hundreds of "observer-anthropologists," while, as a scholar and classifier, he aggregated under one cover all the data they had accumulated in "big and small centers" of the Russian Empire. Ivanovskii was a "synthesizer" who endeavored to establish imperial hybridity as a general concept (a structuring narrative) that would scientifically objectify the elusive imperial reality. In the language of Neo-Kantian epistemology, this meant combining idiographic descriptions of individual cases into a broader nomothetic structure without their synthesis or "sublation" (*Aufhebung*). It was understood that the whole is not the sum of its parts, nor even their equivalent, but a different plane of perception of the same reality. Ivanovskii saw his generalization as an act of interpretation that allowed "bringing life into the numbers that resulted from measurements, which by themselves were dead."[51]

Like Deniker, Ivanovskii combined the concepts with different analytical statuses: abstract somatic types (elements of nomothetic systematization) with individually established categories of ethnographic difference (products of idiographic description). However, unlike Deniker, he never implied that the elements of his classification were held together by anything more than their relation to a certain "value" proposed by a researcher (in line with Rickert's approach). Ivanovskii compared and systematized not variations of essentially analogous phenomena (e.g., differing races) but relationships between variously defined human groups: some were equally "more close" and others were similar in their degree of relative otherness to each other. His classification relativized the boundaries between collectives and focused on their contacts and interaction, scientifically representing miscegenation as the process that produced racial differences and similarities. As a result, instead of a rigid structure, he proposed a map of dynamic relationships—most accurately representing the empire within which "one physical type gives way to another."

The very point of departure for systematization (by definition, an act of grouping together elements with common traits) was unusual: Ivanovskii introduced as the basic category the notion of the "unit of difference." Equal units of difference calculated on the basis of several criteria indicated the "physical similarity" of respective groups—but it did not imply their common genealogy or direct relationships. The common social sphere described by his classification was united by systematic differences and thus recognized them as the fundamental characteristics of human collectives.

This is how a classification based on this initial epistemological ("value-related") decision looked in practice. Ivanovskii collected as many cases and measurements as possible and selected those physical indicators that featured more frequently in the studies of Russian anthropologists (otherwise poorly compatible in their scope and research design). His classification was based on the following indicators: hair and eye colors, height, cephalic index, height-longitudinal skull index, facial index (a ratio of the maximum width of the face to its length), nasal index (a ratio of the maximum nasal width to nasal length), body length, chest circumference, length of arms, and length of legs. As can be seen, Ivanovskii's selection combined descriptive indicators, such as color of hair and eyes, with precise measurements—however, these kinds of compromises were common to many classifications of the time, including those of Deniker or Virchow. Both served as sources of inspiration for Ivanovskii. Virchow in particular built his classification of the German racial types on the color indicators assembled during the national anthropological survey of German schoolchildren that he supervised in the 1870s. He identified two "pure" types—blonds (*der blonde*

Typus) and brunets (*der brünette Typus*), whereas all their combinations were to be classified only as mixed.[52] Ivanovskii also singled out the light-colored group whose representatives had fair hair (up to light red) and a light-colored iris (gray, blue, light brown, and light green). The second was the dark group with dark hair and dark eye tones. All other variations and combinations belonged to the mixed group. This typology was directly influenced by Virchow, but in general Ivanovskii's borrowings from Virchow or Deniker were never consistent, because neither of the existing classifications satisfied the task of establishing hybridity as a general scientific concept. Thus, deviating from Virchow and Deniker, Ivanovskii did not include skin color in his classification. Most probably he simply lacked data regarding this indicator among different peoples of Russia, but in general his method depended not on any particular indicators, but on their combinations.

Ivanovskii assigned each indicator a letter symbol, for example: A—light type, B—mixed type, and C—dark type. This basic code was developed further to designate smaller subgroups: a—"real blonds," a1—"blonds of the light type," b1—"sharply mixed type," and so on. Using these symbols, Ivanovskii coded each population group measured in the Russian Empire and thus made it possible to compare them. Identical letters indicated similarities of the racial makeup. If in relation to the same racial indicator one group belonged to type A and another to type B, they differed from each other by one unit of difference. If these were A and C, the unit of difference equaled two. On the level of subdivisions coded with small letters, the unit of difference had to be divided by the number of subdivisions (if there were two subdivisions, the unit of difference equaled one-half). Using this mathematically "precise" scheme, Ivanovskii calculated units of difference among all peoples of the Russian Empire but then classified them according to three degrees of "physical similarity." The highest degree of similarity had a ratio of differences between the indicators of less than one; the second degree was less than two; and the third was no more than three. Ivanovskii's classificatory narrative told the story of interconnectedness through variative differences and relative intermixture. This was the story of hybridity conceptualized as a phenomenon in its own right, and, moreover, as a fundamental condition transcending isolationism of individual groups but at the same time not necessarily leading to their eventual amalgamation—neither a salad bar, nor a melting pot.

To avoid building in any implicit teleological scheme, the narration of this imperial hybridity was organized simply in alphabetical order, starting with Afghanis and followed by Aisors, Armenians, Bashkirs, Buriats, Belarusians, Great Russians, and on down to Yakuts. But even the adaption of alphabetic order did not organize Ivanovskii's text into a linear narration. The neat structure of this ABCs of imperial diversity was constantly interrupted by parallel entries for each category. For example, instead of a single comprehensive article for Buriats there were several alternative sets of measurements: "Buriats [Tal'ko-Hrinstevich]"; "Buriats [Portnov]"; "Buriats—integrated indicators" (because each set was produced by different anthropologists). The same pluralism could result from measurements taken in different localities: "Great Russians of Tver province"; "Great Russians of Kursk province"; "Great Russians of Tula province"; "Great Russians of Erevan province"; and "Great Russians—integrated." Some entries implied hundreds of measurements, and others no more than ten; however, Ivanovskii did not evaluate their relative weight. His imperial model was a realization of the totalizing anthropological utopia, and it was apparently so impressive as such that the journal *American Anthropologist* (AA) chose to reproduce the whole list of peoples included in Ivanovskii's study as a meaningful statement by itself. The list amounted to two pages in small print and was published without additional explanations, as a silent image of systematized imperial diversity.[53]

Unlike the list in *AA*, Ivanovskii's actual narrative was multilayered. For example, this is how he classified (or should we say hybridized?) Tatars (roman numbers indicate degree of physical similarity; names in brackets refer to those who took particular measurements; ethnicities in italics signify integrated type as opposed to regionalized types of the same ethnic group

KAZAN TATARS

II. Belarusians of Minsk province (Rozhdestvenskii), *Belarusians*, Poles of the Lublin province, *Poles*

III. Bashkirs (Nazarov), *Bashkirs*, Belarusians of Smolensk province (Eikhgolttz), Great Russians of Tver, Kursk, Tula and Erivan provinces, *Great Russians, Astrakhan Kalmyks, Kalmyks, Little Russians*

KASIMOV TATARS

III. *Great Russians*

CRIMEAN TATARS

III. Armenians (Ivanovskii)

AZERBAIJAN TATARS (DANILOV)

II. *Azerbaijan Tatars*

III. *Persians*

AZERBAIJAN TATARS

II. *Kurds*, Azerbaijan Tatars (Danilov)

III. Kurds (Ivanovskii), *Kurds of Transcaucasia*, Kurds of Persia, *Persians*

ALTAI TATARS

Stands alone[54]

Unlike Tatars, Poles, Samoyeds, Latvians, Lithuanians, and everyone else, from A to Z, "Russians" (without predicates, such as "Great," "Little," "White," or "of a given district") were demonstratively absent from this classification. Ivanovskii did not think that this political concept could be validated as a physical type by the available anthropometric statistics. Moreover, his Slavic group (to which different "Russians" belonged), not unlike Deniker's Slavs, was not a single "somatic type" either. Ivanovskii's "Slavonic anthropological group" included Great Russians, Little Russians (Ukrainians), Belarusians, Poles, and Lithuanians as well as Kazan Tatars, Bashkirs, and Kalmyks, yet excluded Little Russians of Kyiv province and the Kuban Cossacks. To complicate matters even more, those Little Russians, Great Russians, and Belarusians who composed the backbone of the group were themselves characterized by an extremely broad "scope of fluctuation of anthropological traits."[55] As a result of this scientific principle of grouping, a key concept of the imperial social and juridical order, the *inorodets*—the alien, literally "born to a different kin"—lost its function of legally demarcating the Other and hence any sense: If Tatars belonged to the Slavonic racial group, how could they be viewed as *inorodtsy*? Whatever Ivanovskii's primary motivation, the absence of the Russians and Slavs as single types and their representation as an array of regional composite groups related to various non-Russians profoundly undermined imperial hierarchies of power.

As a thoroughly "nomothetic" enterprise based on a more or less statistically valid agglomeration of instrumental "idiographic" measurements, this classification undermined the very idea of objective racial borders. With a few exceptions, Ivanovskii's classification found no peoples (*narodnosti*) that would not be similar to one another in some respect:

> The question arises as to which peoples can be considered so anthropologically homogeneous that they could make up one anthropological group. To answer this question, one needs to establish the location of a border that at some point breaks the chain of transitional forms, thus separating one anthropological group from another. It is easy to a priori predict that this border is not going to resemble a clearly visible and deep furrow. One rather has to expect that this border will be so smoothed and shaded or so sinuous and inextricable that it does not allow one to determine with any precision at which side of such a border one or another people should be located.[56]

This statement, formulated by Ivanovskii as one of the concluding reflections in his classification, must have had a personal dimension to it as well, for Ivanovskii's life experience was defined by constant border-crossing. He lived a genuine "imperial biography" full of relocations and transfers of experience and local knowledge between imperial peripheries and centers (including episodes of "going native"). He was born in the imperial periphery, in the small township of Maiuta in the Biisk district of Altai province in Siberia. In the early nineteenth century, Biisk emerged as a Cossack strong-

Народность.	Типъ по цвѣту волосъ и глазъ.	Ростъ.	Головной указатель и наиб. продольн. діаметръ.	Высотно-продольный указатель.	Лицевой указатель и полная длина лица.	Носовой указатель.	Туловище.	Окружность груди.	Рука.	Нога.	Авторъ.
Грузины	Cc	—	Cc_1	—	—	Aa_2	—	—	—	—	Chantre.
Грузины	Cc	Cc	$2Cc_1$	Aa	$4Bb_2$	Aa_1	—	Bb	—	—	—
Даргинцы	—	Dd	—	—	—	—	—	Bb_2	—	—	Свидерскій.
Дунгане	Cc_1	Dd	$4Aa_1$	Bb	—	Aa	Cc_1	Bb_2	Aa_1	Aa_1	Мацѣевскій и Поярковъ.
Евреи варш.	Cc	Aa_1	2Cc	Aa	$5Bb_1$	Aa_1	Bb	Bb	Cc	Bb_2	Элькиндъ.
„ кіевск.	Cc	Aa_1	Cc	—	—	—	—	—	—	—	Тал.-Гринцевичъ.
„ литов.	Cc	Aa_1	Cc	—	—	—	—	—	—	—	(Тал.-Гринцевичъ.)
„ могил.	Cc	Aa_1	4Cc	—	$4Bb_1$	Aa	—	Bb	Bb_2	Cc_1	Яковенко.
„ ковен.	Cc	Aa_1	$4Cc_1$	—	$4Bb_2$	Aa_2	—	Bb	Cc	—	Blechmann.
„ витеб.	Cc	Aa_1	$4Cc_1$	—	$1Bb_2$	Bb	—	Bb	Cc_1	—	(Blechmann.)
„ курлян.	Cc	Aa_1	$4Cc_1$	—	$4Bb_1$	Aa_2	—	Bb	Cc	—	(Blechmann.)
„ лифл.	Bb_1	Cc	$4Cc_1$	—	$1Bb_2$	Aa_1	—	Bb	Cc	—	(Blechmann.)
„ минск.	—	—	$4Cc_1$	Aa	—	—	—	—	—	—	Stieda.
„ одесск.	Cc	Aa_1	$2Cc_1$	Aa_1	$4Bb_1$	Aa_1	Ab	Bb	Cc	Cc_1	Ивановскій.
„ южн.-рус.	Cc	Cc	$1Cc_1$	Aa	—	—	—	—	Cc	Cc_1	Weissenberg.
„ разл. г.	—	—	Cc	—	—	—	—	—	—	—	Иковъ.
„ горск. Кавк.	—	Dd	—	—	—	—	—	Bb_1	—	—	Свидерскій.
„ закавк.	—	Aa_1	$1Cc_1$	—	$5Bb_2$	Aa_1	—	—	—	—	Пантюховъ.
Евреи	Cc	Aa_1	2Cc	Aa	$4Bb_1$	Aa_1	Bb	Bb	Cc	Cc_1	—
Езиды	Cc_1	Aa_1	5Bb	Bb	—	Aa	—	—	—	—	Горощенко.
Зыряне	Bb	Cc	$1Cc_1$	Aa_1	5Bb	Bb	Cc	Bb_2	Bb_2	Bb	Палимовъ.
„	—	Aa_1	$4Cc_1$	—	—	—	—	—	—	—	Sommier.
Зыряне	Bb	Cc	$1Cc_1$	Aa_1	5Bb	Bb	Cc	Bb_2	Bb_2	Bb	—
Имеретины	—	Cc	Cc	—	$4Bb_2$	Aa	—	—	—	—	Пантюховъ.
„	—	—	Cc_1	—	$2Bb_2$	Aa_1	—	—	—	—	Эркертъ.
„	—	—	Cc	—	—	Aa	—	—	—	—	Chantre.
Имеретины	—	Cc	Cc	—	$4Bb_2$	Aa	—	—	—	—	—
Ингуши	Cc	Dd_1	4Cc	—	$5Bb_2$	Aa_2	—	—	—	—	Пантюховъ.
„	—	—	4Cc	—	5Dd	Aa_2	—	—	—	—	Эркертъ.
„	—	—	—	—	—	Bb	—	—	—	—	Chantre.
Ингуши	Cc	Dd_1	4Cc	—	$5Bb_2$	Bb	—	—	—	—	—
Иштигардцы	Cc_1	Cc	2Bb	Bb	5Bb	—	Cc_1	Bb	Cc_1	Bb_2	Даниловъ.
Кабардинцы	Cc	—	$4Cc_1$	—	—	—	—	—	—	—	Вырубовъ.
„	Cc	Dd	$2Cc_1$	Bb	2Dd	Aa_1	—	Bb_2	Bb_2	Cc	Вышогродъ.
„	Cc	—	—	Aa_1	$5Bb_1$	Aa	—	—	—	—	Эркертъ.
„	Cc_1	—	—	—	—	Aa	—	—	—	—	Chantre.
Кабардинцы	Cc	Dd	Cc_1	Bb	$4Bb_2$	Aa_1	—	Bb_2	Bb_2	Cc	—
Кайтагцы	—	Dd	—	—	—	—	—	Bb_2	—	—	Свидерскій.
Калмыки астрах.	Cc_1	Aa_1	$4Cc_1$	—	—	Aa_2	—	—	—	—	Воробьевъ.
„ „	Cc_1	Aa_1	5Cc	Aa	$5Bb_2$	Bb	Cc_1	Bb_2	Cc_1	—	Королевъ.
„ „	—	Cc	—	—	—	—	—	—	—	—	Мечниковъ.
„ „	—	Cc	5Cc	—	—	—	—	—	—	—	Deniker.
„ „	Cc_1	Cc	5Cc	—	—	—	—	—	—	—	Sommier.
„ *астрах.*	Cc_1	Cc	5Cc	Aa	$5Bb_2$	Bb	Cc_1	Bb_2	Cc_1	—	—
„ ставроп.	—	Aa_1	5Cc	Aa	—	—	—	—	—	—	Эркертъ.
„ донск.	—	—	—	—	$5Dd_1$	Bb	—	—	—	—	Ивановскій.
„ чахары.	Cc_1	Aa_1	$4Cc_1$	Aa_1	—	Aa	Cc_1	Bb_2	Cc_1	Aa_1	Мацѣевскій и Поярковъ.
„ турфан.	Cc	Aa_1	$1Cc_1$	Bb	—	Aa	Bb	Bb_2	Cc_1	Bb	(Мацѣевскій и Поярковъ.)
Калмыки	Cc_1	Cc	4Cc	Aa	$5Bb_2$	Aa_2	Cc_1	Bb_2	Cc_1	Bb	—
Карагасы	Cc	Aa	—	—	—	—	—	Cc_1	Cc_1	—	Залѣсскій.
Караимы	Cc	Aa_1	$2Cc_1$	—	—	Aa	—	—	—	—	Вайсенбергъ.
Каракиргизы	Cc	Dd	$4Cc_1$	Bb	—	Bb	Cc_1	Bb_2	Cc	Aa	Зеландъ.
„	—	Dd_1	$4Cc_1$	—	—	—	—	—	—	—	Ujfalvy.
Каракиргизы	Cc	Dd	$4Cc_1$	Bb	—	Bb	Cc_1	Bb_2	Cc	Aa	—
Карачаевцы	—	—	5Cc	—	—	—	—	—	—	—	Эркертъ.
„	—	Dd	$5Cc_1$	—	—	—	—	—	—	—	Sommier.
Карачаевцы	—	Dd	$5Cc_1$	—	—	—	—	—	—	—	—
Карелы Финл.	Aa_1	Dd_1	4Cc	—	5Bb	—	—	—	Bb	Cc_1	Retzius.
Киргизы Букеев. о.	Cc_1	Cc	$4Cc_1$	—	—	—	—	—	—	—	Харузинъ.
„ Средн. о.	Cc_1	Cc	$2Cc_1$	Bb	2Dd	Aa_2	Cc	Bb_2	Bb_2	Aa_1	Ивановскій.
„ „	—	Aa_1	$2Cc_1$	—	—	Bb	—	Bb_2	Aa	Aa	Троновъ.
„ семирѣч.	—	Dd	$4Cc_1$	—	—	—	—	—	—	—	Зеландъ.
„ кульдж.	Cc	Cc	2Cc	Cc	—	Aa	Cc_1	Bb_2	Bb_2	Aa_1	Мацѣевскій и Поярковъ.
„ сыръ-дар.	Cc	Aa_1	$2Cc_1$	—	—	—	—	—	—	—	Масловскій.
„ „	—	Dd	—	—	—	—	—	—	—	—	Ujfalvy.
Киргизы	Cc_1	Cc	$2Cc_1$	Bb	2Dd	Aa_2	Cc_1	Bb_2	Bb	Aa_1	—
Китайцы	Cc_1	Dd	4Bb	Cc	—	Aa	Cc_1	Aa_1	Bb_2	Aa_1	Мацѣевскій и Поярковъ.
„	Cc_1	Aa_1	—	—	—	Aa	—	—	—	—	Тал.-Гринцевичъ.
Китайцы	Cc_1	Cc	4Bb	Cc	—	Aa	Cc_1	Aa_1	Bb_2	Aa_1	—

Fig 4. An opening page of Ivanovskii's classificatory tables, organized alphabetically. (Source: A. A. Ivanovskii, *Ob Antropologicheskom Sostave Naseleniia Rossii* [Izvestia IOLEAE, vol. 105; Trudy Antropologicheskogo Otdela, vol. 22] (Moscow: Otdel. Tipografii T-va I.D. Sytina, 1904), 171–74.) Columns: ethnicity (*narodnost'*); type according to hair and eye color; height; cephalic index and the largest longitudinal diameter; height-longitudinal skull index, facial index and a full length of the face; nasal index; body; chest circumference; arm; leg; author.

hold in the defense line at the southeastern frontier of the Russian Empire. Kazakh nomads (then identified as Kirgiz) were part of this region's population. After having graduated with distinction from the Tomsk gymnasium, Ivanovskii joined a Kazakh tribe in the Zaisan district (Semipalatinsk region, in today's Kazakhstan) and led a nomadic life for a year, immersing himself in the Kazakh language, oral tradition, and way of life. Then, from the steppes of Semipalatinsk, Ivanovskii headed directly to Moscow University, where he concentrated in anthropology and geography. Equipped with modern knowledge, he again returned to the imperial borderlands. In 1890 he studied Mongols-torgouts; in 1891, together with Anuchin, he traveled to the Caucasus; in 1893 to Transcaucasia; and in 1894 he undertook another expedition to the Turkish border. He visited many of the same "colonial," petroleum-rich regions of the empire that Deniker had visited a decade earlier, as a fresh graduate of Petersburg Technological institute.[57]

Moscow University sent Ivanovskii to Europe to perfect his anthropological training. His base was Leipzig University, and his primary tutors the geographer Friedrich Ratzel and the physical anthropologist Emil Ludwig Schmidt. There, in Leipzig, the young Russian scholar defended his dissertation, "Die Mongolei." However, in Moscow his dissertation topic was totally different and absolutely unrelated to the tradition of Oriental studies. Ivanovskii received his Russian degree in geography (there was no degree in anthropology) in 1904 for his dissertation "On the Anthropological Composition of the Population of Russia," in which he presented his original classification.[58] It took him another nine years to write the second, doctoral (habilitation) dissertation, "The Population of the Globe: An Experiment in Anthropological Classification," which he defended at Moscow University in 1913.[59] After that he was offered a full professorship in Ukrainian Khar'kov, far from the imperial centers. There he survived the First World War, the revolutions of 1917, and the civil war and worked as an anthropologist until the early 1930s. During the lifetime of this one scholar, the epistemic and political contexts that informed the development of Russian anthropology had changed not once.

When Ivanovskii embarked on the task of classifying Russian "racial types" back in the early 1900s, the narrative of anthropology as the classificatory science dominated the field, the nomothetic vs. idiographic debate was still ongoing, and anthropology was a "movement." Some of the Russian "observer-anthropologists" had medical degrees or were trained in natural sciences, whereas others were less competent amateurs. In addition, some of them were known for having a particular political, most often anticolonial, nationalizing agenda.[60] Among those who supplied Ivanovskii with their measurements were non-Russians or even non-Slavs who measured Russians or other Slavs; there were Russians who studied non-Russian imperial groups and there were cases when an anthropologist represented the very group that he or she measured.[61] Such inconsistency of sources would present an equivalent problem for purely nomothetic or idiographic sciences, but not for Ivanovskii, with his conscious methodological orientation toward methodological and social (imperial) hybridity. His method was relational and comparative, and his focus was on miscegenation as the process of hybridization of pure types, however his sources constructed them. In the introduction to his dissertation, Ivanovskii claimed that one cannot study Russians as a racial type without dissolving them in the anthropology of the imperial non-Russians: "Across the vast space of their settlement, Russians came in touch with many non-Russian tribes. In many instances they were experiencing the greater or lesser influence of non-Russian blood. Therefore, the analysis of Russian anthropological traits conducted exclusively on Russians cannot elucidate the meaning of all the elements that compose a given anthropological type."[62]

What was needed instead was the study "of meticization of our population," because this process, so conveniently available to researchers in the Russian Empire, "provides a rare opportunity to examine the very mechanism of formation of new anthropological types."[63] Evident in this passage was the implicit acceptance of the uniqueness of the Russian Empire as a space of racial contact, but this perception was definitely structured by "values" in Rickert's sense. This "idiographic" quality of Ivanovskii's discourse justified his methodological and ideological pantophagy.

After developing a general model for the case of the Russian Empire, Ivanovskii advanced to the next stage and applied his method to classify "the races of Man" and establish their fundamental hybridity, worldwide. Ivanovskii's bold claim of a universal applicability of his classificatory method could reflect his view of the Russian empire as a comprehensive model of global human diversity, and at the same time it could be a way to make a mark on transnational anthropology from a more marginal "corner" of this discipline.[64]

> On April 5, 1913, in one of the Moscow university halls, at a public meeting of the Department of Physics and Mathematics, privat-docent A. A. Ivanovskii defended his dissertation in pursuit of the degree of doctor of geography and anthropology, "The Population of the Globe: An Essay on Anthropological Classification," M[oscow], 1911 (508 columns, two on each page), with a "Supplement" M[oscow], 1912 (52 columns).[65] The author studied an extremely wide range of literature and set himself the task of selecting the relative and absolute body measurements of many tribes and peoples for his work. On the basis of these indicators he attempted to classify "the population of the Globe" or, to be more precise, all of the more or less anthropologically studied groups. Nearly 240 columns of his book contain only tables with numbers and letter symbols, more than 70 columns feature bibliography, and 42 offer an alphabetical index. The rest is a narrative discussing the data presented in the tables. Half of the "Supplement" is occupied by tables and a list of peoples whom the author grouped according to their studied traits.[66]

This time, Ivanovskii's defense generated a heated discussion that lasted four hours. Many among the 150 people present at the defense questioned his method, including Anuchin himself.[67] Anuchin objected to Ivanovskii's reliance on "descriptive indicators," such as hair and eye color, alongside "anatomic" indicators. The science of anthropology, explained Anuchin, had no universally accepted methodology for determining the exact color, and many data used by Ivanovskii were collected by amateurs who ignored even the existing scientific conventions. He also criticized Ivanovskii's readiness to consider peoples represented literally by two or three measurements. Most important, Anuchin questioned Ivanovskii's "synthetic" narrative that ascribed the characteristics of "physical type" to peoples—"ethnological units" defined by culture and history. Anuchin blamed Ivanovskii for mixing up these two analytical categories, while Ivanovskii defended himself by stressing that in reality anthropologists never measure abstract types, only real people, and therefore combining anthropological and ethnographic (or national) categories in their scientific language is inevitable.[68] However, Anuchin received support from a younger generation of anthropologists, such as Sergei Rudenko from Petersburg, who echoed Anuchin when he insisted that anthropological classification cannot be composed of data collected for "peoples" (*narodnosti*): "Classification of races is one of the major tasks of contemporary anthropology. However, today there are almost no pure races. We can deduce them only through a slow and detailed analysis of the elements constituting peoples. . . . Meanwhile, the author of this classification is trying to classify peoples (composite bodies, not their elements) and operates with them as with major units of his analysis. Races, at the same time, are not objects of his analysis; they do not interest him at all."[69]

The discussion that took place in 1913 reflected a new degree of anthropological professionalization and specialization and a turn away from synthetic philosophical paradigms to more technologically oriented or deterministic versions of race science. However, it is important to stress that despite all the voiced criticism, Ivanovskii successfully defended his dissertation, and his classification of the physical types of the Russian Empire continued to serve as a common frame for the development of Russian liberal race science. Russian anthropologists of the Moscow school routinely calculated degrees of difference as indicators of similarity between the population groups that they studied, and Ivanovskii's hybrid imperial model continued to grow. Since the first publication of his classification, the participants in the Moscow network learned to understand the act of classification in Ivanovskii's terms: as producing a scientific model of fundamental imperial hybridity. In many individual cases this scientific choice reinforced a "value" judgment in favor of a democratized empire, reconstituted on the assumptions of modern knowledge. Only such a composite polity was able to accommodate the "mixed physical type" naturalized by Russian liberal anthropologists and to defend hybridity as an essential quality of modernity as they understood it. In their view, Russia, together with the rest of the civilized world, was moving away from exclusivist forms of groupness toward a new humanity, and its "empireness" was a structural advantage on this path toward the postnational humanity anticipated on the eve of the First World War.

Notes

1. A. A. Ivanovskii, *Ob Antropologicheskom Sostave Naseleniia Rossii* [Izvestia IOLEAE, vol. 105; Trudy Antropologicheskogo Otdela, V. XXII] (Moscow: Otdel. Tipografii T-va I.D. Sytina, 1904), 30.

2. For the most comprehensive review of the existing literature and approaches to this problem, see Vera Tolz, "Diskursy o Race: imperskaia Rossia i 'Zapad' v sravnenii," in *Poniatiia o Rossii: K Istoricheskoi Semantike Imperskogo Perioda*, vol. 2, ed. A. Miller, D. Sdvizhkov, and I. Schierle (Moscow: NLO, 2012), 154–93. On the pre-1917 Russian empire, see James A. Rogers, "Racism and Russian Revolutionists," *Race and Class* 14, no. 3 (1973): 279–89; Eugene M. Avrutin, "Racial Categories and the Politics of (Jewish) Difference in Late Imperial Russia," *Kritika* 8, no. 1 (2007): 13–40; Sergei Kan, *Lev Shternberg, Anthropologist, Russian Socialist, Jewish Activist* (Lincoln: University of Nebraska Press, 2009); Marlène Laruelle, "Transferts culturels autour du concept de Race: Lectures de Darwin en Russie," in *Transferts culturels et comparatisme en Russie* [vol. 30, Slavica Occitania], ed. Michel Espagne (University of Toulouse, 2010), 154–93; M. Laruelle, "Regards sur la réception du racialisme allemand chez les panslavistes et les eurasistes russes," *Revue germanique internationale* 3 (2006): 145–55; Vera Tolz, "Response to Alexander Etkind's Review of Marina Mogilner's *Homo Imperii: Istoriia fizicheskoi antropologii v Rossii*," *Laboratorium* 3, no. 2 (2011): 94–96; Konstantin Ivanov, "Replika po povodu diskussii o knige: Marina Mogilner *Homo Imperii. Istoriia fizicheskoi antropologii v Rossii*," *Laboratorium* 3, no. 2 (2011): 97–99; Elena A. Vishlenkova, *Vizual'noe narodovedenie rossiiskoi imperii, ili "Uvidet' Russkogo dano ne kazhdomu"* (Moscow: NLO, 2011); Karl Hall, "'Rasovye priznaki koreniatsia glubzhe v prirode chelpvecheskogo organizma': neulovimoe poniatie *rasy* v Rossiiskoi imperii," in *Poniatiia o Rossii*, 194–258. Some important information on the development of race science in the former Baltic regions of the Russian empire may be found in Bjorn M. Felder and Paul J. Weindling, *Baltic Eugenics: Bio-Politics, Race, and Nation in Interwar Estonia, Latvia, and Lithuania, 1918–1940* (Amsterdam: Rodopi, 2013). On the Soviet period, see Discussion: Eric Weitz, "Racial Politics Without the Concept of Race"; Francine Hirsch, "Race Without the Practice of Racial Poli-

tics"; Amir Weiner, "Nothing but Certainty"; Alaina Lemon, "Without a 'Concept'?"; Weitz, "On Certainties and Ambivalences: Reply to My Critics," *Slavic Review* 61, no. 1 (2002): 1–65; Forum: The Multiethnic Soviet Union in Comparative Perspective: Adeeb Khalid, "Backwardness and the Quest for Civilization"; Adrienne Edgar, "Bolshevism, Patriarchy, and the Nation"; Peter A. Blitstein, "Cultural Diversity and the Interwar Conjuncture"; Mark R. Beissinger, "Soviet Empire as 'Family Resemblance,'" *Slavic Review* 65, no. 2 (2006): 231–303; and Francine Hirsch, *Empire of Nations: Ethnographic Knowledge and the Making of the Soviet Union* (Ithaca NY: Cornell University Press, 2005). At least two recent international conferences should be mentioned in this footnote: "The Born and the Common Criminal. The Discourse of Criminality and the Practice of Punishment in the Late Russian Empire and the Early Soviet Union (1880–1941)" organized by Riccardo Nicolosi (Ludwig-Maximilians-Universität München) and Anne Hartmann (Ruhr-Universität Bochum) in February 2015; and "Russia's Races: A Workshop on the Meaning and Practices of Race in Imperial Russia and the Soviet Union," organized by David Rainbow and New York University's Jordan Center for the Advanced Study of Russia. The later conference, in particular, offers a "who's who" in the field of the history of "race" in Russia and the USSR. See http://jordanrussiacenter.org/event/russias-races-meanings-and-practices-of-race-in-imperial-russia-and-the-soviet-union/+.

3. Alexander Semyonov, "Empire as a Context Setting Category," *Ab Imperio* 9, no. 1 (2008): 193–204; Ilya Gerasimov, Sergey Glebov, Jan Kusber, Marina Mogilner, and Alexander Semyonov, "New Imperial History and the Challenges of Empire," in *Empire Speaks Out: Languages of Rationalization and Self-Description in the Russian Empire*, ed. Ilya Gerasimov et al. (Leiden: Brill, 2009), 3–32.

4. See the latest discussion of imperial repertoire of power in Jane Burbank and Frederick Cooper, *Empires in World History: Power and the Politics of Difference* (Princeton: Princeton University Press, 2010), especially the introduction, "Imperial Trajectories."

5. The body of new historiography of the Russian Empire is growing. It is most comprehensively represented in all its diversity and complexity by publications in *Ab Imperio Quarterly*, which is dedicated to the new imperial history of Russia and the post-Soviet space. For a general overview, see Nicholas Breyfogle, "Enduring Imperium: Russia/Soviet Union/Eurasia as Multiethnic, Multiconfessional Space," *Ab Imperio* 9, no. 1 (2008): 75–129; Gerasimov at al., "New Imperial History and the Challenges of Empire"; and Marina Mogilner, "New Imperial History: Post-Soviet Historiography in Search of a New Paradigm for the History of Empire and Nationalism," *Revue d'études comparatives Est-Ouest* 45, no. 2 (2014): 25–67. Among the main works illustrating the dynamics described above, see Robert Crews, "Empire and the Confessional State: Islam and Religious Politics in Nineteenth-Century Russia," *American Historical Review* 108, no. 1 (2003): 50–83; Richard Wortman, *Scenarios of Power: Myth and Ceremony in Russian Monarchy from Peter the Great to the Abdication of Nicolas II* (Princeton: Princeton University Press, 2006); Ilya Gerasimov, *Modernism and Public Reform in Late Imperial Russia: Rural Professionals and Self-organization, 1905–*

30 (Houndmills: Palgrave Macmillan, 2009); Mikhail Dolbilov, *Russkii krai, chuzhaia vera: etnokonfessional'naia politika imperii v Litve i Belorussii pri Aleksandre II* (Moscow: NLO, 2010); and others.

6. Mogilner, "Beyond, Against, and With Ethnography: Physical Anthropology as a Science of Russian Modernity," in *An Empire of Others. Creating Ethnographic Knowledge in Imperial Russia and the USSR*, ed. Roland Cvetkovski and Alexis Hofmeister (Budapest: Central European University Press, 2013), 81–120.

7. Neil MacMaster, *Racism in Europe. 1870–2000* (New York: Palgrave Macmillan, 2001), 14.

8. A detailed analysis of these schools can be found in Mogilner, *A History of Physical Anthropology in Russia*, Critical Studies in the History of Anthropology (Lincoln: University of Nebraska Press, 2013).

9. Andrew Zimmerman, *Anthropology and Antihumanism in Imperial Germany* (Chicago: University of Chicago Press, 2001).

10. On the Moscow liberal anthropological network, see Mogilner, *Homo Imperii*.

11. See the special forum on liberal race science in *Ab Imperio* 1 (2007): Andrew D. Evans, "A Liberal Paradigm? Race and Ideology in Late Nineteenth-Century German Physical Anthropology," 113–38; Marius Turda, "Race, Politics, and Nationalist Darwinism in Hungary, 1880–1918," 139–64; Christian Marchetti, "Scientists with Guns: On the Ethnographic Exploration of the Balkans by Austrian-Hungarian Scientists before and during World War I," 165–90; Mogilner, "Russian Physical Anthropology in Search of 'Imperial Race': Liberalism and Modern Scientific Imagination in the Imperial Situation," 191–223; and Andre Gingrich, "Liberalism in Imperial Anthropology: Notes on an Implicit Paradigm in Continental European Anthropology before World War I," 224–239.

12. For more on the liberal paradigm in German physical anthropology and Virchow's liberalism, see Andrew D. Evans, "A Liberal Paradigm?"; see also Andrew D. Evans, "Anthropology at War: Racial Studies of POWs during World War I," in *Worldly Provincialism: German Anthropology in the Age of Empire*, ed. H. Glenn Penny and Matti Bunzl (Ann Arbor: University of Michigan Press, 2003), 198–229. On the liberal paradigm, see especially 202–7.

13. Anuchin, "R. Virchow kak antropolog," *Russkii Antropologicheskii Zhurnal* 7–8, nos. 3–4 (1901): xviii.

14. Benoit Massin, "From Virchow to Fischer: Physical Anthropology and Modern Race Theories in Whihelmine Germany," in *Volksgeist as Method and Ethic: Essays on Boasian Ethnography and the German Anthropological Tradition*, ed. George W. Stocking Jr. (Madison: University of Wisconsin Press, 1996), 100. See also Ivan Kalmar, "The Völkerpsychologie of Lazarus and Steinthal and the Modern Concept of Culture," *Journal of the History of Ideas* 48 (1987): 671–90; Glenn Penny, "Bastian's Museum: On the Limits of Empiricism and the Transformation of German Ethnology," in *Worldly Provincialism*, 86–118; Robert Proctor, "From *Anthropologie* to *Rassenkunde* in the German Anthropological Tradition," in *Bones, Bodies, Behavior: Essays*

on Biological Anthropology, ed. George W. Stocking Jr. (Madison: University of Wisconsin Press, 1988), 148–52.

15. This special case is discussed in Marina Mogilner, "Evreiskaia fizionomia v Rossiikoi imperii: predely kolonizatsii i samokolonizatsii v antropologii rossiiskogo evreistva" ("Jewish physiognomy" in the Russian Empire: the limits of colonization and self-colonization of Russian Jewry), in *Tam, Vnutri. Praktiki vnutrennei kolonizatsii v kul'turnoi istorii Rossii*, ed. A. Etkind, D. Uffelmann, and I. Kukulin (Moscow: NLO, 2012), 376–412; Mogilner, "Toward a History of Russian-Jewish 'Medical Materialism': Russian-Jewish Physicians and the Politics of Jewish Biological Normalization," *Jewish Social Studies* 19, no. 1 (2012): 70–106; Mogilner, "Between Scientific and Political: Jewish Scholars and Russian-Jewish Physical Anthropology in the Fin-de-Siècle Russian Empire," in *Going to the People: Jews and the Ethnographic Impulse*, ed. Jeffrey Veidlinger (Bloomington: Indiana University Press, 2016), in press.

16. Riccardo Nicolosi, "Criminality, Deviance, and Anthropological Diversity: Narratives of Born Criminality and Atavism in Late Imperial Russia (ca. 1880–1890)," unpublished paper presented at the workshop "The Born and the Common Criminal: The Discourse of Criminality and the Practice of Punishment in the Late Russian Empire and the Early Soviet Union (1880–1941)," Ludwig-Maximilians-Universität München, February 13–14, 2015.

17. Gillian Beer, *Darwin's Plot: Evolutionary Narrative in Darwin, George Eliot and Nineteenth-Century Fiction* (London: Routledge & Kegan Paul, 1983).

18. Until quite late in the nineteenth century, when biological reductionism became the dominant trend in race science, this naturalization proceeded in multiple modes. See Susanne Lettow, "Modes of Naturalization: Race, Sex and Biology in Kant, Schelling and Hegel," *Philosophy and Social Criticism* 39 (2013): 117–31. For the application of this argument to Russian intellectual history, see Karl Hall's unpublished paper "'I Know You Won't Be Satisfied with My Description of Chuvash Faces, but What to Do if I Was Not Born a Diligent Student of Lavater, Camper, Blumenbach, or Virey?': Entangled Concepts of Race in the Russian Empire before 1859," presented at the workshop "Russia's Races: Meanings and Practices of Race in Imperial Russia and the Soviet Union," New York University, February 26–27, 2015.

19. O. I. Senkovskii, *Listki Barona Brambeusa*, vol. 1 (St. Petersburg: I. I. Glazunov, 1858), 343.

20. J. F. Blumenbach, *Handbuch der Naturgeschichte*, 4th ed. (Göttingen: Johann Christian Dieterich, 1791); *Rukovodstvo k estestvennoi istorii*, trans. Petr Naumov and Andrei Teriaev, vol. 1 (St. Petersburg: Tipografiia Vil'kovskago, 1797).

21. Hall, "I Know You Won't Be Satisfied," 41.

22. On A. P. Bogdanov and his craniometrical studies and publications, see M. G. Levin, "A. P. Bogdanov i russkaia antropologiia," *Sovetskaia etnografiia* 1 (1946): 187–209. Most of his works were published as separate articles in the *News of the IOLEAE* (e.g., "Opisanie kurgannykh cherepov Smolenskoi givernii"; "Cherepa iz starykh moskovskikh kladbishch" etc.), or as a separate volume of the *News*: Bogdanov,

"Materialy dlia antropologii kurgannogo perioda v Moskovskoi gubernii," *Izvestiia Imperatorskogo Obshchestva Liubitelei Estestvoznaniia*, vol. 4 (1867).

23. Dmitrii Anuchin, "Rasy," in *Entsyklopedichekii Slovar*, vol. 26, ed. F. A. Brockhaus and I. A. Efron, 356–60 (St. Petersburg: Izdatel'skoe delo, 1899).

24. There was one aspect of the Pushkin myth that made his case especially important for race science: his father belonged to the ancient Russian aristocratic Pushkin family, whereas his mother was a descendant of the famous "Blackamoor of Peter the Great," a young man of Ethiopian descent and the poet's great-grandfather, Ibrahim Petrovich Gannibal, who made a spectacular career in the Russian Empire. The exotic African roots and "black" ancestors of the "most Russian" poet challenged the scientists who were thinking in racial categories to come out with a theory explaining either the positive or negative correlation of this "racial paradox."

25. As Anuchin explained, "Everything said above justifies my doubts regarding the probability of the story of a pure-blooded Negro, resettled from Africa to Europe and subjected here to the influence of upbringing, who then manifested his abilities on the same scale as did Ibrahim Gannibal. It is doubtful that among the sons of this Negro, the mulattoes, there was one (Ivan Abramovich) who became known not only for his brevity but also for his administrative talent. Finally, it is doubtful that this Negro's great-grandson, A. S. Pushkin, marked a new epoch in the literary-artistic development of a European nation and acquired the reputation of a great poet." Dimitri Anuchin, "Pushkin (antropologicheskii eskiz): Prodolzhenie," *Russkie vedomosti*, May 3, 1899, 2–3.

26. For a detailed analysis, see the chapter "Race-Pushkin: The Anthropology of Russian 'All-Humanity,'" in Marina Mogilner, *Homo Imperii*, 151–64.

27. "Instruktsii dlia prigotovleniia po kafedre geografii i antropologii prof. D. N. Anuchina, 1916 [Instructions for preparing (for doctoral exams) in the Department of Geography and Anthropology]," Moscow State Historical Archive (GIAM), F. 418, Op. 94, D. 488, L. 17–18, 22.

28. Anuchin, "Rasy," 358.

29. I. E. Deniker, *Chelovecheskie rasy*, trans. V. Rantslov (St. Petersburg: Tipografiia Ju. N. Erlikh, 1902).

30. Wilhelm Windelband, *Geschichte und Naturwissenschaft*, 3rd ed. (Strasbourg: Heitz, 1904).

31. Wilhelm Windelband, *Einleitung in die Philosophie* (Tübingen: J. C. B. Mohr, 1914). Quoted from the English edition: Wilhelm Windelband, *An Introduction to Philosophy* (London: T. Fisher Unwin, 1921), 288.

32. Windelband, *An Introduction to Philosophy*, 259.

33. Heinrich Rickert, *The Limits of Concept Formation in Natural Science: A Logical Introduction to the Historical Sciences*, trans. Guy Oakes, Texts in German Philosophy (Cambridge: Cambridge University Press [1902] 1986), 86, and others. The Russian translation of this work appeared already in 1903: G. Rikkert, *Granitsy estestvennonauchnogo obrazovaniia poniatii* (St. Petersburg: Izd. E. D. Kuskova, 1903).

34. In the Russian translation, this paragraph from Deniker's work demanded to clarify the meanings of such terms as "narod, natsiia, plemia, rasa, vid . . . " Deniker, *Chelovecheskie rasy*, 4.

35. Joseph Deniker, *The Races of Man: An Outline of Anthropology and Ethnography*, 3rd ed. (London: Walter Scott, 1913), 345.

36. Anuchin, "Rasy," 359.

37. His three European races were much easier to fix and politicize, which eventually happened with his Teutonic race in particular. At the same time, Richard McMahon claims that "Ripley was more a transitional figure, accepting that his own term Teuton confused ethnicity and race more than Deniker's Nordic did." Richard McMahon, "Anthropological Race Classification of Europeans, 1839–1939" (PhD diss., European University Institute, Florence, 2007), 150.

38. McMahon, "Anthropological Race Classification of Europeans," 69, 151.

39. A letter from Deniker Osip Egorovich to A. P. Bogdanov, March 22, 1888, Archive of the Russian Academy of Sciences (ARAN), F. 466, Op. 2, D. 196, L. 2.

40. Letter from Deniker to Bogdanov, September 26, 1888, Archive of the Russian Academy of Sciences (ARAN), F. 466, Op. 2, D. 196, L. 8–8rev.

41. Sh. M. Levin, "Vospominaniia I. E. Denikera," *Katorga i ssylka* 11 (1924): 20. Deniker wrote his memoirs in the early 1880s, and since then they have been preserved in the archive of the underground populist organization, "People's Will."

42. I. E. Deniker, "Vospominaniia," *Katorga i ssylka* 11 (1924): 25.

43. Deniker, "Vospominaniia," 26.

44. Rickert, *The Limits of Concept Formation in Natural Science*, 85.

45. On the Moscow liberal anthropological network, see Mogilner, *Homo Imperii*.

46. Anuchin, "Beglyi vzgliad na proshloe antropologii i ee zadachi s Rossii," *Russkii antropologicheskii zhurnal* 1 (1900): 41.

47. Ivanovskii, *Ob Antropologicheskom Sostave Naseleniia Rossii*, 7.

48. Ivanovskii, *Ob Antropologicheskom Sostave Naseleniia Rossii*, 8–9.

49. Ivanovskii, *Ob Antropologicheskom Sostave Naseleniia Rossii*, 9.

50. Anuchin, "O zadachakh i medodakh antropologii," *Russkii antropologicheskii zhurnal* 1 (1902): 72.

51. Ivanovskii, *Ob Antropologicheskom Sostave Naseleniia Rossii*, 8.

52. Rudolf Virchow, "*Gesammtbericht über die von der deutschen anthropologischen Gesellschaft veranlassten Erhebungen über die Farbe der Haut, der Haare und der Augen der Schulkinder in Deutchland*," *Archiv für Anthropologie* 16 (1886): 275–475.

53. Ales Hrdlicka, "Review: Physical Anthropology of Russia by A. A. Ivanovskij," *American Anthropologist* 9, no. 2 (1907): 400–403. For the list of peoples, see 401–2.

54. Ivanovskii, *Ob Antropologicheskom Sostave Naseleniia Rossii*, 190.

55. Ivanovskii, *Ob Antropologicheskom Sostave Naseleniia Rossii*, 196.

56. Ivanovskii, *Ob Antropologicheskom Sostave Naseleniia Rossii*, 192.

57. For more on Ivanovskii, see Mogilner, *Homo Imperii*, 101–20.

58. On the dissertation defense of April 22, 1904, see "Opyt novoi antropologicheskoi klassifikatsii i disput A. A. Ivanovskogo," *Zemlevedenie* 1–2 (1913): 335–36; "Ob'iavlenie" in the Moscow Central Historical Archive (TSIAM), F. 418, Op. 82, D. 178, L. 1; "Predstavlenie fiziko-matematicheskogo fakul'teta o utverzhdenii A. A. Ivanovskogo v stepeni magistra geografii," TSIAM, F. 418, Op. 82, D. 178, L. 4; "Svidetel'stvo o prisvoenii A. A. Ivanovskomu stepeni Magistra geografii," TSIAM, F. 418, Op. 82, D. 178, L. 7.

59. Ivanovskii, "Naselenie zemnogo shara: Opyt antropologicheskoi klassifikatsii," *Izvestiia IOLEAE* 121 [Trudy Antropologichekogo otdela, 27] (Moscow: Tipografia P. P. Riabushunskogo,1911), 1–262.

60. Many such cases are considered in Mogilner, *Homo Imperii.*

61. Most of the anthropologists whose data were included in the classification were listed in the introduction to Ivanovskii, *Ob Antropologicheskom Sostave Naseleniia Rossii*, v—vi.

62. Ivanovskii, *Ob Antropologicheskom Sostave Naseleniia Rossii*, 15.

63. Ivanovskii, *Ob Antropologicheskom Sostave Naseleniia Rossii*, 30.

64. I am grateful to Richard McMahon for this observation. He suggested placing Ivanovskii within a group of race anthropologists from the margins of the normative "western Europe" who compensated for their relative marginality to the field by advancing radically new classificatory methods which received little acclaim from representatives of the mainstream trends and established centers in their science.

65. Ivanovskii, "Naselenie zemnogo shara."

66. "Opyt novoi antropologicheskoi klassifikatsii i disput A. A. Ivanovskogo," 235.

67. Anuchin, "Rasy," 359.

68. McMahon, "Anthropological Race Classification of Europeans, 1839–1939."

69. Letter from Deniker to Bogdanov, September 26, 1888, Archive of the Russian Academy of Sciences (ARAN), F. 466, Op. 2, D. 196, L. 8–8rev.

SEVEN

Physical Anthropology in Colonial Korea

Science and Colonial Order, 1916–1940

ARNAUD NANTA

This chapter examines physical anthropology in colonial Korea, focusing in particular on the Anatomy Section of the Imperial University in Keijō,[1] as Seoul was known while under Japanese rule (1910–45).[2] This institution, which existed from 1924 to 1945, joined the network of Japanese imperial universities, which were national universities prior to 1945. It was founded after the imperial universities of Tokyo in 1877 and Kyoto in 1897. My aim is to illustrate how the Anatomy Section strove to validate discourse about the "common ancestral origins" of Koreans and Japanese (*nissen dōso-ron*), a theory advanced around 1910 to justify Japan's annexation of the peninsula. Despite sharing similarities with its counterparts in the metropole, Keijō Imperial University had its own specific chairs and was entrusted with missions that had no equivalent in Japan. Indeed, three chairs were created within the Anatomy Section, two of which were held by physical anthropologists studying the physical characteristics of Koreans.

Racial taxonomies and modern classificatory logic were not applied to the Japanese colonies with the aim of differentiating them from the home nation—as with European colonies in Africa and Asia—but rather to link them to it.[3] As in Ireland and Slavic Eastern Europe, the rationale for this was "continental imperialism," an "annexationist" logic claiming cultural and racial proximity between conqueror and conquered.[4] These theories pervaded both the human sciences and the field of medicine, notably physical anthropology and serology. Keijō Imperial University's Anatomy Section—led by professors Ueda Tsunekichi (1887–1966) and Imamura Yutaka (1896–1971)—and the Forensic Medicine Section were instrumental in developing a Japanese colonial science devoted to serving ideology.[5] The discourse supported by anthropologists in Korea constituted the dominant paradigm and the official colonial ideology in Japan until approximately 1940. It would nonetheless come into conflict with eugenicist scholarship as of 1930. Whereas colonial researchers claimed "racial" proximity to justify the annexation, the eugenicists sought to prevent any intermixing between the metropole and its colonies. This "autochthonist" trend—which was opposed to imperial integration and reasserted Japan's supremacy over possessions it felt should not be assimilated—came to dominate in around 1940, thanks to the war. In the pages that follow, I hope to shed light on an example that perfectly illustrates the links that existed between science and ideology in pre-1945 colonial Japan, while exploring this chapter in the history of Keijō Imperial University and the studies this institution produced.

The opening section will explore the history of Japanese anthropological research as well as the founding of the imperial university in Korea and its chairs in physical anthropology. The second section will then present the fieldwork conducted by these anthropologists on the populations of colonial Korea and the tensions that brought them into conflict with the eugenicists, notably during a symposium held in Tokyo in 1934, at a time when theories on the autochthonous origins of the Japanese were becoming increasingly prominent. Finally, the third section will examine the most significant texts published by these scholars between 1935 and 1940.

Creating an Imperial University in Korea: From Metropolitan Anthropology to Colonial Chairs in Physical Anthropology

A Brief History of Japanese Physical Anthropology

The history of modern Japanese biological anthropology dates back to the 1870s and 1880s.[6] The Anthropological Society of Tokyo was founded in 1884 at Tokyo Imperial University.[7] With no university chairs yet in existence, anthropology was at that time a "composite" science embracing a variety of subfields: the society's founder, Tsuboi Shōgorō (1863–1913), who was appointed to the Anthropology Section at the university in 1892 and was a former student of Edward B. Tylor (1832–1917) in London, championed an anthropology focused more on culture, while Koganei Yoshikiyo (1859–1944), who hailed from the Faculty of Science and was a former student of the leading German anthropologist Rudolf Virchow (1821–1902), was instrumental in developing Japanese physical anthropology.[8] Although this section only became a full-fledged department within Tokyo Imperial University in 1938, it nonetheless trained many anthropologists and prehistorians in the 1920s and 1930s. Modern Japanese anthropology thus encompassed three approaches: cultural-linguistic, purely biological, and prehistoric studies. However, if all these aspects of the research appeared within the society, physical anthropologists had a clear inclination toward the French and—more and more from the end of the nineteenth century—the German school. This importance of the German school within Japanese physical anthropology through the first half of the twentieth century reflected Germany's leading role in world medicine at the time. Japanese anthropologists did not incline toward the elaboration of "racial hierarchies," but, rather, had a strong tendency to measurement and racial classification. This situation would be different in a colonial context, where scientists had to "continuously and vigilantly craft a grammar of difference." However, as it supported assimilation policies, the position of Japanese physical anthropology in Korea in fact perfectly illustrates the tensions of empire.[9] The year 1893 saw the founding of the Japanese Association of Anatomists. This was followed in 1899 by the Faculty of Medicine at Kyoto Imperial University, where three chairs in anatomy were created between 1899 and 1906. The first of these was held by the physical anthropologist Adachi Buntarō (1865–1945), who studied for five years at the university of Straßburg, which was a part of Germany at that time. Almost all Japanese physical anthropologists of the first half of the twentieth century studied in Germany. A huge amount of Japanese research papers would thus be written in German during the interwar period that I will discuss below. Together, these two scholarly societies and two universities formed the framework within which Japanese physical anthropology evolved at the dawn of the colonial era in Korea in 1905, when the country became a Japanese protectorate.

Between 1884 and the annexation of Korea in 1910, physical anthropologists and prehistorians were for a time obsessed with understanding the "origins" of the Japanese people, a question that was linked to the issue of national identity. This debate sought to establish the "racial" (*jinshu*) connections between the Japanese and neighboring "ethnic groups" (*minzoku*), such as the indigenous Ainu or the Koreans. It led to disputes between Tsuboi and Koganei, and also with the anthropologist, ethnologist, and archaeologist Torii Ryūzō (1870–1953).[10] One of the most famous field researchers of his time, Torii wrote fluent French, had close relationships with Paris researchers, and was chosen as Japan's representative for the Institut International d'Anthropologie in 1920. This notwithstanding, at the beginning of the twentieth century there was general agreement among scholars that the Ainu of Hokkaidō and other northerly islands were descended from the prehistoric populations of Japan, and that the Japanese were a multiethnic and non-native people who had arrived during the protohistoric period from the Asian continent via the Korean peninsula, with which they supposedly shared a close biological proximity. This idea remained central throughout the entire colonial period—a point that now brings us to the annexation of Korea.

From Keijō Medical College to the Colonial University of Korea

Keijō Medical College was founded in 1916, after the creation of the Government-General in 1910, and developed from the medical school at the Imperial Clinic of Korea, itself established in 1899. The first professorial position in anatomy, held by Kubo Takeshi (1879–1921), was created at the college in 1917.[11] Right from this early period, anatomical research in colonial Korea was concerned with the study of "race." The colonial newspaper *Keijō Nippō* had carried an article by Kubo on the "Racial Characteristics of Koreans" the previous year, and Kubo subsequently published several studies on "Koreans Considered from the Perspective of Racial Anatomy" in the journal *Chōsen oyobi Manshū* (Korea and Manchuria).[12] In June 1921 he found himself embroiled in controversy after his Korean students objected to his negative conclusions on the position of Korea in the racial hierarchy.[13] Racial anthropology in Korea in this opening phase was still imprecise, blending general impressions with measurements in insufficient quantity.[14]

The establishment of Keijō Imperial University, which would subsequently eclipse the medical college in the sphere of research, came about as part of a move to reform the Korean education system following the March First Movement against Japanese colonization in 1919. The resulting "cultural policy" saw authorization granted in 1922 for the opening of universities that would also be made accessible to Koreans.[15] In 1926, two years after it welcomed its first cohort of students, Keijō Imperial University established a Faculty of Law and Letters, as well as a Faculty of Medicine. A Faculty of Science followed in 1941. These would work in tandem with Keijō Medical College, which remained in place along with its staff. In 1929 the university possessed forty-nine chairs in the Faculty of Law and Letters, twenty-six in the Faculty of Medicine, and some five hundred students—a third of them Korean—following a curriculum taught entirely in Japanese.[16] This proportion of colonized students is high when compared, for example, to the colonial university in Algiers.[17] However, Korean students occupied subordinate positions and merely assisted Japanese researchers.

The Faculty of Medicine was distinctive for its three chairs in anatomy, the first and third of which were specialized in physical anthropology. Accordingly, "the Anatomy Section at Keijō Imperial University could pride itself on being the largest prewar Japanese research facility in biological anthropology."[18] Ueda and Imamura, who, respectively, held chairs one and three, were at that time the only Japanese scholars working specifically in the field of "physical anthropology" (*taishitsu jinruigaku*). This was the first—and, in fact, the last—time in colonial Korea that university chairs would take this name, at a moment when Japanese anthropology was splintering into biological and cultural studies.[19] The Anatomy Section trained fourteen people between 1926 and 1945, when Japan's colonial empire was dismantled. They included the Korean scholar Na Sejin (1908–1984), who would later become a renowned physical anthropologist in South Korea after decolonization.[20]

A Forensic Medicine Section was also created within the Faculty of Medicine in 1929 and placed under the leadership of Satō Takeo (1895–1958).[21] This new discipline—established in Japan with the founding of the Society of Forensic Medicine in 1916 and practiced at Keijō Medical College as of 1922—was to play a vital role in blood group research during the interwar period.[22]

The Boom in Biometry and the Keijō Anthropology School

During the interwar period Japanese physical anthropology experienced a boom in biometry, which was seen as a means of ensuring the field's scientific objectivity. Anthropological studies in the realm of serology were also gradually taking shape, the aim being to classify populations according to their blood type. Significantly, the first doctoral dissertation in anthropology was written in the field of raciology. In 1924 Matsumura Akira (1880–1936), who headed the Anthropology Section between 1925 and 1936, defended a dissertation entitled "On the Cephalic Index and Stature of the Japanese and their Local Differences"[23] at Tokyo Imperial University before a jury composed of Koganei, a geneticist, and a mathematician.[24] Increasingly during this period, major studies in the field of biological anthropology were conducted on skeletal remains, including prehistoric, and on blood groups, beginning with the metropole.[25] The discipline experienced a radical mathematization and henceforth strove to be cartographic. It was also during this time that mass censuses of the population were carried out in Japan and in the colonies.[26]

Ueda and Imamura defined their research as "the study and statistical treatment of physical racial characteristics."[27] During a lecture describing "Physical Anthropological Research on Koreans," published in 1934 in the *Korean Medical Association Journal*

(*Chōsen igakkai zasshi*), they stated that the aim of their work was "to provide a medical explanation for data relating to the anatomy of Koreans and to contribute to anthropological research on their racial constitution."[28]

While this was not the first research to be conducted on the anatomy of Koreans, it broke new ground through the sheer number of people measured, offering a comprehensive view of the colonized population via peninsula-wide studies. Ueda was instrumental in the development of Japanese biometry. His papers applying statistics to physical anthropology were regularly cited. Indeed, the history of the discipline sets him apart as "the statistics specialist among the pre-1945 anthropologists."[29] Just like their late nineteenth-century predecessors, Ueda and Imamura drew on German research by the likes of Rudolf Martin (1864–1925), a Swiss-born anthropologist working in Munich, who published race anthropology's most influential textbook in 1914. In 1935 Ueda published a technical text entitled *Seibutsu tōkeigaku* (Biometry),[30] which was featured prominently in scientific bibliographies.[31]

Ueda and Imamura's work in Seoul must be considered in tandem with the studies on religious anthropology, conducted notably by Akamatsu Chijō (1886–1960), who held the chair in religious anthropology, and Akiba Takashi (1888–1954), a specialist in Korean shamanism.[32] Cultural anthropological research in colonial Korea—which falls beyond the scope of this chapter—constituted, along with raciology, the other cornerstone of colonial anthropology. It also illustrates new developments within Japanese cultural anthropology during the interwar period and links with the Chicago and Vienna schools. Akamatsu and Akiba covered the same geographical terrain as the physical anthropologists and, like them, widened their field of study to include the whole of northeast Asia,[33] ultimately identifying links between the religions of Korea and Japan.[34] Collectively this body of research, composed of religious studies on the "dual soul" of Koreans and raciological inquiries into their physical traits, has been referred to as the "Keijō Anthropology School." This colonial anthropology was thus united around a common discourse of the "shared origins" of Koreans and Japanese.

The Science of Race: The Korean Surveys and Justification of Annexation

The Large-Scale Studies of Koreans of the 1930s

The Anatomy Section at Keijō initiated a vast program of research on the populations of Korea shortly after chairs one and three were established in 1926.[35] The aim was to determine the physical characteristics of Koreans, as well as their regional variations, and to situate them biologically in relation to the Japanese. The survey was undertaken by fieldwork expeditions in the summers of 1930 and 1931.[36] In 1933 Arase Susumu, an associate professor in the Anatomy Section, published a field diary in the Tokyo journal *Dolmen* that revealed how these expeditions worked.[37]

In order to ensure a representative sample of measurements, two teams of researchers, led by Arase and his colleague Kohama Mototsugu, proceeded to select one county (*kun*) for each of the thirteen provinces (*do*) in colonial Korea. The teams, accompanied by interpreters and Korean collaborators familiar with the areas visited, were systematically aided by police and the Japanese hygiene services in forcing locals to submit to measurement. Those carrying out the survey did not hesitate to claim they were conducting medical exams or having peasants sign letters of consent that they were unable to read, while the police explained that "the great university doctors have come from Keijō and will cure you of any illness.[38] In his notes for July 1931 Arase reports having distributed tobacco, medicine, and money or relied on police to deal with recalcitrant villagers.[39] Racial anthropologists were little concerned with the ethics of their surveys and believed that they flattered these populations by studying them.[40]

The researchers avoided areas with highly mixed populations, such as the cities where regional headquarters were located, preferring rural areas deemed difficult to access. In total 1,532 men and 684 women aged twenty years or over were measured, sometimes in very limited numbers in the case of females, who seem to have been more difficult for the anthropologists to approach.[41] The survey focused on the subjects' bodies (stature, limbs, face, and skull) and blood groups (see below). Fieldwork was supplemented by laboratory research, with some two hundred skeletons being measured at the university. Matsumoto Kiyoshi, who joined the Anatomy Section as a student in 1931, recalled in 1974 that "the teams led by Imamura and Ueda worked together to conduct an anthropological study on the physical traits of Koreans. They began by measuring two hundred skeletons, for which a huge pile of skulls, trunks, and limbs had been laid out on tables in the research rooms."[42]

The results were published in the *Korean Medical Association Journal* (*Chōsen igakkai zasshi*) in 1934, in two reports entitled "A Physical Anthropological Study of Koreans."[43] Following the sequence adopted when the study was conducted, these reports were separated into the north and the south of the peninsula. Nevertheless, the anthropologists would soon discover regional varieties. These publications were followed by more detailed articles on specific parts of the skeleton or certain organs, either in the aforementioned journal or in the *Journal of Anatomy* (*Kaibōgaku zasshi*).[44]

In coordination with Imamura and Ueda, the Forensic Medicine Section conducted a survey to determine the blood types of Koreans and the racial group to which they belonged. Blood samples were collected from 24,929 individuals between the summers of 1930 and 1934.[45] Assisted by local authorities, serologists selected five provinces and urban areas whose inhabitants were theoretically "indigenous." Blood samples were also taken from children. The results were published from 1931 on in scientific publications such as the *Journal of Criminology* (*Hanzaigaku zasshi*) at Tokyo Imperial University.

In Japanese biological anthropology of the period, these research programs are only comparable with the "Biological and Medical Study of the Ainu," led by the eugenicist scientists Nagai Hisomu (1876–1957) and Uchimura Yūshi (1897–1980) at Tokyo Imperial University. This program, financed in 1934–35 by the Japan Society for the Promotion of Science (JSPS), aimed to reassert the unique racial attributes that distinguished the Japanese from neighboring populations, including the Koreans, and bore witness to the growing influence of a counter-discourse in 1930s metropolitan Japan.[46] The eugenicist group thus tried to demonstrate that the Japanese "nation" (*kokumin*)–which encompassed Ainu and, at that time, Korean—was in fact composed of biologically different "people" (*minzoku*). For the eugenicists, mainland Japanese were the only "real" Japanese, considered as a race. At the same time, various state organizations and private foundations provided financing to Keijō Imperial University. Between 1928 and 1939, numerous studies at the university were funded by the JSPS and the Imperial Academy, and, in the private sector, the Society to Commemorate the 300th Anniversary of the Tōshōgū and the Hattori Hōkōkai foundation. The Hattori Foundation granted Ueda and Imamura 2,000 gold yen in 1934–36 for a program entitled "The Physical Anthropological Study of the Koreans and Neighboring Races."[47] Along with a similar-sized grant awarded to finance archeological research, this was the largest outside funding ever provided to the university. The research conducted by Satō's team, entitled "The Study of Blood Groups in Korea,"[48] was financed by the Tōshōgū Society (450 gold yen in 1931) and the Imperial Academy of Sciences (900 gold yen in 1933–34).[49]

The 1934 Anthropological Congress and the Eugenicist Challenge

The different trends in anthropological research each corresponded to ideological groups, which became clearly distinguished in the latter half of the 1930s. The studies conducted in colonial Korea on cultural continuities with the continent or the biological links between the Japanese and neighboring peoples were considered by peers within the scientific community to be the most accomplished of their time, as evidenced by the interest shown in Ueda and Imamura's work. In 1934 the Anthropological Society of Tokyo commemorated its fiftieth anniversary with a congress held in the Japanese capital. It brought together researchers from the discipline's two opposing schools of thought and saw "annexationist" colonials rub shoulders with medical scientists from the metropole's new eugenics movement. Twenty-five of the forty-six papers presented at the congress dealt with physical anthropology.[50]

Metropolitan Japanese medicine at the beginning of the 1930s was marked by a growth in eugenicist thought.[51] This movement developed independently of "conventional" racial and colonial anthropology, which were born of the nineteenth century and were closely linked to the debate on the "shared ancestry" of Japanese and Koreans. The annexationist discourse would become the target of those adhering to the eugenicist school, which first emerged in Japan during the 1880s but truly took shape around 1910 through the work of scientists such as Ōzawa Kenji (1852–1927) from the Faculty of Medicine at Tokyo Imperial University.[52] Ōzawa asserted the predominance of nature over nurture and advocated the introduction of a sterilization campaign modeled on that of the state of Michigan.

In 1924 Nagai Hisomu, who in 1915 succeeded Ōzawa as the chair in physiology and had close links to Koganei, created a movement that drew on the work of geneticists. This led in 1930 to the founding of the Japanese Association of Racial Hygiene (Nihon Minzoku Eisei Gakkai), and then in 1931 to the journal *Minzoku eisei*.[53] The association's title used a literal translation of the German word *Rassenhygiene* rather than *yūseigaku*, the usual rendering of "eugenics" in Japanese. Its members included numerous metropolitan scientists and renowned physical anthropologists from the autochthonist school of thought, such as Kiyono Kenji (1885–1955) or Hasebe Kotondo (1882–1969), an influential theorist on blood purity. Kiyono and Hasebe nevertheless remained restrained in their opinions during the interwar period.[54]

In 1936 the association's journal, *Minzoku eisei*, in a fever about the 1933 German law, explained in its editorial: "It has been now thirty years since the United States established a sterilization law. But only some twenty thousand sterilizations have been realized. However, since the Nazi regime established such a law, they carried out more than one hundred thousand sterilizations in only three years, including 56,244 in the last year alone. What enthusiasm! We too must shout Heil Hitler!"[55] This movement would spread an ethnocentric nativist discourse, promoting the "racial" purification of a Japanese people only comprised of "real" Japanese.

Although the eugenics movement enjoyed a strong base among university scholars in the metropole, it was only in the second half of the 1930s that it posed a serious challenge to the annexationist discourse on "shared origins." It eventually came to dominate after 1938 through the Ministry of Health, created that year to strengthen the control of citizens' bodies, and through the introduction of the National Mobilization Law. In addition to research, the eugenicists organized public lectures for the population and lobbied the government to express their opposition to the intermixing of metropolitan Japanese and colonized populations.[56] During these years Nagai and his group repeatedly supported the idea of a Eugenic Protection Law of the Japanese People, which would enable sterilizations in order to purify the Japanese people of its racial blemishes. The eugenicists' aim was not the whole subject population of the emperor (that is to say, mainland Japanese *and* colonized people), but merely the "real" mainland Japanese Volk (*minzoku*). Following a lengthy campaign, these activities saw the Imperial Diet pass a National Eugenic Law (*Kokumin yūsei hō*) in 1940.[57] Theoretically concerning the whole nation, this law would only be applied inside mainland Japan. Despite this, the annexationist discourse was not called into question by the Japanese state until the dismantling of the colonial empire in 1945. Instead, beginning in 1937, it was greatly strengthened via the introduction of "imperialization" policies (*kōminka*) aimed at "Japanizing" Koreans and Taiwanese to an extent never achieved during the interwar period.[58]

The colonial authorities in Korea heavily criticized the eugenicists, likening them to the Nazis, who they also attacked. In 1941, for example, Furukawa Kanehide, head of the security office at the police department in Korea, criticized the actions of the newly created Ministry of Health and compared those of the eugenicists to the anti-Semitic policies of the Nazis. Furukawa saw their actions as an obstacle to amicable relations between Korea and Japan, as well as contrary to the view of the Japanese as a "composite people" (*fukugō minzoku*) sharing common origins with the populations of Asia.[59] In 1937 the Government-General of Korea began to publish critical pamphlets stressing the need for a "concept of multi-ethnic harmony" (*minzoku kyōwa shisō*) in the Far East, and tirelessly defended the "shared origins" thesis.[60] The annexationist and autochthonist ideologies thus clashed from the latter half of the 1930s.

During the 1934 anthropological congress, medical scientists from colonial Korea upheld the continental annexationist discourse by presenting comparative studies stressing the racial proximity between neighboring populations in East Asia, in particular between Koreans and Japanese.[61] Keijō scholars such as Shima Gorō and Ueda, who had become a member of the Anthropological Society's scientific board, delivered presentations on subjects like biometry and Korean physical anthropology.[62] Imamura delivered a paper on the "Differential Relations between East Asian Races."[63] His taxonomy classified Asian races into four groups. Group three established a link between Koreans, eastern Chinese, Taiwanese, and Japanese—in other words, the northeast Asian populations controlled by Japan, thereby legitimizing the colonial order. Furthermore, Imamura already saw a strong proximity between these peoples and his fourth group, which included the people of the Philippines, Borneo, Java, and Burma, regions that were occupied after 1940. However, if Japanese physical anthropology—or other colonial knowledges—produced particular discourses about Koreans at this time, these discourses were developed within an interaction between the colony and the metropole as well as on the transnational level.[64]

Nevertheless, a plurality of viewpoints was apparent at the 1934 symposium, betraying the oppositions between colonial researchers from the Anthropological Society of Tokyo on the one hand, and, on the other, scholars affiliated with the Japanese Association of Racial Hygiene, who defended the specificity of Japan. The eugenicist scientist Koyama Eizō (1899–1983), for example, discussed the "degeneration" of the Ainu and the Taiwanese aborigines. Koyama's views would become increasingly radical during the war, when he argued against the intermixing of metropolitan Japanese and colonial natives.[65] In 1934 the Association of Racial Hygiene also held its own symposium, at which Kiyono upheld the theory of the uninterrupted biological continuity of the Japanese since Protohistory.[66] The mid-1930s was thus an important time in the rise of autochthonist—or Japan-centric—discourse, although, as I noted earlier, this narrative would only come to dominate after 1940.[67]

The Japanese People and the Surveys in Asia: The Search for a Racial Continuum

Beginning in 1935 Ueda and Imamura turned their attention to the links between the Japanese and the peoples of northeast Asia, using Korea as a staging ground for their work on the continent.

Colonial Anthropology and The Japanese People

In 1935 the Anthropological Society published a lengthy book entitled *The Japanese People*, which combined physical and cultural anthropology, past and present, and devoted a significant section to the Korean peninsula.[68] As an emanation of the Anthropological Society, this book upheld the colonialist position; the eugenicists, who were critical of Japan's assimilation policies, took no part in its writing. Throughout its pages, arguments in support of the "mixed racial origins" and "common ancestry" discourses were put forward by the anatomists Ueda, Imamura, Shima, and Kanaseki Takeo (1897–1983) from the Imperial University of Taipei; by the archaeologists Hamada Kosaku (1881–1938) and Umehara Sueji (1893–1983) at Kyoto Imperial University; and by Shimada Sadahiko, head of the museum in Port Arthur, thus underlining once again the weight these theories carried in the academic community.[69]

In his "Comparison of the Korean and Japanese Constitutions," Ueda criticized the idea that the "Japanese" formed a distinct biological unit, arguing instead that they fell along a racial continuum with the continent.[70] He drew in particular on craniometric analysis in order to corroborate this theory: "Who are the Japanese? Many researchers have attempted to answer this question using racial studies. Yet after numerous debates, [science] has so far been unsuccessful. This is only natural, given the extent of the problem. Resolving it will necessarily involve studying neighboring peoples—Koreans, Chinese, Manchurians, Tungus, Ainu, and the peoples of the Southern Seas."[71] The term "relationship" (in Japanese, *kankei*)—a keyword in the writings of Ueda and Imamura—made it possible to assert the "natural" unity between Japan and northeast or Southern Asia. The idea that the Japanese had arrived in the archipelago during the protohistoric period was central to the discourse on the "common ancestral origins" of the Japanese and continental Asians. This conclusion was "substantiated" by racial anthropology as a means of legitimizing Japan's continental imperialism. Ueda combined the nineteenth-century model of racial substitution during the protohistoric period (see the first section of this chapter) with the "shared origins" theory developed in the run-up to the annexation. In his view, "ethnic groups" (*minzoku*) were defined by physical characteristics rather than by culture. If physical similarities allowed the Japanese to be likened to the Koreans, then they constituted one single "ethnic group." In this way, anthropology provided scientific evidence of the "shared origins" linking Koreans and Japanese.

In the aforementioned article, Ueda presented twenty-four measurements and indices: sixteen for the skull and eight for the rest of the skeleton. The entire set of data—presented in graphic form, using dotted lines in the style of the Nazi raciologist Theodor Mollison to express the standard deviations for each entry—made it possible to determine the "coefficient of racial likeness" (*shuzoku ruiji keisū*): in other words, the biological distance from a particular standard value. This method, which was central to Ueda's argument, allowed him to illustrate the racial distance separating the Japanese from the populations studied, and then to minimize it. According to Ueda, while the "Chinese and Koreans differed remarkably," the physical characteristics of the Koreans—namely, a clear brachycephaly (broad headedness) in the north and south of the peninsula, a high neurocranium, and a high upper face—made them similar to the Japanese. He went on to explain that "it must be stressed that Koreans from the center of the peninsula most resemble the Japanese, through numerous characteristics, and that Japanese from the Kinki and Chūgoku regions, the birthplace of Japanese civilization, are the most Korean. Does this not suggest the ancient racial links connecting the Japanese and Koreans?"[72]

With its view of ethnic groups as anatomically isolable entities and skeletons as units that had remained unchanged since prehistory, Ueda's fixist biology was able to establish links between the Japanese and Koreans and provide scientific evidence to support the official ideology of the period.[73] At the same time, while Ueda legitimized Japan's colonial domination of Asia, his "radical theory on the common origins" of Koreans and Japanese also had the effect of deconstructing the "Japanese nation" as a biological entity.[74]

Shared Origins and the Northeast Asian Shift in Research

In 1935 Imamura published two studies on Korea in the *Journal of the Anthropological Society of Tokyo*, in which he reflected on the whole of East Asia.[75] Developing the theory he presented at Tokyo's fiftieth anniversary symposium, these studies on races in prehistory, antiquity, and the present day constituted a turning point in Imamura's work, from a narrower focus on Koreans to a broader, regional scope.[76] In one article he set out his view of the regions bordering the Korean peninsula. Through Imamura's discourse, the notion of "East Asia"—which would reappear later in the ideology of the "Greater East Asia Co-Prosperity Sphere"—became a political concept: the idea of a racial unity between the conquered "Asian" populations.

The article synopsized the conclusions of Imamura's fieldwork and attempted to empirically demonstrate the median position of the Japanese among the peoples and races of East Asia, as well as their proximity to Koreans and eastern Chinese (Fujian, Beijing, and Fushun). Imamura scientifically reasserted the "composite and multi-ethnic" nature of the Japanese, to borrow the expression used to affirm their racial links with the continent.[77] Unsurprisingly, the "racial geography" produced by Imamura and Shima revealed that the Japanese almost perfectly matched the Koreans.

The first of the four groups identified by the authors consisted of "Koreans, Japanese, and Chinese from the north and south, all of them very similar." Sketches showing the front and upper sections of the skull were used to compare these three populations: the Koreans were deemed to have "a slightly shorter head than the baseline [represented by Japanese from the Kinki region] but they have high faces and on this point resemble the Chinese." However, according to the authors, these differences could be classed as infra-groupal. Although Imamura "regretted" that contemporary science had yet to sufficiently explain the "hereditary links between the different

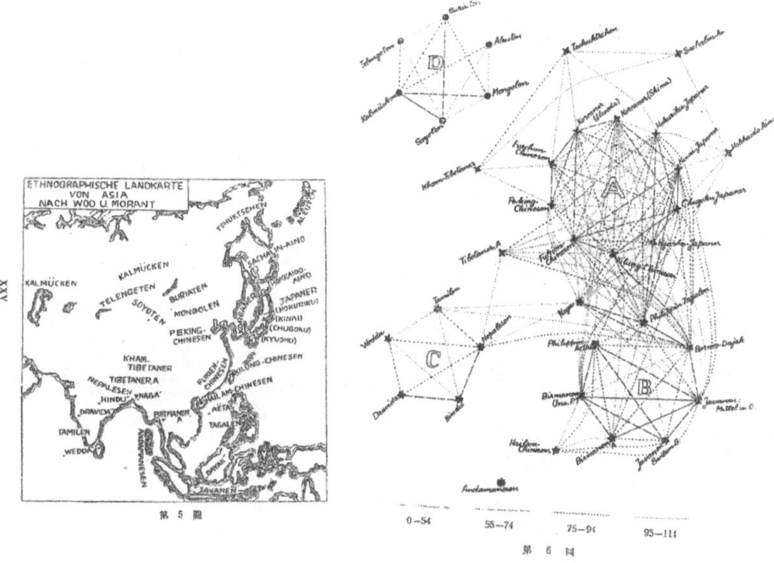

Fig 5. Map from "The Differential Relations between East Asian Races" by Imamura and Shima (1935), visualizing the links between the four racial groups. Courtesy of the Anthropological Society of Nippon.

characteristics of the skull," he did not hesitate to conclude that cranial morphotypes were genetically transmitted and formulated the "general hypothesis that people with a similar size or shaped skull also shared some proximity in their blood relationship." Science thus provided a means of upholding the "shared ancestry" between Japanese and Koreans, or even between the populations of northeast Asia. He ultimately expanded its scope to embrace the Pacific Islanders. This area had been the focus of Japanese cultural and biological anthropology ever since the League of Nations had made Micronesia a Japanese mandate in 1921.

On the Eve of War on the Continent: The Research Missions in Northeast Asia

It was in this context that, in June 1935, the journal of anthropological and archaeological studies *Dolmen* published a special issue on the "Japanese Stone Age," with a third of the volume devoted to the

114　今村・島—東部アジア諸種族の相互關係

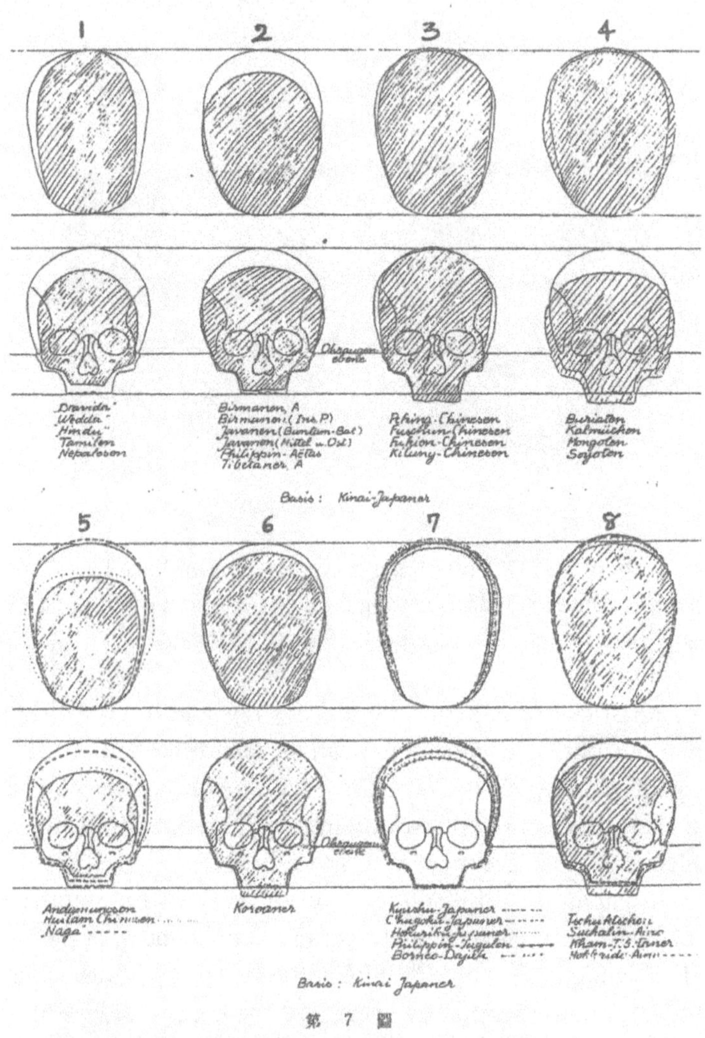

第　7　圖

き、指數のみでなく、外廓線の恰好をも考慮すべきであるが今回は之を省いた。

第7圖 (1) の印度族及び Nepalesen は著しく長頭であるが顔が小さい。

(30)

Fig 6. Skull sketches from "The Differential Relations between East Asian Races" by Imamura and Shima (1935), using Kinki Japanese as criterion. Courtesy of the Anthropological Society of Nippon.

Asian continent or the colonies.[78] The list of study areas reveals a "Japan" that was not confined to the archipelago but rather expanding into the new "East Asia." Just like *The Japanese People*, *Dolmen* drew on both the network of colonial researchers and the Anthropology Section at Tokyo Imperial University but excluded scientists from the eugenicist movement. Once again, science from the imperial universities defended the colonial status quo.

In this special issue Imamura discussed the subject of "Stone Age Man in Korea."[79] It was his third publication in six months in one of the most important journals of the capital. His article analyzed skeletons from the peninsula, other prehistoric skeletons, and anthropometric measurements taken from contemporary populations and classified them into racial groups. He identified what in his view were clear similarities between Korean prehistoric people, the populations of Manchuria, and Japanese from the west of the archipelago.[80] Inevitably, Imamura's craniometric paleoanthropology concluded that a racial proximity existed between the Japanese and the colonized populations.

The outbreak of war in the summer of 1937 sparked an increase in scientific research on the continent. In parallel with his study of Koreans, Imamura turned his attention toward Mongolia and the north of Manchuria. The many texts published by his team in 1940 show a clear expansion of the territories studied. In that year Imamura published *The Constitution of the People of Manchuria and Mongolia*, edited by the Society for the Study of Continental Cultures at Keijō Imperial University (founded in 1933).[81] The concept of "Man-mō" grew out of the war, creating the illusion of a natural cultural area formed by Manchuria and Mongolia, just as the concept "Man-sen" had done previously for Manchuria and Korea. In 1941 the religious anthropologists Akamatsu and Akiba published a book with an identical geographic focus (see the first section of this chapter). Researchers from the Forensic Medicine Section also studied the populations of Manchuria, then Mongolia, between 1934 and 1940.[82]

Following another monograph in 1940,[83] Imamura's team published three articles in the *Lectures in Anthropology and Prehistory* series edited by the prestigious archaeological publisher Yūzankaku.[84] After 1940, as the war spread into southeast Asia, these research expeditions and comparatist studies were extended to Thailand and New Guinea, the aim still being to situate the Japanese biologically.[85]

Conclusion: Colonial Assimilation and Insular Isolation

When Japan colonized Korea in the early twentieth century, it introduced policies designed to increase its knowledge of the peninsula, beginning in 1906 with the "Survey of Ancient Customs and Institutions." In parallel, scientific inquiry into the culture and race of the Koreans had been a constant preoccupation of physical anthropologists and medical scientists since the 1880s, with fieldwork being conducted in Korea around 1900 at the behest of Tokyo Imperial University.

The creation of colonial institutions such as the Medical College and, above all, the Faculty of Medicine at Keijō Imperial University in 1926 caused a shift in the direction and scope of anthropological research on the Koreans. While it resembled its counterparts in the metropole, the imperial university in Korea was also a colonial institution like the one founded in Taihoku (Taipei) in 1928. This duality was a fundamental characteristic of the institution. Viewing it as an "imperial" university emphasizes the idea of a Japanese empire that successfully managed to "integrate" its overseas territories, mirroring the propaganda of the period. However, perceiving it as a colonial institution provides insight into its role in legitimizing the Japanese domination of Korea.

This brings me to the question of the way bodies were controlled and utilized for political purposes, at a time when the Korean population was perceived and classified as a biological resource whose filiation with Japan needed to be constantly reaffirmed. The theses developed by the Anatomy and Forensic Medicine sections are a perfect illustration of "continental imperialism" as defined by Hannah Arendt: in other words, they constitute annexationist practices legitimized by an alleged ethnic proximity between conqueror and conquered.[86] The science at work here appears to be eminently political in nature. Physical anthropologists at Keijō University strove to establish links between the Japanese and Koreans, thereby maintaining the political illusion of "one single people" (*dōitsu minzoku*), one sole and unique nation of subjects united around the emperor, as asserted as of 1931 in the official slogan *Naisen ittai* (Korea and Japan, one body). Trapped in a circular discourse with predetermined conclusions, raciology used skeletons and blood groups to demonstrate the idea of racial proximity between the two populations, as underscored by colonialism since 1910. This theory became increasingly prominent after the uprising of March 1, 1919. The comparative studies on northeast Asia saw Japan as constituting a microcosm of Asia, the aim being to better defend the colonial order. And yet in their work Ueda and Imamura continually differentiated between "Metropolitans" and "Koreans": the need to compare Koreans and Japanese meant that they were always in principle distinguished.

The research undertaken by the Keijō Faculty of Medicine was also conditioned by the context of the 1930s. In some ways, this colonial science was fighting a rearguard action: Keijō Imperial University was founded late in the history of modern colonization, which spanned the final third of the nineteenth century into the mid-twentieth. It fought to defend the legitimacy of the colonial empire during the interwar period, at a time when the global colonial order was growing weak. Evoking the context of the aftermath of the First World War and the economic depression of 1929 may be a commonplace, but the ensuing weakening of nation-states intensified the desire to affirm national identity. In Japan these tensions resulted in the creation and subsequent consolidation of a eugenicist discourse on the "Japanese race." This movement would become dominant in Japan around 1940. The other factor explaining the shift toward an "insularist" discourse is the creation of the "Greater East Asia Co-Prosperity Sphere" in 1940. The idea of Japan's supremacy over Asia—a discourse that had not existed vis-à-vis the colonies—appeared at this time, thus paving the way for the ethnicist theories proposed by the eugenicists.[87]

The disappearance of the colonialist discourse underscoring the unity between metropolitan Japan and Korea highlights the process by which Japan since 1945—or, in reality, since 1940—has come to refocus on the archipelago. Stripped of its colonies, it would reconstruct an "island" identity devoid of links to the Asian continent.[88] Supporters of the ethnicist discourse, who during the colonial period had contrasted "pure Japanese" with the colonized populations (notably the Koreans), occupied key positions in wartime Japan, positions they retained until approximately 1970. Ueda and Imamura meanwhile took up posts in the Tōhoku region, Shima worked as an engineer at Osaka City Medical University, and Kanaseki swapped Taipei for Kyūshū. With the colonial school retreating to these provincial posts, the discourse linking Japan to "Asia" disappeared from postdecolonization mainstream scholarship, while the capital's main universities were dominated by scholars from the ethnicist school of thought. At the same time, in the new South Korea founded in 1948, Ueda's former student Na Sejin, now a professor at Seoul National University, argued that the Korean "racial pool" was entirely distinct from neighboring countries.[89] In Japan the postdecolonization period saw the emergence of the myth of Japan as a "homogeneous nation." This was the main conclusion now defended by physical anthropology, by an insularist archaeology (which suddenly "discovered" a Japanese Paleolithic period in 1946), and by a "re-nationalized" historical science.[90] The memory of the colonies and the shared ancestry with Korea was forgotten.

Notes

1. For more information on the university, see Keijō Teikoku Daigaku, ed., *Keijō teikoku daigaku ichiran* (Keijō Imperial University annual reports, 1924–1942, National Library of Korea); Abe Hiroshi, "Nihon tōchi-ka Chōsen no kōtō kyōiku" (Higher Education in Korea under Japanese Rule), *Shisō* 565 (1971): 920–41; Keijō Teikoku Daigaku Dōsōkai, ed. [KTDD], *Konpeki, haruka ni* (Far Away, Deep Blue [= Korea]), (Tokyo: Keijō Teikoku Daigaku Dōsōkai, 1974); Okamoto Takuji, "Keijō teikoku daigaku to kagaku" (Scientific Practices at Keijō Imperial University), *Kagakushi kagaku tetsugaku* 11 (1993): 70–84; Han Yongjin, "Il'che singmin t'ongch'i-ha ŭi taehak kyoyuk" (University Education under the Colonial Regime of Imperial Japan), *Hanguk sa simin kangjwa* 18 (1996): 94–112; Chŏng Sŏn'i, *Kyŏngsŏng cheguk taehak yŏn'gu* (Keijō Imperial University) (Seoul: Mun'ŭm-sa, 2002); Chŏng Kŭnsik et al., *Singmin kwŏllyŏk kwa kŭndae chisik* (Colonial Power and Modern Knowledge) (Seoul: Seoul National University Press, 2011).

2. Numerous studies have been written in Japanese, Korean, and English on Japan's colonization of Korea. See the classic study by Ramon H. Myers and Mark R. Peattie, eds., *Japan's Colonial Empire, 1894–1945* (Princeton: Princeton University Press, 1984); or Alain Delissen and Arnaud Nanta, "Sociétés et possessions coloniales japonaises (fin xixe à mi-xxe siècles)," in *Les sociétés coloniales à l'âge des empires*, ed. Dominique Barjot and Jacques Frémeaux (Paris: Armand Colin, 2012), 173–82. On the colonial historiography, see Arnaud Nanta, "The Japanese Colonial Historiography in Korea (1905–1945)," in *History at Stake in East Asia*, ed. Rosa Caroli and Pierre F. Souyri (Venice: Libreria Editrice Cafoscarina, 2012), 83–105.

3. On the subject of Western European racial anthropology see, in addition to the introduction to this book, Patrick Tort, *La raison classificatoire* (Paris: Aubier, 1989); Claude Liauzu, *Race et civilisation: l'autre dans la culture occidentale* (Paris: Syros, 1992); Léon Poliakov, *The Aryan Myth: A History of Racist and Nationalist Ideas in Europe* (New York: Barnes & Noble, 1971); Stephen J. Gould, *The Mismeasure of Man*, rev. ed. (New York: W. W. Norton, 1996); Claude Blanckaert, ed., *Les politiques de l'anthropologie en France* (Paris: L'Harmattan, 2001); and Carole Reynaud-Paligot, ed., *Histoire comparée des pensées raciales. 1860–1930* (Munich: Oldenbourg Verlag, 2009). See also the classic study by Benedict Anderson, *Imagined Communities*, rev. ed. (London: Verso, 1991), chapter 8, 141–54.

4. Hannah Arendt, *The Origins of Totalitarianism*, vol. 2: *Imperialism* (New York: Harcourt, 1973).

5. As is customary in the Sinicized world, family names precede given names.

6. On the history of physical anthropology in Japan and in connection with colonial Korea, see Terada Kazuo, *Nihon no jinruigaku* (Japanese anthropology) (Tokyo: Shisakusha, 1975); Ch'oe Kilsŏng, "Nihon shokuminchi jidai no minzokugaku—jinruigaku" (Ethnography and anthropology in colonial Japan), in *Nihon shokuminchi to bunka henyō* (Japanese colonies and cultural transformations) (Tokyo: Ochanomizu Shobō, 1994), 3–32; Arnaud Nanta, "Koropokgrus, Aïnous, Japonais, aux origines du peuplement de l'archipel: Débat chez les anthropologues, 1884–1913," *Ebisu* 30 (2003): 123–54; Chŏn Kyŏngsu, *Kankoku no jinruigaku hyakunen* (One hundred years of anthropology in Korea) (Tokyo: Fūkyōsha, 2004); Arnaud Nanta, *Les débats sur les origines du peuplement de l'archipel japonais dans l'anthropologie et l'archéologie (décennies 1870–1990)*, PhD diss., Faculty of Geography, History, and Social Sciences (GHSS), Paris 7, 2004; Sakano Tōru, *Teikoku Nihon to jinruigakusha* (Imperial Japan and the anthropologists) (Tokyo: Keisō Shobō, 2005), 295–353; Kim Okchu, "Kyŏngsŏng chedae ŭihakpu ŭi ch'ejil illyuhak yŏngu" (Physical anthropology at Keijō Imperial University's Faculty of Medicine), *Ŭi-sa hak* 17, no. 2 (2008): 191–203; Chŏn Kyŏngsu, "Keijō gakuha no jinkotsu kenkyū to senji jinruigaku" (Wartime anthropology and research on skeletal remains by the Keijō school), *Kokusai kenkyū shūkai hōkokusho* 42 (2012): 73–113; Chŏng Chunyŏng, "P'i ŭi injongjuŭi wa singminji ŭihak: Kyŏngsŏng chedae pŏb'ŭihak kyosil ŭi hyŏlaek-hyŏng illyuhak" (Colonial medicine and blood racism: blood group anthropology at Keijō Imperial University's Forensic Medicine Section), *Ŭi-sa hak* 21, no. 3 (2012): 513–50 (a Japanese

translation of this text was published in *Kokusai kenkyū shūkai hōkokusho*, 42 [2012]: 151–71); and Ch'oe Sŏg'yong, *Il'che ŭi Chosŏn yŏngu wa singminji-jŏk chisik saengsan* (Japan's colonial process of knowledge-making on Joseon) (Seoul: Minsok-wŏn, 2012), 254–81.

7. The University of Tokyo was formed in 1877 by the merger of several specialized schools and became an imperial university in 1886. For further information on the Anthropological Society, see Terada, *Nihon no jinruigaku*; Nanta, "Koropokgrus"; and Sakano, *Teikoku Nihon*.

8. Foreign medical professors during the 1870s and 1880s were all German.

9. Frederick Cooper and Ann Laura Stoler, eds., *Tensions of Empire: Colonial Cultures in a Bourgeois World* (Berkeley: University of California Press, 1997), 3–4.

10. The term *jinshu*, employed by anatomists, was more biologically determined, whereas *minzoku* was defined more by culture. However, *minzoku* also took on a biological connotation when contrasted with the word "nation" (*kokumin*). The racial taxonomies used in Japan at the time mirrored those employed by the other colonial powers and were characterized by the same vagueness and imprecision. Compare Sakano, *Teikoku Nihon*; and Arnaud Nanta, "L'altérité aïnoue dans le Japon moderne (années 1880–1900)," *Annales HSS*, January-February (2006): 247–73.

11. Chŏn, "Keijō gakuha no jinkotsu," 78.

12. Kubo Takeshi, "Chōsen-jin no jinshu teki tokuchō" (The racial characteristics of Koreans), *Keijō nippō* 55 (June 9, 1917); Kubo Takeshi, "Jinshu kaibōgaku yori mitaru Chōsen-jin" (Koreans considered from the perspective of racial anatomy), *Chōsen oyobi Manshū* 115 (1917): 72–77; 117: 58–61.

13. Kim Hoi-eun, "Anatomically Speaking: The Kubo Incident and the Paradox of Race in Colonial Korea," in *Race and Racism in Modern East Asia*, ed. R. Kowner and W. Demel (Boston: Brill, 2013), 411–30; Mark Caprio, "Abuse of Modernity: Japanese Biological Determinism and Identity Management in Colonial Korea," *Cross-Currents*, 10 (2014): web.

14. See Chŏn, "Keijō gakuha no jinkotsu," 78n1.

15. See Abe, "Nihon tōchi-ka," 927–28. Nevertheless, these institutions had to remain under the control of the Government-General, as illustrated by a failed Korean attempt to create a 'national" university in 1922. KTDD, *Konpeki, haruka ni*, 3–9; Abe, "Nihon tōchi-ka," 927–36; Ch'oe, "Nihon shokuminchi"; Han, "Il'che singmin," 102–4.

16. See Chŏng et al., *Singmin kwŏllyŏk kwa*; Kim, "Kyŏngsŏng chedae ŭihakpu ŭi," 193; and Tsūdō Ayumi, "Keijō teikoku daigaku igakubu no shokuminchi teki tokuchō. Kōsatsu no tame ni" (Elements for reflection on the colonial characteristics of Keijō Imperial University's Faculty of Medicine), *Kokusai kenkyū shūkai hōkokusho* 42 (2012): 53–58.

17. Pierre Singaravélou, "L'enseignement supérieur colonial: Un état des lieux," *Histoire de l'éducation* 122 (2009): 71–92.

18. Sakano, *Teikoku Nihon*, 328; Shima Gorō, "Jōdai igakubu kaibōgaku kyōshitsu sono ta no kotodomo" (The Anatomy Section at Keijō Imperial University's Faculty of Medicine), in KTDD, 239–41; Chŏng et al., *Singmin kwŏllyŏk kwa*.

19. Ueda had previously been a professor at the Tokyo Medical School as of 1919. Imamura graduated from the Faculty of Medicine at Kyoto Imperial University in 1919, where he obtained a PhD in anatomy. Ueda and Imamura both served as deans of the Keijō Faculty of Medicine.

20. KTDD, *Konpeki, haruka ni*, 244–45; Chŏng, *Kyŏngsŏng cheguk taehak*; Kim Hoi-eun, "Reauthenticating Race: Na Sejin and the Recycling of Colonial Physical Anthropology in Postcolonial Korea," *Journal of Korean Studies* 21, no. 2 (2016): 449–83.

21. Kobayashi Hiroshi, "Hōigaku kyōshitsu ni tsuite" (On the Forensic Medicine Section), in KTDD, 197–200; Kim, "Kyŏngsŏng chedae ŭihakpu ŭi," 198–200.

22. Chŏng et al., *Singmin kwŏllyŏk kwa*, 532–34.

23. Matsumura Akira, "On the Cephalic Index and Stature of Japanese and their Local Differences," *Journal of the Faculty of Science, Imperial University of Tokyo* 1, no. 1 (1925).

24. The geneticist in question was Fujii Kenjirō (1866–1952), a famous cytologist who founded the first Japanese chair in genetics at Tokyo Imperial University in 1918. The mathematician was Yoshie Takuji (1874–1947).

25. Examples include the publications by the *Journal of the Anthropological Society* in Tokyo, the studies by Kiyono Kenji at Kyoto Imperial University, those by Miyamoto Hiroto on Japanese skeletons (Nanta, *Débats sur les origines*), and those by Sunada Sotoharu at Kanazawa Medical University.

26. Three censuses were carried out by the Japanese in colonial Korea: in 1925 (intermediate), 1930 (complete), and 1935 (intermediate).

27. Terada, *Nihon no jinruigaku*, 212.

28. Quoted in Kim, "Kyŏngsŏng chedae ŭihakpu ŭi," 195.

29. Ueda occupied a position of superiority over a professor like Kiyono, whose methodological errors he threatened to expose (KTDD, *Konpeki, haruka ni*, 243; Terada, *Nihon no jinruigaku*, 202; Sakano, *Teikoku Nihon*, 328–29).

30. Ueda Tsunekichi, *Seibutsu tōkeigaku* (Biometry) (Tokyo: Iwanami Shoten, 1935).

31. KTDD, *Konpeki, haruka ni*, 241; Terada, *Nihon no jinruigaku*; Sakano Tōru, "Kiyono Kenji no jinshu ron" (The racial theory of Kiyono Kenji), *Kagakushi kagaku tetsugaku* 11 (1993): 85–99; Nanta, *Débats sur les origines*; Arnaud Nanta, "Kiyono Kenji: anthropologie physique et débats sur la 'race japonaise' à l'époque de l'empire colonial (1920–1945)," in *Histoire comparée des pensées raciales*, ed. C. Reynaud-Paligot (Munich: Oldenbourg Verlag, 2009), 43–58.

32. Akamatsu graduated from Kyoto Imperial University, and Akiba, from that of Tokyo. In 1937 they published their famous work *Chōsen fuzoku no kenkyū* (A study of Korean shamanism), which has since been translated into Korean. See Chŏn, *Kankoku no jinruigaku*; Kikuchi Akira, "Chijō no jijō–Kindai Nihon bukkyō to shokuminchi jinruigaku" (The circumstances of Akamatsu Chijō: Buddhism and colonial anthropology in modern Japan), in *Teikoku no shikaku / shikaku* (The perspectives/blind spots of the empire), ed. Sakano Tōru and Shin Ch'anggŏn (Tokyo: Seikyū-sha, 2010), 80–112; Sakano, *Teikoku Nihon*.

33. In 1941 they published a book entitled *Manmō no minzoku to shūkyō* (The peoples and religions of Manchuria and Mongolia). Refer to the third section of this chapter.

34. Sakano, *Teikoku Nihon*, 320–28.

35. KTDD, *Konpeki, haruka ni*, 239–40.

36. KTDD, *Konpeki, haruka ni*, 243.

37. Arase Susumu, "Chōsen-jin seitai sokutei ryokō nisshi" (Travel diary [during fieldwork] to measure the bodies of Koreans), *Dolmen* 8 (1933): 80–83; 9 (1933): 24–28; 10 (1933): 28–37; see also Ch'oe, *Il'che ŭi Chosŏn yŏngu*, 266–67.

38. Arase, "Chōsen-jin seitai sokutei," 8:82.

39. Arase, "Chōsen-jin seitai sokutei," 10:33.

40. KTDD, *Konpeki, haruka ni*, 243.

41. Arase, "Chōsen-jin seitai sokutei"; Kohama Mototsugu, Arase Susumu, Tanabe Hidehisa, and Takamure Osamu, "Chōsenjin no taishitsu jinruigaku-teki kenkyū," *Chōsen igakkai zasshi* 24 (1934): 60–110; Kohama M., Arase S., Shima Gorō, Nishioka Tatsuzō, Tanabe H., and Takamure O., *idem*, *Chōsen igakkai zasshi* 24 (1934): 111–53; Ch'oe, *Il'che ŭi Chosŏn yŏngu*, 266–67. This national survey aimed to study between 90 and 168 males, and between 6 and 110 females, depending on the county visited. Some Koreans questioned why the doctors merely observed them without distributing medicine (Arase, "Chōsen-jin seitai sokutei"; Sakano, *Teikoku Nihon*, 328–30; Kim, "Kyŏngsŏng chedae ŭihakpu ŭi").

42. KTDD, *Konpeki, haruka ni*, 242.

43. Kohama et al., "Chōsenjin no taishitsu."

44. Kohama Mototsugu, "Chōsenjin no kotsuban no jinruigakuteki kenkyū" (Anthropological study on the pelvis of Koreans), *Chōsen igakkai zasshi* 25 (1935): 136–82; Kondō Michiru, "Chōsenjin chōkankotsu no sōkan narabi ni kanren 1. Chōsenjin jōshi narabi ni kashi kotsu no kenkyū hoi" (The correlations and links between the long bones of Koreans: 1. Supplement to the research on the upper and lower limbs of Koreans), *Chōsen igakkai zasshi* 9 (1937): 1004–17; Kawaguchi Toshitsugu, "Gendai Chōsenjin no chūkō nō maku dōmyaku-kō no kenkyū" (The mean meningeal arteries of modern-day Koreans), *Kaibōgaku zasshi* 8 (1935): 141–67.

45. Kim, "Kyŏngsŏng chedae ŭihakpu ŭi," 198–200; Chŏng, "P'i ŭi injongjuŭi wa singminji ŭihak," 534–540.

46. "Ainu no igakuteki seibutsugakuteki kenkyū." The results were set out in 1936 and 1937 during a congress held jointly by the Anthropological Society and the Japanese Society of Ethnology, which was founded in 1934. Kinase Takashi, "Ainu 'metsubō' ron no shosō to kindai Nihon" (Overview of the debate on the "extinction" of the Ainu in modern Japan), in *Kindai Nihon no tashazō to jigazō* (Images of the Other and the Self in Modern Japan), ed. Shinohara Tōru, 54–84 (Tokyo: Kashiwa Shobō, 2001).

47. "Chōsenjin oyobi kinrin shuzoku taishitsu jinruigakuteki kenkyū." The sum of prewar 1,000 gold yen is the equivalent today of around 28,000 dollars.

48. "Chōsen no ketsueki-gata kenkyū."

49. Chŏng, *Kyŏngsŏng cheguk taehak*, 199–201.

50. Ethnology and folklore were explored in eight papers, and archaeology, in eighteen (Nanta, *Débats sur les origines*, 516–530). A second series of commemorations took place on October 12, 13, and 14, 1934. The Anthropological Society was founded in October 1884.

51. For further information on Japanese eugenics, see Suzuki Zenji, *Nihon no yūseigaku* (Eugenics in Japan) (Tokyo: Sankyō Shuppan, 1983); Oguma Eiji, "Tsumazuita junketsu shugi, yuseigaku seiryoku no minzoku seisaku ron" (The failure of eugenicist forces and Völkisch pure-blood discourses), *Jōkyō*, 2nd series, 11 (1994): 38–50; Oguma Eiji, *Tan'itsu minzoku shinwa no kigen* (Tokyo: Shinyō-sha, 1995), 235–70 (translated by David Askew as *A Genealogy of "Japanese" Self-Images*, Melbourne: Trans Pacific Press, 2002); Fujino Yutaka, *Nihon fashizumu to yūsei shisō* (Japanese fascism and eugenic thought) (Tokyo: Kamokawa Shuppan, 1998); Yonemoto Shōhei, Matsubara Yōko et al., *Yūsei undo to ningen shakai* (Eugenics and human societies) (Tokyo: Kōdansha, 2000); Nanta, *Débats sur les origins*, 504–514.

52. In 1884, Takahashi Yoshio (1861–1937) published *Nihon jinshu kaizō ron* (On reforming the Japanese race), in which he argued for an interbreeding between the white and yellow races.

53. Instances of the word "race" (*jinshu*) being translated as *minzoku* in Japanese, meaning ethnic group or *Volk*, can be found during this period but are unusual. Nagai used the two terms interchangeably. See Nagai Hisomu, *Yūseigaku gairon* (Introduction to eugenics) (Tokyo: Yūzankaku, 1936), 22–24.

54. Arnaud Nanta, "Physical Anthropology and the Reconstruction of Japanese Identity in Postcolonial Japan," *Social Science Japan Journal* 11 (2008): 29–47; French version revised and published in 2010, *Cipango* 17 (2010): 151–83.

55. "Kantō-gen" (Editorial), *Minzoku eisei* 5, no. 1 (1936), quoted in Suzuki, *Nihon no yūseigaku*, 160–62.

56. Nagai Hisomu, "Minzoku no konketsu ni tsuite" (On mixed-blood ethnicity), *Minzoku eisei* 2 (1932): 395–96.

57. This law was followed in 1947 by a Eugenic Protection Law (*Yūsei hogo hō*), which remained in force until 1996. The Eugenic Protection Law was intended notably to control the behavior of women and served to intern people suffering from leprosy.

58. Oguma, *Tan'itsu minzoku*; Komagome Takeshi, *Shokuminchi teikoku Nihon no bunka tōgō* (Cultural integration within Japan's colonial empire) (Tokyo: Iwanami, 1996); Oguma Eiji, *"Nihonjin" no kyōkai* (The boundaries of the "Japanese") (Tokyo: Shinyō-sha, 1998); Nanta, *Débats sur les origines*; Sakano, *Teikoku Nihon*.

59. Oguma, *Tan'itsu minzoku*, 243.

60. In 1941 for example, a pamphlet entitled "Naisen ittai no rinen oyobi sono gugen hōsaku yōkō" (Outline of the ideal of unity between Korea and Japan, and the policy necessary for its realization) stressed the common ancestral origins of the Japanese and Koreans, and defended the assimilation policies (Oguma, *Tan'itsu minzoku*, 242).

61. Tōkyō Jinruigakkai, ed., "Tōkyō jinrui gakkai sōritsu gojū nen kinen kōenkai kiji" (Congress to celebrate the fiftieth anniversary of the Anthropological Society of Tokyo), *Jinruigaku zasshi* 49, no. 5 (1934): 173–99; 49, no. 6 (1934): 215–40.

62. Ueda Tsunekichi, "Sōkansū r no kanben naru shin keisan hō ni tsuite" (A new and simpler method of calculating the correlation coefficient *r*); Shima Gorō, "Gendai chōsen-jin taishitsu jinruigaku ho'i (zugaikotsu no bu)" (Supplements in physical anthropology on modern-day Koreans [skulls]); Tanabe Hidehisa, "Heian nandō Chōsen-jin no taisei ni tsuite" (The physical tendencies of Koreans from Pyŏng'an namdo Province).

63. "Kyokutō shuzoku no sōgo kankei." This paper, coauthored with Shima, was published in the *Journal of the Anthropological Society* the following year: Imamura Yutaka and Shima Gorō, "Tōbu Ajia shoshuzoku no sōgo kankei," *Jinruigaku zasshi* 50, no. 3 (1935): 1–32.

64. See the remarks in Cooper and Stoler, *Tensions of Empire*, 14–15.

65. In 1943, while discussing "The problem of mixed marriages and assimilation" (Zakkon oyobi dōka mondai) at the Institute of Ethnology (Minzoku Kenkyūjo), a public organization founded that year, Koyama criticized these two options and argued for a unity of race. See Koyama Eizō, "Zakkon oyobi dōka mondai," in *Kokusai jōmin bunka kenkyū sōsho* 11 ([1943] 2015): 97–108.

66. Kiyono Kenji, "Nihon ko jūmin no taishitsu ni kan suru gentō" (Insight into the physical constitution of the ancient inhabitants of Japan), *Minzoku eisei* 3, no. 6 (1934).

67. Oguma, *Tan'itsu minzoku*, 243; Sakano, *Teikoku Nihon*, 134–52; Nanta, "Physical Anthropology"; Nanta, "Kiyono Kenji: anthropologie physique."

68. Tōkyō Jinruigakkai, ed., *Nihon minzoku* (The Japanese people) (Tokyo: Iwanami Shoten, 1935).

69. Hamada, who served as president of Kyoto Imperial University in 1937, asserted the similarity between Korean and Japanese archaeological sites.

70. Ueda Tsunekichi, "Chōsen-jin to Nihon-jin no taishitsu hikaku," in *Nihon minzoku*, ed. Tōkyō Jinruigakkai (Tokyo: Iwanami Shoten, 1935), 111–64.

71. Ueda, "Chōsen-jin to nihon-jin," 114.

72. Ueda, "Chōsen-jin to nihon-jin," 139–40.

73. Ueda, "Chōsen-jin to nihon-jin," 114.

74. Oguma, *Tan'itsu minzoku*, 245.

75. They were respectively titled "Han Dynasty skeletons in Lelang, Stone Age skeletons in Unggi" (Imamura Yutaka, Kunifusa Fumi, Kuroda Ka'ichirō, and Nomura Shōichi, "Rakurō Kandai jinkotsu Yūki sekki jidai jinkotsu no chiken," *Jinruigaku zasshi* L-1 (1935): 1–17), and "The Differential Relations between East Asian Races" (Imamura Yutaka and Shima Gorō, "Tōbu Ajia shoshuzoku no sōgo kankei," *Jinruigaku zasshi* L-3 (1935): 1–32). In 1963 Kuroda published a book entitled *Ketsueki kagaku* (Hematology) with the publisher Asakura Shoten; Imamura and Shima, "Tōbu Ajia shoshuzoku."

76. Imamura and Shima, "Tōbu Ajia shoshuzoku," 1.

77. This expression was used during the annexation by the historian Kita Sadakichi (1871–1939) from Kyoto Imperial University, a well-known figure in debates from the 1900s to 1930s who endorsed the annexation of Korea and defended Japan's assimilation policies.

78. The journal *Dolmen* was published between 1932 and 1939.

79. Imamura Yutaka, "Chōsen no sekki jidai-jin," *Dorumen* 4, no. 6 (1935): 188–92.

80. See Imamura "Chōsen no sekki jidai-jin," 191.

81. Imamura Yutaka, *Manmō minzoku no taishitsu, Keijō teikoku daigaku tairiku bunka kenkyūkai pamufuretto*, 3, 1940.

82. See Chŏng et al., *Singmin kwŏllyŏk kwa.*

83. Imamura Yutaka, *Kita Ajia jinshu gairon* (Presentation of North Asian races), in *Tairiku bunka kenkyū-zoku* (Further studies on continental culture), ed. Keijō Teikoku Daigaku Bunka Kenkyūkai (Tokyo: Iwanami Shoten, 1940).

84. Shima Gorō, "Chōsenjin kokkaku" (The Skeletal Structure of Koreans), in *Jinruigaku—senshigaku kōza*, 19 vols. (Tokyo: Yūzankaku, 1940), vol. 4; Kohama Mototsugu, "Chōsenjin no seitai sokutei" (The anthropometry of Koreans), in *Jinruigaku—senshigaku kōza*, vol. 4; Imamura Yutaka and Shima Gorō, "Hokuman shominzoku no taishitsu jinruigaku" (Physical anthropology of the peoples of north Manchuria), in *Jinruigaku—senshigaku kōza*, vol. 4.

85. Shima Gorō, "Jōdai igakubu kaibōgaku kyōshitsu," 240.

86. Arendt, *The Origins of Totalitarianism.*

87. Oguma, *Tan'itsu minzoku*; Fujino, *Nihon fashizumu*; Nanta, *Débats sur les origines*; Sakano, *Teikoku Nihon.*

88. Sakano, *Teikoku Nihon*; Nanta, "Physical Anthropology."

89. Kim Hoi-eun, "Reauthenticating Race." Na drew on the study reports written during the colonial period to arrive at exactly the opposite conclusion to Ueda and Imamura.

90. Oguma, *Tan'itsu minzoku*; Oguma, *"Nihonjin" no kyōkai*; Nanta, "Physical Anthropology"; Arnaud Nanta, "Histoire de l'archéologie paléolithique et de l'homme fossile au Japon," *Extrême-orient Extrême-Occident*, (2010) 32: 193–220.

EIGHT

Racial Anthropology on the Eastern Front, 1912 to the mid-1920s

MACIEJ GÓRNY

Loosening the Rules of Science

The First World War in Europe saw boundlessly fascinating (and rather seldom noted by scholars) input from representatives of sciences such as psychology, psychiatry, and geography. However, it was physical anthropology that developed a particularly powerful bond with the Great War. There is a certain irony in the fact that the year 1914 saw the publication of the first edition of Rudolf Martin's handbook of anthropology.[1] The Swiss-based German anthropologist patently rejected the popular tendency to identify race with nation.[2] In Martin's view the foundations of the "norm" of physical anthropology research—notions of humanity's progressive racial degeneration, dating back to de Gobineau—were unscientific. He stressed that, like many similar generalizations, they could only be verified through very extensive measurements. In fact, a description of various techniques for collecting biometric data forms the core of Martin's work. Among other things, it describes how to make gypsum casts of living people's heads and notes the most commonly accepted scales for assessing eye, skin, and hair color. In his handbook Rudolf Martin repeatedly emphasized that "tact and great seriousness on the part of the researcher are vital for all kinds of measurements on living people."[3] In wartime anthropological research, particularly in Austria-Hungary and in Germany, this element of Martin's rules was entirely abandoned. One of physical anthropology's main objects of inquiry—the racial typology of humanity—proved to be a powerful tool in symbolic distancing from the enemy, which was foreign not only in a spiritual or a metaphorical sense, but also in its biology. Andrew D. Evans observes that in both Austro-Hungarian and German wartime research, the fundamental anthropological boundary between race and nationality was obliterated. The hated European opponents increasingly came to be perceived as non-European "others" rather than as members of the same racial community.[4] While "liberal" physical anthropology still persisted in international academia and even in war-related research, the militant atmosphere and overall mobilization of intellectuals facilitated the growth of the politicized and racialized variety of the discipline.[5] The second aspect of anthropologists' involvement in the war effort extends beyond scientific or political discourse; the practice of physical anthropology during the war often entailed physical violence, which was committed against persons subjected to analysis. The most unnerving example was the use of prisoners of war (POWs) as subjects of anthropological research. In Martin's view coercion ran counter to the rules of the art. Yet, at the same time, coercion was part and parcel of the prisoners' existence. The ambiguity of their situation is reflected in the contradictory observations of the anthropologists. The published works of the latter typically include warm remarks on their research objects; Egon von Eickstedt claimed that, due to their open and welcoming nature, the Sikhs he had measured during the war had won his sympathy forever.[6] Viktor Lebzelter opened his work on Serbs by thanking "all men who *willingly* [italics in the original] devoted their time of rest to participation in scientific research."[7] On the other hand, private letters of the self-same anthropologists are replete with complaints about prisoners who tried to avoid participating in the measurements and fabricated responses to questions about their origins.[8] Without a doubt, at least some of the procedures were carried out without the consent of the research objects.

The Great War in the east had some special features that gave this evolution in physical anthropology an original color. Though this fact has been widely recognized by specialists, the scale and character of anthropology's wartime engagement still requires some clarification. According to Andre Gingrich, the "uniquely intense engagement of German-speaking anthropologists in World War I-related activities" makes Germany and Austria-Hungary a special case of departure from liberal anthropology.[9] In my view this assessment largely ignores an important parcel of research conducted by non-German and non-Austrian anthropologists along the Eastern Front both in the time of the Great War and immediately thereafter. Some characteristic features of this phenomenon were partly in concord with German-language wartime anthropology, while others made it a distinctive category of politicized racial science. Starting with the campaigns of 1914, this research blurred the line between civilians and the military. In addition to POWs, this research—and the racial stigmatization that it often brought about—was also visited upon civilians: refugees and the inhabitants of conquered or occupied territories. There were some signs of the persistence of the liberal paradigm in anthropology; Krum Dronchilov, the most distinguished Bulgarian anthropologist of the period (and a student of Felix von Luschan), produced scholarly works based on detailed studies that did not feature POWs or conform to the national ideology.[10] Yet, as in Germany and Austria-Hungary, politicization of the discipline ceased to be a marginal phenomenon. Finally, racial anthropology became a means of including an ethnic substratum in contested territories in one's own nation. The supposed racial traits of different groups of people served to justify territorial demands made during the Great War. Especially in East Central Europe and in the Balkans, racial anthropology's "golden age" starts on the eve of the continental conflict but goes far beyond its end. The "wars of the Pygmies," to use Winston Churchill's intentionally arrogant term, included independent wars in the former Romanov and Habsburg Empires and border wars between the nascent national states, as well as attempts at introducing communist regimes into the region. In many ways these conflicts represented the continuation of the First World War on a local level. The professional activities of anthropology experts at least up to the mid-1920s should be looked at in the context of the Great War, and thus with respect to the belated beginnings of peace in that region. Correspondingly, East Central

European racial anthropologists followed and developed ideas and techniques of wartime German and Austro-Hungarian racial science. In terms of scale, intellectual output, and political instrumentalization, their influence on their region's history is comparable to that of their German-speaking colleagues.

Research Continuity

In 1915 the German anthropologist Georg Buschan published an address to his peers in the *Deutsche Medizinische Wochenschrift* that stated: "Under their banners, our enemies collected such a colorful mixture of peoples that nearly all races of the world can be found to be represented in it. . . . Perhaps we may never again be granted such an opportunity of finding so many tribes, especially those from Eastern Europe, in the same place and at the same time, as we have now in our prisoner of war camps."[11] Making use of a short leave from the front, Buschan examined seventy-five prisoners from the camp in Stettin (nowadays Szczecin) and testified to the necessity of state support for similar endeavors in other locations. The Austrian anthropologists Rudolf Pöch and Eugen Oberhummer reached similar conclusions during their visit to the Wegscheid camp near Linz. Oberhummer recounted that even a passing acquaintance with the wealth of racial types collected in the area led the scholars to acknowledge "the enormity of the possible rewards anthropological study could reap there."[12]

Interestingly, these representatives of leading western European scholarly institutions were not the first to exploit this opportunity. Recall Rudolf Virchow, who addressed German anthropologists in October 1870 with a plea that matched, nearly word for word, one delivered by Georg Buschan forty-five years later, exhorting them to acquire photographic images of the *turcos* found in German field hospitals during the war with France.[13] But even shortly prior to Pöch's and Oberhummer's observations, Niko Županić, a Slovenian student of geographer Albrecht Penck, took the occasion to study the European enemy's racial makeup. In 1913 Županić conducted measurements on well over one hundred Turkish POWs, held in Belgrade since the First Balkan War. He managed to publish his observations in Serbia that same year. Soon afterward, he published the results of measurements he had conducted on Bulgarian POWs in captivity since the Second Balkan War.[14] The conclusions of these pioneering undertakings were due to be presented at the German anthropological congress in August 1914. However, the outbreak of yet another war hampered Županić's plans, and his research did not ultimately attract significant attention.[15] Among the few responses to his findings was an extensive review penned by a Polish anthropologist, Julian Talko-Hryncewicz, in *Kosmos* in Lemberg, which included details of the biometric data Županić had gathered during his research on Pontic Bulgarians.[16]

In the rivalry for precedence, Austrian and Hungarian anthropologists significantly outpaced both Županić and their German colleagues. From the outset, they were also granted the privilege of more extensive support from authorities, especially the military hierarchies. Pöch oversaw measurements conducted by a team of scientists supported by soldiers specifically assigned to the task. Several thousand POWs were examined, most of them from Russia. During this gargantuan project, the director published extensive reports describing the techniques used and hinting at early conclusions. First, measurements of arm span and head and body size were taken. After that, naked prisoners were subjected to an analysis of their skin and hair color and the extent of their body hair. The instruments and reference tables that were used were selected in accordance with Rudolf Martin's guidelines. Some of the research subjects were also photographed, always in the nude, in a separate, well-lit room. Gypsum casts of the heads of chosen POWs were also made. In the case of particularly "exotic" nationalities, linguists from Budapest, who were also employed in the project, recorded stories and folksongs. Films were shot depicting prisoners carving wood, dancing folk dances, and even while engrossed in Muslim prayer.[17]

Pöch's research became a source of inspiration for anthropologists throughout the monarchy. During the winter of 1915–16, Georg Kyrle, a member of Pöch's research team, conducted measurements on prisoners of war in immediate proximity to the frontline, even before they were delivered to camps.[18] Viktor Lebzelter examined several hundred Serbian prisoners held at the Kraków prison camp, and several Serbian Roma prisoners from the Dąbie camp.[19] Kraków was also the sphere of activity of a Polish anthropologist, Adam Wrzosek, one of whose postwar achievements was the founding of the *Przegląd Antropologiczny* (Anthropological Review). In his research, Wrzosek cited measurements conducted on nearly a thousand Russian and Serbian prisoners.[20] Pöch's assistant, Josef Weninger, concentrated on measuring black soldiers (access to them having been granted by the German ally).

The same methods and techniques were also applied to other groups. Rudolf Pöch's wife (and doctoral student), Hella (born Schürer), supplemented the data collected at prisoner-of-war camps with analyses of refugees from Volhynia—mainly women and children, interned at the Niederalm camp near Salzburg.[21] Due to having access to entire families, her observations focused in particular on the question of heredity. After the capture of Serbia, Lebzelter and Arthur Haberlandt conducted similar research on Albanians who joined volunteer units supporting the Austro-Hungarian army.[22] Projects based directly on the Austro-Hungarian research were also conducted after the war; some of the most significant were the Polish measurements of several tens of thousands of recruits, conducted in the early 1920s. "Anthropological photography" was in this instance overseen by a former officer of the Austro-Hungarian army, Jan Mydlarski. Precisely the same course of action was accepted and identical procedures—also taken from Martin—followed.[23] The only significant addition to the methodology of measurement was the introduction of serological tests, based on the research Hanna and Ludwik Hirszfeld conducted on allies, POWs, and locals in military field hospitals on the Salonika front.[24] From the perspective of the creators of racial hierarchies, the major virtue of the tests the Hirszfelds established was in furthering the connotation between blood type and race.[25]

Mongolization

The term that became the focus of the wartime debates about race in Eastern Europe was "Mongolization." From its inception, Pöch's research was aimed at capturing the particular features of anatomy which were identified as Mongolian. Attention was drawn to, for example, bowed legs and the "Mongolian fold" (on the eyelids). Characteristically, Pöch's analyses almost entirely leave out of the discussion those nationalities of the Tsar's empire that also inhabited Austro-Hungary. The sole exception was the "Little Russians," whose national identity remained unresolved. Numerous journals noted the triumph of Austro-Hungarian science.

As Andrew Evans observes, one could see this as anthropology's contribution to the national integration of the monarchy. In spite of linguistic and racial diversity, as well as numerous mutual conflicts, these nationalities consistently maintained unity in the face of the "Mongolized" enemy.[26] In the eyes of Otto Pfeifer, an Austrian publicist, who based his opinion on the results of the research, this unity was confirmed in the heroism displayed by the army during the recapture of L'viv: "Here, Russia threw in its entire arsenal of barbarous Siberian tribes, and they were met by . . . units composed of all Slavic peoples of the monarchy working in perfect union with German, Hungarian, Romanian, and Italian regiments, valiantly and loyally defending Central European culture."[27]

Attempts to forge national unity on an image of a racial enemy were, however, encumbered by certain risks. Claims of Russia's Asiatic character, it seemed, needed no particular explanation. They were consistent with the dominant tropes of Russia's wartime stereotyping, with only minor alterations and a veneer of professional terminology. The anonymous author of a 1915 article about the Mongolization of Russia in the *Zeitschrift für Socialwissenschaft* compared the process to the emergence of the Finnish nation out of the mixing of Slavic and Ural-Altaic racial elements and concluded that, while the Finns had achieved a high level of civilization, Russians were actually experiencing a degeneration, with a growing number of "somatic and psychic" Mongoloid elements becoming apparent. Russians, it was alleged, had a tendency to adopt traits characteristic of peoples of lower racial standing. The "Yakutization" of Siberian Russians (i.e., the alleged dominance of Asian racial features in the offspring of mixed Russian-Asian couples) was cited as proof in that regard.[28] At the margins of this line of thinking emerged a related problem: the question of the effect centuries of living side-by-side with Tartar nomads had on Ukrainians in terms of their Mongolization.[29] This notion was furthered in a work by Hella Pöch, published after her husband's death. Rejecting wholesale the imperial unity paradigm of Austrian wartime anthropology identified by Evans, she concluded that Ukrainian refugees from Volhynia were, in fact, deeply Mongolized:

> Although our familiarity with Mongoloid features remains imperfect, the characteristics described below . . . compel me to accept their characterization as a Mongoloid people. These are: the heavy fold of fat over the eyelid; the concave, short nose with a blunt tip and upturned nostrils; the big earlobes with lobules grown into or extending up to the cheeks; the long, straight upper lip; the large gap between the inside corners of the eyes; the asymmetrically bulging cheeks with characteristic fat pillows; the receded lower part of the face, with a poorly developed chin. Height no greater than medium, stocky build, with short legs and arms. . . . Women exhibit a tendency to an excess in the fat pillow. Scant bodily hair, with hair on the head scant and straight.[30]

In 1924 Hella Pöch and Josef Weninger, the former assistant to Rudolf Pöch, published a methodological article concerned with the anthropological evaluation of facial features and skull shape. The revised racial valuation of Ukrainians by Austrian scientists was borne out even in the choice of photographs to accompany the text. The authors placed images of "typical" Vietnamese, Hindu, Senegalese, and Georgian specimen next to a picture of a Ukrainian.[31]

The early response came from the Ukrainian geographer Stepan Rudnytskyi. His work from 1914, written in German, included an entire chapter devoted to the racial makeup of Ukrainians. While he agreed that—like any other nation—Ukrainians were of mixed origin, he stressed that their particular racial mixture differed decisively from either the Russian or the Polish mixture. He also vehemently rejected the conjecture that the country was forced into the Mongolian sphere of influence by history. In general, he claimed, invaders were in Ukraine only briefly, not affecting the local inhabitants in any way.[32] For Rudnytskyi, claims to any kinship between Ukrainians and Poles, Russians or Mongols were univocally invalidated by the biometric data gleaned from publications devoted to the Russian Ukraine.

Rudnytskyi's assertion that Ukrainians represented the Dinaric (or Adriatic) race did not contradict the state of knowledge at the time. His statements were a direct reference to claims put forward by the French anthropologist Joseph Deniker in the early twentieth century.[33] All Rudnytskyi did was, in effect, shift the accents, making Ukraine the central and relatively racially homogeneous kernel of a type Deniker located primarily in the Balkans. Another novelty was the association of the Dinaric race with the primordial Slavs. A similar edge was given to another of Deniker's theses, concerned with the emergence of the so-called Vistulian type (*race Vistulienne*) among Poles and, to a far lesser extent, Russians. Rudnitskyi proposed that this type differed from the Dinaric race in exhibiting a significant admixture of Mongolian blood. The Ukrainian anthropologist also cited measurement data that, in his view, documented the similarity between Poles and Russians. Having concluded that Ukraine's Polish and Russian neighbors were worthless in racial terms, in a book written after the war Rudnytskyi advocated a program of national eugenics for the Ukrainian intelligentsia. Aside from recommending social hygiene, he urged his fellow Ukrainians to refrain from marrying representatives of racially inferior nations: Poles, Russians, Romanians, Jews, Turks, and Tartars. On the other hand, he advocated marriages with Nordic Germans, Dinaric Southern Slavs, and Bohemians.[34]

Rudnytskyi's theses were wholeheartedly embraced by Ukrainian nationalist activists of the early twentieth century, especially insofar as his ideas reflected on the relationships between Ukrainians, Poles, and Russians. For the same reasons, these claims were vehemently rejected by Polish authors. Rudnytskyi achieved a commanding victory in Germany, where his theses were eagerly published while also—even more important—earning inclusion into the more general arguments penned by German anthropologists (including Fritz Lenz) and geographers.[35]

"War of the Races"

Stepan Rudnytskyi's claims met with approval from the practitioners and amateurs of racial anthropology in Germany primarily because they perfectly suited a particular racial historiosophy that enjoyed huge popularity at the time. Reflections on the character and psychology of one's own people and one's enemies were often informed by the idea of war as a clash between races that pitted the Nordic-Aryan Teutons against a variety of different, less notable anthropological types. Contemporary scientific studies supplied a crucial distinction between dolichocephalic and brachycephalic human skulls (with intermediary types). The former were identified as a marker of Nordic origins. Brachycephaly, on the other hand, was ascribed to numerous anthropological types (including Dinarics) and—as we shall see below—did not prohibit the formation of a positive identity: a fact illustrated by Rudnytskyi's theory.

Hans F. K. Günther, soon to become one of the main authors of Nazi racial theory, helped to create this genre of racial historiosophy—for instance, in his *Rassenkunde des deutschen Volkes* (1922). Unjust accusations were raised on both sides of the front, he claimed; now that the war was over, it had to be openly admitted that the popular claim made in the Reich, to the effect that Frenchmen did not have a single drop of Teutonic blood in them, was untrue. Günther identified a similar error in claims that the English, and even Germans themselves, had non-Teutonic origins. For him, such theories ignored the basic findings of anthropology.[36] Indeed, German publications on the racial origins of the nations involved in the war—even when produced by professional craniologists—rarely admitted Aryan origins to anyone other than the Germans. The wartime edition of Ludwig Wilser's popular *Die Überlegenheit der germanischen Rasse* interpreted the conflict as the result of the aggression of racially worthless elements against the Reich.[37] In the eyes of the German chauvinist Wilser and many other authors, the Aryans created the entire human "*Kultur*" and were the direct ancestors of contemporary Germans. Other nations could not claim such an esteemed genealogy, and, besides, they were subject to the perilous influences of "civilization." The owner of Breslau's anthropological publishing house, Ferdinand G. Faßhauer, noted a dilution of the remnants of Aryan blood, leading to wholesale degeneration of entire nations—in both England and in France, for example. In fact, France already faced a complete cultural collapse on the eve of the war; the English, despite having set out from a better, more Teutonic position, developed neurasthenia as a result of alcoholism, industrialization, and urbanization.[38] In 1907 the racist polemicist Ludwig Woltmann had already claimed, on the basis of extensive illustrative material, that all major figures of human history had Teutonic origins, even if they lived and worked in non-Teutonic surroundings.[39] Jörg Lanz-Liebenfels, a prolific author of brochures published in the "Ostara" series, went furthest in the cult of the Aryan race and its concurrent identification with contemporary Germans.[40] Even while some anthropologists—for instance, Karl Classen—stressed the racially mixed character of nations and the impact of the environment on the evolution of primary, "clean" racial types, their conclusions did not deviate significantly from the established pattern. Germans, albeit racially mixed, were always judged to be far more homogeneous than the southerners or Slavs, and hence more talented and intelligent.[41] In the eyes of staff physician Ferdinand Münter, "Germans have indeed become by and large racial mongrels, since mixed types enjoy certain superiority [in terms of genetic reproduction]. Still, one would continue to claim that, as a national organism, we consistently represent the Teutonic orientation, both in terms of physical features and psychology."[42] Regardless of the meanderings of German anthropological thought, the racial inferiority of wartime enemies served continuously as the object of its ruminations.[43] Interestingly, even the ultimate, humiliating defeat of Germany did not lead to a retreat from these racial claims. Instead, German authors set out to detect Aryan-Teutonic racial types among the military and political leaders of the victorious powers. Thus, after 1918 it suddenly turned out that a purely Aryan heritage and a long, narrow, noble skull typified not only Hindenburg and Ludendorff, but also Joffre, Foch, Lloyd George, and Wilson.[44] On the other hand, as had often been claimed both during the war and after, the exceptional valor and tendency to bravura that characterized the Aryan race marked it out for glory but also repeatedly put it under threat. Otto Hauser illustrated this claim with supposedly first-hand observation of the battlefields of the Great War. While those who fell in the first line of fire were primarily the racially superior blonds, the less worthy dark-haired types hid in the rear. This racial variant of the *Dolchstoßlegende*, which consisted of accusing Jews and other non-Aryans of capital treason, was to achieve greater popularity over the following decades.[45]

But the perception of war as a struggle between races was not exclusive to Germany. Both during the war and immediately thereafter, Finland proved an incredibly fascinating test ground for racial theories. According to a belief shared almost universally among well-educated Europeans, the country was inhabited by a Mongoloid people. In 1918 Finland saw the eruption of a civil war between "whites" and "reds," with the former emerging victorious. Clashes were neither extensive (the war lasted about three and a half months in all) nor bloody, particularly in the context of the continuing Great War and the Russian Revolution. For some observers the conflict was not so much a symptom of a class struggle as of a race war. In simplified terms, the oppressed, primitive Finnish folk rose up in rebellion against its Swedish masters. The claim was fitted into a racial theory by Lars Ringbom, who stated that the war broke out between two distinct nationalities inhabiting Finland. The western part of the country was populated by those who claimed an admixture of Germanic blood, while the east was the dwelling of Finnish-Slavic mongrels. The former were individualists, the latter primitive collectivists.[46] In the pages of Woltmann's *Politisch-Anthropologische Monatsschrift*, the following racist interpretation was accepted: "The civil war, in the end, was nothing more than a war between races, with the whites reliant on Swedish backing, and the reds unable to mobilize more than a passive support among Swedes."[47] The eventual victory of the whites was sometimes treated as a form of atonement—limited, but still soothing—for the German failure in the Great War. According to this interpretation, the heroism of "the Swedish youth, the core of the yeoman class" made victory over the "Asiatic hordes" advancing from the east possible, which meant that "Baltic became a German internal sea!"[48]

New Pretenders in the Hierarchy of Races

The intellectual structure based on the division of peoples into dolichocephalic and brachycephalic types, operating by means of the disqualifying notion of Mongolization, owed its attractiveness, for the most part, to its consistency with the state of contemporary anthropology. As a result, the discourse that grew so exponentially in Germany drew in authors from other countries, looking for the most elevated station available for "their" racial types. Such an operation hardly caused any trouble to Swedes, who enjoyed the status of the most Nordic of all Nordics. However, representatives of other nations could play this game as well, a fact proved by Stepan Rudnytskyi. In his racial theory, the Ukrainian anthropologist and geographer made good use of a term successfully applied in other contexts. The Dinaric race, though viewed as inferior to the Nordic race by most French and German anthropologists, was typically seen as more elevated than other brachycephalous types. The image of the Dinaric type was also affected by wartime experiences; in later years, the Nazi race ideologue Hans Günther associated it with Bavarians and Serbs, whom he acknowledged as "particularly trustworthy due to their sense of dignity, patriotism, courage and a peculiar self-confidence. These traits made soldiers originating from the Dinaric regions the best warriors of the south-eastern front during the war."[49] They were supposedly characterized by a stern morality, typical for highlanders, and a patriarchalism of which the South Slavs Jovan Cvijić and Niko Županić took note, as well (see Yeomans in this volume).

There was, of course, a world of difference between the significance ascribed to the Dinaric race by Deniker, as well as by Županić, and the meaning Rudnytskyi gave to it. Only the Ukrainian anthropologist perceived it as a primordial race and identified it with the Slavic type. In the eyes of other anthropologists, the race was more likely a product of mixing. However, in the context of a European "spiritual war," such differences paled before a general, immeasurably positive assessment of the Dinaric type. Significantly, it seemed immune to the charge of Mongolization. Polish anthropologists faced a much more problematic situation, as they entered a discourse in which their nation occupied a subservient position. Of course, one could always join the debates without instigating a major polemic; such was the disposition of Walenty Miklaszewski in an essay that discussed a poll he conducted among over 1,500 officers of various national backgrounds who had served in the Russian army and received treatment at the Ujazdowski Hospital in Warsaw during the war.[50] In practice, the conclusions of his research were limited to a corroboration of the advanced degeneration of Russians, who generally started smoking earlier than Poles, smoked more, and masturbated from an earlier age and more frequently. For an army whose cadres were mostly made up of such shoddy material, victory was a virtual impossibility: "It is beyond any doubt that no officer of the Russian army . . . could have stood up to that task."[51] Efforts to highlight differences in the biological quality of Poles and Russians did not, however, help solve the key problem of Mongolization.

The Polish anthropologist Jan Czekanowski's reply consisted in skillful merging and separating of anthropological types. Whereas his Austrian and German colleagues were prone to see a great mass of a Mongolized *Ostrasse*, he defined three clearly discernible types. He stressed that the postwar research asserted "that the Nordic element is not less numerous in Poland than in Germany."[52] He concluded, however, as did his numerous students in Poland, that most of the inhabitants of the country exhibited a mixed Nordic-Lapponoid—also known as the Subnordic—type. One could say that, in this way, he supported the contention of his German colleagues, who saw Slavs as Mongolized Nordics. In this case, though, the form of the message was more important than its content. The dominant racial type among the population of Poland was consequently assigned the appropriately ennobling name of the "Sarmatian" type in Polish treatises. Czekanowski had already used the term before the war, claiming that the typical division into Nordic, Mediterranean, and Alpine types was inapplicable to Central and

Eastern Europe. When applied, it could only mislead the researcher, unable as it was to effect agreement between different parameters: cranial indices with hair and eye colors. In place of the received division, he suggested another that also took into account the Dinaric and pre-Slavic types alongside the Sarmatian type. He treated the other categories as supplementary, devoting the most attention to the Nordics of northern Poland.[53] From a historical point of view, he perceived Slavs as a primordially Nordic racial type and compared their prehistoric expansion to that of the Germanic tribes.[54] While Czekanowski vehemently criticized all attempts at identifying racial types with nationalities, the tripartite division he put forward generally respected boundaries between the nationalities of the Second Polish Republic: Poles, Ukrainians, and Belarusians.[55]

Responding to the none-too-favorable image of Poles in the racial discourse dominant in Europe at the time, Polish anthropologists took the initiative. With the aid of the structures of their young state, they conducted widespread anthropological research and used it as a source for illustrating their new classification of racial types in the region. In a way, by reinterpreting received categories and introducing their own, they obliterated the previous dogmas. It is quite telling that the term Mongolization, so crucial during wartime, disappeared almost completely in their thought. Nor could there be any doubt as to the hierarchy of dominant racial types in the country. In his summary of research into the relationship between race and school education, Ludwik Jaxa-Bykowski concluded that, psychologically speaking, the Sarmatian race most closely resembled the Nordics: "First of all, as far as gymnasia are concerned, there is a striking abundance of the Nordic race and . . . the Sarmatian type, even in places where they do not enjoy numerical superiority among the population. Furthermore, these proportions grow with every passing year. This is a fact undeniably related to the high level of ability within those components, which makes it easier for them to sustain competition during classificatory selection."[56]

In an article published in the *Przegląd Antropologiczny*, Jaxa-Bykowski made it abundantly clear that of the two privileged races, superior talents and dominance could only be ascribed to the Sarmatian race, "whose characteristic mark is evident among the young people in gymnasia and the entire Polish intelligentsia."[57] The name itself, which could be seen in particular by foreign scholars as an admission of Asiatic roots, actually related to an entirely different period of history. The Sarmatian type, wrote Jaxa-Bykowski, "which has, in the past, characterized that lively and abundant community of the nobility (*szlachta*), shines through today among our intelligentsia . . . It is undeniably an effect of a rapid physical development, but also of that 'cruel fantasy of knighthood' immortalized by Sienkiewicz in his literary creation, Kmicic [hero of the novel *The Deluge*]."[58] Such glorious traits of character were beyond the reach of representatives of the Dinaric type, but the bottom of the Polish racial hierarchy was reserved for Belarusians, commonly ascribed to a pre-Slavic type. Although Czekanowski made no comment to that effect, the term was understood as a synonym of the so-called Eastern race (*Ostrasse*), which, in turn, was identified with the Vistula race (*Weichselrasse*) cited by Rudnytskyi.[59] Polish anthropological research suggested that the number of representatives of this type in schools of the Second Republic dropped with every year of education. In accordance with the logic of the science he practiced, Jaxa-Bykowski was inclined to explain that fact on purely biological grounds: "Apparently, that type is incapable of maintaining the struggle for survival in schools and gives in to the more accomplished types."[60] He invoked the same reasons when debating the relationship between race and intellectual faculties in the whole country: "Here, the harmony is striking: the intellectual profile . . . rises with the number of Poles living in the given township and along the line drawn from the south-east toward the west."[61]

Finnish anthropologists followed a similar path. The young country was at odds with the interpretation of the civil war provided by Swedish and German authors, who perceived it in racial terms. This interpretation shattered unity among citizens of the state, many of whom found themselves associated with the non-European Mongoloids. The anthropological research conducted in Finland from 1924 onward was a deliberate attempt at debunking this categorization. Yrjö Kaarlo Suominen claimed in his 1929 summary of the research that the Swedish-speaking inhabitants of the country differed from the rest only in tongue, not in race.[62] Light skin color was deemed a primordial characteristic of the type inhabiting Finland and consequently could not be the result of an influx of Nordic blood. According to Suominen, Finns did not exhibit the slightest marks of any kinship with Mongols. Though the Finnish research did not reference Czekanowski's findings directly, his publications appeared in Finnish periodicals and scientific journals.[63] The manner of solving the racial dilemma that the Finnish anthropologists went on to apply was, to a rather large extent, an application of the method put forward by the Polish anthropologist. Following in his footsteps, Czekanowski's Finnish counterparts refrained from applying the generally approved racial division of Europe, introducing in its stead a new category, which they called the "East Baltic race." In a fashion strikingly similar to the Sarmatian type, this race was said to be closely related to the Nordics, though better adapted to the natural conditions prevalent in Finland.[64] In other words: the noble *Ostrasse*.

Conclusion

The First World War constitutes one of the most seminal periods in the history of anthropology. It divides a period of "internationalist" science from its purely national guise—especially, though not exclusively, in German-speaking racial science. As far as research practice is concerned, the paradigm change found expression in an almost universal disregard for the distinction between racial and national orders, heretofore a basic tenet of the science. The efforts of the Austrian anthropologists, who endeavored to use measurements on prisoners of war in order to depict the conflict as a war between races, inspired numerous followers. Ukrainians, Poles, and Finns obviously do not exhaust the list of the nations whose political strivings were legitimized by the use of racial arguments. A number of analogies to the ideas described above can be found in Latvia, where the Finnish conception of race was used to determine the racial definition of the ruling nation: Nordic, with admixture of East Baltic blood.[65] The conception was even more markedly influential in Estonia, where racial anthropology, developing locally in the 1920s, focused on combating arguments advocating a Mongolian descent of Finno-Ugric peoples.[66] Racial anthropology, with particular focus on serological testing, was quite thoroughly exploited to provide grounds for the racial unity theory used in the enlarged Romania.[67] Elsewhere, ideas of a similar sort manifested themselves less powerfully but were always present. In Czechoslovakia the leading Prague anthropologist Jindřich Matiegka argued that his fellow countrymen represented a Celto-Slavic type, which he found was most closely related to western Romance peoples. The Czechs' innate courage was, apparently, proven by the martial deeds of the Czechoslovak legionnaires; and their intelligence (somewhat surprisingly, perhaps, to a Polish or German reader) by the Bohemian lineage of Jan Hus and Nicolaus Copernicus.[68] Voices were also raised in defense of the anthropological quality of Belarusians, whom Czekanowski identified—not at all flatteringly—with the pre-Slavic type. Konstancja Skirmuntt, an activist in the Polish Eastern Borderland (and, in the 1920s, a quite elderly woman), did not cease fighting in her last years for acknowledgement of the racial distinctiveness of Belarusians from her hated "Muscovites," to whom she afforded "pre-Slavic" traits.[69] This inevitable manifestation of racial claims ensued from the drive to legitimize either the states or national movements concerned—a preoccupation that was shared by many proponents of these ideas.

No less important than the political incentives of these scholars are their scientific ambitions, including those awakened during their studies at German universities at the turn of the century. It was the striving for professionalism that incited the anthropologists (and, because of them, the young and not-quite-rich countries) to conduct far-flung biometrical studies. This same motive played a crucial part in the shaping of new racial theories. It would have been rather easy to overturn the racial hierarchies recognized in Europe and to establish, in lieu of them, others that offered the top position to "our people." Reconciliation of legacy theories, conceptions, and ideas with the actual needs of East Central European national movements and local researchers' sense of patriotism called for real craftsmanship. Moreover, only an operation of this kind would have allowed one to count on international success. The incoherence and logical contradictions within the Nordic theory (or, perhaps, the differences between the apostles of Nordic theories) excellently facilitated this hard effort. Still, the exercise was not easy at all.

The notion of a correlation between race and class origins, which played a prominent role in racial discourse before the war, was pushed to the margins, as the unity of nations was considered key to beating one's enemies. From the perspective of an American racist, all such particular efforts were entirely pointless. "From a race point of view," wrote Madison Grant in 1916, "the present European conflict is essentially a civil war and nearly all the officers and a large proportion of the men on both sides are members of this [Nordic] race. . . . It is the modern edition of the old Berserker blood rage and is class suicide on a gigantic scale."[70] The postwar racial discourse in Europe and North America was dominated by the notion of biopolitics—a program by the state to raise the racial quality of the nation.[71] In its most radical guises, biopolitics embraced a way of thinking typical during wartime, moving on to identify an enemy within the society, in that society's others: the maladjusted, the antisocial.[72]

Notes

1. Rudolf Martin, *Lehrbuch der Anthropologie in systematischer Darstellung, mit besonderer Berücksichtigung der anthropologischen Methoden* (Jena: Fischer, 1914).

2. Martin, *Lehrbuch der Anthropologie*, 9.

3. Martin, *Lehrbuch der Anthropologie*, 106.

4. Andrew D. Evans, *Anthropology at War: World War I and the Science of Race in Germany* (Chicago: University of Chicago Press, 2010), 145–46.

5. Wolfgang J. Mommsen, "Die europäischen Intellektuellen, Schriftsteller und Künstler und der Erste Weltkrieg," in Mommsen, *Bürgerliche Kultur und politische Ordnung. Künstler, Schriftsteller und Intellektuelle in der deutschen Geschichte 1830–1933* (Frankfurt am Main: Fischer, 2000), 196–215.

6. Egon von Eickstedt, "Rassenelemente der Sikh," *Zeitschrift für Ethnologie* 52–53 (1920–21): 317–94, 318.

7. Viktor Lebzelter, "Beiträge zur physischen Anthropologie der Balkanhalbinsel," *Mitteilungen der Anthropologischen Gesellschaft in Wien* 53, nos. 1–2 (1923): 3–22, 3.

8. Britta Lange, *Einen Krieg ausstellen. Die „Deutsche Kriegsausstellung" 1916 in Berlin* (Berlin: Verbrecher Verlag, 2003), 319–20; Evans, *Anthropology*, 144–48.

9. Andre Gingrich, "After the Great War: National Reconfigurations of Anthropology in Late Colonial Times," in *Doing Anthropology in Wartime and War Zones: World War I and the Cultural Sciences in Europe*, ed. Reinhard Johler, Christian Marchetti, and Monique Scheer (Bielefeld: transcript Verlag, 2010), 355–80.

10. See Christian Promitzer, "'Betwixt and Between.' Physical Anthropology in Bulgaria and Serbia until the End of the First World War," in *Doing Anthropology in Wartime and War Zones*, 141–68, 157–59.

11. Georg Buschan, "Krieg und Anthropologie," *Deutsche Medizinische Wochenschrift* 41, no. 26 (1915): 773.

12. Eugen Oberhummer, "Rudolf Pöch (gestorben am 4. März 1921)," *Mitteilungen der Anthropologischen Gesellschaft in Wien* LI, nos. 4–5 (1921): 96–102, 100. See also Maria Teschler-Nicola, "Rudolf Pöch's osteologische Lehr-und Forschungssammlung im Spannungsfeld von Wissenschaft und Ethik," *Mitteilungen der Anthropologischen Gesellschaft in Wien* 141 (2011): 51–66.

13. Rudolf Virchow, no title, in "Verhandlungen der Berliner Gesellschaft für Anthropologie, Ethnologie und Urgeschichte," *Zeitschrift für Ethnologie* 3 (1871): 16.

14. Niko Županić, *Pontijski bugari* (Beograd: Prosvetni Glasnik, 1913).

15. See Promitzer, "'Betwixt and Between,'" 141–68, 157–59.

16. Julian Talko-Hryncewicz, "Niko Županič. Pontijski bugari. Prilog fizyckoj antropologiji balkanskog istoka," *Kosmos* nos. 4–6 (1914): 476–79.

17. Rudolf Pöch, "Bericht über die von der Wiener Anthropologischen Gesellschaft in den k. u. k. Kriegsgefangenenlagern veranlaßten Studien," *Mitteilungen der Anthropologischen Gesellschaft in Wien* 6 (1915): 219–31.

18. Rudolf Pöch, "III. Bericht über die von der Wiener Anthropologischen Gesellschaft in der k. u. k. Kriegsgefangenenlagern veranlaßten Studien," *Mitteilungen der Anthropologischen Gesellschaft in Wien* 47 (1917): 99.

19. Viktor Lebzelter, "Beiträge zur physischen Anthropologie der Balkanhalbinsel," *Mitteilungen der Anthropologischen Gesellschaft in Wien* 53, nos. 1–2 (1923): 3–22; Lebzelter, "Anthropologische Untersuchungen an serbischen Zigeunern," *Mitteilungen der Anthropologischen Gesellschaft in Wien* 52, nos. 1–3 (1922): 22–35.

20. Olga Willerowa, "Spostrzeżenia nad barwą oczów i skóry u Tatarów, Ormian, Gruzinów, Mołdawjan, Serbów i Macedończyków," *Przegląd Antropologiczny* 1, no. 2 (1926): 84–91.

21. Hella Pöch-Schürer, "Beiträge zur Anthropologie der ukrainischen Wolhynier," *Mitteilungen der Anthropologischen Gesellschaft in Wien* 56 (1926): 289–333.

22. Arthur Haberlandt & Viktor Lebzelter, "Zur physischen Anthropologie der Albanesen," *Archiv für Anthropologie* n.s., 17 (1919): 123–43.

23. Jan Mydlarski, "Sprawozdanie z wojskowego zdjęcia antropologicznego Polski," *Kosmos* 50, nos. 2–3 (1925): 530–83.

24. Ludwik Hirschfeld and Hanna Hirschfeld, "Essai d'application des méthodes sérologiques au problem des races," *L'Anthropologie* 29 (1918–19): 504–37. On the history and interpretations of Hanna and Ludwik Hirszfeld's wartime research, see Katrin

Steffen and Maciej Górny, "'Böses Blut: Die Blutgruppenforschung und der Serologe Ludwik Hirszfeld in Deutschland und in Polen," *Historie: Jahrbuch des Zentrums für Historische Forschung Berlin der Polnischen Akademie der Wissenschaften* 7 (2013–14): 97–119.

25. See Marius Turda, "The Nation as Object: Race, Blood, and Biopolitics in Interwar Romania," *Slavic Review* 66, no. 3 (2007): 413–41; and Myriam Spörri, *Reines und gemischtes Blut. Zur Kulturgeschichte der Blutgruppenforschung, 1900–1933* (Bielefeld: transcript Verlag, 2013).

26. Evans, *Anthropology*, 149.

27. Austriacus Observator [Otto Pfeifer], *Germanentum, Slaventum, Orientvölker und die Balkanereignisse: Kulturpolitische Erwägungen* (Kempten: Verlag der Jos. Kösel'schen Buchhandlung, 1917), 33–34.

28. "Die Mongolisierung Rußlands," *Zeitschrift für Socialwissenschaft* 6, no. 2 (1915): 126–32, 129–31.

29. "Die Mongolisierung Rußlands," 129.

30. Pöch-Schürer, "Beiträge," 35. See also Beate Fuchs, *"Rasse," "Volk," Geschlecht: Anthropologische Diskurse in Österreich 1850–1960* (Frankfurt am Main: Campus, 2003), 250–61.

31. Josef Weninger and Hella Pöch, "Leitlinien zur Beobachtung der somatischen Merkmale des Kopfes und Gesichtes am Menschen," *Mitteilungen der Anthropologischen Gesellschaft in Wien* 54, no. 6 (1924): 232–70.

32. Stefan Rudnyćkyj, *Ukraina und die Ukrainer* (Wien: Verlag des Allgemeinen Ukrainischen Nationalrats, 1914), 12–13.

33. Joseph Deniker, *Les races et les peuples de la terre. Éléments d'anthropologie et d'ethnographie* (Paris: Schleicher frères & Cie, 1900).

34. Степан Рудницкий, *Чому ми хочемо самостійної України*, 2nd ed. (Львів: Світ, 1994), 300–307.

35. See Max Friederichsen, *Die Grenzmarken des Europäischen Rußlands: Ihre geographische Eigenart und ihre Bedeutung für den Weltkrieg* (Hamburg: L. Friederichsen, 1915), 89–90; and Eugen Oberhummer, *Die Türken und das Osmanische Reich* (Leipzig: Teubner, 1917), 21.

36. Hans F. K. Günther, *Rassenkunde des deutschen Volkes*, 2nd ed. (München: Lehmann, 1923), 7.

37. Ludwig Wilser, *Die Überlegenheit der germanischen Rasse. Zeitgemäße Betrachtungen* (Stuttgart: Strecker & Schröder, 1915), vi.

38. Barelhako [Ferdinand G. Faßhauer], *Der Weltkrieg 1914/15 als Siegszug der germanischen Kultur: Der Aufstieg der deutschen Kultur* (Breslau: Anthropologischer Verlag F. G. Faßhauer, 1915), 16–39.

39. Ludwig Woltmann, *Die Germanen in Frankreich. Eine Untersuchung über den Einfluss der germanischen Rasse auf die Geschichte und Kultur Frankreichs. Mit 60 Bildnissen berühmter Franzosen* (Jena: Diederichs, 1907); see also Paul Schultze-Naumburg, *Kunst und Rasse* (München: Lehmann, 1928); and Heinrich A. Schmid, *Deutschtum und bildende Kunst. Rede am 22. März 1915* (Berlin: Heymann, 1915).

40. Jörg Lanz-Liebenfels, *Rasse und Adel* (Mödling: Ostara, 1918).

41. Karl Classen, "Beiträge zum Indogermanenproblem," *Korrespondenz-Blatt der Deutschen Gesellschaft für Anthropologie, Ethnologie und Urgeschichte* 49, nos. 1–4 (1918): 7.

42. Ferdinand Münter, "Über Rasse," *Politisch-Anthropologische Revue* 13, no. 6 (1914): 306–14.

43. See Pirmin Coar [Hans Roselieb], *Über das Wesen französischer Macht* (Mönchengladbach: Sekretariat Sozialer Studentenarbeit, 1916), 6–7.

44. Otto Hauser, *Rasse und Politik* (Weimar: Duncker, 1922), 111; Erwin Bauer, Eugen Fischer, and Fritz Lenz, *Grundriß der menschlichen Erblichkeitslehre und Rassenhygiene*, vol. 1 (München: Lehmann, 1921), 293.

45. Hauser, *Rasse*, 113.

46. Lars Ringbom, *Inbördeskriget i Finland. Psychologiska anteckningar* (Helsingfors 1918), quoted in Aira Kemiläinen, *Finns in the shadow of the "Aryans": Race Theories and Racism* (Helsinki: SHS, 1998), 150.

47. Freiherr von Born, "Finnland und die 'russische Pest,'" *Politisch-Anthropologische Monatsschrift* 18, no. 5 (1919–1920): 220–24.

48. Freiherr von Born, "Völker-und Sprachenverhältnisse in Finnland," *Politisch-Anthropologische Monatsschrift* 17, no. 6 (1918–19): 276–81, 280–81.

49. Hans F. K. Günther, *Kleine Rassenkunde Europas* (München: Lehmann, 1925), 57.

50. Walenty Miklaszewski, "Oficer armji rosyjskiej ze stanowiska rasy," *Zagadnienia Rasy* 1, no. 2 (1918): 1–6; *Zagadnienia Rasy* 2, no. 3 (1919): 8–14.

51. *Zagadnienia Rasy* 2, no. 3 (1919): 13.

52. Jan Czekanowski, *Zarys antropologji Polski* (Lwów: K. S. Jakubowski i S-ka, 1930), 432.

53. Jan Czekanowski, "Beiträge zur Anthropologie von Polen," *Archiv für Anthropologie* n.s., nos. 2–3 (1911): 187–93.

54. Jan Czekanowski, *Anthropologische Beiträge zum Problem der slawisch-finnischen Beziehungen* (Helsingfors: K. F. Puromiehen Kirjapaino, 1925): 12–13.

55. Czekanowski, *Zarys*, 454.

56. Ludwik Jaxa Bykowski, *Antropologiczne podstawy wychowania* (Warszawa: Nasza Księgarnia, 1933), 17–18.

57. Ludwik Jaxa Bykowski, "Stosunki rasowe wśród naszych abiturientów gimnazjalnych," *Przegląd Antropologiczny* 6 (1932): 31.

58. Ludwik Jaza Bykowski, "Przyczynki do znajomości ras wśród naszej młodzieży szkolnej," *Kosmos* 51 (1926): 935–40, 935–36.

59. This omission was undone by his student Gizela Lempertówna, "Przyczynki lwowskie do antropologii Żydów," *Kosmos* 52 (1927): 782–820, 811.

60. Bykowski, "Przyczynki," 936.

61. Bykowski, "Przyczynki," 939.

62. Yrjö K. Suominen, "Physical Anthropology in Suomi (Finland)," *Journal of the Royal Anthropological Institute of Great Britain and Ireland* 59 (1929): 207–30, 209.

63. Jan Czekanowski, *Übersicht anthropologischer Arbeiten in Polen im Laufe der Jahre 1913–14–1924–25* (Helsinki: Suomalaisen Tiedeakatemian Kustautama, 1925).

64. Suominen, "Physical," 206.

65. Björn M. Felder, "'God Forgives—but Nature Never Will': Racial Identity, Racial Anthropology, and Eugenics in Latvia 1918–1940," in *Baltic Eugenics: Bio-Politics, Race, and Nation in Interwar Estonia, Latvia and Lithuania, 1918–1940*, ed. Björn M. Felder and Paul J. Weindling (Amsterdam: Rodopi, 2013), 115–46.

66. Ken Kalling and Leiu Heapost, "Racial Identity and Physical Anthropology in Estonia 1800–1945," in *Baltic Eugenics*, 83–114.

67. See Marius Turda, "In Search of Racial Types: Soldiers and the Anthropological Mapping of the Romanian Nation, 1914–44," *Patterns of Prejudice* 47, no. 1 (2013): 1–21.

68. Jindřich J. Matiegka, *Vznik a tělesný stav národa československého* (Prague: Československý cizinecký úřad, 1920), 9–10. The argument whereby Copernicus was of Bohemian origin was not Matiegka's original concept, as it dates back to the nineteenth century.

69. Konstancja Skirmuntt, *Fascynacja nazwy i potęga litery* (Wilno, 1928), quoted in Jerzy Garbiński, ed., *Myśl białoruska XX wieku: Filozofia, religia, kultura (antologia)* (Warszawa: PAN, 1998), 236–40. For more on Skirmuntt, see Dariusz Szpoper, *Gente Lithuana, natione Lithuana: Myśl polityczna i działalność Konstancji Skirmuntt (1851–1934)* (Gdańsk: Arche, 2009).

70. Madison Grant, *The Passing of the Great Race or the Racial Basis of European History* (New York: Charles Scribner's, 1916), 200.

71. Turda, "The Nation," 413–15.

72. Philipp Sarasin, "Zweierlei Rassismus? Die Selektion des Fremden als Problem im Michel Foucaults Verbindung von Biopolitik und Rassismus," in *Biopolitik und Rassismus*, ed. Martin Stingelin (Frankfurt am Main: Suhrkamp, 2003), 60–75, 67.

NINE

Racial Politics as a Multiethnic Pavilion

Yugoslavs, Dinarics, and the Search for a Synthetic Identity in the 1920s and 1930s

RORY YEOMANS

When the Belgrade architect Dragiša Brašovan was selected to design the pavilion for the Yugoslav entry at the 1929 International Exposition in Barcelona, it came at a tumultuous time. In January of that year King Aleksandar had declared a personal dictatorship, and by October he had renamed the former Kingdom of Serbs, Croats, and Slovenes the Kingdom of Yugoslavia, to emphasize the sweeping away of "tribal" divisions and the incarnation of a new synthetic identity. Brašovan had been commissoned to design a pavilion that would serve as an expression of the "national architecture" of a reborn Yugoslavia. Partly owing to a small budget and a tight deadline, the architect had opted for a modernist structure, but one constructed in wood, the traditional building material of Serbia. Despite its external modernism, the interior of the structure represented a primeval form of dwelling. Designed by the Croatian artist Tomislav Krizman, it was filled with traditional handicrafts, folkloric art, and embroidery from throughout the state. The pavilion's success in winning the "absolute majority" of the Grand Prix at the Exposition and attracting at least 200,000 visitors was covered extensively in the national press, which interpreted the pavilion as a symbol of the dynamic new Yugoslavia and a sign that it would be experimental in form and multinational in content. The avant-garde poet Stanislav Vinaver, reporting for *Politika* newspaper, argued that, in championing a modernist style constructed with traditional materials, the pavilion had captured the authentic expression of Yugoslavism. The pavilion was a synthesis of the "patriarchal household" and "the modernism of daring calm monumentality." As such, it was a "precisely-used national emotion" and a "sum, an integral of experience and inspiration." He continued breathlessly, "It immediately became clear to each one of us that this was the route that can be taken, that has to be taken. The national moment isn't here a hindrance to modernist sentiment but acts as a stimulus for it. The whole national originality used with nothing held back in creation of one completely modern idea." For wider Europe and not just Yugoslavia, the wooden pavilion stood as a symbol of how "national style" had become an "integral part of the contemporary" and had found a path through which they could "unite, synthesize and become one."[1]

In the 1920s and 1930s race was an essential building block in the creation of a modern Yugoslav state: as much as civil engineering schemes, construction projects, and the building of new transport systems, the creation of a synthetic Yugoslav racial identity was a central element in the project of bringing Yugoslavia up to the standards of other European states. Over time, the terms of that project evolved, reflecting changing political and state-building priorities as well as the growing influence of racial scientific ideas from Nazi Germany and fascist Italy. Examining the work of a disparate group of researchers and ethnologists in interwar Yugoslavia who contributed to the search for a synthetic Yugoslav racial identity, this article explores how Yugoslav racial theory evolved from its largely archaelogical and ethnographic roots in the 1920s toward a more explicitly racial-biological direction in the 1930s. In the early 1920s, before a unitarist state had been created, ethnographers and racial anthropologists advocated the fashioning of a Yugoslav race that would embody the best qualities of the different nations ("tribes") and regions in Yugoslavia. By contrast, after a synthetic state had been founded in 1929, the search for a "core" race in the shape of the Dinaric population, as the nucleus of a new Yugoslav person, gained in legitimacy. This addressed underlying concerns that, while a synthetic state had been realized, a unified racial and cultural identity had not. From this perspective, the Dinaric theory of Yugoslav racial uniqueness not only had the potential to bring together large numbers of inhabitants over a wide geographical area but to provide a racially unifying explanation for their traditions, cultural habits, and psychology.

This transition reflected a specifically national context, but it was also a reaction to external factors. These included territorial challenges from neighboring revisionist states, especially Fascist Italy and Hungary, and increasing vulnerability to political pressure and ideological influence from, and the economic dominance of, Nazi Germany. Nonetheless, one aspect remained fundamental among almost all racial scientists, ethnographers, and anthropologists: the belief that the superiority of Yugoslav persons derived from their racial heterogeneity. True, National Socialist racial biological influences became increasingly evident as Yugoslav race theory adopted specific concepts of racial purity and the superiority of the Nordic race. However, these ideas never became dominant, because they couldn't work as a legitimizing device in a multiethnic state. In fact, sometimes it worked the other way around with Nazi and, to a lesser extent, Fascist racial biological concepts being used by Yugoslav racial scientists and ethnographers as a means of reinforcing the inevitability of racial hybridity and the autarchy of the Yugoslav race. By the end of the 1930s, with the Yugoslav ideal—and the state itself—in crisis, one major anthropological study envisioned a future Yugoslav nation through the synthesis of Dinaricism and the principles of Yugoslav racial hybridity.

Contemporary nationalist Croatian historiography, especially, tends to emphasize the repression that Croatians and other non-Serbs were subjected to in interwar Yugoslavia, often reducing the Yugoslav state of the 1920s and 1930s to little more than a hegemonic Greater Serbia.[2] Clearly, the writing and ideas of a narrow cohort of scientists and anthropologists is not a reliable guide to how most ordinary citizens felt, not least because they were writing in journals that were not accessible to the general public in a country where more than a third of the population was illiterate.[3] On the other hand, the fact that many of the scientists, anthropologists, and ethnographers involved in the construction of a racial Yugoslav consciousness were Croats and Slovenes—who themselves identified strongly as Yugoslavs rather than according to their "national" identities—suggests that, for some Croats and Slovenes, at least, the construction of a Yugoslav race represented idealism and opportunity.[4] The researchers under discussion here believed, as did many other advocates of a Yugoslav race, that the mixing and amalgamation of the inhabitants' diverse racial attributes could overcome the national differences standing in the way of modernity. Moreover, they argued that the heterogeneous and exotic nature of the racial and cultural composition of the Yugoslavs already represented a synthesis of the East and the West. This, they believed, provided Yugoslavs with a unique view of the world—one that was progressive and informed by Western values but that also drew on its own autarchic racial traditions and customs. In this sense, the 1929 Yugoslav pavilion was emblematic of the wider racial project. Unlike the Soviet Union, which viewed ethnic particularism as a "communal apartment" containing separate rooms for each nationality, Yugoslavia was to be like the Brašovan pavilion: modern in form, with each exhibit embodying the national and racial characteristics of all its peoples.[5]

Research Networks, International Collaboration, and the Limits of Biological Concepts of Race

The cohort of anthropologists, racial scientists, and ethnologists that made up Yugoslavia's racial research network in the 1920s and 1930s was drawn from research institutes and universities across the state. Whether they ever comprised a genuine network, however, is debatable. It is true that a number of the researchers most actively engaged in the search for a Yugoslav identity—such as Niko Županič, Božo Škerlj, Branimir Maleš and Boris Zarnik—were listed together under the Yugoslav section of the 1938 international directory of anthropologists.[6] Maleš and Zarnik were also included along with Škerlj in the list of members of the International Federation of Eugenic Organizations, which Yugoslavia joined under Škerlj's leadership in 1936.[7] Some of them—like Maleš, a professor of anthropology at Belgrade University and head of the Section for Anthropology and Racial Physiology at the Central Hygiene Institute in Belgrade, and

Škerlj, a researcher in the Anthropological Section of the Hygiene Institute in Ljubljana—were linked institutionally, even when they did not work together. In other instances, as was the case with Zarnik and Škerlj, they were regular collaborators in campaigns to further the cause of anthropology and eugenics at a Yugoslav-wide level. Moreover, most of them had studied at foreign universities, coming into contact with racial scientific concepts then gaining currency in both Nazi Germany and wider Europe. This was particularly true of the younger generation of racial anthropologists like Škerlj who had undertaken fellowships at German racial science institutes such as the Kaiser Wilhelm Institute for Anthropology, Human Hereditary, and Eugenics (KWI). In the 1930s international institutional and academic links became increasingly important for Yugoslav researchers. Maleš and Škerlj, for instance, were both contributors to European racial science journals such as Egon Freiherr von Eickstedt's *Zeitschrift für Rassenkunde* and Telesio Interlandi's *Difesa della Razza*, trading polemics with foreign colleagues and with each other. Maleš, who had trained at the University of Rome, was also a member of a number of Italian anthropological societies, including the Italian Society for Anthropology.[8] Likewise, Škerlj developed a close working relationship with anthropologists and anthropological institutes in Czechoslovakia, where a number of his anthropological studies were published, and Poland, where he conducted research with Jan Czekanowski on the menstrual cycle and fertility of female athletes.[9] Furthermore, in their work on Dinaric race and blood groups, Yugoslav researchers frequently borrowed from studies from Germany, Austria, France, and Poland. Yet not all of those engaged in discussions about the Yugoslav race were part of this professional network, and some worked outside scientific institutions altogether. One of the more idiosyncratic contributors to the field of racial research was Vladimir Dvorniković, a young professor of ethnopsychology at the University of Zagreb and a keen amateur photographer. Nevertheless, his monumental 1939 study of the traditions, folklore, and physical characteristics of the peoples of Yugoslavia was viewed at the time by critics as a significant contribution to the Dinaric theory of Yugoslav racial origins.

How far Yugoslav racial researchers genuinely endorsed National Socialist (and, after 1938, Italian fascist) biological concepts of Nordic racial purity, and to what extent they simply instrumentalized this terminology in order to promote Yugoslav national interests and enhance their own international professional standing, is not clear. Certainly, the Dinaric model of physical and intellectual perfection claimed by researchers like Maleš and Škerlj, with its mixed racial origins and dark features, hardly fit in with the blond Nordic ideal, even if it did conform to German racial scientists' ideas about Dinaricism. Among some historians there is a tendency to read such scientific appropriations uncritically and to underplay the context in which they emerged and, even more so, the agendas that motivated them.[10] However, it is likely that on some level the utilization of racial biological terminology by Yugoslav researchers and, for instance, the inclusion of the Dinarics in the Nordic racial family, were attempts to secure for the Yugoslav state an equal status with those European states it aspired to emulate in the postwar European hierarchy, as a way of announcing its modernity and progressive values.[11] In addition, utilizing the terminology of modern racial science, contributing to German and Italian racial science journals, and attending international conferences enabled Yugoslav researchers to feel part of a mainstream network of researchers in Europe, bringing prestige to their state and their field of research. Inevitably, during the late 1930s and early 1940s these transnational intellectual interchanges became more polemical. This was particularly clear in the exchanges with scholars from revisionist states as questions of borders, territorial integrity, and the rights of diaspora communities became ever more contested. Nevertheless, the relationships Yugoslav researchers established with their German, Italian, and Eastern European counterparts exposed them to cutting-edge racial ideas that seemed to offer answers to questions thrown up by the Yugoslav state's national conflicts. Ultimately, many of these concepts had only limited applicability, even for a younger generation of researchers working, as they were, in a multiethnic polity in search of a synthetic identity that could unite the state's ethnic groups. Consequently, their reproduction of the international science of race was inevitably partial and contradictory, veering between notions of a dominant Dinaric race and the benefits of racial heterogeneity.

That is not to suggest that the scientific research and fieldwork of anthropologists and ethnologists such as Škerlj and Županič was driven solely by national questions or political concerns; in fact, some in this cohort, such as Škerlj and Dvorniković, had a problematic relationship with the Yugoslav authorities, especially during the 1930s. Furthermore, many of them were driven by a fundamental interest in discrete scientific questions and aspired to answer the social and demographic challenges being posed in Yugoslavia and Europe more broadly. Their research networks reflected this. For example, by the mid-1930s Škerlj, as he set out in an essay of 1935 for a German racial science publication, was carrying out substantial research on the Dinarics with young Yugoslav colleagues, including the Slovenian researcher Bojan Pirc and the Croat anthropologist Boris Rasuhin, and with scholars at the Polish Central Institute for Physical Education (Centralny Instytut Wychowania Fizycznego; CIWF) in Warsaw. In both projects, he aimed to address questions related to female fertility, demographics, and economic efficiencies.[12] More broadly, many of the cohort were attempting to understand how racial science and anthropology could be made use of in resolving a range of social and economic questions in Yugoslavia and the region in sectors like education, agriculture, health and economic exchange. They all undoubtedly believed that they were working at the cutting edge of scientifically rigorous research and to that extent were producing what Franz Boas termed "good science." Nevertheless, it is important to appreciate that, as a whole, their primary focus was not science for science's sake, nor did the scientific and disciplinary breakthroughs they aspired to exist in a political vacuum. For most of them, including members of both the older and younger generation, their research ultimately aimed at understanding more about the state in which they lived in order to apply this knowledge and the research techniques they had studied and learnt abroad to help create a modern and progressive Yugoslav state.

How scholars at the various institutes at which this cohort studied in Germany, Italy, and elsewhere reacted to the subjective adaptation of their ideas to the Yugoslav context is not clear. Despite the fact that some, like Günther, had acted as mentors for members of this group, it is likely they did not approve. As this study shows, reactions to their ideas from German and Italian scientists and researchers could be sharp, especially when they came into conflict with core tenets of National Socialist or fascist racial science. Still, the fact remains that throughout the 1930s Škerlj and other young Yugoslav researchers continued to publish in National Socialist race journals and edited volumes, some of which were specifically dedicated to the state of racial and anthropological research in the region. Consequently, German and Italian peers and colleagues in particular must have been aware of the various imaginative means by which Yugoslav scientists were adapting the ideas they had learned at foreign race and ethnographic institutions and universities to their own national context, in so doing deviating significantly from the orthodoxies of National Socialist and Italian fascist racial science and anthropology.[13] In fact, in Škerlj's case, he continued contributing regularly to the *Zeitschrift für Rassekunde* until 1942. It was two years later, while working as an associate professor of anthropology at the University of Ljubljana, that he was arrested by the German occupation authorities on the charge that he had been in contact with the Partisan resistance movement and was deported to Dachau.[14]

Niko Županič and the Blood and Race of the Yugoslavs

Few states created in the aftermath of the First World War were accompanied by such an atmosphere of optimism and experimentalism as the Kingdom of the Serbs, Croats, and Slovenes (Kraljevina Srba, Hrvata i Slovenca; SHS). This mood of excitement was eloquently expressed in an article of 1919 by Milan Pribičević, a writer and youth leader in the Organization of Yugoslav Nationalists (Organizacija jugoslovenskih nacionalista; ORJUNA). In *Književni jug* he set out his vision of the "ideal Yugoslavia," which would be modern, progressive, and united, with all national and religious divisions swept away.[15] At the same time, few other states were so beset by divisions, competing agendas, and squabbling politicians. From the beginning there were disagreements about every aspect of national life. Even the name of the state became a matter of dispute. Those who believed in the existence of a single Yugoslav nation were especially dissatisfied, arguing that, far from contributing to the construction of a synthetic Yugoslav identity, the name reinforced national differences, obstructing the creation of a common Yugoslav consciousness. As the journalist Juraj Demetrović argued dismissively in *Jugoslovenska njiva* in 1919, "No, with this conservative Croatdom and Serbdom, we shall not get very far. Es-Ha-Es or, if you like, Se-Ha-Se is yet another formula, and one which supports and encourages unrest, jealousy, agitation and megalomania. For the creation of a state and the building of national unity, what is needed is one united state of Yugoslavia and one united national Yugoslav consciousness in which all accursed hereditary tribal opposites are reconciled. A united Yugoslavia and in it only Yugoslavs—that is the solution."[16]

It was in this disputatious atmosphere in 1919 that Niko Županič, director of the Ethnographical Museum and professor of ethnology at the King Aleksandar I University in Ljubljana, published a French language study of the Yugoslav "race," *Le Sang et le Race Yougoslaves* (The blood and race of the Yugoslavs). Županič had studied history and anthropology at the University of Vienna before completing a doctorate on the early settlements of the Slavs in southeastern Europe. In 1906 he began working at the Ethnographic Museum in Belgrade, interspersed with anthropological field trips to border regions to study the populations that lived between Serbia and Albania and, during the Balkan Wars, Bulgaria and Turkey. In 1914 the museum appointed him an anthropological researcher, with the task of "measuring the Serbian people and only after that foreigners on the Balkan Peninsula."[17] Županič spent the First World War in London lobbying for the establishment of a Yugoslav state, partly predicated on his belief in a single Yugoslav race. In the 1920s Županič became the leading racial ethnologist and researcher in Yugoslavia, writing prolifically on the subject of ethnography and archaeology. It was during this time that he completed his most famous book *Etnogeneza Jugoslavena* (The ethnogenesis of the Yugoslavs) in 1922.[18]

On the surface, Županič's theory about a single Yugoslav race seemed to be an ideal scientific answer to the search for common racial unity. For Županič, a Yugoslav race had existed ever since Slav tribes settled in the region. While Županič's work endorsed the value of racial mixing, like that of many Yugoslav ethnographers and racial anthropologists of the 1920s, he differed from them in his insistence that a Yugoslav race did not have to be made: the inhabitants of Yugoslavia simply had to become conscious of a racial reality that already existed. In *Le Sang et Race Yougoslaves*, he claimed an illustrious prehistory for the Yugoslav races in the Balkans, one characterized by their "poise, democratic spirit, their love of nature and agriculture as well as by their idealism." His study was illustrated throughout by photographs of typical examples of the young vigorous Yugoslav race, and he claimed that when the Yugoslav race established itself in the Balkan Peninsula in the sixth century, the "Illyrian" name given to it by strangers demonstrated "the unity of the territory, the language and the race." He also argued that the Yugoslavs' linguistic unity demonstrated that between the Adriatic and the Black Sea there resided "the same people and the same homeland and that the language above all is their real homeland." As far as Županič was concerned, "the similitude of the language of the Yugoslavs corresponds to the consanguinity, the unity of their race." Županič, like many Yugoslav ethnographers of the 1920s, embraced the diversity of the Yugoslavs' racial origins as an example of the heterogeneous nature of all national races while nevertheless insisting that the Yugoslav race was unique. He wrote that while there were no pure races in Europe, particular racial groups did dominate. In northern Europe, for example, the xanthodolichocephalic race, characterized by blond hair and long skulls, was prominent, while in the Mediterranean, the melanodolichocephalic race, with brown hair and long heads, predominated. In the Alps and the Balkans, meanwhile, the melanobrachycephalic type, characterized by brown hair and short heads, was the most common. However, the Yugoslav race stood outside all of these groups, being "a mixture of the blood of the different tribes and nations from the Neolithic period until today."[19]

Paradoxically, despite his theories about the racial heterogeneity of the Yugoslavs, Županič ascribed to them a pure racial lineage, tracing their origins to two interrelated races: the *homo adriaticus* and *homo dinaricus*. This, in turn, drew on the research of the French naturalist and anthropologist Joseph Deniker, whose *Les six races composant la population actuelle de l'europe* (The six races comprising the population of present-day Europe) in 1904 had identified a common Adriatic-Dinaric race as one of the six main European races.[20] Županič consciously adapted this theory in the name of incarnating the Yugoslavs as a new dominant race, destined to be the leading nation in the Balkans as a result of their physical resilience, deep affinity for culture, and racial heterogeneity. Županič argued that the *homo adriaticus* were distinguished by their tall stature, rounded head, wavy hair, long legs, fine nose, aquiline features, and slightly brown skin, and lived mostly in the mountains of the Dinaric region. While the amalgam of anthropological features from the *homo adriaticus* were characteristic of the Yugoslav race, they also corresponded "to the frontiers of Yugoslavia" and thus were dispersed more widely throughout the region. This explained why their features were present in Venice and some parts of Albania. Although in Albania the Yugoslav tribes had lost their language almost completely, they had, he wrote, "refreshed their descendants with the blood of Aryans." Consequently, the Serbs and Albanians formed a unique race, and while they contained Asiatic and "a little" Hamitic blood, "corporally and physically they are more Aryan than, for example, the Greeks and Italians, the Spanish, the southern French, the Germans and Romanians." In particular, the Serbs resembled in the "structure of their bodies, their limbs and their faces the Aryans generally, but the form of their brains (especially their cerebellum) and their complexion showed an element of melanobrachycephalism." Županič extended his idea that the Yugoslav race was both similar to other European races but also exotic and unique in the cultural field. For example, he was among the first ethnographers to argue that the Yugoslav race had a cultural mission in regenerating European civilization. Županič noted that, despite the fact that the Yugoslavs had been studied less intensively from an anthropological perspective than some other nations, the Balkan Peninsula had long been a meeting place of different African, Asian, and European civilizations. The region could be compared to ancient Greece, where different races lived together harmoniously under the rule of the nature-loving and art-creating Hellenes. Similarly, he continued, "fate has destined the Yugoslavs, more vigorous in their bodies and in their souls, to take the place of the Hellenes in regenerating the Byzantine world." This mission had been precipitated by the invasion of the Balkans by the Ottoman army, under whose rule the Yugoslavs had endured torture and suffering, "personified in their thoughts and their sentiments," their national poetry, and "patriarchal mores." By shedding their blood, the Yugoslavs hoped that they would be able to fulfill their destiny "in the regeneration of the East and the introduction of new elements in European civilization."[21]

In 1932 Županič returned to the theme of the racial origins of the Yugoslav race in an article published in the anthropological journal *Etnolog*, of which he was the editor and founder. On the one hand, his conclusions clearly showed the influence of German racial science—in particular the studies of the racial philosopher Houston Stewart Chamberlain, on his analyses of Yugoslav racial origins. Yet Županič's findings also demonstrated how archaeological research could be used to construct an ethnographical simultaneity between different national groups and serve the cause of a Yugoslav race. In his article, Županič aimed to show how the racial makeup of the Yugoslavs had changed over time, becoming less Nordic and Aryan as a result of an influx of "foreign blood" beginning before the birth of Christ and continuing to the present day. Županič explained that as the proportion of dolicecephalic skulls declined and the proportion of brachycephalic skulls increased, the number of Illyrians with blond hair and fair complexions also fell. The South Slav masses that had settled in the Balkan Peninsula also constituted by this time a united linguistic group. It was interesting to note, he added, that they possessed recognizable racial characteristics. The Byzantine historian Procopius observed that in their appearance and characteristics the Southern Slavs did not differ. "Their skin was neither completely white and nor was their hair completely blonde but neither was it too brown or dark either, usually having a red shimmer," Župančič recorded him as writing. In their stature the Slavs were so tall and strong that Emperor Mauricius was astonished at their "imposing appearance, excellent dimensions and the extremity of their proportions." Arab historians likewise recorded the characteristics of the Slavs and, in the eighth century, according to Župančič, one Arab writer, Aber-Rahman ibn Habib, was known as the "Slav" on account of his blond hair, blue eyes, and muscular build. As Župančič pointed out, such observations had been confirmed by excavations of skulls in areas of present-day Yugoslavia as well as Austria and Germany. Alluding to the influential nineteenth-century theory proposed by scholars such as the American economist William Z. Ripley that the Yugoslavs were originally brachycephalic migrants from central Asia, Župančič asked rhetorically, "Were the Southern Slavs an ethnic element which brought to the Germans and Greeks brachycephaly as well as a dark complexion and so robbed these people of their dolichocephalic and blonde complexion?" On the contrary, the analysis of skulls from local necropolises suggested that nearly 40 percent of the South Slavs were dolichocephalic and less than 10 percent brachycephalic. This compared with 14 percent of brachycephalic skulls among Germans found in mass graves from the second to fifth centuries. Moreover, according to Byzantine historiographies, many of the Slav skeletons were over one meter and seventy centimeters high, indicating that South Slavs of the early middle ages were a people of high stature, dolichocephalic skull shape, and fair complexion. The "racial character" of the ancient Yugoslavs, Župančič surmised, therefore resembled that of the Germanic and Celtic tribes from the time of their wanderings in the South, but the South Slavs of the early middle ages were almost as pure as the similarly tall xanthodolichocephalic Aryan and Nordic races. Furthermore, Župančić continued, excavations of skulls from the necropolises of the late middle ages in Bosnia and Croatia had demonstrated that even at that stage the inhabitants of the region were still tall with dolichocephalic heads.[22]

He pointed out, however, that by the time Ernest Zuckerkandl, a Viennese anthropologist, was carrying out examinations on South Slav skulls in the late nineteenth century, barely 20 percent of excavated skulls were dolichocephalic, while the vast majority were brachycephalic. In 1912 another anthropologist, Arthur Weisbach, had published his own study of sixty Slovenian skulls and cranial indices, which showed that nearly 50 percent of skulls were brachycephalic. By contrast, a mere 2 percent of skulls were dolichocephalic. True, when Weisbach later examined the racial characteristics of nearly four thousand soldiers from Bosnia, he found that while dolichocephalism accounted for only 2 percent of those examined, many of these soldiers nevertheless retained the long facial features representative of the ancient inhabitants of this region. This was something that set them apart from other Slavs. "With justification, Weisbach noted that there were almost no small so-called turned-up noses on Serbo-Croats of the kind one often observes on Czechs and Poles," Županič commented. From the same examinations, Weisbach found that the South Slavs were tall, with dark hair, swarthy skin, and brown eyes predominating. On the other hand, there was no denying that only a tiny minority of the soldiers examined were dolichocephalic. This showed that the brain shape of the south Slavs had "changed completely and in place of the long skull the short and high brain shape are now present to a greater extent." The formerly fair complexion had also changed to dark, with only the tall stature remaining from the physique of the primordial Yugoslavs.[23]

Unlike Houston Stewart Chamberlain, though, Županič did not see this racial evolution as negative. On the contrary, in *Etnogeneza Jugoslavena* he robustly countered Chamberlain's contention that mixing with other races had diluted the racial strength of the prehistoric blond Slav tribes. Instead, he appealed to the virtues of racial mixing in producing a genetically more resilient nation. The peoples of the Balkans, he wrote, had never only constituted one race. Indeed, racial mixing, far from diluting the Nordic racial component of the South Slavs, had produced an "alloy" that was tougher, more durable, and physically superior. Comparing the mixing of races to the making of gold coins, he asserted that "precious gold is not more beautiful or coveted because it is pure. In such cases, it is too fragile and too soft. That is why one places it in the copper mint and adds other less valuable metals to it to give it a tough enduring colour and a beautiful shine."[24] Moreover, Županič argued—as a number of other Yugoslav researchers later would—that the unique and heterogeneous racial characteristics of had made them peculiarly attuned to culture. Writing in 1923 in the Slovene art history journal *Umetnostno zgodovino* Županič claimed that the famed Renaissance artist Pellegrino di San Daniele was, like many apparently foreign painters and writers, "an artist of our blood." Županič went further, claiming that "among the artists of the Renaissance, many of the men were of the Yugoslav race but because of the times in which they lived passed themselves off as Italian and German." Despite this, he maintained that the race of these artists played an important role in their work and the "individual traits of these Yugoslav artists of the Italian Renaissance" could be traced to their Yugoslav racial heritage, in di San Daniele's case as the son of the Udinese Giovanni Schiavone da Zagrabia, an immigrant from Dalmatia originally called Ivan Beljan.[25]

Županič's positive persepective on ethnographic diversity and plurality in the Balkans put him sharply at odds with many European travelers to the region in the nineteenth and twentieth centuries. They viewed the same diversity as dangerous: the melange of races and languages threatened to disrupt the "European order" in which ethnicity was associated with a common language and a clearly demarcated territory.[26] By contrast, Županič's research in the 1920s continued to demonstrate a wide-ranging interest in the racial composition of various national groups, and he often used his anthropological field work to reinforce his theories about the heterogeneous racial origins of the Yugoslavs. Among the communities he surveyed most extensively was the Serb settlements on the borderlands of the state. As part of a 1924 Festschrift for the human geographer Jovan Cvijić, a pioneer of the Dinaric theory, Županič reported on his findings from a research trip to Kosovo, where he had examined anthropological features of the Serb inhabitants in Kosovo Polje. Recruiting seventy-six men aged between twenty and twenty-nine and forty-seven children who had been born in Pristina or the Gračanica region, he set out to measure a range of physical features. These included height, length and width of head, complexion and hair color, skull index, facial morphology, and the length of limbs, as well as overall physiognomy, to better understand the racial composition of the Serbs of Kosovo Polje in comparison to other Yugoslavs. He concluded that, as elsewhere, the Serbs of Kosovo Polje were "no pure race" and "represent no pure racial element," but were a mixture of "numerous races." This had produced a new race composed of the mixing of numerous dark, brachycephalic, and dolichocephalic near-eastern races and "Mediterranean and Armenoid" groups with Nordic races and blond Thracians, Illyrians, and Hellenes.[27]

A little later, Županič also undertook research trips to examine the physiognomy and racial characteristics of other minorities in Kosovo Polje. One of these was the Circassian community. In his field report of 1933 Županič noted their racial hetereogeneity, demonstrated in their distinctive combination of light eyes and brown hair, or, alternatively, light hair and dark eyes. Županič also ascribed to them a range of behavioral characteristics and personal qualities and spent some time analyzing their habits and customs. For a long time they were known for "their intrepidity as brave warriors and courageous brigands": men who "observed scrupulously the commands of hospitality and the vengeance of the blood." Their songs, meanwhile, celebrated the famed beauty of Circassian women. According to Županič, the Circassians loved to eat horsemeat and were expert equestrians. The author recalled that in 1919 he had assisted in the recruitment of six Circassians for the Yugoslav infantry, who were later transferred to the cavalry for their prowess. However, by the time Županič traveled to Kosovo for his field work he could see that the Circassians were no longer dangerous brigands but "instead demonstrated a desire for progress and civilization." In this sense, they were becoming progressive Yugoslavs.[28]

Why the fascination with the Circassians? On one level, Županič's subject choice was not surprising, since their claimed ethnographic links to the Serbs and isolated geographical location had made Circassians a favorite group for study by Yugoslav ethnographers and anthropologists, especially those living and working in the state's borderlands.[29] Similarly, Županič explained that the Circassians were particularly valuable in terms of ethnographic research about the Serbs because the first people to carry the Serbian name had been from the Caucasus and were probably Circassians. These Circassian-Samartians might have lost their identity and language but in the movement of Slavic peoples they had retained their name and ideas about state organization as they migrated from the Dnieper to the Elbe and Saale along with the Croats and Celts. As such they represented a living museum of the prehistoric roots of the Yugoslav race. Unfortunately, by the time of his trip to the Circassian settlements of Velika Reka, Miloševo, Donje Stanovce, and Gornje Stanovce in 1929 it was clear, Županič observed, that the community was dying out, most of it having already emigrated to Syria and the Middle East. By 1929 there were only three hundred people left in the villages of Kosovo Polje: consequently, his sample size was restricted to twenty-one men aged between ten and twenty. He measured height, the diameter and radius of the head and frontal lobe, width of the face, diameter of the nasal cavity, distance of the zygomatic arch, cephalic index of the head and face, and color of the eyes, hair, and skin. He found that the Circassian males were generally in the brachycephalic range but with underlying dolichoid and mesocephalic elements. This reflected "the mixture of blood, the mixture of heterogeneous ethnic elements" evident in the distinctive combination of dark hair and light eyes so characteristic of Circassians. "From such facts," Županič concluded, "one can deduce that the Circassians of Kosovo are a mixture of at least two or more ethnic elements. One of these must have been a Nordic element (xanthodolichocephalic) which has left its vestige in the high percentage of blue and green eyes and light skin. As regards the colour of the hair, dark hair predominates with 52%, demonstrating "one or more dark ethnic elements," which concurred, he added, with travel writer Jakob Peinegg's descriptions, during his travels in the Caucasus, of Circassian girls with their slim figures, fair skin, and dark hair.[30]

Racial Mixing and the Search for the Dinarics

The idea of "blood mixing" was an important aspect of the quest for a synthetic Yugoslav racial identity. If, as Županič argued, a unique Yugoslav race with a racial consciousness already existed, other ethnographers, anthropologists, and racial eugenicists countered that a Yugoslav race could be formed only through an active policy of mixing national groups; this would not only support the building of a Yugoslav consciousness, but through combining the best qualities of the various national and regional groups construct a Yugoslav superman. In the early 1920s officials in the Ministry of National Health were already looking at racial hybridity in other states and considering what lessons could be applied to Yugoslavia. Early advocates of racial mixing linked these ideas to eugenics. In 1920, for example, Vladimir S. Stanojević, a researcher at the Central Hygienic Institute in Belgrade, published a study of eugenic principles that was clearly aimed at health officials, scientists, and policy makers. *Eugenika* provided an overview of the international state of eugenics and discussed what the Yugoslav state could benefit from learning. In particular, Stanojević praised the United States for its extensive eugenic policies. In his view, America's rigorous and unsentimental eugenic policies—which included the segregation and sterilization of the disabled and mentally defective—was helping it become the dominant world power. As such it provided a model for Yugoslav health officials. Yet, he added, there was another factor working in America's favor: the racially hybrid nature of its population. Stanojević did not believe that pure races were stronger or healthier, or would enjoy greater longevity. On the contrary, he cited the example of the cross-breeding of animals and trees to assert that the more a race was mixed, the more virile it became. The "new ideal race" created by the Americans was destined for hegemony precisely because it was a synthesis of a number of different racial groups. The implications for the future Yugoslav race were clear: race mixing—synthesizing the strengths and qualities of all its peoples and regions—would make the state more powerful, dynamic, and better able to protect its borders against revisionist neighbors.[31]

By 1924 Jovan Zubović, an anthropologist, was proposing that race mixing should become a systematic state program. Writing in the intellectual Zagreb journal *Nova Evropa*, Žubović prophesied that a "national unit" was emerging in the form of a new Yugoslav person. He conceded that there were many environmental, geographical, national, economic, cultural, political, and religious factors that separated the embryonic Yugoslavs from each other. Nevertheless, he wrote, while it would be "unnatural, impossible and unnecessary" to wipe away all such differences, the essence of the new Yugoslav person meant "the coming together, unity and synthesis of different tribal elements." Using the metaphor of the Yugoslav state as a healthy tree on which the best national and tribal qualities should be transplanted, he argued that "blood mixing" held out the promise not just of national unity but racially and eugenically perfect Yugoslavs. While Žubović believed that there could be no real unity without the mixing of the different Yugoslav elements, he acknowledged that racial mixing would produce "complicated intellectual and moral results," not least since eugenics commonly stressed "pure races and strict selection." His solution was the implementation of a process of "rational mixing." This meant the selection of the most "capable" individuals for mixed breeding while at the same time maintaining the Yugoslav character traits "which we define as Slavic morals, justice and social conscience." Žubović reasoned too that the principles of racial eugenics should be applied to marriage and family law in order to make "mixed" marriages easier, decoupling matrimony from religion, which served to frustrate intermarriage by encouraging tribal particularism. Ultimately, though, he concluded, a new Yugoslav person could only be realized through *total* social, economic, educational, and geographic mixing by means of internal colonization: city dwellers would mix with villagers; the urban middle class with workers; valley inhabitants with mountain populations; and populations from the less-educated regions with the educated. He insisted that if there could be no "national or racial unity" without equally blending different Yugoslav elements and attributes, total mixing by combining the different physical and psychological qualities of Yugoslavia's diverse groups would also increase the productivity of commerce, agriculture, and industry.[32]

Proposals such as Zubović's were not taken up by Yugoslav politicians in the 1920s: Serbs, Croats, and Slovenes continued to be represented by their own ethnic parties until the introduction of King Aleksandar's personal dictatorship and the reconstitution of the state as synthetically Yugoslav in 1929. All manifestations of "tribalism" were then outlawed and the internal borders of the state redrawn on a supra-ethnic basis. For committed Yugoslavs, October 3 represented a kind of national revolution, one that was embodied in the state's new name. As novelist Jovan Dučić exclaimed triumphantly in *Politika*, "One blood and one ideal! One destiny and one life formula! One fatherland and one patriotism! One future and one duty! One language and one culture! One tradition and one history! Or, in a short and splendid definition: one history and one state! That's the new and powerful energy which has been given the name Yugoslavia."[33] *Pobeda*, the newspaper of ORJUNA, hoped for the construction of a racially engineered Yugoslav person. In an editorial of June 28, 1933, under the title "The Indestructibility of our Race," *Pobeda* argued that the new synthetic Yugoslav state should be a symbol of the regeneration of the Yugoslav race, demonstrating its racial strength through the centuries in its struggle for liberation. In contrast to Županič, who had evoked images of a melange of invading armies mixing with the autochthonous population to produce something racially unique, *Pobeda* likened the Yugoslav race to a frequently cultivated field with deep roots that had protected its cultural and racial uniqueness and "Slavic spirit" from foreign intrusion. No matter how many civilizations had ploughed its fields, their "spiritual unity and oneness opposed the Roman legionaries and Asian and African races. On the mountainous Balkans, in the fertile Balkans, in the bloody Balkans, there remained a tough, healthy and independent part of the great Slav family; there remained the Yugoslav nation."[34]

The broader program to incarnate a Yugoslav racial consciousness resulted in the penetration of the value of racial hybridity into many aspects of the new state's cultural life, including novels, songs, tourism advertising, even beauty competitions. In a dispatch before the final round of the 1929 Miss Yugoslavia competition, for example, the competition's sponsor, the editor of the popular Belgrade news magazine *Vreme*, asked: "Which region will provide the most beautiful woman in Yugoslavia?" The writer, noting that the winner of the competition would go to Paris to compete in the Miss Europe finals, predicted that the voting of the international jury would be influenced by the racial characteristics of the competitors, since the intention of the jury would be to assess the beauty of individual nations. This posed a problem for Yugoslavia, given its regional variation. Yugoslav racial beauty drew its strength, he wrote, from its heterogeneity, combining the attributes of the Slavic race, defined by blond hair and blue eyes, with admixtures of northern Asian and Indid races, Slav tribes, and old Balkan races such as the Thracians. This meant that no typical Slavic racial type existed any longer and, to make the situation even more complicated, racial mixing had taken a different form in each region, resulting in an "overwhelmingly mixed" beauty standard. If the photographs of the finalists reinforced the claims of Yugoslav racial hybridity, from Serbia's statuesque brunets and Slovenia's blonds to Vojvodina's multiethnic melange and Dalmatia's "Roman mixture," *Vreme* was nevertheless struck by the "extraordinary beauty" of Yugoslav women and the preponderance of black hair, dark eyes, tall height, and "classical racial faces" among the entrants.[35]

With the establishment of a synthetic Yugoslav state, proposals for racial mixing seemed to fade into the background and, with it, Županič's preeminence. The emphasis of Yugoslav racial discourse also began to change, from one that insisted that a Yugoslav "race" either already existed or could be created through the mixing of the different national groups, in the quest for a dominant and superior racial prototype capable of assimilating the state's diverse national and religious communities. That prototype was the Dinaric. What explains this evolution? First, the strongly racialized discourse of the new Yugoslav state and its policies of national synthesis—which included internal colonisation—rendered discussions about racial mixing irrelevant. The recasting of citizens' identity as Yugoslavs meant that debates about whether a Yugoslav race existed evolved. Evidently it did exist, and had existed since prehistory, as historians such as Viktor Novak, Ferdo Šišić, and Vladimir Ćorović made clear. The challenge now was to ensure that citizens were conscious of their Yugoslav biological superiority and learned how to think "racially."[36] Since the Dinaric was geographically and regionally distributed and possessed a range of psychological and physical attributes common to peasant communities throughout the state, Dinaric appeared to provide another means by which to achieve racial synthesis. Moreover, as the scholarship of Jovan Cvijić demonstrated, the Dinaric had been identified as an anthropological phenomenon long before the foundation of the state by foreign as well as South Slav anthropologists and ethnographers and hence enjoyed, at least potentially, a legitimacy not applicable to other Yugoslav racial theories. The influence of National Socialist and *völkisch* concepts of race was also an important factor, exemplified in the discourses of an emerging generation of Yugoslav researchers. Some of the younger anthropologists, such as Božo Škerlj, who most energetically championed the Dinaric theory of Yugoslav racial origins, had completed their education at German universities under racial scientists like Eugen Fischer, director of the Kaiser Wilhelm Institute for Anthropology, Human Research, and Eugenics, and Hans Günther, professor of racial theory at the University of Jena. Both of these German scientists had written extensively on the subject of the Dinaric race. In his 1922 study *Rassenkunde des deutschen volkes*, Günther had identified the Dinaric race as one of the five constituent "Aryan" races—an idea that members of a new generation of more biologically minded Italian racial scientists returned to in the early 1940s. Chief among them was the young anthropologist Guido Landra, director of the Office of Racial Studies and author of the anti-Semitic "Race Manifesto," which argued for the Aryan rather than Mediterranean origins of the Italian people.[37]

Finally, placing the Dinaric race in the framework of Nazi and, later, Italian fascist racial science provided Yugoslav ethnographers and racial anthropologists with international scientific kudos and bolstered the legitimacy of the Yugoslav state. Publishing in prestigious race journals such as *La difesa della razza* and *Zeitschrift für Rassenkunde* not only brought young researchers' ideas about a synthetic Yugoslav race to a wider audience but, through the process of intellectual exchange, enabled Yugoslavia to restate its territorial integrity. This was a task that seemed urgent after the outbreak of the Second World War, as a revisionist Italy made increasingly noisy claims to the Dalmatian region. In late 1939, for example, Božo Škerlj, by now an associate professor of anthropology at the University of Ljubljana, penned an article for Interlandi's La *difesa della razza* in which he pointedly drew attention to the Dinaric (in other words, Yugoslav) racial origins of Dalmatia's inhabitants.[38] However, while National Socialist concepts about race classification and biological purity clearly influenced researchers during the 1930s, as Škerlj's polemic illustrated, they were typically integrated within the existing Yugoslav context. In this sense, National Socialist theories were arguably appropriated by Yugoslav race researchers to provide a scientific framework for their notions of racial hybridity as synthesis.

The shift toward a more biological understanding of race symbolized in a "white" Dinaric race was illustrated in a 1931 essay by Boris Zarnik in the journal *Priroda*. A zoologist and professor of medicine at the University of Zagreb who, though of the same generation as Županič, had spent long periods of his academic career in Germany, Zarnik had also founded the Morphological-Biological Institute and was a co-founder of the Anthropological Section of the Sociological Society. In 1925, along with other members of this society, he undertook a two-year racial anthropological project examining schoolchildren in the Zagreb area. Ten years later, with researchers from the anthropological section of the Central Hygiene Institute in Zagreb, he carried out racial scientific measurements on 560 peasants from ninety villages in northwest Croatia and central Bosnia in order to categorize their racial characteristics and anthropological features.[39] In his essay, Zarnik stated that the "white race" was not one pure race but a combination of four different races: the Nordic race in the north; the alpine race in the center; the Mediterranean race on the Mediterranean Coast; and the Dinaric race in the Balkans, an idea that owed a great deal to the theories of German racial scientists and anthropologists such as Hans Günther and Egon Freiherr von Eickstedt. Zarnik certainly made a distinction between nationality and race, observing that "in every nation there are found members of those races, particularly mixed breeds, that show the characteristics of the race in varying combinations.[40]

Unlike earlier interpretations of Yugoslav racial definition, Zarnik's essay emphasized the differences between white and nonwhite races in ways that seemed to militate against racial mixing. As evidence of this difference, he pointed to the psychometric tests the U.S. army had asked its recruits to undertake during the First World War. The fact that blacks and mixed-race candidates had scored significantly lower than whites was more striking because of the high number of Americans who were a combination of white and black, something he suggested did not bode well for the country's future. This directly contradicted the argument of eugenicists such as Vladimir Stanojević in the early 1920s, that racial mixing had strengthened the United States.[41] In an essay four years earlier in *Hrvatsko kolo,* just after completing his project measuring Zagreb schoolchildren, Stanojević had appeared to argue for the racial superiority of the Yugoslav Dinarics as derived from their supposed Nordic ancestry. In his article, which was illustrated with photographs of typical Dinaric, Alpine, Nordic, and Mediterranean types, he stressed the racial closeness of the Dinaric-Adriatic and Nordic races in height, build, and facial shape. "Apart from Sweden," he asserted, "no other state in Europe has a population with such a relatively equal racial composition as our land which . . . manifests everywhere the same Dinaric-Nordic core. The superhuman deeds of bravery and daring, of which the history of the South Slavs is filled from the oldest times until today, shows that our racial composition produces the most excellent virtues." However, this did not necessarily imply racial purity, since, as he explained, the supremacy of the Dinarics was based on their heterogenous racial origins. He pointed out that while the average Yugoslav inherited twenty three Dinaric and fifteen Nordic chromosomes, he was the recipient of a range of other assimilated chromosomes, including Alpine, Mediterranean, and Mongoloid genetic markers. Furthermore, Zarnik's championing of Dinaricism was not to imply that a Yugoslav race did not exist. In fact, as Zarnik showed, the two concepts were often complementary and could be employed together as a geopolitical justification for the maintenance of the state's existing borders and the expansion of those borders to include all the diaspora "Yugoslav" populations. While the Yugoslavs constituted three distinct people on the basis of language, religion, and tradition, Zarnik argued, "from the biological perspective they are one unit who will, without doubt, draw to themselves and assimilate all those of equal racial composition who today live outside our borders." Yugoslavia's enemies could "build towers and wire fences, bridges and aeroplanes, fire cannons and grenades," but the genes of the Yugoslavs would remain essential to the future of the state. For that reason it was the duty of all Yugoslavs "to get to know in its entirety the racial composition of our inhabitants so that we are empowered to protect the unchangeability of our race, our greatest national worth."[42]

By the time Zarnik's essay was published in *Priroda* in 1931, he was increasingly concerned with understanding the link between race and intellectual differences among Europeans. He suspected these differences were linked to environmental and social conditions. Fortunately, Zarnik wrote, the intellectual features of the Dinaric race had been rigorously assessed. Racial anthropologists attributed to them "a developed fantasy, having as a consequence a great talent for art, especially music; significant intelligence; great self-awareness, courage and militancy and sensibility for heroism, in other words all those characteristics which embody the Nordic race." As the essence of the Dinaric race, he pointed out, Hans Günther had identified their "toughness, strength and sincerity" while others stressed their "good nature and honesty as well as talent for business."[43]

Like many German scientists, Zarnik believed that the Nordic race possessed exceptional intellectual qualities and was the producer of all culture. Zarnik argued that Nordic races, especially the old Germanic and Slavic tribes, had conquered the whole of southern and central Europe. That the Slavs were Nordic had been decisively shown, he argued, through excavations by archaeologists of Slavic graves and examinations of their dolichocephalic skulls. In this he echoed Županič's theories about the blond dolichocephalic origins of the South Slavs. Zarnik cautioned against racial exclusivity, however, stressing that it was the mixing of the Nordic with other races that had produced such strength and vitality. Indeed, a cursory examination of the racial makeup of European novelists and thinkers proved his point:

> If, for example, we look at the physiognomy of diverse men who on the intellectual field have achieved great success, in the vast majority of cases they are mixed types such as Socrates, Leibniz, Kant, Schopenhauer, Goethe, Schiller, Voltaire, Tolstoy, Pushkin, Dante, Luther, Karl Ernst von Baer, Darwin, Caesar, Napoleon, Michelangelo etc. The truth is that with few exceptions, we find in their physiognomy diverse Nordic characteristics but at the same time characteristics of other races, especially the Dinaric (for example, Leibnitz, Goethe, Schiller, Voltaire, Baer) so that I have come to the conclusion that the Nordic-Dinaric mixture produces the most exceptional qualities.[44]

To support his arguments about the benefits of the mixing of Nordic and other races, he cited studies by the scientist Karl Gerlach, who had traced the birthplaces of "various illustrious Germans" on a map and found that the majority of these locations "lie in the belt where there is the strongest mixing between the Nordic and Dinaric and Alpine races." Zarnik noted that as well as racial maps for German poets, Gerlach had produced similar maps for painters, musicians, doctors, mathematicians, and generals, showing that their birthplaces were in regions of "the most intensive racial mixing."[45]

Other Yugoslav advocates of Dinaricism traversed the same line between racial biology and the Yugoslav principles of racial heterogeneity. One of the most prolific was Branimir Maleš,the author of two studies about the "biodynamics" of the Dinaric race. In 1935 Maleš had authored a scientific study in which he argued that the key to the racial uniqueness of the Dinaric man was found in his body shape and the formation of his skull. These features, he contended, had nothing in common with the Alpine race "or even worse with American Indians and Asiatic Mongols, part of the great yellow race, though all of these were, like the Dinaric, brachycephalic."[46] Maleš's biological explanations of race also featured in the mass media. In the mid-1930s Maleš began writing for the Serbian novelist Miloš Črnjanski's short-lived populist racial science journal *Ideje* and for a number of other publications on the radical right, including *Otažbina*, the newspaper of the Yugoslav National Party, known as ZBOR. When, under pressure from Nazi Germany the Yugoslav government introduced a raft of unpopular anti-Semitic laws in 1938, Maleš penned a number of articles for the Belgrade journal *Vreme* on the otherness of the Jewish "race."[47] For all that Maleš's research incorporated fashionable racial-biological concepts, like Zarnik he endeavored to adapt them to the Yugoslav context, especially the idea that the strongest races were created through mixing diverse racial groups. That said, in his 1936 study *O ljudskim rasama* (On human races), based on a series of public lectures at Kolarčev Public University, his discussion of Dinaricism and the Yugoslav race was grounded in paradox. On the one hand, Maleš stressed the ethnic homogeneity of the Yugoslavs. The Dinaric race, he asserted, was not a combination of "Nordic and Armenoid elements," as some racial scientists had mistakenly assumed. Rather, all the characteristics of the Dinaric race were "exclusively Dinaric." This meant that, while other comparable nations were racially divided, "the vast majority of our people, without regard to name, religion or earlier administrative or state division are members of one racial community. What divides others unites us. They know that we came together under the same biological influences, that even in the prehistoric period we were one as today we are one too." Nevertheless, he acknowledged the existence of many subsets of Dinarics and the existence in Yugoslavia's "mountainous regions" of populations "with features characteristic of foreign races." Meanwhile, in coastal Dalmatia, the Montenegrin Primorja, and southern and eastern Serbia, the Mediterranean influence could be felt and, as his colleague Škerlj had pointed out, the presence of "negroid features." These were traces, Maleš explained, of Roman legionaries of "black origin."[48]

Likewise, Maleš emphasized that the racial compositon of nations was complex and that there were not many people who "in their biological breakdown belong to one race." Nations were racial mixes just as much as individuals were. Nonetheless, there *were* cases, he continued, where one race dominated over others and imbued the nation with its characteristics. In the case of Yugoslavia, this had resulted in the hegemony of the Dinaric race. Rather than "non-national" groups being eradicated, however, Maleš argued that they would be incorporated into the dominant Dinaric race, making it stronger. It would be a mistake, he wrote, "to place the race above the nation, to exclude from the national community all those members of 'non-national' races." Since every race had instrinsic worth, it was imperative to protect those "racial collages" that created races, to ensure the nation enjoyed "a healthier and better biological, cultured and social future." On the other hand, he emphasized that in the Yugoslav case it was necessary "to safeguard the 'hegemony' of the Dinaric race" and the "psychological characteristics of the people" that had provided "Dinaric kinship." By contrast, he argued for the removal of of those groups that "are unsuitable for life, the products of illness and degeneration, the incurably ill and those races to which such genetically-burdened people belong" in order to prevent harm to the nation. "We must enable the posterity of healthy families, both physically and spiritually, especially the posterity of racially-pure types with greater physical and spiritual harmony and not allow the development of individuals and generations of weaker biological and character value."[49]

Being a Yugoslav the Dinaric Way

By 1939 the idea of a common Yugoslav identity was in crisis. The assassination five years earlier of its guiding symbol King Aleksandar by the Ustasha movement, an émigré Croatian terrorist organisation, and successive years of political crises had brought the Yugoslav state to a breaking point. In Croatia separatism was on the rise, and ideological extremism was increasing throughout Yugoslavia as interethnic tensions and economic difficulties intensified. In September of that year an agreement was reached between the Yugoslav Prime Minister Dragiša Cvetković and the leader of the Croatian Peasant Party, Vladko Maček. The treaty created an autonomous Croatian unit comprised of Croatia and parts of Bosnia and the formation of a coalition government between Cvetković's Yugoslav Radical Union and Maček's party. This existential crisis did not deter enthusiasts for a synthetic Yugoslav identity, however, among them the young ethnopsychologist Vladimir Dvorniković. His *Karakterologija Jugoslovena* (The characterology of the Yugoslavs), published the same year, was the most extensive study to date of the Dinaric roots of the Yugoslav race. The author of several books about race, psychology, and character among the Yugoslavs, Dvorniković had a particular interest in the Dinaric man as a symbol of resistance to the individualistic ethos of the West. The superior moral virtues of the Yugoslav man and the Dinaric was a common theme in Dvorniković's writing: as early as 1925 he had identified the Dinaric man, with his instincts for social justice and the rights of the community, as a natural replacement for the managerial Nordic man.[50]

Karakterologija Jugoslovena was grounded in the progressive assumptions of a committed Yugoslavist. While it employed some of the tropes of racial biology and drew on the racial theories of Nazi and German racial scientists and anthropologists, it was not a racial scientific study per se. Rather, it was an example of *Völkerpsychologie*, a form of cultural psychology that stressed the role of national identity, geography, society, and culture in the development of mentalities.[51] Dvorniković's book offered a spirited exploration of Balkan folklore, patriarchal culture, history, and social practices through the study of collective mentalities and race. It advocated protecting the best elements of Dinaric culture and racial attributes from the encroachment of Western influences, especially urbanism, which was, he argued, taking Yugoslavs away from their patriarchal roots and also transforming their physical features. While, on the face of it, Dvorniković's study endorsed fashionable notions of racial science and ethnobiology, it also frequently undermined them. Dvorniković argued, for example, that it was important to mix up the different nations of Yugoslavia, and that while genuine national, cultural and anthropological differences existed between the peoples of Yugoslavia, they were "contingent and temporary and masked a deeper and more profound racial unity." Like Zarnik and Maleš, he argued for the Dinaric as the core of the emerging Yugoslav race, but elsewhere his study alluded to the artificial nature of racial characteristics. Indeed, at the outset he explicitly rejected notions about racial superiority and racial purity, warning of the dangers of succumbing to the "blonde beast" concept of the perfect racial society.[52] His magnus opus about the Yugoslav Dinaric man and woman as the nucleus of an embryonic Yugoslav race can, then, itself be read as a synthesis of Yugoslav ideas about race, representing a bridge between the early work of Županič and the later research of Maleš and Zarnik. Dvorniković argued that it was important to mix up the different nations of Yugoslavia, since only through integration could the Serbs, Croats, and Slovenes survive as a dynamic nation. While his book explored the profound national, cultural, and anthropological differences that existed between the peoples of Yugoslavia, he continually stressed, as Andrew Baruch-Wachtel has written, that these were "contingent and temporary," masking "a deeper and more profound racial unity." Like Zarnik and Maleš he argued that the Dinaric race was the foundation of the Yugoslav race coming into existence while at the same frequently suggesting the intrinsic artificiality of much racial theory.[53]

An important aspect of *Karakterologija Jugoslovena* was its defense both of Dinaric folk belief and the racial worth of contemporary Yugoslav against the superiority of the Nordic type: this marked a contrast to the studies of Zarnik and Maleš, who assumed that the racial superiority of the Dinaric stemmed partly from his Nordic heritage. Dvorniković noted that "Nordic long headedness is viewed especially by the Yugoslav Dinaric as something ugly, inferior, 'gypsy' . . . The ideal is the short head and if possible 'as round as an apple.'" In regions such as Dalmatia, he wrote, the mother or grandmother of a newborn would manipulate its head to ensure that it would be round and the nose not too long, in the belief that only a brachycephalic-shaped head "was normal and beautiful." Hence, he observed, citing the Serbian anthropologist Milovan Filipović, "at least one part of our brachycephalic people must be ascribed to artificial deliberate deformation and the percentage of natural brachycephalic must be far less." Under Dvornikovič's microscope, Dinaric traditions could challenge notions about the genetic and evolutionary origins of racial characteristics and highlight their mutability and artificiality.[54] Dvorniković, nevertheless, underlined the favored status of black hair and dark eyes, as confirmed by the anxious reaction of mothers to babies with blond or reddish hair, as well as by folk poetry of the region. This was not a new idea. In a speech to colleagues in Berlin at the International Congress for the Research of Ethnology in 1935, Županič, whose research strongly influenced Dvorniković, claimed to have identified the emergence of a new aspect of ethnology: the "racial aesthetic." He proposed to study its embodiment in peasant life, through Yugoslavia's national poetry and art, arguing that this racial aesthetic could provide an insight into the unique nature of the Yugoslav racial composition. Observing that possessions of great rarity were always highly coveted, he noted that those with dark brown hair were prized in north European cities while those with fair hair were valued in Italian cities. However, this rule did not apply to Yugoslavia, particularly its rural regions, where peasants "look through very different eyes on racial types which find themselves a minority in the countryside or constitute an exception." In Bosnia those with dark hair and eyes represented "the overwhelming majority" while, by contrast, blue eyes were "the exception." As a result, one would expect that "blue eyes as a rarity in Bosnia would be of greater value than darker-colored irises." But that was not the case. A Serbian folk ballad *Mujo i Uma* (Mujo and Uma), he explained, told how a "besotted" youth Mujo goes to his death after his "bashful betrothed" opens her eyes in response to his pleas and shows blue, not black eyes, the promise of which, as a "simple peasant boy" under the spell of "accepted tastes," has "seduced and enraptured" him. In this preference, Županič explained, the Yugoslavs were more like the Arabs, Turks, and Chinese, who were all dark-eyed and dark-haired and who not only did not favor blue eyes but actually found them "extremely ugly." Traditional folk songs, Županič pointed out, also reinforced the disdain Yugoslavs felt for blond hair and fair complexions. One began: "For two golden blondes I would not give a cent,/and for a flaxen blonde I would not give one dinar:/ but for one black-eyed girl I would give a thousand ducats." Admittedly, different standards of physical beauty seemed to apply in the city and the village. As a result, while country inhabitants valued the typical, the "refined and spoilt city dweller" prized the unusual. Despite this folkloric and ethnographic material, one could surmise that "in the Yugoslav people there lives a strong racial feeling." Moreover, he concluded, this sentiment, reflected in the "anthropological-aesthetic moment of South Slav songs," persisted in the contemporary era as a direct result of "diverse kinds of blood mixing."[55] In other words, prehistoric blood mixing had resulted in the production of a dark racial prototype, which because it was typical became, paradoxically, favored.

Folk culture—popular songs in particular—was widely used in Yugoslav culture in the interwar period, not just by ethnographers and anthropologists, who often collected and published folk songs, but also by public health officials such as Andrija Štampar, the director of the Yugoslav health service, who believed that they could be used to spread awareness of hygiene, social medicine, and disease prevention.[56] And if the songs cited by Županič appeared to contradict the central message of Yugoslav racial hybridity by valorizing dark features and excluding fairer ones, they paradoxically, in another way, reinforced a fundamental tenet of Yugoslav racial science: namely, the exoticism of Yugoslav racial origins, which had only been achieved through the mixing of races from Africa and Asia as well as Europe. In his characteristic manner, Dvorniković, noting the "coveted" status of dark features and the disdain for blue eyes, wrote that one of the most well-known sayings of the legendary brigand Hajduks was that "the ideal of manly beauty was dark (like the wolf!)." The Hajduk needed to be "dark of eye and wide of head." Thus, he concluded, a dark complexion was still "the most fundamental of all racial types" and had "inserted itself" into "national racial tastes."[57]

In his search for the essence of the Dinaric man, Dvorniković identified his masculinity and patriarchal patriotism as the characteristics that placed him on a superior level to many other racial groups in Europe. Unlike Županič, Dvorniković perceived the evolution of the Yugoslav from blond dolichocephalicism to dark brachycephalicism as an unambiguously positive development, a testament to the success of widely dispersed racial mixing between Nordic and Asian peoples. In fact, in opposition to Zarnik and—to an extent—Maleš's hegemonic Nordic myths, Dvorniković insisted that the superiority of the Yugoslav Dinaric was in large part due to the fact that his Nordic racial element had been assimilated by a dominant Asiatic and Armenoid core, creating a distinct hybrid race. The idea that some Europeans were descended from Asiatic and Armenian populations had first been articulated by William Z. Ripley, professor of political economy at Harvard University. In his 1899 racial-sociological study *The Races of Europe*, first presented as a series of lectures at Columbia University's Lowell Institute, he maintained that Europe was divided into just three races: Nordic, Alpine, and Mediterranean. While he ignored the existence of an Armenoid race entirely, he theorized that the Mediterranean race (in which he included southeastern Europeans) was closely connected to African and Middle Eastern races. He stated bluntly that "beyond the Pyrenees Africa begins." He characterized the Mediterranean race, rather incongrously, as being dolichocephalic, short in stature, and dark-skinned, a description that clearly conflicted with Yugoslav researchers' own theories about the physical characteristics of the Dinaric.[58] It was also directly challenged by the Polish ethnographer Jan Czekanowski, who, in a 1928 five-part study, identified the Dinaric as being a mixture of the Nordic and Armenoid races. Unperturbed, Dvorniković, as a number of his colleagues had previously done with the work of other European and American racial anthropologists, appropriated both theories, in the process transforming Ripley's negative notions about the inferiority of the inhabitants of Mediterranean, Africa, and the Middle East into a positive marker of racial uniqueness. In this way, Ripley's ideas were reconceptualized to serve Dvorniković's narrative of an emergent synthesized Dinaric Yugoslav super race. He wrote:

> Perhaps no other race in Europe has succeeded in such great proportions as the Dinaric Yugoslav has in establishing his own new type and racial ideal. In his racial transformation from blonde long faced to dark pigmentation and short faces, the Yugoslavs have been accepted as a racial ideal and taste. Perhaps this is one of the reasons why the Nordic Slavs from the time of their arrival in the south relatively quickly adapted themselves to the racial type which they found in their new surroundings. Our ancestors were overwhelmingly dolichocephalic, blonde, tall and with long skulls. These same characteristics, in other words Nordic features, were alien to the racial ideal which today lives in the blood and flesh of our people.

Instead, Dvorniković argued, the "Armenian, Asia Minor foundation of the old Balkan inhabitants was imposed primarily on the Nordic Yugoslavs as their racial ideal. And the Dinaric form of face was imbued through Slavic Nordicism and Balticism not only as a result of the laws of biological dominance of one race over another but the sculptured and select strength of this Armenoid taste and racial ideal." While height and an imposing physique were the essential characteristics of the Dinaric racial ideal, reflected in the folk saying that "small men don't take wives!", being a man imbued with masculine virtues was vital and Dvorniković cited illustrious figures throughout Yugoslav history who had typified this ideal. "A handsome, real picture of a man—above all, that's what the Dinaric Yugoslav should be," he declared. "As the authentic embodiment of this type of male beauty the life of [Prince-bishop] Njegoš is noteworthy. Vuk Karadžić [the famous Serbian nineteenth-century linguist] was enraptured when he first saw him as a twenty year-old youth. And Njegoš himself was conscious of his manly beauty. 'Thank you, mother of God, that you blessed me, above millions of others on this earth, with this intellect and this body,' he wrote in his famous last will and testament."[59] Dvorniković bolstered his argument about the heroic masculinity of the Dinaric man with plentiful citations from German anthropologists and racial scientists such as Günther and Hans Weinert. The conclusions of their investigations of Dinarics in Austria, southern Germany, and Switzerland, he maintained, could also be applied to the South Slav Dinarics. He pointed out that while Günther and Weinert agreed that in terms of their psychological character Dinarics throughout Europe possessed common characteristics such as an "energetic and open spirit," they maintained that other features such as "a love of noise and distinct masculinity" fit better with southern regions, marking "a strong relationship with the Mediterranean and Oriental races." If Günther argued that the southern German Dinaric was a completely separate type of southern German man, "of robust strength, a warlike and liberated temperament, with passionate local patriotism . . . masculinity and artistic sensibilities, energy and business qualities," Dvorniković added that this "was a characteristic of the Dinaric race in all nations where they are found. The Dinaric, whether a Little Russian [i.e., Ukrainian] or Yugoslav, yearns with a special fervour for his fatherland. He is a born warrior." Meanwhile, Dvorniković noted with satisfaction that another German anthropologist, Wilhelm Böhle, had identified the chief characteristics of the Dinaric as "bravery, energy, pride, self awareness and love of freedom," producing men who were "tough and ungovernable," rash, irascible and of "fiery resistance."[60]

As much as Dvorniković eulogized the heroic qualities of the Dinaric and the quality of manliness, his study was also a lament for the increasingly disappearing world of the Dinarics and the sense that the old racial and patriarchal values, in an era of modernization, were being lost. Whereas previously the "tribal-patriarchal life of struggle and competition" had protected "this racial ideal," the essential spirit which had "sculpted the contours of this type" was no longer alive in all its "true tremors." Increasingly in classic Dinaric regions "the specific racial ideal is being lost and in its place a new broader European or racially-alien ideal is appearing. In Slavonia and the Vojvodina, for example, there is almost nothing of the old Dinaric racial idea to be observed; on the whole the Dinaric Slovenians are becoming fewer and fewer." What was to be done? Dvorniković envisaged the mobilization of folk songs and poems in the service of racial consciousness. He suggested that out of Yugoslavia's "rich folklore material, proverbs, sayings, parables and especially traditional national literature (poems!), material and sources for the development of racial ideals and racial aesthetics in Yugoslavia must be chosen." The question, he stressed, deserved dedicated study:

> So for example when we read in an epic poem how a terrified woman approaches Marko [Kraljević] and describes to him a wolf—'It has something black in its teeth—like a six month-old lamb'—we must remember the racial characteristics and the racial ideal of the Dinarics: so that we can even more strongly emphasize his secondary sexual masculine features . . . We should integrate certain racial elements into the framework of the national character and, if there is no place for certain other elements, we should eliminate them as the situation demands.[61]

An important part of Dvorniković's discussion considered the impact of increasing urbanization on the physiogonomy of the Dinaric. Using a series of photographs of Yugoslav politicians, artists, and intellectuals throughout the Dinaric region, he guided the reader through what amounted to an evolutionary national family tree. Like many Yugoslav racial scientists and anthropologists, Dvorniković believed that the peasant was the most authentic reflection of the nation. Nonetheless, he also insisted that many of the Dinaric peasants' racial attributes were so intrinsic that moving to the city had not diluted or degenerated them. As a result, the urban population, the majority of which, he claimed, was of peasant origin, was still marked by regional racial characteristics; as he noted, "we come across the racial Dinaric, Alpine, Turanian on city asphalt as well as on village roads." One of the first photographs in the book was of a typical Dinaric peasant, who was used as the standard for the images of Dinaric dilution that followed. There was, Dvorniković wrote, "no urbanisation or intellectual outline" in him and everything was still in an "essentially racially-expressed harmony: the bearing and sharp outline around the mouth and the bulging beard on a hard and heavy jaw as well as the peasant hooded eyes." By contrast, in the next picture, of a politician, the reader could see "a less coarse and sharply Dinaric stylised face," though still in the framework of the "Dinaric racial style." In the photographs that followed, the subjects, Dvorniković wrote, had all retained something of their Dinaric origins. Thus, a photograph of a second Yugoslav politician demonstrated the incremental impact of urban life on racial features, but it also illustrated how "in becoming accustomed to city life and intellectualism," the Dinaric could remain strong enough to emphasize certain characterologically important racial features: "Here a heavy and especially distinguished moustache which veers almost entirely into caricature" while the "defiantly emphasized lower part of the face," although somewhat urbanized, "communicates clearly that in this Dinaric there is no talk of 'sentimentality.'" However, he was troubled by a characteristic common to all of them: "All these racial forms contain something conventional, European about them. In place of heroism which would suit the basic shape of this physiological profile model, there remains a somewhat self-conscious and managed pose." While in the first and second example "something of the Dinaric soul and the epic man who is living under this peasant and tough outline" could still be felt, in the third there was a fragment of the Dinaric "energy and roughness," but his soul was not "touched by heroism," his hooked nose and pronounced moustache notwithstanding. Preoccupied with the "earthly side" of life, the heroic view of the world and "tribal agony" no longer directed his "soul."[62]

In contrast to his perhaps predictably unflattering portraits of Yugoslav politicians, his discussion of the evolving faces of Yugoslav intellectuals, artists, and scientists spoke in more ambivalent terms of the impact of urbanization and Europeanization on their features. In their cases there had been a more pleasing synthesis of Dinaric and non-Dinaric attributes. For example, in his commentary on a photograph of a Yugoslav intellectual, Dvorniković wrote that the subject's more "synthesized" face with its "new intellectualised Dinaric physiognomy" retained many features of the Dinaric, including "vigilant lively falcon's eyes," which were also now shrewd, energetic, and slightly fierce, and with no "coarse formation" of the lips. In the next example of a Yugoslav fine artist, the outlines of his face expressed the "irascible but intellectualised Dinaric soul." The nose, in turn, Dvorniković wrote, had become "a sharp eagle's beak," the eyebrows frowned, and the mouth curled in perfect mimicry of the "rough Dinaric mouth." Then there was a photograph of a Yugoslav actor, whose visage attested to "a comprehensive Europeanization of the Dinaric profile, sharp, but without the traces of the Dinaric tension, completely aestheticised." With his straight eyebrows and a refined sharp moustache, he had discreetly taken on the face of "Dinaric toughness" and given it something "classically Mediterranean," a Dinaric inheritance with a "Mediterranean twist." Similarly, Dvorniković conceded, the transformation of the Dinaric racial physigonomy under the influence of urbanization could indicate an "undiluted obsession" with intellectual inquiry, a feature of the greatest Dinaric minds. As an example he cited the "plump deformed profile of the celebrated Jesuit mathematician, astronomer and philosopher Ruder Bošković," as opposed to the "elongated nose and thick beard" of his Hercegovinan peasant ancestors. A better example of transformation, perhaps, was the "entirely Dinaric figure" of Nikola Tesla, "the genius scientist" carved out of "the most explicit Dinaric racial material." These preliminary examinations suggested that intellectualism had synthesized with "the old racially-expressed characteristics" to create a new kind of Dinaric.[63]

Like Zarnik and Maleš, Dvorniković acknowledged the importance of the Nordic race to the Dinaric racial physiogonomy, but, similar to Županič, he stressed that what made the Yugoslav race unique was its mixing with Asiatic blood, placing the Yugoslav race simultaneously in the Nordic North and the "Armenoid Asiatic East." This had led them into a "false kinship" either with the Nordic race on the one hand or the Armenian race on the other. In fact, it was precisely this synthesis of the Nordic and Asiatic worlds in the Dinaric—in other words, the Yugoslav, the "joining of two racial souls"—that was the "central dilemma" of the Yugoslav national psyche. This, he continued, explained why European anthropologists had labeled the Dinarics an "unfinished race." It constituted the "central problem" of the Yugoslav national psyche, since, as Dvorniković observed, it "sends us from one side to the Nordic North and the other side—in large part!–to the Near East." Through the Dinarics, a fusion of the "blonde Nordics" and the "swarthy Asiatic-Levantine element," at the lowest ebb of the Yugoslav ideal, Dvorniković had returned to Županič's idea of a synthetic Yugoslav race incarnated through a combination of the best qualities of the Asiatic East and the Nordic North—a vision Županič had set down twenty years before in what must have already seemed a different era.[64]

Conclusion

The search for a viable Yugoslav race was bound up with notions of modernity and racial hybridity. At the same time, Yugoslav racial theories stressed autarchy and uniqueness. Over time, partly due to domestic politics but also because of international factors and intellectual developments—most obviously, the growing influence of National Socialist ideas about race—the discourse changed and scientists and race researchers began to emphasize more biological concepts, as encapsulated in the concept of a Dinaric core race. In the same way that the advocacy of racial mixing in the early 1920s had reflected priorities about the construction of a Yugoslav person by drawing on the attributes of all its national groups in a state under construction, for Yugoslav ethnographers and anthropologists in the 1930s unitarist state Dinaricism appeared to provide an end to the search for a synthetic racial consciousness in a multiethnic state. While studies of Dinaricism drew on the writing of German and Italian race experts, their ideas never became dominant among Yugoslav researchers. This not only reflected the multiethnicity of the state but also spoke to the role Dinaricism played in providing Yugoslavs with a framework for claims of racial and national autarchy, a means of constructing a supranational Yugoslav identity and defending their state's territorial integrity. Even among those racial anthropologists and ethnographers who enthusiastically appropriated biological concepts of race, the belief that racial heteroegeneity, including non-European influences, was key to the strength of the Yugoslavs remained for them a marker of their unique consciousness.

Vladimir Dvorniković's *Karakterologija Jugoslovena*, published twenty years after Niko Županič's *Le sang et la race Yougoslaves*, testifies to the persistence of narratives of racial hybridity in synthetic Yugoslavism. Dvorniković and Županič's studies can be viewed as staging posts in the evolving story of Yugoslav thinking about race. They suggest that sometimes the incarnation of new racial identities can be liberalizing and secularizing enterprises aiming to overcome ethnic, national, and religious differences in the long march toward modernity rather than to reinforce them. The quest to construct a Yugoslav person, like the search for the Dinaric race, endeavored to build a new synthetic identity, integrating Yugoslavia's prehistoric heterogeneous past with the Yugoslav racial project of the 1920s and 1930s. Despite the insistence of ethnographers and anthropologists like Županič, Dvorniković, and even Maleš about the inevitability of a synthesized Yugoslav person, by the late 1930s that vision had corroded from within—and with it, the project to make the state a racial pavilion, Yugoslav in form and multiethnic in content.

Notes

1. Of the 180 grand prix awarded, ninety-seven were awarded to the Yugoslav pavilion. The pavilion was also counted "among the three most successful" in the entire exposition. J., "Naš uspeh na međunarodnog izložbi u Barcelona," *Politika*, November 5, 1929; Tomislav Krizman, "Uspeh naše izložbe u Barceloni," *Politika*, October 24, 1929; Stanislav Vinaver, "Veliki uspeh našeg pavilijona," *Politika*, July 5, 1929; Ljiljana Blagojević, *The Elusive Margins of Belgrade Architecture: 1929–1941* (Cambridge MA: MIT Press, 2003), 97–99.

2. See, for example, Bošiljka Janjatović, *Politički terror u Hrvatskoj, 1918–1941* (Zagreb: Institut za hrvatsku povijest, 2012).

3. These figures are contained in Dragoljub J. Tasić, "Uvod," in *Definitivi rezultati popis stanovištva od 31 Marta 1931 godine, vol. 2: prisutno stanovništvo po pismenih i starosti* (Belgrade: Državna štamparija, 1938), v–vii.

4. Studies of the cultural politics of unitarist Yugoslavism include Christian Axboe Nielsen, *Making Yugoslavs: Cultural Politics in Yugoslavia under the Dictatorship of King Aleksandar* (Toronto: University of Toronto Press, 2014); Ljubodrag Dimić, *Kulturna politika u Kraljevine Jugoslavije, 1918–1941*, vols. 1–2 (Belgrade: Stubovi kulture, 1996–97); and Predrag Marković, "Die 'Legitimierung' der Königsdiktatur in Jugoslawien und die öffentliche Meinung," in *Autoritäre Regime in Ostmittel und Südösteuropa 1919–1944* (Paderborn: Ferdinand Schöningh, 2001), 586–622.

5. Yuri Slezkine, "The USSR as a Communal Apartment, or How a Socialist State Promoted Ethnic Particularism," *Slavic Review* 53, no. 2 (Summer 1994): 414–52.

6. Entries for Maleš, Škerlj, Zarnik and Županič under "Jugoslavia," in *International Directory of Anthropologists*, ed. Alfred V. Kidder (Washington DC: National Research Council, January 1938), 223–34.

7. Ana Cergol Paradiž, "Yugoslavia (Slovenia): Overview," in *The History of East-Central European Eugenics, 1900–1945: Sources and Commentaries*, ed. Marius Turda (London: Bloomsbury, 2015), 373–74.

8. Ilija Malović, "Eugenika kao ideološki sastojak u fašizma u Srbiju 1930-ih xx veka," *Sociologija* 50, no. 1 (2008): 85n4.

9. Cergol Paradiž, "Yugoslavia (Slovenia): Overview," 372; Marko Farić, "Božo Škerlj (1904, Vienna–1961, Ljubljana)," in *The History of East-Central European Eugenics*, 381–82. In Czechoslovakia, Škerlj was on the editorial board of the journal *Anthropologie* and maintained particularly close ties with Czech anthropologists and eugenicists, first and foremost his mentor Jindřich Matiegka.

10. See, for example, Nevenko Bartulin, *The Racial Idea in the Independent State of Croatia: Origins and History* (Leiden: Brill, 2014).

11. Christian Promitzer, "Vermessene Körper: 'Rassenkundliche' Grenzzeihungen im Südöstlichen Europa," in *Europa und der Grenzen im Kopf*, ed. Karl Kaser, Dagmar Gramshammer-Hohl, and Robert Pichler (Klagenfurt: Wieser Enzyklopädie des europäischen Ostens II, 2003), 376–79.

12. Božo Škerlj, "Die Leibesübungen der Frau als bevölkerungspolitisches Problem," *Zeitschrift für Rassenkunde* 1, no. 2 (1935): 178–85.

13. See, for example, Božo Škerlj, "Rassenforschung in Jugoslawien," *Rassen im Donauraum: beiträge zur Rassenkunde Erbbiologie und Eugenik der Donauvölkes* 1, no. 1 (1935): 8–11.

14. Petar Vlahović, "Dr. Božo Škerlj in njegov pomen za etnično antropologijo," *Slovenski etnograf* 23–24 (1970–71): 101–4.

15. Milan Pribičević, "Naš idejal Jugoslavije," *Književni jug* 3, no. 1 (1 January 1919): 1–2.

16. Juraj Demetrović, "Hrvatstvo, Srpstvo i Jugoslovenstvo," *Jugoslovenska njiva* 3, no. 4 (1919): 45. The "Es-Ha-Es" and "Se-Ha-Se" refer to the Serbo-Croatian acronyms for the Kingdom of the Serbs, Croats, and Slovenes (SHS and CHC, as written in the Latin and Cyrillic scripts).

17. Monika Milosavljević, "Niko Županič i istorijska antropologija balkanskih naroda," *Etnoantropološki problemi* 7, no. 3 (2012): 681–708.

18. There is an extensive literature on the life and scholarship of Županič. Among recent studies are Monika Milosavljević, "Niko Županič i konstrukcija jugoslovenske etnogeneze," *Etnoantropološki problemi* 8, no. 3 (2013): 717–46; Christian Promitzer, "Niko Županič in vprašanje jugoslovanstva: med politiko in antropologijo (1901–1941)," *Prispevki za novejšo zgodovino* 41, no. 1 (2001): 7–30. See also Rajko Muršič and Mihaela Hudelja, eds., *Niko Županič: njegovo delo, čas i prostor* (Ljubljana: Filozofska fakulteta, 2009).

19. Niko Županič, *Le sang et la race Yougoslaves* (Paris: Sociétié d'Editions Lévé, 1919), 5–11.

20. Joseph Deniker, *Les six races composant la population actuelle de l'europe* (London: Anthropological institute of Great Britain & Ireland, 1904).

21. Županič, *Le sang et la race Yougoslaves*, 11, 12, 17–19.

22. Niko Županič, "Zur physio-ethnischen Metamorphose des Völkes mit besondere Rücksicht auf der Südslaven," *Comitato Italiano per lo Studio dei problemi della Popułazione* 10 (1932): 3–9.

23. Županič, "Zur physio-ethnischen Metamorphose des Völkes," 10–12.

24. Niko Županič, *Etnogeneza Jugoslavena* (Zagreb: Jugoslavenska akademija znanosti i umjetnosti, 1922), 146, as cited in Promitzer, "Vermessene Körper," 376.

25. Niko Županič, "Pellegrino di San Daniele-umetnik nase krvi," *Zbornik za umetnostno zgodovino* 3, nos. 3–4 (1923): 113–23.

26. Tanja Petrović, "The Serbs of Bela Krajina between Local and National Identity," in *Developing Cultural Identity in the Balkans: Convergence versus Divergence*, ed. Raymond Dexter and Pieter Plas (Brussels: Peter Lang, 2005), 65–68.

27. Niko Županič, "Antropološki opis Srbov Kosovega polja," in Županič et al., *Srbi Plinja i Ptolemeja: pitanje prve pojave Srbe na svetskoj pozornici sa historijskoj, geografskog i etnološkog stališta* (Belgrade: Državna štamparija, 1924), 65–85.

28. Niko Županič, *Etnološki značaj kosovoskih Čerteza* (Ljubljana: Etnolog, 1933), 245–47.

29. See, for example, Tihomir R. Djordjević, "Certezi u našoj zemlji," *Glasnik skopskoj naučnoj društva* 3 (1925): 141–55.

30. Županič, *Etnološki značaj kosovoskih Čerteza*, 247–53.

31. Vladimir S. Stanojević, *Eugenika: higijena čovečeg začeča i problem nasledja* (Belgrade: Ministarstvo narodnog zdravlja, 1920), 149–51.

32. J. Zubović, "Jugoslovenski čovjek," *Nova Evropa* 10, no. 6 (August 21, 1924): 145–47, 152–53.

33. Jovan Dučić, "Reč Jugoslavija," *Politika*, October 30, 1930.

34. "Neslomljivost zdrave rase," *Pobeda*, June 28, 1933.

35. ABH, "Koje će pokrajina dati najlepši ženu u Jugoslavije?" *Vreme* 14 (January 15, 1929): 5.

36. See, for example, Viktor Novak, "Jugoslavenska misao," in Novak, ed. *Antologija jugoslavenske misli i narodnog jedinstva (1390–1930)* (Belgrade: Državna štamparija, 1930), ix–lxv; Ferdo Šišić, *Jugoslovenska misao: istorija ideje jugoslovenskog narodnog ujedinjenja i oslobodjenja od 1790–1918* (Belgrade: Balkanski institut, 1937), 5, 273; and Vladimir Ćorović, *Istorija Jugoslavije* (Belgrade: Narodno delo, 1933), 1.

37. See Hans F. K. Günther, *Rassenkunde des deutschen volkes* (Munich: Lehmanns-Verlag, 1922); and Guido Landra, "L'antropologia nel quadro della politica della razza," *La difesa della razza* 3, no. 18 (July 20, 1940): 12–15.

38. Škerlj's article was accompanied by critical notes from the editors, who shot back that the Dinarics were, clearly, racially Italian. See Božo Škerlj, "Rapporti di razza fra Jugoslavia e Italia," *La difesa della razza* 3, no. 1 (November 5, 1939): 46–51.

39. Božo Skerlj, "Jugoslawien," *Zeitschrift für Rassenkunde* 1 (1935): 111.

40. Boris Zarnik, "Rasa i duševna produktivnost," *Priroda* 21 (1931): 129–30.

41. Zarnik, "Rasa i duševna produktivnost," 130–31.

42. Boris Zarnik, "O rasnom sastavu evropskog pučanstva," *Hrvatsko kolo* 1, no. 8 (1927): 61–64, 71, 79–80.

43. Zarnik, "Rasa i duševna produktivnost," 132–34.

44. Zarnik, "Rasa i duševna produktivnost," 135–36.

45. Zarnik, "Rasa i duševna produktivnost," 135–38. This was also the view of some other Yugoslav racial scientists and eugenicists. For example, Svetislav Stefanović, president of the Yugoslav Doctors' Society, who during the 1930s interpreted Dinaricism in increasingly racist and eugenicist terms, argued that many famous European artists, writers, generals, and musicians throughout history had been Dinarics. See Svetislav Stefanović, "Über die Rassenfrage als Kulturproblem," *Rassen in Donauraum: Beiträge zur Rassenkunde, Erbbiologie und Eugenik der Donauvölkes* 1, no. 1 (1938): 15.

46. Branimir Maleš, "Nekoliko napomena o dinarskoj rasi," *Socijalno-medicinski pregled* 7 (April–June 1935): 1–7.

47. Malović, "Eugenika kao ideološki sastojak u fašizma," 85n4. For public criticism of the anti-Semitic laws, see, for example, Ć [Laza Popović], "Molitva svirepnog Slovenina za Jevreje," *Nova Evropa* 31, no. 11 (November 26, 1938): 375–84.

48. Branimir Maleš, *O ljudskim rasama* (Belgrade: Biblioteka Kolarčevog narodnog univerziteta, 1936), 50–56, 60–62. Similarly, in an article of 1937 in a German race journal, Svetislav Stefanović, a frequent contributor to Črnjanski's *Ideje* journal, argued that it was important to make sure that "higher races, the major European races like the Nordics and the Dinarics do not degenerate through mixing with lower quality races." He compared the "positive mixing of the Nordic and Dinaric races" with the "dramatically degenerative results of the mixing of Germans and Jews." He also submitted that "racist elements" played an important part in "young" Yugoslav nationalism. Paradoxically, he rejected the idea of racial purity, writing that it is the job of the serious academic researcher in the area of race research to ensure that exaggeration and the salaciousness of racism are avoided." See Stefanović, "Über die Rassenfrage als Kulturproblem," *Rassen in Donauraum*, 12–15.

49. Maleš, *O ljudskim rasama*, 48–49.

50. Vladimir Dvorniković, *Psiha jugoslovenske melanholije* (Zagreb: Z. & V. Lašić, 1925), 58–63.

51. Egbert Klautke, *The Mind of the Nation: Völkerpsychologie in Germany, 1850–1955* (London: Berghahn, 2014).

52. Vladimir Dvorniković, *Karakterologija Jugoslovena* (Belgrade: Kosmos/Geca Kon, 1939), 192; Promitzer, "Vermessene Körper,"384.

53. Andrew Baruch Wachtel, *Making a Nation, Breaking a Nation: Literature and Cultural Politics in Yugoslavia* (Stanford: Stanford University Press, 1998), 92–94.

54. Dvorniković, *Karakterologija Jugoslovena*, 247.

55. Županič, "O rasni esesteski ljudstva pri jugoslovenih," *Etnolog* 7 (1935): 74–76, 80–81.

56. See, for example, Andrija Štampar, "Politika o populaciji," in Štampar, ed., *Socijalna medicina*, vol. 1 (Zagreb: Institut za socijalnu medicinu, 1925), 30–31.

57. Vladimir Dvorniković, *Karakterologija Jugoslovena* (Belgrade: Kosmos, 1939), 247. The term "Hajduk" was commonly used for a brigand, outlaw, or rebel, but its meaning could be positive or negative depending on the context and the author. On the changing meaning of the Hajduk in southeast European history, see Wendy Bracewell, "'The Proud Name of Hajduk': Bandits as Ambiguous Heroes in Balkan Politics and Culture," in *Yugoslavia and its Historians: Understanding the Balkan Wars of the* 1990s, ed. Norman Naimark and Holly Case (Stanford: Stanford University Press, 2003), 22–36.

58. See William Z. Ripley, *The Races of Europe: A Sociological Study* (New York: D. Appleton, 1899), 205. In 1939, the same year that Dvorniković's study was published, *The Races of Europe* was "rewritten" by Carleton S. Coon, a professor of anthropology at the University of Pennsylvania and president of the American Association of Physical Anthropology who had conducted extensive field work in the Balkans, North Africa, and Arabia. In his rewritten version Coon developed Ripley's theory of the non-European roots of the Mediterranean race, arguing that the Caucasian race was to be found not just in Europe but also in North Africa, Asia, and Arabia, with its homeland in the Middle East. However, unlike Ripley, who made no mention of the Armenoid race, Coon postulated that the Armenian and Dinaric races were closely related. See Carleton. S. Coon, *The Races of Europe* (New York: Macmillan 1939).

59. Dvorniković, *Karakterologija Jugoslovena*, 247–48.

60. Dvorniković, *Karakterologija Jugoslovena*, 216–18.

61. Dvorniković, *Karakterologija Jugoslovena*, 246, 249. Marko Kraljević was the Serbian king between 1371 and 1395 and subsequently became a key figure in Serbian mythology and the Kosovo literary cycle.

62. Dvorniković, *Karakterologija Jugoslovena*, 212–13.

63. Dvorniković, *Karakterologija Jugoslovena*, 215–17.

64. Dvorniković, *Karakterologija Jugoslovena*, 219–22.

Conclusion

From National Races to National Genomes

CATHERINE NASH

In an era in which genomic research on human evolutionary origins, early human migration, and the origins and migration histories of specific groups is one dominant strand of the biological sciences, this book is a timely reminder of the prehistories of contemporary research on human biological variation. It is especially useful in historicizing the construction of the national in recent genomic research, given the degree to which national genomic projects feature within and in part constitute the wider transnational practice of bioscience. State-led or state-funded genomic projects to study the national population are an increasing priority for governments, since they are viewed as offering the promise of biomedical advancement; economic growth through the biotech industries; national prestige in excelling in, or keeping up with, scientific advances; and, in many cases, insight into the national past. It is increasingly the case that national genomic knowledge—of the pattern of genetic variation within the populace—is seen as a national imperative. As a result, national genome projects have proliferated over the last decade.

However, much of the critical engagement with human population genetics has focused on race, rather than on the intersections between race, ethnicity, and nation. Yet the nation as the scale and site of genomic research is deeply relevant in terms of cultural, social, and legal delineations of belonging. Studies of genetic variation within a state that are figured as national projects raise complex and compelling questions about how the people of that country are imagined and represented in terms of ideas of what is shared—culturally, historically, ancestrally—and the social relations and patterns of inclusion shaped by those ideas of shared and differentiated heritages. The focus on the national population and on the national past in genomic terms foregrounds the fundamental issue of the national as an imaginative scale of identity and identification. States are naturalized in terms of a collective identity that legitimizes governance and sovereignty. This is so when collective identity is based on a traditional idea of the ethnically homogenous nation-state based on shared ancestry. It is also the case when that model of national identity has been reworked, with varied inflections and to different degrees in various national contexts, in response to immigration through ideas of multiculturalism. Alternatively, the national community can be defined through the concept of a distinctive pattern of diversity or mixing that characterized the nation-state from its foundation, as in Latin American ideas of *mestizaje* (race mixture).[1] Ideas of both racial purity and mixing were often mobilized in the making of national races in modern nation-states, but purity is now rarely part of the lexicon of liberal nationhood. Instead, ideas of variation and distinctiveness are the entangled terms that dominate national genomic projects. While ideas of the distinctiveness of the national population are still potent in political, cultural, and genomic discourse, that distinctiveness is more often a matter of a distinctive pattern of *variation* that reflects a specific national history of settlement, state formation, and immigration. National genomic projects are presented as both exploring how those histories are reflected in patterns of genetic variation and can be known more fully through analysis of that variation.

National projects are of particular public interest because they are engaging alternatives to both the less compelling extended universalism of the human or global family tree, as in the Human Genome Project and accounts of universal human origins, and to the extreme singularity of individual genetic uniqueness, as in forecasts of a future of personal genetic histories and personalized biomedicine. Like accounts of ethnically particular genetic histories, national genomic projects work at a potent scale of public and scientific interest, since they deal in ideas of a distinctive collective history and geography of identification. National projects promise ways in which an individual might locate themselves in national "imagined genetic communities," whether these genetic communities are imagined in terms of a majority population-sharing ancestry, an amalgam of different strands, or a mosaic of diverse groups.[2] The significance of the nation-state continues even if it has a complex relation to other models and scales of identity and forms of governance. This is despite and often in response to the intensified mobilities of the last half century or more.

Over the last decade or more, reports of research in the field of human genomics have featured prominently in the media, whether focusing on biomedical genomics, including efforts to map patterns of genetic variation; studies that explore those patterns to reconstruct the timing and geography of human origins and settlement; or the histories and relationships between specific human groups, in what is sometimes called evolutionary or anthropological genetics. More specifically, the idea that research on human genetic variation is a resource for addressing questions of the national past and national identity and heritage as well as personal "deep ancestry" has been more and more prevalent in public culture, through popular science, radio and television, books, and the commercial development of ethnically specific genetic ancestry testing companies, such as IrelandsDNA. National genomic knowledge is presented as a resource for collective national self-knowledge, as a way of knowing our "genetic heritage": a way of "who we are and where we come from." Marianne Sommer has used the term "biohistories" to describe the science and popular culture of genetic accounts of the past, and the way studies of the patterns of human genetic variation are formulated and interpreted to reconstruct histories of ancestral origins and migration. It also refers to the discourses of the gene as historical document and DNA as archive that are commonly employed both in popular accounts and the scientific presentation of research results.[3] As I reflect on the continuities and differences between late nineteenth- and early twentieth-century racial anthropology and late twentieth- and early twenty-first-century projects of mapping and describing human genetic variation, two reports of national "biohistories" that appeared weeks apart confirm this book's importance in informing historicized and critical engagement with the making of ideas of commonality and difference in national genomics.

In March 2015 research published in *Nature Genetics* analyzing "the "genetic code" of an entire nation," Iceland, was widely reported.[4] This was the outcome of the well-known decODE genetics project, which analyzed a large sample of the genomes of people in contemporary Iceland in combination with detailed genealogical and medical records. By sequencing the entire genomes of ten thousand people, the researchers were able to extrapolate the findings to represent "the genome of the entire nation."[5] There is much that is exceptional about this case: what is described as Iceland's largely homogenous population; the depth and comprehensive nature of its genealogical records; and the similar thoroughness of its medical records. It is, nonetheless, an influential model for national genomic research, and, as many have already argued, a test case for exploring questions of commodification and privacy in relation to genetic information and the ethics of disclosing risks of genetic susceptibilities to disease.[6]

The focus of this project is primarily biomedical, since the relatively recent settlement of Iceland is already known through historical records. Those picking up on this story of national genomics may have already heard of the also widely reported results of another national project published in *Nature* a few weeks before.[7] This project, entitled *People of the British Isles*, began in 2004 and sought to map patterns of genetic variation in the United Kingdom in order to examine the nature and genetic impact of the early settlement of Britain and Northern Ireland, and so provide insight into a collective national past. At the same time the map of genetic variation was envisaged as a tool for biomedical research.[8] Media reporting announced the project as "the first fine-scale genetic map of the British Isles" (though, in fact, this was inaccurate, like the title of the project itself, given its focus on the United Kingdom rather than the British Isles as a whole).

These two national genomic projects share a focus on the national in the study of human genetic variation with the making of national races a century ago, and, like most "positivist" race science of the second half of the nineteenth century—and human genomics more widely—are seen as exemplars of enlightened, progressive science in the service of collective biomedical benefit and collective self-knowledge. In this case, however, they are presented as far removed from racist accounts of hierarchies of human difference and ideas of national races. The science of human genomics is particularly haunted by the worst of racial science as applied in eugenics and in the Holocaust. But a simple contrast between racial science and human genomics is complicated by the varied ways in which ideas of racial superiority and racial purity were in fact avowed by some and renounced by others in the racial science of the late nineteenth century. Furthermore, the collective category of the national is as much entangled with ideas of race and ethnicity and the politics of national identity, inclusion, and belonging in the early twenty-first-century as it was in the late nineteenth and early twentieth, albeit in distinctive ways. These entanglements not only reflect their historical contexts, but also specific geographical contexts, since contemporary accounts of national genetic variation are inflected by the particular configurations of ideas of difference and diversity in different countries. The use of genetic anthropology to research specifically national pasts is now a worldwide phenomenon.[9] For the sake of consistency with the main focus of the race science studies in this book, I concentrate here on European examples, and especially on the *People of the British Isles* study.

Despite the idea of the universality of science, studies of human genetic variation are shaped by and embedded within the particular social, cultural, economic, and political dynamics of the different national contexts in which they are undertaken.[10] This includes how questions of national identity, inclusion, belonging, and diversity in different national contexts have become integral to the practice of what Amy Hinterberger describes as "molecular multiculturalisms."[11] This attention to the ethics of ethnic inclusion and representation within national genomic projects is one key point of differentiation between late nineteenth- and early twentieth-century projects of defining national races. However, this does not mean that there is nothing problematic about the making of categories of human genetic variation in contemporary human genomics. In concluding this volume I argue why this is the case, first by considering the nature and implications of categories of difference in the science of human genetic variation broadly, then by reflecting on the figuring of ideas of shared national genetic heritage, national genetic diversity, and differentiation in national genomic projects.

From National Races to National Genomes

There are considerable differences between the projects of racial science examined in this book and contemporary studies of human genetic variation. These are differences of technologies and knowledges; of scientific ethics, including the process of gathering bodily material and measurement; and in the discourses of human difference that reflect the historical contexts of these knowledge-making projects. The study of variation is now at the molecular level rather than that of morphology or blood type. Samples of blood or saliva may be gathered in order to extract genetic material from blood or cheek cells, but their collection is conducted under the ethical protocols that are now integral to liberal anti-racist genomics instead of through coercion or the use of "captive" subjects, such as the soldiers and inmates of early twentieth-century studies. The aim of contemporary studies is not racial classification. The language of anthropological genetics is one of populations, of diversity, rather than taxonomies of difference. The study of human genetic variation, as Nadia Abu El-Haj has argued, does not reproduce the tenets of racial science; it does not envisage human genetic variation in terms of hierarchies of difference, nor does it read patterns of variation in terms of genetic variants determining the traits or abilities of human groups. Instead, it interprets genetic variation as evidence of collective ancestral histories.[12]

But there are also striking continuities and parallels. Firstly, the interest in mapping human biological variation and in addressing collective origin stories characterized both periods. Contemporary patterns of genetic diversity are studied as a means of reconstructing the timing and geography of the spread of human groups across the world from the evolutionary origins in east Africa, the settlement of specific regions at different scales, and the origins and demographic histories of particular groups. While one prominent argument for the value of studies of patterns of human genetic variation is biomedical and concerns the potential value of this knowledge for understanding and treating disease, it is also paired with claims about its value for providing knowledge of the origins, evolution, and migration of humanity as a whole or the origins of specific ethnic groups. Though the science is presented as revolutionary in its new abilities to know the past (in fact echoing the claims of philology, race anthropology, and race serology in the late nineteenth and early twentieth centuries), it is propelled by very similar interests in seeking evidence in the bodies of the people for regional ancestral differences—and thus the historical geography of migration and settlement—as those that shaped late nineteenth-century ethnographic surveys of the British Isles and other European countries. The overtly national *People of the British Isles* project builds on a significant strand of research since the late 1990s that explores the early settlement history of Britain and Ireland in relation to the broader patterns of migration to and across continental Europe. It tests historical accounts of settlement and the ideas of ancestral difference that, traditionally, at least, underpin ideas of national or ethnic difference. The biomedical dimension of this project also reflects the continuation of longstanding concerns about the health of the national population that are now being addressed through new genomic technologies.

Secondly, while the overt language of racial types and taxonomies were largely eschewed in both anthropological and biological studies of human variation following the horrific application of racial science in the Second World War, as Jenny Reardon has shown, much scientific work in delineating human biological difference continued but was reframed as the study of human populations rather than race. While science took on the role of disabusing wider society about the genetic existence of races as bounded and genetically distinctive groups, the shift from typological to population-based approaches in the 1950s did not signify a simple and complete transition. Debates persisted about the most appropriate models and methods for studying human genetic variation and the terminology for describing patterns of variation.[13] The shifts from morphology to blood types to molecular genetics mark the evolution of studies of human difference rather than constitute neat ideological breaks; anthropological genetics, for example, emerged from sero-anthropology, which had close links to earlier anthropometric raciology. Nevertheless, by the 1990s the study of human genetic variation via molecular genetics was largely characterized by an explicit commitment to foregrounding the genetic unity of humanity. Many contemporary geneticists are mindful too of the criticisms of the human genome diversity project of the 1980s. The field is now overtly anti-racist and framed by ethical concerns about the practice of science.[14]

Anthropological genetics, and human population genetics more widely, is often portrayed as the corrective to earlier studies of race, not only in terms of technical sophistication and deeper knowledge, but also of its departure and distance from the racist ideologies of the past. Scientific research on patterns of genetic difference and their relation to deeply political national, subnational, or transnational categories of ethnicity and identity is not framed by ideas of fixed racial types, racial hierarchies, competition between nation-states, or ideas of national stock in need of protection, improvement, and managed reproduction.[15] These biohistories—addressing the genetic evidence for longstanding popular histories of origin and migration or using popular histories to interpret patterns of genetic variation—may apply science to knowing the past in ways that echo earlier accounts of the people and peopling of Europe. But the aim is certainly not to delineate races.

However, this is not to say that this research on human genetic diversity does not mobilize ethnic, racial, and national categories in practice or is not implicated in the making of ideas of ethnic or racial categories as categories of shared ancestry and genetic similarity. An important strand of critical work on biomedical genomics and human population genetics has challenged overly simplistic diagnosis of the implications of these fields either as the return to racial science or the overturn of race through the science. Instead, race has a complex place in human genomics. This reflects the public cultures of the science, the internal differentiation among scientists in the field, and broad issues and approaches in the practice of the science itself.

Firstly, the making of race and, indeed, other categories of difference (including gender as well as ethnicity and nationhood) through accounts of human genetic variation is not simply a matter of scientific practice conducted in isolation from wider concerns. Human genomic science is inflected by wider public interests and approaches and at the same time interpreted through those concerns and mediated by the ways in which the science is reported, featured in the media, commercially applied, and taken up in different ways by different communities of interest. This is not to argue that the problem of the "misinterpretation" of scientific "facts" lies with the media; the results of research projects can, of course, be oversimplified and distorted. However, scientists, research units, and universities also often actively engage with the wider public, due to intense pressures to demonstrate the public value of their research and gain media attention, and the potential to develop "spin-offs" in the form of genetic genealogy companies. This can shape research project development as well as the dissemination of results. Highly technical scientific results can be converted by journalists into public interest stories by evoking ideas of ethnicity or identity, for example, but these kinds of stories are often in mind already at the research planning stage and served up via university press offices. The blurred boundaries between science, commerce, and culture and, indeed, state security practices via forensic genetics means there is no single neat field within which to track the contemporary science of race.

Secondly, those working in the field of anthropological genetics—and human population genetics more widely—vary in terms of their own standpoints on questions of biological or ancestral categories of identity and in terms of their different perspectives on the public dissemination, interpretation, use, and implications of their research in relation to the politics of biological or ancestral versions of national identity, ethnicity and race. While some geneticists are acutely conscious of the political dimensions of their work and warn of the spurious assumptions that underpin much of the genetic genealogy sector, others are very willing to assert the value of their work in relation to national histories, ethnicity, or even local or regional identities, depending on the scale of the research area or the resolution of the analysis. They work from different positions as well as with different intentions and analytical frameworks, albeit within the broadly shared paradigms of human genomics.

Thirdly, race has a complex place in human genomics because of the continued scientific interest in the categorization of human biological difference, the focus on sociocultural populations as objects of research, and the practices of differentiating samples and genetic variants according to ethnicity, race, nation, or region in surveys of genetic variation for use in biomedical genomics. These issues are complicated but crucial to evaluating what is politically at stake in accounts of the geographies of human genetic variation. It is therefore worth elaborating on them briefly here by setting out key issues in understandings of, and approaches to, the geography of human genetic diversity.

A key element of the deconstruction of races as biological subgroups within humanity is the argument that research has shown human genetic variation to be continuous across space—or "clinal"—with gradients of variation rather than abrupt breaks. Gene frequencies vary gradually with very few sharp discontinuities and the particular spatial gradient of frequencies for one set of genetic variants (e.g., southwest to northeast or east to west) will not be the same for another. This is paralleled by the similarly "non-concordant clinal variation" of biological features traditionally used to define race groups, such as hair texture and skin color.[16] There may be subtle differences in gene frequencies that relate to the effects of localized, random genetic changes or physical barriers, but these patterns do not coincide with racial, ethnic, or national groups.

The complex place of race in science derives from the ways in which some human population geneticists seek to delineate the geographical pattern of human genetic variation and then identify categories or clusters of genetic similarity within broad patterns of clinal variation. The identification of these clusters is dependent on the sampling schemes used to produce databases of variation and the techniques through which categories are derived. Some geneticists, social scientists, and public commentators readily relate these categories to racial, ethnic, or national groups. In the U.S. context this has been deeply shaped by the racial politics of health care, leading some researchers and activists to see the focus on the genetics of ethnic or racial groups as redressing the neglect of nonwhite groups in biomedical research and the treatment of disease.[17]

In contemporary studies, as in the old race anthropology, human genetic variation is both represented in maps of geographical gradients of variation and in terms of clusters of distinctive patterns.[18] Diagrams, maps, and written descriptions of gradients and clusters are entangled with questions of how to describe variation—of what labels can be used—that are themselves caught up with the political question of the coupling of ideas of genetic variation and difference with ideas of nation and ethnicity. The degree to which these differentiated ancestries relate to categories of nation or ethnicity depends on geneticists' choices about how to describe the patterns of variation that they derive from their surveys, and this is crucial in terms of their wider public dissemination and effects.

But this is not just an issue of what to name clusters of genetic variation that simply preexist in nature, since these clusters are the product of the analysis. The making of categories within patterns of continuous variation will always be arbitrary, an artifact of the technologies of their production and interpretation.[19] As critics have importantly argued, genetic clusters are as much socially produced as are ethnic, racial, or national identities.[20] Researchers regularly rely on social categories of ethnicity, race, or nation in describing individual samples or clusters of genetic similarity in surveys of genetic variation in biomedical studies and international genetic mapping projects. Though geneticists are now much more wary about the use of ethnic labels in survey strategies, issues persistently arise over where to sample and how to name the sample groups or particular genetic markers in terms of ethnicity or geographical origin.[21]

In other strands of human genomics, especially in anthropological genetics, the issue is not the identification of clusters within patterns of variation. Instead, sociocultural groups are the starting point of genetic analysis. This is because their pattern of genetic variation is taken to represent an ancient pattern that has survived unchanged in contrast to wider mixing and thus is thought to be valuable for the insight it offers to understanding early human migration, as was the case in the proposed Human Genome Diversity Project and the subsequent research that took up its aims. This assumption has been heavily criticized and resisted, especially for its depiction of "indigenous" groups as "relict" populations and as genetic resources for Western science, and also for the arrogance, intrusiveness, and inappropriateness of subjecting indigenous origin stories to scientific analysis.[22] Furthermore, much research has been and is being undertaken in which patterns of genetic variation of and between ethnic or national groups are studied in order to reconstruct the migratory histories of and demographic relationships between these groups. Again, this approach is at odds with understandings of the fluid, dynamic, performed, and always political nature of group identities. It assumes a natural correlation between shared ancestry, shared patterns of genetic variation, and shared identity, even if the science is figured as a neutral tool for confirming or refuting these assumptions. Scientists may robustly deny that their work implies a correlation between ethnicity or national identity and biology, but at the same time treating ethnic groups or national categories as objects of analysis suggests a scientific authority in proving or disproving an assumed ancestral, and thus genetic, foundation to identity and identification.

Thus, the issue of the making of genetic categories of difference is not just a matter of the translation of the science into the public by media actors eager to link genetics to sociocultural identities. In fact, it is integral to the scientific technologies of categorization and differentiation. It is also integral to the ways in which sociocultural groups are constituted as objects of scientific analysis. By suggesting that their histories can be reconstructed genetically, and by emphasising the value of this reconstruction for collective self-knowledge, these studies imply that there is a natural correlation between ancestry, genetic similarity, and identity.

National Genomics: Diversity and Differentiation

National genomic projects are both national in their focus and framing, and situated within and in relation to the international science of genomics. Increasingly, national governments actively pursue national genomic projects because of the perceived value of knowing the population in this way, in relation to biomedical futures or the national past. National genomic projects are seen as indicative of a country's engagement in and contribution to scientific progress and its membership in a prestigious international network of countries at the forefront of cutting-edge science.[23] Among the growing number of studies explicitly articulated as national projects in terms of scale, focus, and significance are national biobanking projects gathering genetic material and medical and lifestyle information for the sake of biomedical research, and studies undertaken in order to provide insight into the national past, or what has been called "genetic heritage." These projects are often depicted as creating national archives of genetic, genealogical, and in some cases medical knowledge, or more spatially, as national genetic atlases. In some cases, as in the *People of the British Isles* project, the research is framed both in terms of its biomedical value and of its value for collective national self-understanding.

The significance of these projects also lies in the potency of their appeal to the "national," not through an old model of national struggle against other nations and ideas of national races, but through ideas of collective effort and endeavor. Both national biobanking initiatives and anthropological genetic projects often appeal to potential participants on the basis that their individual contribution is of benefit to the national population more widely.[24] Something of larger value above the individual is suggested. Individual acts of donation, for example, are cast as part of a wider collective contribution. This image of individual contribution to wider collective effort is often coupled with claims that the genomes of the population will be a shared national resource, of use now and also of prospective value. Participants are thus donors to a collective national resource of genetic information that will serve the development of biomedicine, be capitalized through further scientific and pharmaceutical investment, and position the nation as at the forefront of the technoscience frontier.

The national genome—the pattern of genetic variation in a country—is presented by those seeking funding for or announcing national gemome research projects as a national asset for prospective national scientific development. At the same time, and again echoing the doubly national and international ambitions and intentions of national race science, the particular character of national patterns of variation are also valued for its potential toconstitute useful data to international genomic research. So, while it is the relative homogeneity of the population of Iceland as well as the depth of medical and genealogical records that is represented as a resource for biomedicine, it is the genetic heterogeneity of the United States or the United Kingdom that is presented as a national resource, offering new prospects for medical genomics. Different articulations of the genetic character of the national population are mobilized to render national genomes as national assets and of value to international genomics in different places.[25] The national genome is not described in terms of a national homogeneity but in terms of a nationally distinctive pattern of variation. The particular ways in which this is described are shaped both by the specific demographic histories of different states and their particular national configurations of ideas of race, ethnicity, and diversity.

But they are also shaped by the ways in which states are situated in relation to the globalized science of human genomics, dominated by Europe and North America. Some national genomic projects are undertaken in response to the perceived neglect of their specific national contexts in large-scale, international (but Euro-American–dominated) human genomic projects and are pursed by less powerful countries in order to ensure that they also benefit from the value of genomic knowledge for biomedical and pharmaceutical developments. This involves the assertion of national sovereignty over the DNA of their populations, which is seen as vulnerable to the exploitation by more powerful nations. Policies of "genomic sovereignty" assert a national politics of self-determination and resistance, but in contradictory ways, in what has been described as "postcolonial genomics." They figure the nation as a biopolitical entity, one based on a unique national pattern of heterogeneity in relation to other states (again reiterating late nineteenth-century ideas of national uniqueness through specific mixtures of racial ingredients). But the process of mapping that heterogeneity involves deploying existing national discourses about patterns of ethnic variation in ways that can reify ethnic categories as genomic entities and elide the differentiated positioning of subnational groups, such as indigenous people, in relation to the potential health or economic benefits of national genomic initiatives.[26] The process of mapping the diverse national genome through identifying and studying—and, so, effectively producing—subnational "populations" is mediated by national imaginaries of history, ancestry, and heritage, as well as the politics of difference. This national genomic mapping, in turn, enables the country to contribute to international genomic science.

The potential implications of national genomic projects for the wider politics of national unity, belonging, diversity, and difference can be considered further in two ways: firstly, in terms of how these projects produce accounts of the national population by constituting certain groups or individuals as representatives of the national genome; and secondly, through ways the results of national surveys of geographical patterns of variation are interpreted in relation to sociocultural categories of difference. The first issue is a matter of identifying groups or individuals as suitable donors of genetic material and of the relationship between inclusion in these projects and ideas of national inclusion and belonging. Studies of genetic variation of a the population of the state—and, even more ideally, where, in the minority of cases, the state boundaries are also natural topographical boundaries—may seem to offer a sense of neatness and completeness. The Icelandic case seems to offer just that:

all genealogies, all medical histories, and, now, enough fully genotyped individuals to stand for the population as whole in a country whose island geography offers an ideal laboratory for genetic research.[27] The reporting of the completion of a key stage of the project, announced in March 2015, presents Iceland as a model for future research. But the features of this exceptional case—its small population, its particular history of settlement by a founding population and limited immigration, and the depth and extent of genealogical and medical record keeping—are also largely not replicable.

Most national projects are being undertaken in countries that have complex and distinctive patterns of ethnic diversity through historical patterns of migration and settlement and more recent immigration, and whose histories of state formation have involved different configurations of majority and minority groups, of the newcomer and the indigenous, diversity, and of mixing and difference. Since studies of genetic variation within a large population are always based on sampling from that population rather than gathering genetic material from each member, this raises key issues of how the sample is constituted as representative of the population at large, or of subnational ethnic groups. The national populace may in fact be conceived of as containing a number of distinct ethnic groups that are deemed to be populations for analysis and, in the process, produced as genetically identifiable ethnic groups. Decisions about how studies are constructed in terms of sampling regions, groups, and appropriate participants are never simply methodological issues. They are entangled with wider social and cultural understandings of ethnic difference and the politics of identity and belonging to, or distinction within, the national community.[28]

National biobanking projects adopt different strategies for balancing the tension between the scientific challenge of ethnic diversity within national biobanks and the principle of ethnic inclusiveness through the screening or ethnic labeling of samples.[29] UK Biobank was established to reflect the ethnic diversity of Britain as a whole and this genetic diversity is emphasized in accounts of its scientific value. In contrast, and as a reflection of the project's historical focus, the researchers undertaking the *People of the British Isles* project adopted a different sampling strategy, one that is widely used in studies that seek to reconstruct early histories of settlement from the analysis of the genetic material of contemporary residents of a study region: participants must live in the rural locality in which their four great-grandparents lived. The rural sampling sites avoid the obviously wide and complex mix of ancestral origins in cities as focal points for in-migration within and beyond the state, and the requirement for grandparental presence in rural locations further screens out those who have moved within and to the United Kingdom over the last one hundred years or so. The project's accounts of the national past are thus the product of analyzing the genetic material of people who are genealogically rooted. This matters in terms of how the "people of the British Isles" are constituted through the project and in terms of the degree to which this implies that national "genetic heritage"—knowledge of the national past—is the heritage of,or indeed imagined to be embodied within, those who are ancestrally British.

The map of genetic variation in the United Kingdom published in 2015 is effectively the product of an attempt to map patterns of genetic diversity that preceded twentieth-century immigration and that are assumed to be long-standing patterns of variation in Britain over the preceding centuries. The project leaders were aware of sensitivities about this focus on "indigenous Britons," in relation to ethnic diversity in Britain and there is no sense in which the project is an effort to produce a genetic version of a national race.[30] Instead, accounts of the project and its findsing combine ideas of the nation as a collective community of identification with an emphasis on a geography of regional diversity. The press release of the project key research papers links regionally distinctive patterns of genetic variation to regional identities. It states: "Many people in the UK feel a strong sense of regional identity, and it now appears that there may be a scientific basis to this feeling." It directs public attention to cases in which patterns of variation seem to differ in ways which correspond to county boundaries. Much is made of the genetic difference between Cornwall and Devon, for example, but not of all the cases where this apparent correlation between county identities and genetic difference is not found. This attention to regional diversity in the study and in the results might at one level be valued as for its potential to challenge ideas of natural, primordial, and pure national identities. Regional identities could foreground internal diversity rather than national homogeneity, However, the problematic issue of producing categories of genetic distinctiveness within broad gradients of variation and relating them to ideas of collective identity pertains here too.

Moreover, while it may be widely thought that it is inappropriate to talk of national identity as having a scientific basis, the press release and subsequent reporting indicate that it appears to be acceptable to suggest that the project has found evidence for a genetic or genealogical basis to regional or "tribal" identities. This is despite the fact that the logic of linking identity, genetics and genealogy at the regional level could simply be scaled up to suggest that the nation itself can be considered a genetic community of shared ancestry, identity and interests. The idea that regional identities are in some sense genetic provides resources for discourses of exclusion at different scales and can play into more racialized versions of difference—a genetically proven English Anglo-Saxon ancestral heritage, for example.

But, at the same time, other national regions are described as containing genetic contrasts—for instance, between North and South Wales. Some sorts and some scales of identity are presented as matching a regional geography of shared ancestry and genealogical depth while others are featured as if they mistakenly assume this linkage, such as people from Celtic regions of Britain, who are presented as genetically dissimilar despite their cultural affinities. The study is reported as finding that there is not a single "Celtic" genetic group implying that the ideas of shared ancestry has no foundation in scientific truth. So while the project seemed to undermine some assumptions of that a shared identity has some sense genealogical basis, in other respects it emphasizes what was described as the "genetic component" of others. In this national biohistory, connectedness and difference are figured in different ways in relation to differently scaled categories of identity; some are reified, others dispelled, some are evoked, others reworked.

However, though the discourse of regional diversity clearly counters ideas of a single pattern of genetic variation for the United Kingdom as a whole, and even if, in some cases, the results challenge an assumed correlation between genetics, ancestry, and identity and purportedly demonstrate it in others, the predominant message is of distinctive regional categories of genetic variation that are aligned with ideas of regional identity. In this way the study of patterns of human genetic variation is presented as contributing to collective national understanding without recourse to problematic ideas of national genetic homogeneity or national ancestral identity—that politically suspect model of the alignment of genealogy, genetics, geography, culture, and national community. However, ideas of the genetic and cultural character of subnational regions can prove divisive at the regional level, if they naturalize ideas of indigenous locals and denaturalize the attachments and forms of belonging of newcomers. Furthermore, if ideas of local genetic communities are scaled up to the subnational ethnic region, nation, or international region (Europe, for example), they produce national, ethnic, and racial cartographies of natural belonging and exclusion by naturalizing an equation of geography, genealogy, genetics, and identity, just as race anthropology regularly did. Projects like this can thus serve as resources for both liberal critiques of xenophobic nationalism through ideas of diversity and illiberal assertions of local, regional, or national distinctiveness under threat of dilution through immigration. The way the results of the project have been used to support progressive ideas of diversity in some media reporting should not make the research itself and its presentation by institutional press offices immune to critique. Critical scrutiny needs to be directed at the projects themselves and not just cases of their "misuse."

Genomic research in national contexts can thus suggest different ways of figuring what is shared and what is distinctive, both producing ideas of national diversity and more bounded differentiations within that diversity, which may or may not be racialized. This is also the conclusion of research on human genomics in Brazil. In the Brazilian context, studies of genetic variation have been interpreted as evidence of quite different models of unity or diversity. In some studies the interpretation of patterns of genetic variation strongly emphasize shared diversity without differentiation according to race. Other studies focus on and highlight distinctive regional patterns of variation in Brazil, and so produce more differentiated accounts of the national genome than generalized diversity. The science has been used to shore up racial identities as well as undermine them and the political claims around them.[31] The disappearance of the language of "racial types," hierarchies, and typologies thus does not mean that contemporary genomics is beyond race. Instead, these cases indicate the multiple ways in which national genomics projects mobilize, rework, and remake categories of difference—race, nation, ethnicity—across the geography of human genetic variation with different sorts of political effects.

Conclusion

Studies of human genetic variation occur at many different scales, from the world as a whole to continental regions, or smaller regions or localities. They thus intersect with different scales of collective identity and how these cultural and spatial imaginaries configure human difference and similarity. These range from the progressive associations of universal humanity at the global scale to ideas of racial difference when the global is dissected into apparently natural continental geographies of genetic difference. The implications accounts of patterns of variation that are reported to "prove" the existence of races certainly deserve critical scrutiny. At the same time, the making of ideas of unity, diversity, and difference within national genome projects, which take the pattern of genetic variation within the state as the object of investigation, also need critical attention. Ideas of race, nation, and ethnicity are being made and remade in different ways in national projects that are established to simultaneously address national interests, signify national scientific achievement, and create potential competitive advantage within the transnational practice of genomics.

Studies of genetic variation in national genome projects are now framed strongly by ideas of diversity rather than pure national races and often inflected by multicultural politics of inclusion and inclusiveness rather than antagonistic difference. Yet, though the idea of the nation as a natural community of shared ancestry or blood would no longer go unchallenged in public discourse, accounts of national genetic self-knowledge evoke also ideas of genealogical or genetic belonging in the nation in ways that are deeply problematic, but perhaps less easily recognized as such. It is important to consider how different groups within the nation can be differently situated in relation to ideas of the national community of shared descent, as, for example, genetically distinctive immigrant newcomers to an established national geography of genetic variation. National genomes are not presented in terms of pure races; however, ideas of a distinctive patterns of variation within them can be racialized. Histories of nation building can be understood in terms of waves of migration, but distinctions can be made between foundational waves that have shaped the national pattern of genetic variation and new immigrants, and these distinctions can also be racialized. However, accounts of national genetic variation (at different degrees of resolution from national to regional) do not need to be overtly or even implicitly racialised to be exclusionary; ideas of shared ancestry as the basis of collective identity at the national or subnational scale also produce exclusive models of belonging. The pursuit of geographically located clusters of genetic similarity in gradients of genetic variation, and attempts to relate them to social categories of identity and identification such as the nation or the region, produces mixed results in terms of the politics of identity and difference. The multicultural and anti-racist framing of this science of difference and arguments about the apparently progressive effects of studies of patterns of national genetic variation should therefore not be taken to mean that this field is either broadly positive in its political effects nor a reliable authority on questions of history, heritage, and identity. Advocates of national genome projects assert the power of genomics to address questions of collective identity, but these are questions that would be much better explored culturally, politically, socially, and historically rather than scientifically.

Notes

1. Peter Wade, Carlos López Beltrán, Eduardo Restrepo, and Richardo Ventura Santos, eds., *Mestizo Genomics: Race Mixture, Nation, and Science in Latin America* (Durham NC: Duke University Press, 2014).

2. Bob Simpson, "Imagined Genetic Communities: Ethnicity and Essentialism in the Twenty-First Century," *Anthropology Today* 16 (2000): 3–6.

3. Marianne Sommer, "DNA and Cultures of Remembrance: Anthropological Genetics, Biohistories, and Biosocialities," *BioSocieties* 5 (2010): 366–90, 369.

4. Daniel F. Gudbjartsson et al., "Large-scale Whole-Genome Sequencing of the Icelandic Population," *Nature Genetics* 47, no. 5 (2015): 435–44.

5. James Gallagher, "DNA of 'An Entire Nation' Assessed," BBC, March 26, 2015, http://www.bbc.co.uk/news/health-32024158.

6. See, for example, Gísli Pálsson and Paul Rabinow, "Iceland: The Case of a National Human Genome Project," *Anthropology Today* 15 (1999): 14–18.

7. Stephen Leslie et al., "The Fine-scale Genetic Structure of the British Population," *Nature* 519 (2015): 309–14.

8. "Who Do You Think You Really Are? The First Fine-scale Genetic Map of the British Isles," Wellcome Trust press release, March 19, 2015, http//www.wellcome.ac.uk/News/Media-office/Press-releases/2015/wtpo58941.htm.

9. The reconstruction of national population histories through studies of genetic variation is often linked to biomedical and health-care research. See, for example, Dhavendra Kumar, ed., *Genomics and Health in the Developing World* (Oxford: Oxford University Press, 2012), and Béatrice Séguin, Billie-Jo Hardy, Peter A. Singer, and Abdallah S. Daar, "Human Genomic Variation Initiatives in Emerging Economies and Developing Countries," *Nature Reviews Genetics* 9, no. 1 (2008): S3–S4.

10. Karen-Sue Taussig, *Ordinary Genomes: Science, Citizenship, and Genetic Identities* (Durham NC: Duke University Press, 2009).

11. Amy Hinterberger, "Categorization, Census, and Multiculturalism: Molecular Politics and the Material of Nation," in *Genetics and the Unsettled Past: The Collision of DNA, Race, and History*, ed. Keith Wailoo, Alondra Nelson, and Catherine Lee (New Brunswick NJ: Rutgers University Press, 2012), 204–24.

12. Nadia Abu El-Haj, *The Genealogical Science: The Search for Jewish Origins and the Politics of Epistemology* (Chicago: University of Chicago Press, 2012).

13. Jenny Reardon, *Race to the Finish: Identity and Governance in an Age of Genomics* (Princeton: Princeton University Press, 2005); Lisa Gannett, "Racism and Human Genome Diversity Research: The Ethical Limits of 'Population Thinking,'" *Philosophy of Science* 63 (2001): 1–8.

14. Jenny Reardon, "The Democratic, Anti-Racist Genome? Technoscience at the Limits of Liberalism," *Science as Culture* 21 (2012): 25–47.

15. Nikolas Rose, "The Politics of Life Itself," *Theory, Culture and Society* 18 (2001): 1–30, 13; Nikolas Rose, *The Politics of Life Itself* (Princeton: Princeton University Press, 2007).

16. Joan H. Fujimura et al., "Clines Without Classes: How to Make Sense of Human Variation," *Sociological Theory* 32 (2014): 208–27.

17. Catherine Bliss, "Genome Sampling and the Biopolitics of Race," in *A Foucault for the 21st Century: Governmentality, Biopolitics, and Discipline in the New Millennium*, ed. S. Bickley and J. Capetillo (Boston: Cambridge Scholars, 2010), 320–37; Gannett, "Racism and Human Genome Diversity Research."

18. David N. Livingstone, "Cultural Politics and the Racial Cartographics of Human Origins," *Transactions of the Institute of British Geographers* 35 (2010): 204–21; Heather Winlow, "Mapping, Race and Ethnicity," in *International Encyclopaedia of Human Geography*, ed. Rob Kitchin and Nigel Thrift (Oxford: Elsevier, 2009), 398–408.

19. Fujimura et al., "Clines."

20. Fujimura et al., "Clines." See also Amade M'charek, *The Human Genome Diversity Project: An Ethnography of Scientific Practice* (Cambridge: Cambridge University Press, 2005).

21. Jenny Reardon, "Democratic Mis-haps: The Problem of Democratization in a Time of Biopolitics," *BioSocieties* 2 (2007): 239–56; Joan H. Fujimura and Ramya Rajagopalan, "Different Differences: The Use of 'Genetic Ancestry' versus Race in Biomedical Human Genetic Research," *Social Studies of Science* 41 (2011): 5–30; Duana Fullwilley, "The Biologistic Construction of Race: 'Admixture' Technology and the New Genetic Medicine," *Social Studies of Science* 38 (2008): 695–735.

22. These criticisms can also be applied to research that took up the aims of the Human Genome Diversity Project even if it was more cognizant of the ethical issues involved. I discuss this more fully in Catherine Nash, "Genetics, Race and Relatedness: Human Mobility and Human Diversity in the Genographic Project," *Annals of the Association of American Geographers* 102 (2012): 667–84.

23. See, for example, Amy L. Fletcher, "Field of Genes: The Politics of Science and Identity in the Estonian Genome Project," *New Genetics and Society* 23 (2006): 3–14.

24. Helen Busby and Paul Martin, "Biobanks, National Identity, and Imagined Communities: The Case of UK Biobank," *Science as Culture* 15 (2006): 237–51.

25. Amy Hinterberger, "Publics and Populations: The Politics of Ancestry and Exchange in Genome Science," *Science as Culture* 21 (2012): 528–49; Amy Hinterberger, "Investing in Life, Investing in Difference: Nations, Populations and Genomes," *Theory, Culture, and Society*, 29 (2012): 72–93.

26. Ruha Benjamin, "A Lab of Their Own: Genomic Sovereignty as Postcolonial Science Policy," *Policy and Society* 28 (2009): 342–54. See also Ernesto Schwartz-Marin and Eduardo Restrepo "Biocoloniality, Governance, and the Protection of 'Genetic Identities' in Mexico and Colombia," *Sociology*, 47 (2013): 993–1010.

27. Beth Greenhough, "Assembling an Island Laboratory," *Area* 43 (2011): 134–38.

28. Margaret Sleeboom-Faulkner, "How to Define a Population: Cultural Politics and Population Genetics in the People's Republic of China and the Republic of China," *BioSciences* 1 (2006): 399–419.

29. Andrew Smart et al., "The Standardization of Race and Ethnicity in Biomedical Science Editorials and UK Biobanks," *Social Studies of Science* 38 (2008): 407–23; Richard Tutton, "Biobanks and the Inclusion of Racial/Ethnic Minorities," *Race/Ethnicity: Multidisciplinary Global Perspectives* 3 (2009): 75–95.

30. Catherine Nash, "Genome Geographies: Mapping National Ancestry and Diversity in Human Population Genetics," *Transactions of the Institute of British Geographers* 38 (2013): 193–206. I also discuss this project within a wider critical engagement with genetic accounts of shared and distinctive origins in Catherine Nash, *Genetic Geographies: The Trouble with Ancestry* (Minneapolis: University of Minnesota Press, 2015).

31. Michael Kent, Ricardo Ventura Santos, and Peter Wade, "Negotiating Imagined Genetic Communities: Unity and Diversity in Brazilian Science and Society," *American Anthropologist* 116 (2014): 736–48.

Contributors

Maciej Górny has been a professor at the Historical Institute of the Polish Academy of Sciences since 2006. Currently he is also a visiting professor at the German Historical Institute in Warsaw. After studying history, Polish studies, Slavic studies, and Hungarian studies in Warsaw, he received his doctorate in 2006 from the Polish Academy of Sciences and habilitated in 2014. Górny held a scholarship at the Berlin Kolleg for comparative European historical studies from 2004 to 2006 and Imre Kertész Kolleg Jena, in 2011–12 and 2016–17. He was a research associate at the Centre for Historical Studies in Berlin from 2006 to 2010. His publications include *The Nation Should Come First: Marxism and Historiography in East Central Europe* (2013; Polish edition, 2007; German edition, 2011; Czech edition, forthcoming). His main areas of research are central and eastern Europe in the nineteenth and twentieth centuries; history of historiography; discourses on race; and the First World War. He is the editor-in-chief of *Acta Poloniae Historica*; a member of the editorial board of the *Czech Journal of Contemporary History*; and an advisory board member of *Europeana 1914–1918*.

Ageliki Lefkaditou is senior curator at the Norwegian Museum of Science and Technology and a historian of science. At the museum, she is the lead curator of the exhibition "Folk—From Racial Types to DNA Sequences." Lefkaditou writes on the history of physical anthropology and human population genetics research, race, and racism from the late nineteenth century to the present, with a special focus on Greece. Her research interests include the development of museum theory, methods, and practices, as well as science communication. Lefkaditou received her first PhD from the Department of Biology at Aristotle University of Thessaloniki and is currently completing her second PhD in the history of science at the University of Leeds. From 2014 to 2017, she held a three-year postdoctoral research position in Oslo with the project "From Racial Typology to DNA Sequencing: 'Race' and 'Ethnicity' and the Science of Human Genetic Variation, 1945–2012." She has recently published the following papers: "'That Wonderful People': Darwin, the Victorians, and the Greeks," *Journal of Modern Greek Studies* 36 (2018): 97–124; and "Observations on Race and Racism in Greece," *Journal of Anthropological Studies* 95 (2017): 329–38.

Richard McMahon lectures in EU politics at University College London. Previously he has been a senior lecturer in European Studies at the University of Portsmouth, a Georg Bollenbeck Fellow at the University of Siegen, in Germany, a Marie Curie senior research fellow in Portsmouth (working with Professor Wolfram Kaiser; and with IR scholar Richard Little), and an ESRC fellow at the University of Bristol. At University College Cork and the Universities of Bath, Portsmouth, Chichester, Siegen, and Birkbeck, he has taught subjects ranging from Chinese history and EU politics to political ideologies and racial subtexts in the work of J. R. R. Tolkien. He also worked for two years in Brussels as a journalist of EU external relations. In 2016 Palgrave published his monograph, *The Races of Europe: Construction of National Identities in the Social Sciences 1839–1939*, based on his PhD research at the European University Institute in Florence. The book focuses on interchanges between the network geography of the transnational scientific community of race classifiers, including its power relations, and the politicized race geographies, histories, and psychologies that classifiers devised. McMahon has published several articles and edited volumes on race classification, European integration, and cultural interaction.

Marina Mogilner is an associate professor of history at the University of Illinois, Chicago, where she holds the Edward and Marianna

Thaden Chair in Russian and East European Intellectual History. Since 1999 she has been a coeditor of *Ab Imperio Quarterly*. She is the author of a number of books, including, most recently, *Homo Imperii: A History of Physical Anthropology in Russia* (Lincoln: University of Nebraska Press), Critical Studies in the History of Anthropology series, 2013. She coedited volumes on different aspects of imperial history. Mogilner's most recent publications include: "Racial Psychiatry and the Russian Imperial Dilemma of the "Savage Within," *East Central Europe* 43 (2016): 99–133; "Between Scientific and Political: Jewish Scholars and Russian-Jewish Physical Anthropology in the Fin-de-Siècle Russian Empire," in *Going to the People: Jews and the Ethnographic Impulse*, ed. Jeffrey Veidlinger (Bloomington: Indiana University Press, 2016), 45–63; "Toward a History of Russian-Jewish 'Medical Materialism': Russian-Jewish Physicians and the Politics of Jewish Biological Normalization," *Jewish Social Studies* 19, no. 1 (2012): 70–106; with Ilya Gerasimov and Alexander Semyonov, "Russian Sociology in Imperial Context," in *Sociology and Empire*, ed. George Steinmetz (Durham NC: Duke University Press, 2012); and others. She is currently working on the history of Russian-Jewish race science.

Amos Morris-Reich is an associate professor in the Department of Jewish History at the University of Haifa and the director of the Bucerius Institute for Research on Contemporary German History and Society. His dissertation and first book (published in 2007 by Routledge as *The Quest for Jewish Assimilation in Modern Social Science*) looked at "assimilation" at the intersection between Jewish history, German history, and the history of the social sciences. He then worked on photography as scientific evidence in the study of "race." This appeared in 2016 as *Race and Photography: Racial Photography as Scientific Evidence, 1876–1980* (Chicago: University of Chicago Press). He is coeditor, with Dirk Rupnow, of *Ideas of Race in the History of the Humanities* (Palgrave: London Macmillan, 2017) and coeditor, with Margaret Olin, of *Race and Imagination* (forthcoming from Routledge), as well as the author of many articles. His current book project studies five cases drawn from Jewish history and the history of photography. With particular focus on the roles of photography for sensual, cognitive, and political education, the book is intended as a reflection on some of the diverse ramifications of photography on modern Jewish history.

Arnaud Nanta is a historian and full-time researcher at the French National Center for Scientific Research (Institut d'Asie Orientale, UMR 5062, Lyons). He works on the history of the humanities and social sciences in modern and contemporary Japan, and in colonial Korea and Taiwan. He has a special interest in the histories of archaeology, anthropology, and historical studies, with a focus on political ideologies and on the making of national identities. He previously worked at EHESS (Paris) and in Maison Franco-Japonaise (Tokyo), and he has lived in Japan more than ten years. His works include "Ethnic Shows and Racial Hierarchies in Modern Japan," *Journal of Taipei Fine Arts Museum* 30 (2015): 85–103; "The Anthropological Society of Tokyo and the Ainu: Racial Classifications, Prehistory, and National Identity (1880–1910)," ed. N. Bancel et al., *The Invention of Race* (New York: Routledge, 2014), 158–69; and "La décolonisation japonaise (1945–1949): le démontage de l'empire colonial, les occupations et replis, les politiques d'assistance aux rapatriés," in *Démontages d'empires*, ed. D. Lefeuvre et al. (Paris: Riveneuve, 2013), 257–83. He has also translated into French T. Takahashi's *La Question du Yasukuni* (Paris: Les Belles Lettres, 2012).

Catherine Nash (School of Geography, Queen Mary University of London) is a feminist cultural geographer whose work explores geographies of identity and relatedness, especially in relation to ideas of the nation, diaspora, and indigeneity. Her recent work has focused on genetic accounts of ancestral origins and shared descent in relation to the politics of belonging and difference. This has included recent research on the sociocultural and biomedical making of relations through human remains in the case of Charles Byrne ("the Irish Giant"), and the politics of genetic and genealogical models of national belonging, with a particular focus on their implications for Irish Travelers and Irish society. She is interested in geographies of kinship of different kinds and is currently pursuing this through research on human-animal relations; the practices, ideas, and relations that make an animal breed; and entangled human and animal histories and genealogies, through a focus on horses and people. Recent publications include *Of Irish Descent: Origin Stories, Genealogy, and the Politics of Belonging* (Syracuse NY: Syracuse University Press, 2008) and *Genetic Geographies: The Trouble with Kinship* (Minneapolis: University of Minnesota Press, 2015).

Maria Sophia Quine studied at Smith College, Oxford University, and the University of London. She has written extensively on the history of population politics, Italian Fascism, the welfare state, women and the family, the science and politics of race, eugenics, and biopolitics. She held a Senior Lectureship in Modern European History at Queen Mary, University of London, before her retirement. Since then, she has held research fellowships in Modern History at the University of East Anglia and in the History of Science and Ideas at the School of Advanced Studies, University of London. She currently holds a Senior Research Fellowship in the History of Fascism and Race, at the Centre for Medical Humanities at Oxford Brookes University. She has been a leading member of the Research Group for the History of Race and Eugenics (HRE) at Brookes. Currently, she researches how Italian neuroscientists sought to liberate humanity from mental illness without recourse to sterilization or "euthanasia." She is also editing a major new volume on the condition of women, globally, past and present. The authors are scholars and activists from fields such as law, politics, sociology, and history.

Maria Rhode emigrated in the 1970s to Germany, where she completed her higher education at the University of Freiburg (Brsg.). Trained as a historian and philologist, she received her PhD in 1994, presenting a study of the Polish interregna during the sixteenth and seventeenth centuries, *Ein Königreich ohne König. Der kleinpolnische Adel in sieben Interregna* (Wiesbaden: Harrassowitz, 1997). Since 2001 she has been teaching (East) European History in the Department of Medieval and Modern History at the Georg-August-University in Göttingen as a senior lecturer. Her early research focused on early modern parliamentarism and modern nationalism. She published articles on early modern self-government in the Polish-Lithuanian Commonwealth. However, her focus of interest recently shifted toward the history of knowledge and knowledge production. She published articles about Russian and Polish colonial entanglements and scientific transfers: "Russische Äthiopienexpeditionen 1889–1896," in *Von Käfern, Märkten und Menschen. Kolonialismus und Wissen in der Moderne*, ed. Rebekka Habermas/Alexandra Przyrembel, (Göttingen: Wallstein 2013), 297–310; and "Zivilisierungsmissionen und Wissenschaft. Polen kolonial?," *Geschichte und Gesellschaft* 39 (2013): 5–34. At the moment, she is preparing a book on European-Polish transfers of knowledge in the nineteenth and twentieth centuries.

Rory Yeomans received his PhD in political science and history at the School of Slavonic and East European Studies, University College London. He is the author of *Visions of Annihilation: The Ustasha Regime and the Cultural Politics of Fascism, 1941–1945* and coeditor, with Anton Weiss-Wendt, of *Racial Science in Hitler's New Europe* (both 2013). Most recently, he is the editor of *The Utopia of Terror: Life and Death in Wartime Croatia* (2015). He is currently a member of the School of Historical Studies at the Institute for Advanced Study at Princeton University and has previously held fellowships at the University of Oxford; the Centre for Advanced Study, Bulgaria; and the Wiener Wiesenthal Institute for Holocaust Studies, as well as an EHRI fellowship with the Bundesarchiv in Berlin. His main research interests lie in the interdisciplinary cultural, social, and economic history of the Independent State of Croatia, interwar and socialist Yugoslavia, and comparative fascism, with an emphasis on nonelite histories. He is currently researching a project about transnational fascism and ideological exchanges in wartime Europe and has recently completed a book manuscript about literature, martyrdom culture, and Croatian nationalism in the twentieth century, for Harrassowitz Verlag.

Index

In the Critical Studies in the History of Anthropology series

Invisible Genealogies: A History of Americanist Anthropology
Regna Darnell

The Shaping of American Ethnography: The Wilkes Exploring Expedition, 1838–1842
Barry Alan Joyce

Ruth Landes: A Life in Anthropology
Sally Cole

Melville J. Herskovits and the Racial Politics of Knowledge
Jerry Gershenhorn

Leslie A. White: Evolution and Revolution in Anthropology
William J. Peace

Rolling in Ditches with Shamans: Jaime de Angulo and the Professionalization of American Anthropology
Wendy Leeds-Hurwitz

Irregular Connections: A History of Anthropology and Sexuality
Andrew P. Lyons and Harriet D. Lyons

Ephraim George Squier and the Development of American Anthropology
Terry A. Barnhart

Ruth Benedict: Beyond Relativity, Beyond Pattern
Virginia Heyer Young

Looking through Taiwan: American Anthropologists' Collusion with Ethnic Domination
Keelung Hong and Stephen O. Murray

Visionary Observers: Anthropological Inquiry and Education
Jill B. R. Cherneff and Eve Hochwald
Foreword by Sydel Silverman

Anthropology Goes to the Fair: The 1904 Louisiana Purchase Exposition
Nancy J. Parezo and Don D. Fowler

The Meskwaki and Anthropologists: Action Anthropology Reconsidered
Judith M. Daubenmier

The 1904 Anthropology Days and Olympic Games: Sport, Race, and American Imperialism
Edited by Susan Brownell

Lev Shternberg: Anthropologist, Russian Socialist, Jewish Activist
Sergei Kan

Contributions to Ojibwe Studies: Essays, 1934–1972
A. Irving Hallowell
Edited and with introductions by Jennifer S. H. Brown and Susan Elaine Gray

Excavating Nauvoo: The Mormons and the Rise of Historical Archaeology in America
Benjamin C. Pykles
Foreword by Robert L. Schuyler

Cultural Negotiations: The Role of Women in the Founding of Americanist Archaeology
David L. Browman

Homo Imperii: A History of Physical Anthropology in Russia
Marina Mogilner

American Anthropology and Company: Historical Explorations
Stephen O. Murray

Racial Science in Hitler's New Europe, 1938–1945
Edited by Anton Weiss-Wendt and Rory Yeomans

Cora Du Bois: Anthropologist, Diplomat, Agent
Susan C. Seymour

Before Boas: The Genesis of Ethnography and Ethnology in the German Enlightenment
Han F. Vermeulen

American Antiquities: Revisiting the Origins of American Archaeology
Terry A. Barnhart

An Asian Frontier: American Anthropology and Korea, 1882–1945
Robert Oppenheim

Theodore E. White and the Development of Zooarchaeology in North America
R. Lee Lyman

Declared Defective: Native Americans, Eugenics, and the Myth of Nam Hollow
Robert Jarvenpa

Glory, Trouble, and Renaissance at the Robert S. Peabody Museum of Archaeology
Edited and with an introduction by Malinda Stafford Blustain and Ryan J. Wheeler

Race Experts: Sculpture, Anthropology, and the American Public in Malvina Hoffman's Races of Mankind
Linda Kim

The Enigma of Max Gluckman: The Ethnographic Life of a "Luckyman" in Africa
Robert J. Gordon

National Races: Transnational Power Struggles in the Sciences and Politics of Human Diversity, 1840–1945
Edited by Richard McMahon

Franz Boas: The Emergence of the Anthropologist
Rosemary Zumwalt

Maria Czaplicka: Gender, Shamanism, Race
Grażyna Kubica

Writing Anthropologists, Sounding Primitives: The Poetry and Scholarship of Edward Sapir, Margaret Mead, and Ruth Benedict
A. Elisabeth Reichel

www.ingramcontent.com/pod-product-compliance
Lightning Source LLC
Chambersburg PA
CBHW030635270326
41929CB00007B/83

* 9 7 8 1 4 9 6 2 2 5 8 4 9 *